"The Case
Against Congress

is at once interesting, compelling and shocking. No outsider could imagine the facts the authors have unearthed, and believe that the men involved could still hold high public office.

"This is a book you've simply got to read."

—*Miami Herald*

"A fascinating exposure of what the people's senators and representatives get away with when they go to Washington. Especially excellent is a tracing of the rise and fall of Senator Thomas Dodd of Connecticut." —*Denver Post*

"The two reporters name names, dates and places in the top ranks as they disclose 'the shame of Capitol Hill' within both parties. They go into conflicts of interest; loophole legislators (the oil depletion allowance); the abuses of privilege; the fine art of 'junketing'; padded payrolls; the senility system; nepotism; and Potomac Pitchmen, where lobbyists, both foreign and domestic, are explored in all their sordid maneuvering."

—*South Bend Tribune*

"The book will make you crying mad and it should."

—*Cosmopolitan*

THE CASE AGAINST CONGRESS
was originally published by Simon and Schuster.

THE CASE AGAINST CONGRESS

A Compelling Indictment of Corruption on Capitol Hill

BY
Drew Pearson
AND
Jack Anderson

PUBLISHED BY POCKET BOOKS NEW YORK

THE CASE AGAINST CONGRESS

Simon and Schuster edition published August, 1968

A *Pocket Book* edition
1st printing............July, 1969

Some of the material included in this book appeared
in a different form in the authors' syndicated column.

This *Pocket Book* edition includes every word
contained in the original, higher-priced edition. It is printed
from brand-new plates made from completely reset, clear, easy-to-read
type. *Pocket Book* editions are published by Pocket Books, a division
of Simon & Schuster, Inc., 630 Fifth Avenue, New York, N.Y. 10020.
Trademarks registered in the United States and other countries.

L

CONTENTS

v

PART II: CONFLICTS OF INTEREST

Chapter Four CROSSING THE BAR: LAWYERS IN CONGRESS

Chapter Five LOOPHOLE LEGISLATORS: THE OIL DEPLETION ALLOWANCE

Chapter Six CROOKED FURROWS: THE WASHINGTON FARMER

Chapter Seven CURBING WATCHDOGS: CONGRESS AND THE REGULATORY AGENCIES

Chapter Eight ADDED DIVIDENDS: BANKERS IN THE CLOAKROOM

PART III: THE ABUSES OF PRIVILEGE

PART IV: POTOMAC PITCHMEN

Chapter Thirteen   LOBBYISTS: FOREIGN

PART V: STRAIGHT AND NARROW

Chapter Fourteen   THE GOOD GUYS

Chapter Fifteen   THE AGONY OF REFORM

INDEX

PREFACE

The Congress of the United States is a group of 535 men and women, each with strengths and failings typical of the human character. The most base among them have, on occasion, served the public worthily. And the most noble have not always risen above pettiness. No attempt is made here to pass eternal judgments.

This work is, rather, a telescopic look at some of the major abuses of power prevalent on Capitol Hill, and at some of the most flagrant offenders. There may well be room for argument about the personalities chosen for examination. Some readers may suggest that, although the Congressmen mentioned are guilty of abuses, others are equally guilty or possibly more guilty.

Other readers may attempt to find partisan political significance in this book. Although it is being published in an election year, no aid to either party is intended, and neither Democrats nor Republicans can take comfort from the disclosures. If there is an imbalance here that favors one party over the other, it is not intended. It is a sad fact that both parties strive to preserve the weaknesses in the Congressional system that make the abuses possible, and that politicians of both labels sometimes seem to vie with one another to reap the most benefits from these abuses.

Members of Congress have talked for years about enacting a code of ethics for themselves. When the press is able to document outrageously unethical conduct on Capitol Hill, the talk becomes louder. Yet there is no real desire to change the double standard that countenances behavior in Congress that would not be tolerated elsewhere within the Federal structure. The inertia is bipartisan; so is the effort to cloak Congressional abuses.

During our years of covering the Washington scene, we have developed a number of reliable sources who have helped us report the words and deeds that powerful men would like to keep hidden. Many of these sources contributed information for this book. They must, of course, remain anonymous.

Some of the information is drawn from our files; some has been developed from new investigations especially for this book. Some of it will undoubtedly be denied. All of it can be documented.

The book, finally, has one purpose: to bring the shady doings on Capitol Hill into the full light of the sun and thus, perhaps, to stimulate a public demand for genuine Congressional reform.

DREW PEARSON
JACK ANDERSON

Washington, D.C.
January 3, 1968

THE CASE
AGAINST
CONGRESS

THE AUTOCRATS:
AN INTRODUCTION

1. Privileges of Rank

Long jaded by exposure to pretenders to greatness, the unenfranchised residents of the District of Columbia still find the view of the Capitol dome inspiring in the morning light. The dome is the symbol of man's most intensive effort to subject the function of governing to the will of the governed—a cathedral to the memory of the nation's founders, a breast to nourish the hopes of Americans who will follow. In the full sun, the rays reflect off the dome's gray enamel, projecting a look of pure whiteness. Beneath the dome as well, and in the five great white marble buildings surrounding it, less natural illusions give the look of whiteness to vast patches of gray morality. For Washington's neoclassic temples of government shelter petty thieves and bold brigands—the political Pharisees of modern America.

It would be as naïve to suppose that the members of the United States Senate and House of Representatives are unaware of the dark stains on their institutions as it would be to pretend that all of them entered politics out of a genuine fervor for public service. Politics is as honorable a career as any other. Yet the honorable men in Congress demean themselves by ignoring the corruption that flourishes in their midst. Many members who might be tempted to speak out against the abuses around them find that they cannot. They have been compromised by the small favors they have done, or intimidated by the wielders of power, or bought off by the necessity of seeking funds for re-election, or hushed by a code of com-

1

radeship that ignores morality. Their silence is complicity in the deeds of the corrupt.

Congressmen, no matter how lofty their motives, have been flattered into believing that they are different from the rest of us, as if the process of election has somehow lifted them above other Americans and made them more knowing, more worthy and less subject to reproach than the people who elect them. Congressmen, too, can easily become insulated from the world around them. Their office staffs act as buffers between them and disagreeable news; the aides who have survived are those who have learned not to make waves. Wherever Congressmen go, they are treated with adulation. Many ordinary men among them are lulled into believing they receive this treatment because they deserve it, and even those who resist the narcotic of flattery are not entirely immune to the heady atmosphere on Capitol Hill.

For a small fee, tourists can follow a guide through the corridors of the Capitol, hear about the history of the building and of the men who have occupied it. The tours pause briefly in the chambers of Congress, where the droning, out-of-context oratory often makes little sense to the listeners. The tour ends where it begins, under the vastness of the Capitol dome. For their coins, the tourists can see much of Congress but discover little about its processes.

There are no guides to the real workings of Congress. Least instructive of all, perhaps, is the literature offered to tourists. The seating charts available to visitors in the galleries of the Senate and House chambers are not footnoted to explain to the casual observer the hidden interests, the friendships, the ambitions, the power relationships, the economic dependencies, the political pressures, or the personal prejudices that motivate the men who suddenly appear on the floor, conduct their business, and just as suddenly disappear.

A casual tour of the Congressional compound can be somewhat more enlightening about the atmosphere in which Congress lives than a guided tour. The unescorted visitor will encounter the spoils system—a system contrived, that is, to spoil the Congressmen. Elevators in the Senate wing, marked SENATORS ONLY, quickly impress the anointed with their own importance. More regal, perhaps, is the treatment of Senators in their office building elevators. They can summon immediate service by pushing the bell three times. Other passengers are forgotten by the college students who man the lifts; a Senator's command is the operator's only priority. Indeed, the ancillary benefits of election to Congress are overwhelming. Taken individually, many of these prizes can be excused as the trappings of rank. As a whole, they form a pattern of living that can be likened to the excesses of the Roman emperors, whose palaces gave birth to the architectural form of Capitol Hill. Behind these walls Congress has created a citadel of privilege.

The Senate alone has spawned a dozen restaurants to feed its members and its workers on meals subsidized for $365,000 in the latest budget year by the taxpayers. It also provides a beauty salon and a number of barbershops for employees where the price is about half what a haircut costs elsewhere in Washington. When the fee was raised recently from $1 to $1.25, there were cries of anguish from the pampered patrons. Only the Senators did not complain; they have their own private barbershop where the haircuts are free.

The Senate stationery shop is a drab basement room that has unusual appeal for Senators and their staffs. The store has nothing but bargains, since all items are sold at their wholesale cost. There is no markup for overhead or salaries. Besides office supplies, the store provides items like cut-rate Christmas cards and engraved wedding invitations for its patrons. This basement bargain counter at one time purveyed auto tires and whisky to its select clientele, but the rules were finally stiffened when the stock list became an embarrassment to the Senate.

Other rooms are dedicated to the further comfort and convenience of Senators. The Senate has its own shops for carpentry, electrical work, and, to insure that Senatorial bottoms are properly cushioned, an upholstery shop. There are also steam baths to help Senators recover from the after-hours duties of their office, and two swimming pools where Senators can cavort in the nude to soothe tired muscles.

On the House side of Capitol Hill, Representatives enjoy similar privileges in their own cloistered surroundings, often with embellishments designed to compensate for the inferiority complex felt by House members who have neither the prestige nor the power of the Senate. The behemoth Rayburn House Office Building is a monument to self-indulgence. The design and appointments reflect both a lack of taste and a lack of propriety, and its $122-million cost—the highest price tag in history for an office building—demonstrates the members' low regard for the public. The building, completed in 1965, is named for the late Speaker Sam Rayburn, and he is blamed for most of its extravagances. Representatives who have offices in the monstrosity will admit privately, however, that they enjoy its comforts.

No one would deny Congressmen sufficient office space to house their staffs. Before the Rayburn Building was completed, some House offices were crowded to the bursting point. Representative Dante Fascell, D-Fla., conscientious about his responsibility to a million citizens of the Miami area, had to mount desks for secretaries inside his own private office and store his files in the bathroom. For a while, he had a woman working in the narrow corridor that led to the bathroom. The woman was pregnant, and gave up her job when she could no longer squeeze into her chair space.

Fascell's problem did not, however, justify a vulgar, $122-million building with a $9.3 million parking lot for 1,220 cars, a 20-by-60-foot indoor swimming pool, a gymnasium, offices equipped with private kitchens, plus a 700-seat cafeteria and five dining rooms. There have been numerous charges of political payoffs in the construction of the building, but little evidence has been offered other than the fact that Matt McCloskey, the former treasurer of the Democratic National Committee, was the builder. A greater crime than the possible financial chicanery, however, is the damage the building has done to the reputation of Congress, just by its existence. Its false grandeur fails to inspire confidence in the ability of Congress to manage the affairs of the nation, and serves to perpetuate the caricature of Congressmen as luxury-loving, free-spending wastrels who are for sale to the highest bidders. Such an image is unquestionably unfair to many hardworking men who are true to their convictions and honest in their dealings. For many, service in Congress is both a personal sacrifice and a proud honor. For others, however, the caricature fits.

By itself, the $30,000 annual salary paid to members of Congress is modest enough. Those who have been required to live on their salaries believe it is just about right. "I don't think that a Congressman should get too far from the people in what he earns," explained Paul Douglas, who, until his defeat by Charles Percy, was the Democratic Senator from Illinois. But less scrupulous legislators have discovered a dozen ways to skin the taxpayers. The unpublicized but officially countenanced benefits of membership in Congress are worth noting.

Pensions—Since even a Southern duchy on occasion has been known to throw out its Representative, Congress has provided a pension plan for those who fail to get re-elected. It has all manner of clauses rarely found in a private-industry contract. By contributing 7.5 percent of his annual emolument, the 30-year man can qualify for as much as $18,000 a year. Pensions are also paid on top of any Social Security or private retirement plans. To become eligible, the political pensioner need serve only five years in Congress.

Life Insurance—For $10.83 a month, a Congressman's life is worth at least $20,000, and it doesn't matter a whit what his health chart shows. A physician's report isn't necessary.

Tax Break—A Congressman who maintains two houses—one in Washington, another in his home state—pays no Federal income tax on up to $3,000 of his $30,000 income.

Stationery Allowance—Each member is allowed $3,000 during a session for the purchase of office supplies, including stationery. The allowance is credited to his account in the stationery rooms and may be withdrawn in cash or left to pay for office purchases. This is an allowance so curiously unrestricted that a Congressman may pocket the entire amount if he wishes. In 1965, for example, Senator Margaret Chase Smith, R-Me., increased her petty cash with $1,822.01 in stationery funds.

Telephone and Telegraph Allowance—A Senator is now eligible for 2,400 free long-distance calls per year, plus $2,200 worth of calls originating and terminating outside of Washington, plus a telegram allowance based on the size of the state and its proximity to Washington. For Senators from large states over 10 million population, 3,600 no-charge calls per year are permitted. Somewhat differently, both telephone calls and telegrams are lumped together in a House member's allowance under the quaintly arcane "unit" system. For each two sessions of Congress, he receives 100,000 units. For every minute of long-distance chatter, he is charged with four units Californians obviously get more for their "units" than do Marylanders, but it's the rare lawmaker who bleeds his account dry. Even so, for the particularly garrulous member who might find himself running short of units, there is yet another provision. This is the $150 backstop allowance, or what Oklahoma's Senator Mike Monroney has called a "sort of slop-over deal." Senior members may also arrange to charge their excess phone calls to the committees on which they serve.

District Allowance—The legislator's political radar is located in his district office, for which there is also an allowance. Each member is entitled to office space at not more than two places within his constituency. The Sergeant at Arms will arrange for comfortable quarters in some handy Federal building. But if this is not available, a member may look elsewhere for space. Representative Alvin O'Konski, R-Wis., found rental space in his own radio station, WLIN in Merrill, Wisconsin. Representative William Dawson, D-Ill., drew $100 a month to pay office rent in the Second Ward Democratic headquarters on Chicago's South Side. Representative Charles Diggs, Jr., D-Mich., paid $75 a month rental to Diggs Enterprises, Inc., of Detroit. Representative Otto Passman, D-La., paid $100 a month for office space in the Passman Wholesale Equipment Company of Monroe, Louisiana. Ex-Representative Eugene Keogh, D-N.Y., paid his $100 monthly rental to his law firm, Halpin, Keogh and St. John. And Representative Watkins Abbitt, D-Va., signed over his rental allowance to his brother, George Abbitt, Jr., in Appomattox, Virginia. In each case the rent was paid by the Government.

Equipment Allowance—Besides everyday offices supplies, a member may order anything from a mimeograph machine to a dictating machine up to a value of $2,500. He is also entitled to manual typewriters and at least three electric typewriters without any deduction from the equipment allowance. In addition, he can claim $50 worth of photostating service per year.

Travel Allowance—Congress has increased the transportation allowance of a Senator from two to six round trips home each year; of a Representative from two to four round trips. Twenty cents a mile is also paid for one more round trip, calculated separately. Even so, this is a woefully small allowance. "Four trips a year may have been all right during the railroad age," grumbled one member, "but this is a jet era, and I have to fly home thirty times a year." Because the allotment is scant, the mischief is often considerable. For once the travel kitty has dried up, some Congressmen will contrive to go home by any means except one that is paid for out of their own pockets. Every Friday, a fleet of corporation-owned planes is available to whisk Congressmen home for the weekend—a handy service that often pays high legislative dividends to the plane owner.

House Folding Room—The modern lawmaker uses tons of paper. What he decides to put on it, or how much he sends as frankable mail, is a secret the House Folding Room will never reveal. Eli Bjellos, generalissimo in charge of this subterranean operation, says there is no limit to the amount of "bulk printed matter" a Congressman may send out. As long as it is frankable, he will fold, insert or wrap it for immediate mailing. Processing 22 million pieces of mail a month is no strain on the Bjellos machines. When the *Yearbook of Agriculture* comes off the presses, then Bjellos' facilities sometimes become taxed. Each Congressman is allotted 400 of these volumes as gifts to mail to his constituents. If he should run out, he can always offer, as substitutes, free copies of *Infant Care, How to Control Bedbugs, Facts on Communism, Guide to Subversive Activities,* or *The Prayer Room in the United States Capitol.* (Ironically, a "Code of Ethics," suitable for framing, was also available until the summer of 1967, when thousands of copies were unaccountably discarded. The Code was adopted during the Eisenhower age of platitudes by a Congress that had not itself in mind for self-policing but the Federal bureaucracy.)

Senate Service Department—It is a rule of thumb that anything a Representative must buy for a pittance is available free to a Senator. To implement this dictum, Congress has created the Senate Service Department. Its origins are obscure, its services secret. Behind unmarked doors in the Old Senate Office Building, this department is run by John "Buck" Chambers, an uncommunicative man, whose organization is supposed to operate on a nonprofit basis. He is about as chummy with interviewers as Greta Garbo, but insiders claim he has 60 employees under his command, including truck drivers, messengers and offset-press operators, whose salaries are camouflaged in the overall budget of the Senate Sergeant at Arms.

Map Service—Also available to members are free maps of

all sizes and shapes, either for personal use or for mailing to constituents.

Binding Service—For those afflicted by pride of authorship, Congress provides that "Members may have any public document, which has been published during their term of office, bound in a fine permanent binding by the Government Printing Office."

Recording Studios—Both the Senate and House provide radio and television studios, the latter equipped with sets that rival anything on the Warner Brothers lot. The most often used prop is the Congressional "office," designed in boardroom motif, with a stunning view of the Capitol dome beneath a bank of cumulus clouds. Both studios charge less than $20 to make a five-minute television film, which is about $380 less than a commercial outfit would charge. (Senator Everett Dirksen, R-Ill., gained an advantage over other recording stars by cutting his profitable, patriotic recording of "Gallant Men" in the tax-subsidized Senate-studios.)

Franking Privilege—Despite a generous stamp allowance, Congressmen are also granted the franking privilege, which permits them merely to sign their first-class mail. A House member gets 40,000 speech-sized envelopes, all duly franked, for mailing out copies of his speeches; a Senator is allotted 60,000. Though speech-sized envelopes are rationed, letter-sized ones have no limitation. Under the law, franked material must be "official correspondence." The Post Office, however, accepts a broad definition.

Printing Shops—Deep in the ink-splattered rooms of the Old House Office Buildings are two printing shops run by Truman Ward, who is listed on the House rolls as "majority clerk," and Thomas Lankford, "minority clerk." Their titles allow them to be carried on the payroll of the House Sergeant at Arms at annual salaries of $7,950. Needless to say, they pass their bargains on to the Congressmen. Two photographers are also provided by the taxpayers to record such historic events as the Millville High School's senior class calling on their Congressman.

Library of Congress—In addition to all the books a Congressman can borrow, the Library of Congress also provides a Legislative Reference Service whose 220 harried researchers will check out anything from the number of koala bears in Australia to the pesticides best suited for the truck gardens of

Matsuyama. Upon request, the researchers will spend up to 50 hours on a single project. LRS handles upwards of 100,000 Congressional inquiries annually.

Parking—For 100 Senators, there is free underground parking for about 400 cars. The 435 House members also have 1,600 parking spaces underground. Congressional employees use free outdoor lots and reserved spaces on the streets. But the prerogative extends far beyond this. Members of Congress are exempt from parking restrictions when on official business. Over the years, the area of immunity has broadened to include their families, staffs and often visiting constituents as well. Senator Wayne Morse, the vigilant Oregonian, has fumed that 33,739 tickets were fixed in a single year. When the District of Columbia commissioners threatened to change the rules to make the streets passable during the rush hour, however, they were hauled before the House District of Columbia Committee and quickly humbled.

Automobiles—Matched against their equals in the business world, Congressmen have unflashy tastes in automobiles. House Banking and Currency Committee Chairman Wright Patman, D-Tex., still cherishes his 1955 Oldsmobile, so much so that he keeps a picture of it on his wall alongside an inscribed portrait of LBJ. The 1955 DeSoto, which Senator John Tower, R-Tex., drove as a professor, serves him as a Senator now. The fanciest car on Capitol Hill, until it was finally dispossessed from its allotted parking space in March, 1968, was a Jaguar that Representative Adam Clayton Powell, D-N.Y., previously left on the streets wherever he chose to disembark. Congressmen, of course, know what voters think of chauffeured politicos. It is not surprising, therefore, that six of the eleven Senate limousines are assigned to staff employees. But even a Congressman cannot resist a bargain. For a token $750 a year in rent, the chairman of any Congressional Committee can drive a gleaming, new Lincoln Continental. Even a lesser Senator whose vote on auto matters also counts can keep a Chrysler Imperial LeBaron in his garage for the same $750 annual payment. One who snapped up this bargain, Senator Vance Hartke, D-Ind., must have been a disappointment to Detroit. He led the Senate fight to impose safety regulations on the auto industry, no doubt planning strategy as he drove to Capitol Hill in his low-rental Imperial LeBaron.

Health Care—A Congressman growing green about the gills can call up one of the three doctors in the Capitol for free medical advice. Most medicines, too, are absolutely gratis. If he needs hospitalization, he can check in at any military hospital and pay only for his board and room. The chief of the Congressional medical staff is Dr. George Calver, a rear admiral, who draws a $1,500 expense allowance in addition to his Navy salary and commutes in a seven-passenger, air-conditioned Government limousine, replete with chauffeur. Calver's office handles 47,000 patient visits in an average year. He also supervises a pharmacy and a physical therapy room on Capitol Hill as well as a first-aid station staffed by a nurse in each Congressional office building. A resuscitator is kept near each chamber, first-aid equipment and stretchers are available in the Democratic and Republican cloakrooms, and an ambulance is gassed and ready in the Senate garage for any emergency.

On those quiet occasions when Congress gets around to appropriating money for its own creature needs, someone almost always tries to slip through a sleeper to increase the fringe benefits. In an obscure paragraph tucked into a Federal retirement bill, Senator John Williams, R-Del., recently discovered language that would comfort not only the elderly poor but the 535 members of Congress as well. The beneficial wording had been added by Senator Ralph Yarborough, D-Tex., who, looking quite astonished, insisted that he hadn't realized members were covered by the bill. Caught with the blind up, Senators sheepishly excluded themselves from the provisions.

Senator Williams one spring also introduced a Senate resolution decreeing that a stationery fund must be used to buy— well, stationery. A colloquy on the Senate floor, however, stirred up Senatorial indignation. Wyoming's Senator Gale McGee thought it shocking that Williams would "question the judgment of this body on how to spend their money." Tennessee's Ross Bass, wondering aloud how an impecunious solon could get along without a couple of allowances, denounced his colleague for "trying to make this a rich man's club!" But it was Richard Russell, the senior Senator from Georgia, who rose to his feet, beet-faced, and delivered the most devastating comment of all. Some people, drawled the Georgian, still had the jaundiced notion "that the Senate had to be watched with exceeding care." With that, spring madness subsided and Williams gave up the quest.

Repeated attempts to curb the franking privilege have also been shouted down. This has left unresolved the question of how much political propaganda the Post Office should allow to be mailed under the free postal privilege. Was Ohio's Representative Walter Moeller wholly ethical, for example, in sending out copies of his wife's newspaper columns to home newspapers, postage free?

Williams took umbrage, in particular, to the use of the frank to circulate Congressional mail addressed only to "Occupant." He declared, "This means that candidates for reelection could use their franking privilege to circulate the voters of an entire state with the taxpayers paying the postage. In fact, under the old arrangement there is nothing to prohibit a Congressional member who was running for the Presidency from using his franking privilege to circulate the entire United States with political propaganda and letting the taxpayers pay the postage merely by putting his speeches in the *Congressional Record* and having them reprinted."

Although the public is generally unaware of it, anything that appears in the *Congressional Record* automatically becomes "official business" and may be mailed under the franking privilege. Members may insert almost anything they wish in the *Record*. This includes not only speeches they make but some they don't make. By getting permission to "revise and extend" his remarks, a Congressman can also have a speech appear just as if he had held his colleagues entranced. As so often happens, the speech is never uttered on the floor at all but is intended strictly for home consumption.

Just as non-speeches can be inserted into the *Record,* occasionally it will also contain a verbatim report of a non-session. Not long ago the *Record* offered a half page of Senate dialogue that took place after the Senate had recessed. It happened just as Oregon's Senator Wayne Morse was arising for one of his nocturnal orations. The presiding Senator, Daniel Brewster, D-Md., rapped the gavel and declared the Senate adjourned. He explained afterwards that he had an important dinner engagement and could not hang around. Morse, incensed, never got to give his speech, but he saw that his remarks condemning Brewster were entered into the *Record*.

2. "Everyone Knows I Am Honest"

Rank has always had its petty privileges, and so it is perhaps not surprising that Congressmen should relish these trappings of their office. If these privileges are occasionally—and in some cases regularly—abused, they are for the most part only minor excesses when compared with the larger outrages committed and countenanced by the Congress. It is these violations of decent ethical behavior in men we look to as our national leaders and exemplars that are the essence of this book.

The integrity of Congress was enunciated in its earliest days by Thomas Jefferson, who returned a gift to a Baltimore merchant and wrote:

> It is a law, sacred to me while in public character, to receive nothing which bears a pecuniary value. This is necessary to the confidence of my country, it is necessary as an example for its benefit, and necessary to the tranquility of my own mind.

Jefferson's words were read, admired, and quickly forgotten.

From the earliest days of the Republic, the votes of Congressmen have been bought by lobbyists, compromised by women and traded for large and small favors. Over the years, the words of Jefferson have been ignored, and in their place the ideas of John Bricker have often been practiced. Bricker, a Senator from Ohio who ran unsuccessfully as Thomas Dewey's Vice Presidential nominee in 1948, was chairman of the Senate Commerce Committee while he drew $35,000 a year from his law firm, which represented the Pennsylvania Railroad. When his conduct was questioned, Bricker responded, "Everyone knows I am honest."

Everyone does not know. Indeed no one can be sure of the honesty of the 100 Senators and 435 Representatives who sit in Congress today. The censure of Connecticut's Senator Thomas Dodd in 1967 inspired Senate leaders to predict that an ethics bill would be quickly passed. But none was forthcoming. In the House a call for creation of an ethics committee was hooted down in 1966, and passed by a 400-to-0 vote in 1967 after the wrongdoing of Senator Dodd and New

York's Representative Adam Clayton Powell focused attention on this sore subject. But there was no rush to legislate rules of conduct. Speaker John McCormack, D-Mass., loaded the committee with members who could be depended upon not to embarrass their colleagues. He gave the committee stern, private instructions to confine its investigation to altruistic generalities. At an early session, Representative Charles Halleck, R-Ind., who earned the nickname "Two Cadillac Charlie" for his ability to keep his garage filled with cut-rate Cadillacs during the postwar shortages, became incensed over testimony that Congress was not held in the highest esteem by the citizens.

There have been too many members of Congress like Representative Victor Wickersham, D-Okla., who announced, "I am a poor man," when he came to Washington in the 1940s, but who listed his net worth in a 1966 report to the Federal Communications Commission at $1,579,789. Wickersham accumulated his fortune in and out of Congress, but much of it was gathered while he served in the House. He had an unusual knack for acquiring land where the Government wanted to put up new buildings.

There have been other members, like Senator Eugene McCarthy, D-Minn., who came to Washington with little money in the bank, and because of their skill as speakers have reaped large honorariums on speaking tours around the nation—tours that cut deeply into the Congressmen's time. McCarthy has been so successful at the lectern that he was able to buy columnist Walter Lippmann's showplace Washington home for $70,000 in 1967.

Scores of Congressmen have toured the world on the taxpayers' money, ostensibly on fact-finding missions. Some of these junkets have produced useful intelligence. Most have been expense-paid vacations in the fleshpots of Europe and Asia, with Congressmen drawing freely on embassy cash reserves to pay for drinking sprees, nightclubs, theater tickets, and gifts for friends back home.

Capitol Hill has also become a parade ground for reserve officers who, as a reward for valiant service in the annual battle for more military appropriations, find themselves rapidly promoted. They also spend three weeks each summer on active duty inspecting military facilities at such grim outposts as Paris, Rome, London, Tokyo, Hong Kong and Honolulu.

In Congressional offices, wives, sons, daughters, brothers, sisters, and mothers-in-law toil along with the nephews for whom nepotism is named. The practice was banned last year in the House when a bill to outlaw nepotism mistakenly was brought to a vote. The unhappy Representatives dared not be recorded against reform.

Some Congressmen who rail against the unfair tax burden carried by part of the population conspire to help other citizens, particularly those who produce oil, get off with token payments. In return, the oilmen make generous payments to campaign chests and, on occasion, directly to the pockets of Congressmen.

Some members of Congress have enriched themselves through their influence, implicit and explicit, over the nation's regulatory commissions. The list of Congressmen who own broadcasting stations, for instance, is awesome, and their profits enormous.

Still others use their positions as guardians of the public interest to forge financial empires in the banking and savings-and-loan industries, while voting for legislation that makes these industries even more profitable.

Human beings are used even more unscrupulously by the Congressional land barons, who exert their power on Capitol Hill to keep the wages and living conditions of migratory farm workers at an intolerable level while insuring large profits for themselves through high crop-price supports.

While making the nation's laws, hundreds of Congressmen continue to make money on the law, thanks to their legal firms back home. The firms of some lawyer-Congressmen delete the name of their elected partner when the firms handle cases involving the Government, but this subterfuge does not at all diminish the Congressmen's value to the firms, or necessarily the Congressmen's income from the firms.

Presiding over all of this potential and actual chicanery is a small clique of tired old men who have achieved power by their dogged ability to hold on to their seats. Most are from districts or states where the two-party system is virtually non-existent. The ability to stay in Congress under such circumstances and the good judgment demonstrated by picking such states for residency in the first place are the only criteria by which committee chairmen are selected. Their power is almost limitless, and they can stimulate legislation—or destroy it—to suit their friends, contributors or their own financial interests.

Lurking behind the scenes, in the gray shadows of the Capitol, is an army of lobbyists, efficient and well heeled, pushing the interests of their employers. Most lobbyists are better paid than are the Congressmen they influence. They are equipped with arguments and statistics to help make their points, and they add emphasis to their words with their thick bankrolls. It is rather unusual—although not unheard of—for today's lobbyists to pass over their cash in sealed envelopes or in brown paper bags. A more sophisticated approach is through campaign contributions, and for this the Democrats and the Republicans have campaign committees in both the Senate and the House. Contributions can be made to selected Congressmen through the campaign committees, and the records will never disclose the transactions. Employees of the campaign committees work to reinforce the lobbyists' pressures. "I consider myself a lobbyist for the big contributors," one campaign committee staff member admitted. "If they come up with the money, it's my job to see that they get a hearing." It is sometimes possible for a Congressman to win a contribution no matter which way he votes. Opposing groups of lobbyists stake their slush funds against each other and match the competition dollar for dollar.

It is illegal to solicit or accept political funds on Federal property, but the campaign committees of both parties nevertheless occupy space in the Senate Office Building. The Democrats also maintain a campaign committee office on the House side. The Republican Congressional Campaign Committee, well financed and heavily staffed, occupies a vast second-floor suite of rooms in a hotel across the street from the House Office Buildings. "The laws have never been much of a problem," one campaign committee official said. "If the question ever comes up about taking money on Government property, I can always walk across the street to get it."

The only law governing the conduct of Congressmen is the archaic Corrupt Practices Act, which was passed in 1925—long before the costs of radio and television made political campaigns soar beyond the means of all but the most wealthy—and is universally ignored. It demands that Congressmen file a record of their personal campaign expenses and that committees operating in more than one state also file reports. To circumvent this, legislators set up committees in their states to handle their financing. Such a gimmick allowed Senator Edward Kennedy of Massachusetts to report both contributions and expenses at zero after his high-priced 1964 campaign. Under the terms of the law, he neither collected nor disbursed a penny; all transactions were handled by campaign committees.

These are the abuses of power—the transgressions of morality and the law—that are commonplace in Congress today. The members of Congress, of course, are painfully aware of the outrages that occur under the Capitol dome. Yet Congress is anxious to avoid legislating a code of ethics for itself. Like all self-regulating groups, it haughtily pretends that all is well. The symbols of autocratic power with which Congress has armed itself may tend to make Congressmen forget that they are merely employees of the American people—but they would do well to remember that an informed public can bring about a change in the ethical standards of Congress by mandating a change in its membership.

I

PORTRAIT
OF A SENATOR

1
PUBLIC AND PRIVATE

Congressmen on the make have discovered a number of shortcuts to the easy dollar, and Senator Thomas J. Dodd, D-Conn., has tried most of them. But for the temptations and the tolerance on Capitol Hill, however, he might have become a worthy legislator. He was a victim as much of the Senate's shortcomings as of his own, for the failings of the one brought out the failings of the other. Much of the story of Tom Dodd is, in microcosm, the story of Congress.

1. Bridging the Obscurity Gap

Throughout the Senate side of the Capitol, the three-bell alarm clamored urgently, summoning Senators to the chamber. Into the great oval, its antique desks arranged in a graceful arc, they shuffled. After answering to their names,

17

some barged off again with the harried looks of men having more important duties; others lingered on, glancing curiously in the direction of the freshman Senator who was scrambling to his feet. From the thronelike leather chair behind the marble rostrum, Senator Lee Metcalf of Montana, temporarily presiding, intoned, "The junior Senator from Connecticut is recognized." Then, with studied detachment, Metcalf began leafing through the Senate calendar for February 26, 1959.

The newcomer, square-shouldered, silver-haired, his massive bulk too big for his short stature, looked like a larger man standing in a well. He gestured to the pages, and a lectern was hurried to his desk. In the doorway of the Democratic cloakroom, Senator Robert Kerr, the Senate's uncrowned king, loomed massively, his open coat revealing the rumpled blue shirt and Phi Beta Kappa key that were the disparate trademarks of this rustic sophisticate. He cast an imperious eye across the chamber. "Who's that little feller with the big text, Bobby?" There was a blend of mockery and amiability in Kerr's Oklahoma twang.

"That's Senator Dodd of Connecticut," said Bobby Baker.

"Dodge?"

"Dodd."

Kerr frowned. "It seems to me that Mr. Dodge hasn't been around here long enough to warm his seat yet," he said. Having registered his disapproval of Dodd's affront to the tradition that a freshman should be seen and not heard, Kerr shambled off on other business. Dodd was speaking now. "No new Senator relishes the prospect of pitting his views in opposition to the views of wiser men whom he respects and admires," he began, "but . . ."

His voice was resonant, easily heard high up in the press gallery where newsmen were beginning to file in. Ranged around him were his 14 fellow Democratic freshmen, all elected in the 1958 sweep, observing self-consciously the tradition of attending a classmate's maiden speech.

William Fulbright, the Senator from Arkansas, slumped behind his front-row desk and peered at Dodd's prepared text through Ben Franklin glasses resting on the end of his nose. He frowned at what he read. For years he had watched American foreign policy under John Foster Dulles assume what he considered a dangerous rigidity, buttressed by self-righteous moralizing. Fulbright saw in Soviet Premier Nikita

Khrushchev's latest ultimatum to the West to get out of Berlin a dangerous threat to peace that required more from Western leaders than oratory and slogans.

The Connecticut Senator was warming to his subject. "Is our Berlin policy too rigid and inflexible?" he demanded. "I think not. There is no peculiar virtue in flexibility. To me, flexibility implies compromise and concession. When applied to fundamental principles, right principles, flexibility is not only without virtue; it becomes a vice."

Three seats to the right of Fulbright in the leadership chair sat Senator Mike Mansfield, the Democratic Whip, who shared Fulbright's concern. The lean and leathery Montanan, the cares of the world etched on his long, solemn face, his forehead tilted back in polite attention, began to recognize in Dodd's words a point-by-point rebuttal of his own speech made a week ago. But he showed no sign of pique.

Ohio's Senator Frank Lausche, with untamed hair and intense manner, nodded in vigorous approval as Dodd, in measured blasts, assaulted the theory of compromise. Aging Joseph C. O'Mahoney, D-Wyo., blue eyes lustrous behind rimless glasses attached to his coat lapel by a black ribbon, beamed benevolently on the new Irish orator. John F. Kennedy, his February tan turning strangely yellow, looked at the clock and tapped his finger restlessly on the polished desk top. Across the center aisle, on the Republican side, sat New York's Jacob Javits, mechanically signing mail, reminding colleagues of his endless task of representing 18 million people. Behind him, pink and cherubic under a lion's mane of white hair, his colleague Kenneth Keating chatted affably with an aide, bearing the Empire State's burdens in a more relaxed manner.

Some were there to encourage the neophyte, others to see the upstart humbled. Dodd spoke for 55 minutes without interruption, his voice steadily deepening in intensity. He lampooned those who urged concession—"the righteous are called to repentance instead of the sinners"—and proposed a 90-day mobilization of military force to dramatize America's determination to stay in Berlin. He concluded with a fervid appeal: "The hour is late. Our friends in Europe already are discouraged by our appearance of division and vacillation. If we are in fact facing the ultimate test, let us approach it not as a divided people, seeking ways to avoid our responsibility, asking ourselves if the price of freedom is too high, resentful of our fate. Let us rather approach it as a united America, proud of our ideals and traditions, conscious of our great mission in the world, and confident that if we but act aright, the hand of God will sustain us to the ultimate victory."

The Senator folded his text, lowered his head, and steeled himself for what was to follow. Several colleagues leaped to their feet and sought recognition from the chair. Conscious that he was being tested in one of the world's foremost forensic arenas, Dodd mentally discounted the complimentary verbiage with which Senators are wont to adorn one another and listened intently for the bite that might be hidden. But there was no bite; for an hour accolade followed accolade. Not even Mansfield rose in his own defense.

Out in the anteroom, news tickers in mahogany cabinets clicked off paragraph after paragraph of Dodd's remarks and the enthusiastic Senate response. At last Fulbright, troubled over the way the Senate had been carried away by an incendiary speech, sought recognition. He turned to face the fledgling Connecticut Senator across the rows that divided front from back, power from ambition. He opened with a series of "clarifying questions," trying to lead Dodd to less bellicose ground without an undignified clash. But Dodd would not be led; he responded touchily to Fulbright's gentle probes, disdaining any expression of rapport. Fulbright, his patience exhausted, rasped back, "I do not like to hear the Senator announce the principle that he sees no hope of better understanding with the Russians . . . that this is a matter of good and evil, and until Russia changes completely the character of her whole society and her approach there is no hope of adjustment."

The freshman gave no ground but moved to the attack: "Our cause is the good cause. The Russian cause, the cause of murder, enslavement, aggression and falsehood is *not* the good cause. . . . A lot of mumbo-jumbo and mental mush about 'rigidity' and 'inflexibility' will never help us as we face this critical hour." Shifting his gaze from Fulbright to sweep the entire chamber, he declaimed with an oratorical quaver in his voice, "What we need to say, as American people, and say in unmistakably clear terms, is that we *are* right. We must tell the Russians we cannot surrender Berlin. Let us not talk about standing firm, and then in mushy, soft words say that on some basis, somewhere, somehow, we will do nothing [*sic*] *other* than stand fast."

Clearly, Dodd was carrying the day. He was making headlines that would do Fulbright no good back home in simplistic Arkansas. Abandoning hope of injecting moderation into the debate, Fulbright backed off. He complimented the Connecticut Senator, stressing their areas of agreement and adding his own plea for firmness in Berlin. But, looking to the future, he closed with an admonition: "We have already noticed some slight change in the character of this Russian regime over the last one. They have at least up to now abandoned the extreme form of terror. I am suggesting that for the future—not with regard to Berlin itself now—we should be careful not to get into a habit of thought which would exclude the possibility not only of changes in the present regime, as such, but also the possibility of changes in the successor to Khrushchev."

Fulbright sat down. The accolades resumed. The triumph was Dodd's. He had held the floor, controlling the air space above it, from 1:00 until 4:03 P.M. The last encomium acknowledged, he yielded the floor and left the chamber, his aide Jim Boyd hurrying after him. "How did it go?" asked Dodd. "Did I make a fool of myself?" He lit a long cigar while listening to how well it had gone. "Good, I'm glad you think so," he said. "I think so, too. We hit a home run."

Indeed, Dodd had knocked a home run. The radio and television networks carried excerpts from his speech. His name was splashed in printer's ink from coast to coast, and his image peered solemnly from hundreds of front pages. *Life* placed editorial garlands on the new Senator's classic brow; *Vital Speeches* printed the text; praise poured in from across the nation.

Dodd was jubilant. At one leap he had bridged the obscurity gap—an achievement that eludes many Senators for a lifetime—less than two months after entering the Senate. Lenten resolutions were put aside, and the Scotch was brought out. He called in Boyd, who had drafted the speech, and gave him a $1,000 raise on the spot—"to encourage you, not to spoil you." Then he busied himself with plans for an encore. "I think we've stiffened up the State Department," he said. "Now we've got to follow this up with a speech about the Communist menace, worldwide, not just in Europe. The time is just right for it."

2. The Country Squire

Few men have come to the United States Senate with a more colorful past or a more promising future than Thomas J. Dodd. At fifty-one, he presented a study in contrasts. He was still handsome; his finely patrician profile called to mind toga-clad Roman senators of old. Yet his distinguished face sometimes showed the ravages of wear and worry and dissipation. He was elegant in appearance, always well manicured and tailored, in his four-button coats, peg trousers and Italian shoes, with his identifying prop, a good watch fob and chain suspended from his lapel. Yet a rougher-hewn, earthier Dodd lurked beneath the surface, betraying its presence in the big cigars bunched in his inner breast pocket, soup stains left from hurried meals, coat stuffed with papers, tie often askew.

On public display he was stiff and severe, exuding dignity; but his private manner was disarmingly homespun and folksy. He was approachable by anyone, and people sensed it. In his official role he was given to moralizing and to viewing with disdain, but he could be a boon companion. He relished jokes hugely, and his colleagues, knowing of his weakness for stories of all sorts, would approach him regularly with their latest, whispering to him amid the hushed and decorous atmosphere off the Senate floor and leaving him doubled up and scarlet with laughter. Among intimates, he could tell a story surpassingly well, with a rare gift for mimicry and dialect, but he could never be persuaded to employ this talent on the platform beyond the mere telling of formal anecdotes. To tell a joke in public is to risk the rebuff of silence, and Tom Dodd had no stomach for rebuffs.

He systematically broke appointments as a way of life, but he could soothe the most piqued feelings with remarkably original apologies. He would keep distinguished visitors waiting in his office—sometimes for hours, sometimes in vain. Yet he was unusually accessible to obscure people who had personal problems: a Capitol Hill cop in a jam, an aging Western Union messenger seeking marital advice, the down-in-luck daughter of an old friend. He would interrupt a conversation with the Secretary of State to take a phone call from a minor official of a Teamsters local in Putnam, Connecticut. Dodd enjoyed incongruous groupings of people. He would arrange a private luncheon in his office with Archduke Otto von Hapsburg and make it a threesome by inviting a small-time politico from Ridgefield, Connecticut; then he would barge off on some mysterious errand, leaving his guests alone together for more than an hour to discuss their mutual interests. He contemptuously dismissed the advice of learned authorities, but divined the deepest insight in the chance remark of a cab-driver or airport porter.

He was a product of both the brashly secular Yale Law School and the staunchly Catholic Providence College. His emotions and politics were liberal, but his instincts and philo-sophical roots were conservative. He voted unfailingly for welfare measures that would help the underprivileged, the sick, or the aged; but he instinctively distrusted liberals in general and intellectual liberals in particular. His favorite magazine was *National Review*.

For all his surface sophistication, Dodd was nonetheless provincial in outlook. An inveterate world traveler, he held a view of the world shaped by the inherited mystique of small-town, rural Connecticut with its blend of prejudice and certi-tude, severity and escapism. He had lived parts of his life in a dozen different states; he was at ease in the best circles in Washington and New York City. But eastern Connecticut was the place he loved. It was there, in North Stonington, that he went to enjoy his leisure, there that he poured his money into an old abandoned farm on 400 acres, hidden away in a wood-ed valley. He converted it into a small estate, with a private road, a verdant blanket of lawn stretching in every direction to the forest, a restored main house with a rich interior of oak, stone, and glass, a guest house, a stable, a hunting pre-serve, an artificial lake stocked with trout, and a waterfall that murmured restfully through New England summer nights.

And it was the people of this region whom he valued above all others, not as a politician seeking votes, for he also sought votes in industrial centers and swank suburbs, but as a coun-try squire whose roots, predilections and values struck a har-monious chord with his neighbors in the beautiful land of gentle townships that antedate the American Revolu-tion—Mystic, Old Lyme, Lebanon, Preston, Ledyard, Baltic, names that conjured up images to be cherished and trusted.

3. Young Tom

Thomas Joseph Dodd was born on May 15, 1907—the youngest child in a family of five children (the others all girls)—in Norwich, Connecticut, then called "the rose of New England," now a drab little factory town. His parents were second-generation Irish, his mother an elocution teacher, his father a small building contractor and livery stable owner who waxed in good times, waned in bad. Thomas Dodd, Sr., was something of a figure to the town's youngsters who found adventure in the primitive construction practices of the day.

"Who made the world?" the nuns would ask in Catechism class.

"Tom Dodd and his horses," some freckled wag was sure to pipe.

Young Tom was scarcely four when his mother began teaching him to orate. Legend has it that she would place him on top of a washtub in the middle of the kitchen and coach his childish declamations, but when *Reader's Digest* used this story in a favorable biographical sketch, Dodd objected violently. The editors obligingly substituted "kitchen table" in place of "washtub."

He attended the Norwich public schools. Not an overly bright student, he was something of a rebel, at one time leading a short-lived students' strike that was broken summarily when the principal yanked him from a platform in the midst of an impromptu exhortation and gave him a good hiding. Hoping for better results, his father next sent him to St. Anselm's Prep, a Catholic school noted for its discipline. Still the prankster, Dodd was expelled for misconduct, then taken back. He went on, with many of his St. Anselm's classmates, to Providence College, a Dominican institution in Rhode Island. It was here that he assimilated the basic Thomistic view of life as a conflict between good and evil. Later this philosophy was to develop into an Armageddon concept of the struggle against Communism. But in his college days, Dodd was no serious-minded ideologue. In those days of relative innocence before LSD and gambling invaded college campuses, he cavorted with a gang of practical jokers whose high jinks contributed to Providence College lore.

Those were also depression days, and finagling an invitation to someone's home for a good dinner became an art. Dodd, always a voracious eater, was an accomplished sponger. He once masqueraded as a young priest just returned from African missions—collar, dark suit, and all—to gain an invitation to a devout Catholic home known for its good table. All went well until the beatitudinous young missionary was led into the bedroom of an aging invalid for a deathbed confession. "It wasn't easy to get a good dinner in those days" was the most Dodd would say about the incident, shrouding in secrecy what went on in the sickroom.

Steeped in the austerity of St. Thomas Aquinas in the long winter months, the young philosophy major tasted of the high life during the summers, night-clerking at the fashionable Watch Hill (Rhode Island) Beach Hotel. With his Hollywood good looks, wavy black hair, muscular frame, and an endless store of funny stories, Tom became a favorite with waitresses and debutantes alike. One summer he met Mary Grace Murphy of Westerly, Rhode Island, petite, dark-haired, pleasant, who was to become the most important single influence in his life. But for a time there were many girls.

Dodd graduated from Providence College in 1930 with a bachelor's degree in philosophy and a yen to become an actor. It was an ambition his father would not abide; he had struggled to educate Tom's four sisters to be teachers and the boy to be a lawyer. And that was that. The 1930s, in a depression-flattened mill town, offered no indulgence to aspiring Thespians; young Tom was thought lucky to have a chance to go to Yale Law School. There, if he could not perform on the stage, he managed to substitute the platform; he became better known as a political enthusiast than as a student at Yale.

Politics came naturally to him; he had soaked it up as a youngster at play. His father's livery stable had been a local hangout for the town's hard-pressed Democrats back in those dim days when, as Dodd later recounted, "there were so few Democrats in my part of Connecticut that they held their caucuses in kitchens, with plenty of room to spare." He became president of the Yale Democratic Club; along with classmate Bob Wagner, later to become mayor of New York City, Dodd in 1932 organized a group of leather-lunged college orators known as "The Flying Wedge." Each evening during that electric Roosevelt autumn, the group would precede the Democratic candidates along the campaign trail, "warming up" crowds and holding them till the candidates arrived. On the stump night after night Dodd conquered his natural fear of speaking in public. Without the aid of loudspeakers, often in the open air, he learned to project his voice, and he mastered the art of whipping up an audience and trading invective with hecklers. All that the old-style oratory had to teach, he learned, and learned it well.

Before long the aggressive spieler came to the attention of important Democrats. Homer S. Cummings, who was to become FDR's Attorney General, and Francis T. Maloney, a political power in Connecticut, eyed the bombastic young student as a comer. When Dodd graduated from Yale Law School in 1933, the new Attorney General asked him to come to Washington and sent him to J. Edgar Hoover with his strong backing. The strict Hoover, usually wary of political appointments, liked Dodd and made him a Special Agent.

His FBI career was to be short, about one year, but memorable. Those were the days of the kidnapers and the famous bank-robbing gangs, when sensational mobsters like Dillinger and Nelson fired the imagination of the country and commanded the front pages. Dodd was assigned to St. Paul, Minnesota, where, according to his own account, he helped to crack the Bremer kidnaping case and took part in the famous "shoot-out" with the Dillinger gang at the Little Bohemia roadhouse in Rhinelander, Wisconsin. Dangerous Dodd also tracked down and arrested "Doc" May, the gangland medico who had patched up Dillinger.

Somehow, during all these escapades, he found time to woo and win Grace Murphy, a girl he had met years before in Rhode Island. But plans for a big Westerly wedding had to be canceled; the FBI did not give new agents time off to get married. Grace came to St. Paul for a hurried wedding and a weekend honeymoon. She was not to be an FBI wife long, however. Back in Connecticut, the campaign trail was beckoning. Francis T. Maloney was running for the United States Senate, and Dodd happily exchanged J. Edgar Hoover's tough discipline for the rough-and-tumble of political combat. Maloney triumphed in the Democratic rout of 1934, and Dodd was rewarded with an appointment as deputy chief of Connecticut's WPA. Later he was named state director of the newly formed National Youth Administration.

With jobs to hand out, favors to dispense and scores of speaking engagements and publicity opportunities for an attractive youth leader to exploit, Dodd began building a state-wide political base. Along with other NYA leaders, he was invited to Hyde Park to meet the President and attended a national NYA conference in Washington, where he encountered and formed an enduring friendship with a lanky, fast-talking fellow who headed the program in Texas—Lyndon B. Johnson. Across the state Dodd could see tangible results in young lives salvaged and in shattered families tenuously preserved. His natural enthusiasm for social-welfare programs deepened and would never leave him; 30 years later he would look back on these days as the most rewarding of his life.

Growing in influence, he became a leader of the burgeoning and chaotic Connecticut Young Democrats, vying for control with a youthful political operator from Hartford named John Bailey. Still in his twenties, Dodd was prominently mentioned as a candidate for Congress and for lieutenant governor. Instead, in 1938, he was appointed special assistant to the U.S. Attorney General, a post he was to hold for seven years. Now based in Washington, he breathed in the heady atmosphere of the last peacetime days of the Roosevelt era, before the New Deal was replaced by Win-the-War. A new civil rights section was created in the Justice Department, and Dodd was named a charter member. Its purpose: to begin testing the degree to which the guaranties and protections of the Constitution could be enforced in the South. For this mammoth task the new unit had less than half a dozen lawyers and virtually no successful precedents, but it had unlimited enthusiasm. Dodd went into Georgia, Arkansas, and South Carolina to defend the legal rights of laborers to organize, and to prosecute local sheriffs for the arbitrary arrest and shakedown of Negroes. He did battle with the red-neck sheriffs at the height of their ugly power; he learned the frustrations of facing hostile juries in stifling courtrooms where due process of law was a mere curiosity. "We won some cases and lost some, mostly lost," Dodd would say later, "but we helped to lay the foundation for victories that were to be won by others in later years." Once, after successfully convicting local law officers in Crittenden County, Arkansas, Tom and Grace Dodd were escorted to the state line under police protection "for their own safety." These experiences opened new dimensions of understanding for the rising politician; they toughened him and stirred in him a dedication to the cause of civil rights.

War always swallows up peaceful reform, and the darkening clouds over Europe and Asia brought a shift of emphasis within the Justice Department. The civil rights team was dispersed; Dodd was assigned to counterespionage work. When World War II eventually thundered down upon Pearl Harbor, Dodd was thirty-four years old, the father of four. He sought a commission in the Navy but failed his physical (high blood pressure). Dejected, apparently consigned to obscurity at the U.S. Attorney's office in Hartford, he requested assignments closely related to the war effort.

But great events had a way of seeking out Dodd. The FBI apprehended saboteurs crawling ashore at New London and broke a Nazi spy ring operating along the East Coast. Dodd played a key role in the prosecution, which ended in the conviction of the "American Führer," Fritz Kuhn, and other German-American Bundists. He added to his growing reputation as a prosecutor by convicting executives of the Anaconda Wire and Cable Company for selling defective communications wire to the Army. Barred from winning the military laurels that so often advance a political career, Dodd made a name on the home front. The notice he gained for breaking up the Nazi fifth column led in 1945 to a coveted appointment to the American delegation at the Nuremberg war crimes trials.

Dodd flew immediately to Nuremberg and found it in indescribable ruins, the stench of dead bodies still in the air. He started off in a minor position on the prosecution staff, but his zest for the proceedings impressed the chief prosecutor, Supreme Court Justice Robert H. Jackson, who elevated him to executive trial counsel, a post second only to Jackson's. For 18 months the four-power tribunal performed what Dodd was later to call "an autopsy on history's most horrible catalogue of human crimes." Walter Cronkite, then an obscure reporter covering the trial, credited Dodd with being the key figure behind the American effort. Twenty years later Cronkite would say, "Tom always pulled things together when they seemed to be falling apart."

After an 18-month absence, Dodd returned to his family in Lebanon, Connecticut, to find himself a celebrity. He was lionized as an important participant in history's most famous trial and hailed as an international lawyer of the first rank. Honors poured in on him: the U.S. Medal of Freedom, a Presidential citation from Harry Truman, the Czech Order of the White Lion from President Eduard Beneš. He plunged into one-worldism and became president of Connecticut's United World Federalists. Audiences clamored for him as a speaker; his name suddenly became pregnant with political significance. And Tom Dodd wasn't the sort to turn his back on fate. Resigning from the Government, he launched into private law practice, moved to fashionable West Hartford and began laying plans for seizing the 1948 Democratic gubernatorial nomination.

4. Into the Fold

There was one troublesome obstacle in Dodd's path to the governorship: Chester Bowles, an interloper in Connecticut Democratic affairs. An out-of-state renegade Republican with a distinguished Massachusetts family pedigree, Bowles had made a lucrative splash as a Madison Avenue advertising man and had purchased a baronial estate in Essex, Connecticut. He had turned from huckstering to foreign affairs, championing isolationism as war spread across Europe. With a remarkable capacity for phoenixlike resurrections that was to demonstrate itself again and again, Bowles humbled himself by taking a job beneath his station in the Connecticut Office of Price Administration. But he quickly rose to prominence as national wartime OPA boss and helped brain-trust the conversion from war to peace. Likable, with a big frame, Presidential looks, amiable mien, casualness of dress, and a knack for the soft sell, "Chet" Bowles projected Big Ideas. Phrases like "massive program" and "comprehensive planning" dominated his speeches; he was now an enthusiastic internationalist and ADA sparkplug. He had a charisma, a Presidential aura.

Still Dodd was the early front-runner. Looking much like a matinee idol, with prematurely silvering hair, new prestige, old roots, a gracious wife and five small children, he seemed all but anointed. He also appeared to be getting the better of the political rabbit-punching. He needled Bowles about past statements that the domestic Communist menace was a myth. When Red Poland offered Dodd a decoration for services at

Nuremberg, he spurned it, saying he would no more accept an award from the Communists than from the Nazis. When Bowles led an abortive move to dump Harry Truman for the Presidential nomination, on the ground that Truman couldn't possibly win, Dodd saw an opportunity and defended Truman stoutly. Chosen to second Truman's nomination at the Democratic convention, he addressed a national audience with vigor and style. The Bowles effort collapsed, and Dodd's position was correspondingly strengthened. But his old rival, John Bailey, who through long years of unspectacular drudgery had mastered the intricacies of organization politics while Dodd and others were winning public acclaim, was now Connecticut Democratic chairman. His power was precarious but substantial; he held back from a commitment to Dodd.

Bailey knew that the chances for a Democratic victory in Connecticut in 1948 were slim at best. Any division among Democrats would make an unpromising situation hopeless. The Wallace third-party movement was vigorous in the state; Henry Wallace would be on the Progressive ticket, and the new party had announced plans to field an entire state ticket. Estimates of their potential vote ran as high as 100,000, most of it to be weaned away from traditional Democrats. Bailey thought the 100,000 estimate inflated, but *any* defection of Democrats to a Progressive gubernatorial candidate would be fatal. Could the Wallaceites be persuaded to support the Democratic state ticket, despite the national split? The answer would be "no" if the Democratic candidate was Dodd, "yes" if it was Bowles. Dodd was anathema to the Progressive party; he had labeled it a "Communist fifth column." But Bowles was acceptable to the Progressives, and they promised to withdraw their own state ticket if Bowles was the Democratic nominee. At the convention, Bailey pushed Bowles over the top, then offered Dodd the lieutenant governorship. Flushing scarlet, Dodd thundered scornfully that he would have nothing to do with a ticket that was backed by Communists, and he stormed out of the convention.

Bailey's political arithmetic turned out to be correct. Truman lost Connecticut to Dewey by the margin of the Wallace vote, but Bowles narrowly squeaked into office, launching a new era for Connecticut Democrats. Although a political outcast, Dodd was not without honor. The Wallace party indeed proved to be deeply infiltrated by Communists, as Wallace was later to admit. People who had never before taken notice of Dodd admired his stand on principle, and as the nature of the third-party movement was exposed, his stature rose even as his political fortunes sank.

By 1950 the left wing had contracted political leprosy, and Democrats too close to the left were on the defensive. Dodd's anti-Communist reputation was now of some value. Senator Joseph McCarthy, R-Wis., fresh from successful forays against Democratic Senators in Maryland and Illinois, entered Connecticut. His target: Senator James O'Brien McMahon, chairman of the powerful Joint Committee on Atomic Energy. The late McMahon, a far more resourceful politician than the plaster-saint image of him now allows, called on the pariah, Tom Dodd, to answer McCarthy's soft-on-Communism charges. He came through convincingly in a series of blistering statewide broadcasts. McMahon won handily. But Bowles lost his bid for re-election and bustled off to India, resuscitated by an ambassadorial appointment from the strangely magnanimous Truman, while Dodd, Truman's defender, remained in political obscurity, practicing law in Hartford and biding his time.

By September 1952, John Bailey, who by now had consolidated his hold on party leadership, made a bold move to stay the expected Eisenhower ballot blizzard. Bailey, bald, stoop-shouldered, paunchy, with the cigar-chewing look of a backroom operator, seemed the cartoonist's stereotype of a ward politician, but the caricature was unfair. A hereditary millionaire and successful lawyer, he was in politics for the love of the game. He had started in the precincts and had risen steadily from political errand boy to master of Connecticut's traditionally discordant, brawling Democratic free-for-all. He was accessible and fair; his word was good; he wielded power gently; he believed in compromise; his forte was persuasion.

Brien McMahon had died of cancer and left a Senate vacancy. Bailey now chose Abraham Ribicoff, a phenomenally popular Representative from Hartford, to run against Republican financier Prescott Bush. The chairman moved to heal the Dodd schism by offering Ribicoff's Congressional seat to Dodd. Ribicoff would be the first Jewish candidate to run for high office in Connecticut, and Bailey sought to head off anti-Jewish prejudice by bolstering the ticket with ethnic props. In largely Catholic Hartford County, Connecticut's most populous, he needed a candidate with just the right religious and ideological background to run with the liberal Jew. Dodd filled the bill—Catholic, Irish, moderate, anti-Communist. With characteristic realism that rose above pettiness, Bailey held out his hand to Dodd and brought him back into the fold. Dodd grasped it.

Ribicoff made a good run, good enough to assure his future in statewide politics, but the Ike blizzard buried all Connecticut Democrats—except one. In a favorable district, Dodd emerged with his head above the snowdrift and became the lone Connecticut Democrat in Congress. With McMahon gone, Ribicoff and Benton defeated, Bowles in exile and Bailey's organization battered, Dodd's political stock was suddenly bullish.

In Congress, he voted with the Democrats on basic issues, rose above sectionalism by backing the St. Lawrence Seaway, supported internationalism, fought for civil liberties, and steadily built an image as a statesman—moderate and enlightened, above partisanship, independent of political control. In 1954 Dodd led the party's ticket as he won re-election by 36,000 votes—a record for Connecticut in an off-year contest. His strength helped Ribicoff take the governor's chair from John Lodge in a race so close that the Hartford *Times* prematurely declared Lodge the winner.

Clearly Dodd had earned first crack at the 1956 Democratic Senate nomination and got it. Without financial help from his party, which offered him as a sacrificial lamb, without newspaper support, without an optimistic word from anyone, Dodd fought gamely against the second Eisenhower tidal wave. He carried the Democratic message to every corner of Connecticut, earning the admiration of local party workers who would later remember him as a dauntless fighter in bad times. Pursuing an incredible schedule of personal appearances—dropping by railroad commuter stations at dawn and making midnight tours of factory night shifts—he impressed something of his personality and drive on the state's voters. When Adlai Stevenson's aides publicly gave up Connecticut for lost in October, Dodd fought on. Though he had little regard for Stevenson, he resisted the temptation to disassociate himself from an inevitable loser. On election eve, trembling with fatigue, his eyes rimmed with dark Rooseveltian circles,

Dodd startled discouraged aides by adding to his schedule an open-car tour of the state—"to encourage the party workers."

He ran 175,000 votes ahead of Stevenson, but was swept out with the tide. The polls had scarcely closed before his defeat was certain, and a year's effort lay in ruins. Statistically, he received the worst drubbing ever administered to a Senate candidate in Connecticut. But compared to what had befallen Stevenson and all other Democratic candidates in Connecticut, Dodd stood out as the party's strongest figure. Unyielding to the end, he planned a gala election-night victory party in his West Hartford home; it soon turned into a wake. Newspapers later carried stories of the Dodd children crying (this was the last time newsmen were to be allowed unrestricted access to the Dodd home). But Dodd remained unabashed on that night of Democratic disaster; he toured TV and radio stations and made gracious concession speeches to audiences he knew would be at peak size. And then he went to bed.

The next morning he had to face the consequences of defeat. Deprived of his House seat, physically spent, financially ruined, politically tarred with defeat, he nonetheless found encouragement in the morning voting statistics, which in almost all of the state's 169 towns showed Dodd leading all other Democrats. He called his downcast staff to his home for breakfast, and, sitting in pajamas and bathrobe, his ashen, weary face like a death mask, with the political posters of last night's "victory party" looking mockingly down upon them, he delivered a pep talk—"This is a victory, not a defeat"— and began charting plans for a 1958 comeback.

5. *Long Winter Nights*

A full year before the 1958 election campaign, all the political indicators pointed to a Democratic revival. Not only were there national breezes blowing up a Democratic storm, but in Connecticut, Governor Ribicoff's popularity was so great that the pols could scarcely believe the polls. Suave and sure, with Cary Grant looks, a sensitive political antenna, a penchant for the safe issue and a distaste for controversy, Ribicoff had given the people of the Nutmeg State what they obviously wanted in a governor: moderate progressivism, strong administration, dignity, prudence, and an absence of political partisanship. He had also held taxes down; indeed, he seemed almost as strong with Republicans as with Democrats. His re-election by an unprecedented margin seemed unavoidable, and Democratic office-seekers up and down the state began eyeing his coattails eagerly.

Chairman Bailey happily laid plans for the expected election of a Democratic state legislature for the first time since 1890. In every town and district, rival factions armed for combat; ambitious candidates at all levels saw that election would be easy but nomination hard. Though Bailey would try to stop the fratricide through his fabled legerdermain in balancing interests and keeping insurgents off balance, intraparty bloodletting threatened.

Dodd, out of office, had no forum. But he managed to keep his classic profile in the public eye through a complicated lawsuit in which he represented 13 rank-and-file Teamsters Brotherhood members seeking to oust Jimmy Hoffa as president. The issues were confused, but Dodd emerged from the legal fog with the image of a battler against labor racketeers.

His advisers, chastened by the 1956 defeat, urged Dodd to act cautiously, but he would have none of it. He determined to move, swiftly and boldly, and stake all on the result. It is the political folkway for candidates to pretend until the last minute to have no interest in the office they eagerly covet. For an aspirant to get caught with his ambition showing is considered indecent exposure. Yet a full six months before such announcements were expected, Dodd declared himself a candidate for the seat of Republican Senator William A. Purtell, a colorless ex-manufacturer, who was wafted into the Senate on the Eisenhower tide in 1952. Political pundits—including trenchant Jack Zaiman of the Hartford *Courant*, the state's top political reporter—faulted Dodd for bad timing. He would never be able to sustain campaign momentum, they said knowingly, and the first candidate to poke his head above the mob risked having it knocked off by his covert opponents.

But Dodd knew his Connecticut politics better than the pundits and the courthouse seers. He was not going to be cut out of the pie at Bailey's table on the eve of the state convention. If he was to be denied the Senate nomination, he would have to be beaten in the open, not in the smoke-filled rooms. He let it be known that he was prepared to carry his candidacy into a statewide primary—a threat that sent a tremor through the Democratic satrapies accustomed to settling these things by amicable arrangements with Bailey.

Though Dodd was supremely confident he couldn't lose a primary, he also had tremendous respect for the power of the Bailey-Ribicoff organization to defeat him in a convention, even to deny him the minimum 20-percent delegate vote needed to qualify for a primary. His strategy, therefore, was twofold: to bind at least 20 percent of the delegates irrevocably to his cause by intense person-to-person campaigning, and to neutralize the state Democratic organization. He realized the organization wouldn't be for him, but he hoped to keep it from openly opposing him.

From the fall of 1957 to the spring of 1958, while other candidates hesitated and postured, Dodd toiled to build up so much visible strength that there could be no chance for a Bailey consensus to form behind someone else. He had set a brutal task for himself. Connecticut is a land of contrasts. Its western section includes perhaps the richest stretch of suburbia in the world—Greenwich, Westport, Darien, Fairfield, Stamford, the lush retreats of New York City executives and tycoons; its eastern section contains broken-down ex-mill towns, filled with poverty and unemployment. It is a highly industrialized state, yet it has deep roots in old rural New England. It grows the nation's best cigar tobacco and produces mighty space engines. Its population is more than 50-percent Catholic, heavily sprinkled with old-line Yankee Protestants and articulate Jews. Its industrial areas are a melting pot—Poles, Irish, Italians, Hungarians, Ukrainians, even surprising numbers of Portuguese. It has a few small cities over 100,000 population and 160 small towns. Dodd set out to woo 1,000 individual delegates, scattered among these towns, who held his fate in their collective hands. If he lost this one, there could be no more comebacks; there would remain only a dreary small-town legal practice of processing wills and contracts.

He had no money and no organization. His staff consisted of three unpaid volunteers: Joe Blumenfeld, his law partner, whose task was to raise a limited budget; Ed Sullivan, a grizzled political veteran, who once drove a beer truck and would be Dodd's campaign manager; and Jim Boyd, a blue-eyed young disciple who would handle the writing, press work, and chauffeuring.

Opposing him for the nomination, as yet unannounced, were two national figures: Chester Bowles, his old luster as OPA boss and governor now polished up by an acclaimed performance as Ambassador to India, and William Benton, former Senator and Assistant Secretary of State, McCarthy-slayer, founder of Muzak, and head of *Encyclopaedia Britannica*. Both were millionaires. Also lined up against Dodd was the labor movement, partial to Bowles; the political organization of almost all the major cities, down on Dodd; and the Bailey state machine, publicly uncommitted but quietly opposed to Dodd. Outside of his own Hartford County, where his personal popularity assured strong delegate backing, Dodd had to collect his delegates one by one, pressing the flesh in a hundred small towns.

Every night during the severe winter of 1957–58, Dodd dogged the trail with a tenacity that still elicits awe in Hartford, hurrying back and forth over tortuous country roads, speaking to small groups of from six to sixty. He knew the state, all the catwalks and shortcuts. In every town, at every village crossroads, he knew people *personally*. By February Dodd had rolled up strength that troubled the party hierarchy. While Dodd was cadging delegates at dreary town committee meetings in grubby back rooms, Bowles was preparing himself for the campaign in the grand manner, yachting in Caribbean waters. And Benton was playing "After you, Alphonse," waiting for the Bowles announcement before announcing his own bid. In February the big B's let go of their hats, Bowles with the confident pose that his would land in the center of the ring, Benton cautiously advertising himself as an ideal compromise to break a Dodd-Bowles deadlock.

Suddenly the race entered high gear. Bowles and Benton poured in big money. Bowles deluged the 1,000 delegates with copies of his latest book, long-playing phonograph records of "A Conversation with Chet Bowles," glossy pamphlets worthy of a Presidential candidate, and invitations to fancy dinners held in every section of the state. Benton was not to be outspent. He put local leaders on his campaign payroll and sent $10 *Encyclopaedia Britannica* yearbooks to each delegate, with whole sets of the *Encyclopaedia* going to key delegate brokers. Dodd had no money to compete on this level, but he kept plugging. At Woodstock Dodd stole the show from Bowles and Benton at a large gathering of Stevensonian "small-town Democrats" with an eloquent homily on the tradition of FDR. On a sleeting, wintry night in Norwich he drew twice the crowd Bowles had drawn on a clear night a week earlier and ended up with a standing ovation. In the factory town of Bristol, when the Democratic town committee refused to endorse Dodd, his supporters knocked on the doors of the city's 6,000 registered Democrats with Dodd petitions. When 95 percent of the first 3,000 signed up, the town committee took the hint. "Everyone is against Tom Dodd—except the people," editorialized the Bristol *Press*, and the Dodd camp had a new slogan.

The nomination drive was now reaching its decisive stage. Dodd was here, there, everywhere—cajoling, entreating, bluffing, wooing, threatening. He waited impatiently for people to awake in the morning to take his phone calls; he was usually still dropping dimes into roadside pay phones at midnight. Snow and sleet seemed at times his worst enemies, given the hilly, winding course of Connecticut's country lanes. But despite almost impassable roads, Dodd always appeared. On the night of his Norwich triumph, the roads sleeted over while he was driving homeward and his car pitched down a sharp, curving incline. It spun round and round on the slippery road, narrowly missed an oncoming car, and finally plunged headlong into a great snowbank. No one was scratched.

He had nothing to offer his growing entourage; there was no campaign payroll. Yet he drew people to him. He would relieve his tension and fatigue with humor. On the long, lonely journeys across frosted landscapes, he would regale his band with stories from out of his past, half truth, half fancy. His favorite stories had that peculiar brand of humor that appeals to the Irish and often leaves others somewhat mystified. He would tell of attending, as a boy, the burial of one of his father's poor construction laborers and of listening to the conversation of the graveside mourners, fellow workers all dressed up in their Sunday best.

"Mike was a foine man," pronounced one.

"A Christian man," declared the next.

"A God-fearin' man," added a third.

"A good family man," chimed the fourth.

A fifth mourner declined comment, chewing his pipe philosophically. Back at the head of the line, the eulogies began again.

"He was a good shoveler," said the first, turning to the deceased's professional competence.

"A foine shoveler indeed," said the second.

"A steady shoveler," commented the third.

"A very outstandin' shoveler," agreed the fourth.

The discriminating one paused, measuring his words carefully. "True," he said, "he was a good shoveler, a *good* shoveler, but not a *fancy* shoveler."

Dodd would roar uncontrollably at his own stories, reducing his entourage to eye-watering helplessness as he continued. On the road he would peer out the car window and spot a neon sign in a tavern window, a brave glow in the empty night, and suggest, "Let's stop here for a smile." He cut an elegant figure in these rustic taverns. Dressed in black coat and black homburg, with his silver hair and chiseled profile, he always drew admiring stares from the local clientele. He would order Dewar's "on the rocks—and make it a double, my friend, it's a cold night." Out would come the big cigars he loved, and soon he would be enveloped in swirls of acrid smoke, lost in another story. "Did I ever tell you about Ghoula Donahue's lantern party in Essex?" A stool-sitter would approach, haltingly.

"Excuse me, ain't you Tom Dodd?"

"Sure am, sit down and join us."

He had a charisma, striking enough to set him apart from ordinary men, but also a homespun approachableness that drew people to him. Soon his table would be filled with strangers, and Dodd would entertain them until closing. When he left, finally, he would have made another six or eight friends, in Moosup or Colchester or Plainville. "Bowles and Benton have been asleep for hours," he would say with a chuckle.

His support was snowballing. Militant "Dodd men," eager for political combat with the entrenched powers, talked openly of a primary. Dodd, having spurred them on, now held them in check; his aim was victory in a convention, with a primary only as a last resort. Bailey and Ribicoff had lost their capacity to control the situation. If they mobilized against Dodd, they could defeat him at the convention but only at the cost of a fratricidal primary fight. Caught off guard by Dodd's boldness, they now moved to recoup. They declared neutrality among the three candidates, pledged hands off in the race, and demanded that the entire party unite behind the eventual convention nominee; lesser party sachems were free to choose sides. Dodd now had what he wanted.

His delegate count continued to rise, though he was unable to crack the big-city machines. By June, a month before the convention, he had 51 percent and kept saying so, but the press would not take his claim seriously. The political columnists continued to rate Bowles the front-runner. As with most intraparty struggles, there were no real issues; it was a clash of personal ambitions.

On the evening of July 7, 1958, Tom Dodd, Chet Bowles, Bill Benton, and hundreds of lesser-known men and women—delegates, alternates and enthusiasts—jammed into Hartford's downtown hotels around Bushnell Memorial Hall, where the Democratic state convention opened the next day. The air was charged with stimulating expectancy, unknown since John M. Bailey had begun stage-managing conventions 12 years earlier. Hundreds thronged the lobbies, where long-legged girls dispensed buttons and pamphlets in front of massive grinning portraits of the heroes. By the button count on that hot and humid evening, Dodd was ahead. He had exhausted his last available credit to host a massive cocktail party for delegates, a party that rivaled in expense those put on by Bowles and Benton. If he had to carry out his pledge to wage a primary, where would the money come from? He refused to face that question. "Never worry about what's going out," he would say. "Concentrate on what is coming in."

The candidates had headquarters suites on the seventeenth and eighteenth floors of the new Statler Hilton; the hallways leading to them were nearly impassable. Dodd received a steady stream of visitors, steered into his sanctum by Katherine Quinn, the obese, affable Mother Superior of Connecticut Democracy; and by J. Francis Smith, a political wizard from the past, state chairman during the halcyon Roosevelt years, who had returned to the battlefield to give shape and organization to Dodd's final assault. Smith was dying; in a matter of months he would be dead. He had been ordered by doctors to remain in political retirement but had rejected their entreaties to make this last fight for Dodd.

Up on the eighteenth floor, Bailey counseled with his old

pros, moving them in and out with professional dispatch. He
was still counting upon the organization to name a choice
after the first ballot. By midnight the facilities of the Statler
Hilton had collapsed under an unmanageable human crush.
The elevators had stopped completely; the switchboard operators had given up. On every floor boisterous throngs crowded
the halls, mobbing hapless waiters headed for rooms with
trays of stale drinks and melting ice. The only way to move
was on a narrow stairway that wound upward 18 floors. More
than 2,000 people, elbow to elbow, jammed the huge lobby.
The cocktail lounges, usually sleepy and deserted at this hour,
swarmed ·with riotous Democrats. The hum of conversation
rose to a fearful roar; no one seemed ready to call it a day.
Rumors spread magically and frighteningly to those who were
pinned motionless in the mass. "Dodd was involved in a scandal, something about Guatemala" . . . "Ribicoff is going to
call for Benton's nomination after the first ballot deadlock"
. . . "Mulverhill can't hold Bridgeport for Bowles, it's all
over."

Dodd's backers were betting now, backing their claims with
cash. At 1 A.M. there were no takers. At 2 A.M. callers were
told that Bowles had gone to bed. At 3 Dodd was cheered by
inebriated throngs as he was escorted through the seven-
teenth-floor hallway toward a service elevator. At the elevator
he paused and told his worried aide, Jim Boyd, "It's all right,
Jimmy. We've lost thirty and picked up twenty-five. We're
holding the line." And he was gone, to spend a fretful few
hours till dawn.

As he made this last drive through darkened streets to his
West Hartford home, his left eye twitching again uncontrollably, he thought of the hundreds of crude meetings at which
strangers had decided his life, the dozen campaigns that made
him remember all the faces he would like to forget, the thousands of impromptu speeches he had given in squalid little
halls, all the bad meals, the missed birthday parties for his
children, the drunken backslappers who called him "Tommy,"
all the bitter defeats, and the half victories, all the debts and
obligations—all culminating tomorrow.

Crowds began to form at Convention Hall at ten o'clock
on a sunny Saturday. Hung-over delegates munched ice-
cream sandwiches dispensed from vending trucks. The great
organ began to lure them inside from the shaded sidewalks

with "Happy Days Are Here Again." The endless round of speeches and demonstrations drove the temperature in the hall steadily upward. Television lights beamed mercilessly on dripping delegates; for the first time Connecticut's citizenry was to have a TV look at the House That Bailey Ruled. But his rule had never been more shaky. Later in the day he would be picking Congressmen out of his hat with accustomed aplomb, but right now he didn't know what was going to happen. It was that close.

Bowles used a New Orleans jazz band snaking through the convention hall to lead his demonstration. It made a hit with the attractive young Ivy League types, not one of them a delegate, who clapped and chanted under Bowles banners. Dodd's demonstration fired the heart of many an old convention tad with a bold Irish pipe-and-drum marching band that boomed down the broad center aisle in a green-kilted phalanx, playing "The Wearing of the Green." Benton's demonstration was small, as his impact on the delegates had been. It was clearly a two-man race. Bowles did not come to the convention floor; he was aloofly ensconced in an upstairs room, watching the proceedings on television. Dodd took his place on the floor with the West Hartford delegation; his appearance brought a prolonged standing ovation that seemed to include the entire center wing of the hall. As the balloting started, he arose and began pacing the aisle restlessly, watching with an intimidating eye as each delegate cast aloud his individual vote, as required under Connecticut law.

Dodd took a commanding lead in Hartford County, the first to be polled, as a freshly mimeographed Bowles handout had cautioned would be the case. By the time the roll call reached Litchfield County, the great hall was sweltering. Bowles broke even in eastern Connecticut, where both he and Dodd lived. Bowles showed strength in New Haven County and rolled up a big majority in Fairfield County. Benton trailed badly, but the combined Benton-Bowles vote stayed neck and neck with Dodd, who knew he had to win it clean on the first ballot or be counted out in the back room. Bailey hovered in the wings of the stage, ready to take command.

Litchfield County, picturesque, antique, rural, would decide. It was here that Dodd had gone up the catwalks and made his personal pitch to a delegate here, another there. His strength surprised the pros; he might take it on the first ballot.

The tension grew almost unendurable as each delegate shouted his choice, with increasing vehemence. Every "Dodd" vote now drew a roar from the crowd, like a close pass in a bullring. The little town of Plymouth cast all three votes for Dodd. The third put him over the top.

In a corner of the hall a spontaneous, sustained roar began; afterward a hundred different men would claim they ignited it. It spread electrically, exultantly, triumphantly. Dodd delegates stood now and stamped and clapped and shouted, joyfully, defiantly. They had put their man over, and they intended to let the world know it before Bailey or Ribicoff could climb on the bandwagon and take the credit. Bailey, agitated, his thin wisp of hair out of place, sprang to the microphone and demanded the demonstration cease so the roll call could continue. Gleefully they shouted him down. This was their moment; an hour from now the old order would return, but this moment was theirs. At length the crowd subsided, its emotion spent, and the roll call resumed. All the delegates were now switching to Dodd; Governor Ribicoff, who had withheld his vote as part of the convention management strategy, now cast it in a firm, demanding voice for "Tom Dodd." In 20 minutes it was unanimous. There would be no primary.

Dodd's intimates looked at each other almost in disbelief. Ed Sullivan beamed serenely, as though he had known it all along. Jim Boyd, eyes red with emotion, clothes drenched with sweat, embraced the immaculate Dodd—the only gesture of affection that would ever pass between them in 12 years of close association. Numbed with excitement and relief, Dodd was pulled and pushed down the center aisle toward the platform. Suddenly he stopped, symbolically asserting control of his movement; he reached for the hands that stretched out to him from everywhere; the microphones could wait. He had won the great prize; he would be a United States Senator. The thousands of nights on the road had been worth it after all.

In November Dodd won easily over Senator Purtell in an election dominated by Abe Ribicoff, who rolled up the greatest personal victory in Connecticut history. In another two years Ribicoff was to go into the Kennedy Cabinet; Bailey would attain his political goal and become Democratic national chairman; Bowles, ever durable in adversity, would run for Congress, help draft the Kennedy platform at Los Angeles, then move into the State Department as number-two man—

V

only to suffer another fall from grace and be dispatched again to inscrutable India; Benton would go back to his financial empire.

Dodd could now relax; he took Grace with him to the Caribbean. When he returned, tanned and fit, to his retreat in North Stonington, he was unaccountably wearing a ten-gallon hat and Western scarf. Once again he could expand a little and indulge his old flair for the theatrical.

Enthroned behind the eighteenth-century Italian olive-wood desk that dominated his Washington office, framed by the flags of the United States and Connecticut, the new Senator savored the national response to his maiden speech. Stacks of commendatory mail covered the delicately curved desk top. There was a message from General of the Army Douglas MacArthur: "Your Berlin statement was magnificent in its concept and masterful in its execution." *Time* magazine's lead article credited him with having starred in the most important Senate debate in a decade. An image painfully built for a generation now emerged on the national scene: Thomas J. Dodd —FBI crime buster, youth leader, civil rights pioneer, spy smasher, international lawyer and fighter against tyranny, foe of political bosses and labor racketeers, voice of enlightened anti-Communism. The *Reader's Digest* would later sum it all up by canonizing Dodd as the "Crusader from Connecticut." Conservatives had found a new hero; liberals had no cause to be disaffected.

To be sure, there were the inevitable skeptics who had tried to spatter mud on the shining image. They had raised querulous questions but had impressed few listeners. The crime buster, while temporarily out of office, they had said, had accepted a $50,000 retainer from the Guatemalan Government after he had fought in Congress to pump millions in foreign aid into Guatemala. The great international lawyer, they had said, had flunked the Connecticut bar exam, never took it again and could practice law only by virtue of a politically arranged waiver. The fearless foe of Hoffa, they had said, had wound up with a $50,000 fee paid by Hoffa's union as part of a compromise settlement that let Hoffa off the hook. The civil rights pioneer, they had said, had deserted the civil rights bloc on his first vote as a Senator by going along with Majority Leader Lyndon Johnson to squelch the anti-filibuster motion. They had said, too, that the "responsible anti-Communist" had shown witch-hunting tendencies. There had even been those in Hartford who had scoffed at "the man of principle who had whipped the political bosses." They insisted that in John Bailey's safe could be found two unsolicited promises in Dodd's handwriting, the first pledging that Dodd would not declare for the governorship, dated only two days before he did indeed so declare in 1948, and the second dated 10 years later pledging to turn over to Bailey all Federal patronage in return for Bailey's pre-convention neutrality.

"A lot of nonsense," grumped Dodd. "Left-wing propaganda." He could dismiss his critics now and bask in the warm sunshine of adulation.

2

PLAYING THE PART

1. The Junior Senator from Connecticut

Power and prestige and publicity have differing effects on different men. To some they are challenges to growth and responsibility. To others they are temptations to vanity and irresponsibility.

The United States Senate occasionally has produced statesmen of heroic mold, but more typical has been the limited politician with a narrow background and parochial interests. The negative kind of power available to him is often more of a temptation than a challenge. His is not the ennobling power to shape bold national policies or the awesome authority to make great decisions for which he will be held accountable by the country and by history. More characteristically, his is the petty privilege to frustrate and delay the proposals of others, to hold up the appointments recommended by the President, to bargain selfishly for patronage and pork as the price of his support for national programs.

Since the inner workings of the Senate are largely shielded

from the public and since no single Senator can be held accountable for what the whole Senate does, each of the 100 can afford, if he wishes, to be irresponsible. This combination of influence and impotence, of power without responsibility, breeds a pusillanimous atmosphere that is reflected in many of the Senate's practices.

Most Senators are honest and honorable men who serve the nation better perhaps than the voters deserve. Some Senators are exemplary public servants, devoted to the national welfare, whose contributions will never be adequately appreciated. But others are irresponsible opportunists who slide through their careers without ever making any real contributions. The collectivity and secrecy obscuring the unheralded dedication of the former also cover up the dereliction of the latter. Only Senate insiders can truly distinguish the doers from the drones. The rules and customs that prohibit one Senator from disparaging another prevent the public from ever sharing in this knowledge. For the conscientious man, therefore, the Senate can be filled with frustrations. But it is ideally constructed for the man who regards his membership as an avenue to special privilege and personal gain.

For a time, Tom Dodd had seemed destined for the higher road, but slowly he began to take the lower. To the Senate's discredit, he was influenced by what he saw around him. It was not only that political compromises, so essential to lawmaking, made personal compromises seem permissible. In the convivial and confidential atmosphere of the Senate, whose members are fond of calling it the world's most exclusive club, there were also few restraints.

The deterioration of Tom Dodd began the day he was sworn in as a United States Senator. He had pledged during his campaign to work with the Senate liberals to overthrow the filibuster rule, by which one-third of the Senate, plus one, could prevent the majority from voting on taboo issues such as civil rights. But when he arrived on Capitol Hill in January 1959, he was confronted with the Senate power structure dominated by Lyndon Johnson of Texas, Robert Kerr of Oklahoma, Richard Russell of Georgia, and Carl Hayden of Arizona, all Democrats. These men were opposed to more than minor modifications in the filibuster rule.

The issue was brought to a head by Senator Clinton Anderson, the New Mexico Democrat, who contended that after each biennial national election the new Senate could make its own rules by majority vote and was not bound by the hoary precedents of the past. Dodd was committed to support Anderson, but the Senate barons impressed upon him that old promises did not count. If Dodd wanted *their* support in getting on the right committees, he would have to support them on this—an issue crucial to their control of the Senate. As Johnson's bright-eyed young assistant, Bobby Baker, put it, "Sometimes you have to swim upstream."

Such was Dodd's introduction to the United States Senate. With misgivings he abandoned his pledge and the liberal cause, which went down to humiliating defeat. He was rewarded with the choicest committee assignments ever given a freshman Senator; he was appointed to the Appropriations, Judiciary, and Aeronautical and Space Sciences committees.

Thus Dodd had reason to be impressed that it paid to go along with the powers in the Senate. He continued to take his signals from LBJ, who, in turn and in time, helped Dodd to leapfrog over senior Senators into a coveted seat on the prestige-laden Foreign Relations Committee. He was appointed as well to the Democratic Steering Committee, which distributes Senate committee assignments. His selection was intended merely to provide LBJ with another vote, but the position gave Dodd a certain leverage with his colleagues.

Other key posts presented him with unique opportunities to build a strong public image. As acting chairman of the Senate Internal Security Subcommittee, which functioned as a sort of elder House Un-American Activities Committee, he fell heir to the murky kind of influence that Senators such as Joe McCarthy and Pat McCarran had exploited in the past.

Dodd's chairmanship of the Senate Juvenile Delinquency Subcommittee brought him widespread national publicity, first as the champion of efforts to clean up sex and violence on television, then as a crusading foe of narcotics traffickers, finally as the leader of a national effort to control the indiscriminate interstate sale of firearms. He also headed a special unit, set up within the Subcommittee on Antitrust and Monopoly to investigate the insurance industry. This provided him with a club he could hold over some of the nation's great financial empires in his home state, the insurance capital of the world.

By the middle of his first term, Dodd had become the Senate's leading spokesman for hard-line anti-Communism. He became an arbiter of what was loyal and faithful and unsubversive conduct in the United States. He became a judge of who was patriotic and who was not. This made him the new darling of right-wing millionaires such as Patrick Frawley, head of Schick Electric; Tom O'Neil, president of RKO General; and Lewis Rosensteil, chairman of Schenley Industries. The conservative press hailed Dodd as a strong voice in foreign affairs, and anti-Communist groups around the world beseeched him to address their international conferences.

When Lyndon Johnson became President in November 1963, Dodd's power index shot up. Many felt that his close relationship with the new President, enhanced by his backing of Johnson in the 1960 battle for the Presidential nomination, would give him lots of clout in the new Administration. The back door to the White House was, indeed, open to him. After one visit on May 13, 1964, Dodd dictated for his diary:

> The President thought it was significant that the Republicans are starting to say that he is soft on Communism. He thought I should speak to [Senator James] Eastland and then he said to me, "You know I am not soft on Communism. I will show them who is soft." I told him I understood and that I knew he knew that.

Some columnists openly speculated that President Johnson would pick Dodd as his running mate in the 1964 election. Tom Dodd seemed on the threshold of a great public career.

But his heroic public pose no longer fooled his Senate colleagues, who had become wise to his ways. He would perform only when he could be in the spotlight. He would make the loudest of noises about the issues with which he wanted to be identified, then fade away into weeks of anonymity. He rarely attended the committee meetings, where the principal work of the Senate is done. This is sheer drudgery, but it is in the committee rooms that legislation is forged.

Dodd, for instance, publicized himself assiduously, through his press handouts and radio reports to Connecticut, as the chief proponent of President Kennedy's nuclear test ban treaty. Yet out of eleven Foreign Relations Committee hearings on the treaty, Dodd attended only two. On those auspicious occasions he arrived late and left early. As a member of the

Senate Space Committee, he subtly reminded Connecticut's burgeoning space industry of the importance of his membership. Yet during one entire year he attended only two sessions of the committee—one a publicity session during which Senators were photographed with astronaut John Glenn for home-state newspapers. When the cameras stopped, Dodd disappeared. Once during a pique of anger in floor debate, Senator Everett Dirksen, R-Ill., forgot Senatorial courtesy and confidentiality long enough to accuse Dodd of having the worst committee absentee record in the Senate.

Always an erratic individualist, Tom Dodd rejoiced in the ambivalence and permissiveness of the Senate. He would be seen and heard only when he wanted to be. Except for Dirksen's momentary outburst, his colleagues did not give him away; their lips were sealed by the unwritten code. Nor was it the press of office work that kept Dodd from his committee hearings. Intimates began to notice that he either had become lazy or was indulging an inherent laziness. Frequently he would not arrive in the office until 10:30 or 11 A.M., a schedule forcing the cancellation of morning appointments. After he arrived, he would often closet himself with cronies and direct to members of his staff those who had come to see him on official matters. He would often begin his weekend holidays on Thursday and not return to his office until Tuesday, thereby missing more and more votes on the Senate floor. Pleading fatigue, he would vacation while Congress was in session.

But if Dodd had no stomach for the hard chores, he did have a genius for getting publicity. He realized that one timely speech, delivered on the Senate floor in 20 minutes, with copies sent in advance to a thousand newspaper outlets, could result in more press attention than months of devoted but unnoticed work in a committee room. He was able, therefore, to create an image in his state and in the country of a vigorous, effective Senator. Wrote the *Reader's Digest*: "Hard-headed, hard-working Senator Thomas Joseph Dodd is a man with a passion for getting and analyzing the facts. . . . He had become the Senate's most dynamic voice for a foreign policy based on freedom for people everywhere."

Before he came to the Senate, Dodd did indeed have to do his own reading and research; he had to do his own thinking. When he got up on a public platform to speak, he phrased his own thoughts in his own words extemporaneously. Earlier the

speeches he delivered as a lowly Congressman were frequently his own, written late at night in a bold, legible longhand.
But his Senate prerogative and payroll changed all 'that. His
administrative assistant, Jim Boyd, now wrote most of his
speeches; the rest were written by his specialist in anti-
Communism, David Martin. When Dodd first began to use
ghost-writers, he would spend considerable time talking over his
speeches with Boyd or Martin and spelling out in a rough way
what he wanted. But as his staff began to produce effectively,
Dodd declined to make even minor exertions. Soon his public
statements became almost totally a product of his ghost-
writers. He would feign participation, objecting to a word
here and there. He would also insist, in violation of the rules
of rhetoric, that almost every sentence be typed as a separate
paragraph. "I can't seem to teach you fellows the art of para-
graphing," he would say. But there his contribution ended.

Although Dodd studiously avoided the routine working sessions of his committees, he bestirred himself sporadically to
attend investigative hearings. A chance to preside on center
stage was the most likely lure. Such opportunities were presented by the televised sessions of the Juvenile Deliquency
Subcommittee. Yet even for these performances in the spotlight, Dodd would rarely do his homework.

For weeks, Carl Perian, Eugene Gleason and other subcommittee staff members would work doggedly to organize
hearings. They would research the subject matter, locate the
witnesses and prepare the lines of questioning. Painfully
aware of Dodd's aversion to detail, they would set forth the
simplified key points in notebooks. A couple of hours of homework by Dodd, who was perceptive enough, would have
prepared him to conduct these hearings. But he would almost
never submit to more than a ten- or fifteen-minute briefing
just before the cameras began grinding. As a result his investigative hearings, though they produced headlines, frequently
floundered because of his inept questioning and failure to follow through. After a couple of hours Dodd would tire of the
proceedings, and when the cameras were withdrawn, he
would instruct his staff to find some other Senator to preside.

Once Dodd gave the Columbia Broadcasting System an erroneous explanation of his own gun-control bill. The staff discreetly arranged to withdraw the interview. On another occasion he had agreed to participate in a panel discussion before

the Overseas Press Club to discuss the book *Advise and Consent*. Rather than plow through the lengthy narrative himself, he assigned the reading to Jim Boyd, who prepared two reviews, one favorable, the other unfavorable. Dodd selected the unfavorable review as the most likely to attract attention. He reaped the headlines he had expected, but later he began to hear that the book had a strong anti-Communist slant. Troubled over his departure from the anti-Communist line, he apologized to author Allen Drury for a mistake in judgment.

While other Senators toiled in committee rooms or on the Senate floor, Dodd more often could be found sitting in his office, in his elevated chair, surrounded by admiring sycophants. One of his favorite pastimes was reading aloud portions of the speeches and the letters his ghost-writers had prepared for him, then basking in the compliments of his listeners. Many Senators have ghost-writers, and most are frank to admit it. But Dodd always pretended to his fellow Senators, his friends and even his family that he did his own writing. His son, Tom, Jr., remarked one night to an inwardly amused staff, "With all that's going on around here, I don't understand how my father has time to write all those speeches."

So it went with virtually every aspect of Dodd's Senate duties. He did not even look at the legislative mail that poured in from constituents. It was answered by his staff and signed on a machine. Nor did he seriously concern himself with the problems of Connecticut's industries and interests. The staff did what it could, but problems demanding his personal intervention fell by the wayside.

Yet the average Connecticut citizen, who noted the headlines about Dodd's speeches and investigations, who read the professional newsletters from Dodd's office, who listened to his canned television and radio reports from Washington, assumed he was an effective statesman. Indeed, he became far better known throughout the state and nation than the average Senator.

2. The Key to the Cabinet

Long before Tom Dodd came to the Senate, he had a drinking problem. The harsh necessities of his upward struggle had forced him to contain and control it. But his new Senate environment was conducive to indulgence. He now felt, perhaps, that he had "made it" and could relax. He was freed from the hourly necessity to work and produce—demands that discipline the habits of most men. Whenever he wished, he could shut himself behind the thick oaken door of his office. His constituents, his callers—even his wife Grace—could be held off indefinitely with stories of high-level meetings that allegedly occupied his days and delayed his return home at night.

He also found the permissive attitude of his fellow Senators hospitable to elbow bending. The Senate contained a few alcoholics whose identities were carefully concealed with the cooperation of a tolerant press. Many of Dodd's colleagues kept open bars in their offices. When there was voting on the Senate floor, obliging Senators to hang around for roll calls, bars were automatically opened in the ornate offices of the Secretary of the Senate and the Senate Sergeant at Arms. There, under the tinkling cut-glass chandeliers, Senators could find the stimulation that might be lacking in a dull debate. For years Senator Wayne Morse of Oregon led a lonely campaign against these unlicensed bars. The thought of inebriated Senators casting votes on vital national issues appalled him. "There has never been one night session of the Senate in all my experience," Morse once told friends, "that hasn't witnessed at least one Senator making a fool of himself and disgracing the Senate." But colleagues looked on Morse's opposition as a quaint idiosyncrasy, and the festivities between roll calls went happily on, unhindered by the Senate and unreported by the press.

This permissiveness gave Dodd encouragement, if he needed any, in a pursuit he instinctively found agreeable. He would start drinking shortly after he arrived at the office, hung over from the night before. For his private snorts during the morning and early afternoon, he would keep a bottle of Dewar's White Label Scotch in his office refrigerator. It went down easier cold, and he was spared bother with ice cubes. His glass, though always within reach, was hidden from view in the recess of a small telephone table beside his desk. And he kept his office uncommonly dark (replacing the overhead lights with a few dim lamps) so that visitors could not focus on him too clearly.

Dodd thought his morning drinking went unnoticed, but

the staff in his outer office had learned from painful experience to listen for the opening of the refrigerator door. By midafternoon all pretenses were abandoned, and a staff aide, usually Mike O'Hare, would be recruited as bartender. Frequently the Senator would go through the ritual of pretending that the drink handed to him was too strong for his taste. O'Hare, who knew precisely the mix his boss liked, would recognize the cue. "Would you like me to add more water, Senator?" he would ask. Dodd would demur with the amiable reproach: "You're trying to knock me out, Mike."

In the company of admiring companions, Dodd would while away the afternoon. The waiting room filled up with visitors who would sometimes sit around for hours, in vain. By late afternoon Dodd frequently passed out on the red leather divan in his office. It became part of the staff's duties, while making excuses to waiting visitors, to break out cold towels, black coffee and hot soup in an attempt to revive him.

Two witnesses observed Dodd one afternoon staggering out of his office, his hat askew. Departing for the airport, he was about to attempt a precarious descent down the marble steps of the Senate Office Building in broad daylight. While the witnesses gaped incredulously, two of Dodd's frail secretaries, Doreen Moloney and Jean Wegner, teetering on high heels, half dragged and half led their distinguished boss out through the door and down the stairs. The Senator's receptionist, Rose Marie Allen, awaited him outside in an automobile. The stuffing of Dodd into the car was a scene so memorable that the witnesses were able to describe it in detail a year later to the Senate Ethics Committee's chief counsel, Benjamin Fern.

Mike O'Hare and Grace Dodd were waiting at the airport when the Senator's car pulled up two hours late. Slowly and uncertainly, Dodd extricated himself from the automobile and lurched toward his wife. "Oh, Tom," she said, close to tears from anger and disappointment.

"Oh, Grace," Dodd said, raising his hand to cover his face. "I have a terrible toothache."

Inevitably this sort of thing hastened the disillusionment of Dodd's once-loyal staff. Aides who willingly worked 12 to 14 hours a day began to wonder what end their sacrifices served. Perhaps the incident that appalled them most occurred on the day of President Kennedy's assassination. Dodd demanded a special plane from United Aircraft to fly him from Hartford to Washington. He explained that the new President needed him immediately, though the shaken Lyndon Johnson, still in Dallas, had not communicated with Dodd and, so far as can be discerned, did not have Dodd on his mind at all.

The Senator notified his staff to meet his special plane at the National Airport. The plane taxied up in front of the Page terminal, where private planes discharge their passengers, and Dodd, looking like an unmade bed, fumbled out of the door and descended on unsteady feet. A few moments later another private plane arrived carrying Democratic Senator George Smathers of Florida. Informed of this, Dodd said almost gleefully, "Smathers is a friend of the former President. I am a friend of the new President." On the drive to his home, Dodd, his tongue loosened by too much Scotch, told his aides that Kennedy had made as many errors as Pope John and that it would take 50 years to correct the mistakes of both. He seemed delighted over the martyrdom. His staff was dismayed.

Earlier Dodd had joined in an anti-Vatican movement within the Catholic Church. He met frequently with disturbed clerics and laymen who feared Pope John was softening up the Church to Communism. Taking the conspiratorial view, they claimed to have "inside information" that the Pope was manipulated by his personal secretary. Thus there was a secret relief after Pope John's passing, only to be followed by dismay over an apparent appeal from his successor, Pope Paul, to admit Red China to the United Nations. Dodd dispatched a private letter to the Holy Father, hand-delivered to the papal nuncio in Washington, pleading passionately, "This concession to Red China would only inspire the Chinese Communists to step up the tempo and scale of their aggressive and subversive operations."

Dodd's reputation as a drinker became whispered knowledge throughout official Washington. At a party he threw for several friends from the House of Representatives, he was highly miffed when one of them, the irreverent Representative Thomas "Tip" O'Neill, Jr., D-Mass., formally toasted their host, to the roaring delight of the other guests, as "the second nastiest drunk in town." Senator Everett Dirksen, during his outburst against Dodd's absenteeism, also referred obliquely to Dodd's drinking. "Quite a number of things can induce cerebral incoherence," Dirksen remarked caustically in reply to a rambling, insulting discourse by Dodd.

Only the Congress would wink at such behavior from one entrusted with heavy responsibilities for legislation affecting the fields of national security, juvenile crime and foreign policy. Dodd well knew that such conduct would brand anyone else high in government as a security risk. But he had no need to worry; he was in charge of investigating security risks.

As Dodd drank his refrigerated Scotch and passed his days with convivial friends, his staff was employed building up quite another image. A steady stream of press releases poured off the new electric mimeograph and into the efficient envelope-stuffing machines of the Senate mail room, trumpeting the speeches Dodd had not written, the investigations he had not conducted, and the announcements of Federal projects and contracts with which he personally had nothing to do. All Senators have these facilities available. But they can become dangerous, to a man's character and to the public service, when used not as an adjunct to personal effort but as a substitute for it.

Although Dodd basked in the privileges of office, the proximity of power seemed to heighten his innate sense of insecurity and suspicion. He would shake his head ponderously and quote Shakespeare to his friends: "Uneasy lies the head that wears the crown." At times he resembled a man in the grip of paranoia. He was certain, he told aides, that his telephones were being tapped by Attorney General Robert Kennedy. A report that a part-time law student in his office had been seen glancing at the mail in Dodd's "in" box caused him to fire the bewildered employee without explanation. The next day he changed all the locks in his office. He became convinced that two employees, one his office manager, the other a lady file clerk, were CIA plants, so he quietly eased them out. Whenever he was attacked by the press, he would talk about the "Red network"—a string of papers he claimed was under Communist influence, including *The New York Times,* the Washington *Post,* New York *Post,* Providence *Journal* and St. Louis *Post-Dispatch.* "I can always tell when I'm hurting the Communists," he would say. "One by one, these papers attack me. The red lights go on all across the board."

He was encouraged in these suspicions by his anti-Communist specialist, David Martin, an ex-Trotskyite who saw a Red plot behind every setback. When *The Insider's Newsletter,* published by the respected Cowles publications' group, carried a disparaging item about Dodd's failure to pass the Connecticut bar exam, Martin alerted the Senator: "The paragraph in question is so maliciously irrelevant that it is hard to believe it was not motivated. My personal hunch is that the apparatus is trotting out its guns in preparation for a sustained campaign of character assassination." Quickly agreeing, Dodd sent back a note in urgent longhand. "David," he wrote, "immediately check on this outfit. Find out who they are—carefully and thoroughly."

Dodd's suspicions frequently caused him to do ludicrous things. He was convinced that the Communists were out to frame him. "Some night they'll dump a naked blonde in my hotel room," he predicted. "And then they'll take pictures." To prevent himself from being thus compromised, he once took along a seventy-year-old retainer on one of his anti-Communist speaking tours out West to act as a watchdog and witness in case of a blonde attack.

Each night before leaving the office, Dodd's staff was directed to lock up his liquor in a wall cabinet. For a long time the key to the cabinet was hidden in the index finger of a glove Dodd kept in the top left-hand drawer of his desk. But Dodd became convinced that FBI agents were coming into his office at night, taking his key, and measuring his whiskey bottles to determine how much was being consumed each day. So, one night before leaving, he summoned his personal secretary, Marjorie Carpenter, and with one finger to his lips, he pointed mysteriously to a book on his shelves and then to his liquor cabinet. Miss Carpenter did not comprehend his meaning, so he took her out into the hall. "I don't like to talk about it in there," he whispered. "They may have the place bugged." He then related his apprehension about the bottles being measured. Henceforth, he said, the key to the cabinet should be kept behind the book he had indicated. The location of the key, he cautioned, was never to be discussed aloud in his office. "There was a scary look in his eyes," recalled Miss Carpenter. "For days I worried about him, but he seemed to get over his suspicions."

3. For Dodd and Country

A United States Senator commands deferential and obsequious treatment from many quarters. Most Senators learn to discount it, but the prevailing flattery inflated Tom Dodd with self-importance. Outwardly he maintained a humble pose, for he knew the public does not abide arrogance in elected officials. But to his staff he gradually became a petty tyrant. When irritated, he would kick desks in uncontrolled anger. He would even accuse baffled secretaries of conspiring to overload his appointment calendar in order to ruin his health. "I could select ten people at random from the sidewalk," he would roar, "and have a better staff than I have now."

Serving as personal secretary to a Senator is so prestigious a job that a Washington secretary is generally willing to endure the most difficult working conditions to hold on to the position. But Dodd was so abusive and inconsiderate that a dozen personal secretaries came and went in the first three years of his term, probably an all-time record on Capitol Hill.

There were graver misuses of authority. Dodd's position as acting chairman of the Senate Internal Security Subcommittee gave him access to the security and loyalty files maintained by both his own subcommittee and the House Un-American Activities Committee, as well as raw files—those containing unproven allegations—provided by the FBI on request. Dodd exploited this privileged information on many occasions. When his oldest son, Tom, Jr., received a "D" for one of his courses at Georgetown University, Dodd sensed something un-American in the grade and ordered a security check run on the professor by the subcommittee on internal security. It revealed nothing except that young Tom apparently had not done his homework.

When a visiting lecturer, speaking at Windham High School in Willimantic, Connecticut, made a critical reference to Dodd, the Senator became infuriated. He not only ordered a security check on the offending lecturer, but without waiting for the results also excoriated the school principal, H. Chester Nelson, over the telephone. Dodd threatened to denounce him on the Senate floor for permitting a known Communist to address students entrusted to his care by the parents of Willimantic. As it happened, the security report identified the lecturer as a bona fide anti-Communist, a former Hungarian freedom fighter who had escaped from Red tyranny. The promised exposé on the Senate floor was forgotten.

He came to crave attention and could now command it. He insisted, sometimes, on being met at the Washington airport by a retinue of staff members. He adorned the walls of his office with plaques, scrolls and inscribed photographs of the great, all attesting to the excellence and importance of Thomas J. Dodd. He spent increasingly more time with his little circle of truckling applauders.

Had he stopped at indulging his appetites and feeding his ego, the Dodd story might have ended differently. But step by step he passed from prerogative to profiteering, from excess to misconduct. Secure in the sanctuary of the Senate, reassured by the prevailing attitude that a Senator's actions are beyond questioning, Dodd began to misuse and misappropriate the Government facilities and allowances made available to him.

It started with the smallest of things. Lithographs of Connecticut scenes, furnished by the Library of Congress for display in Dodd's office, wound up in his home. The carpentry workshop in the basement of the Senate Office Building, on request, will frame and hang pictures for Senate offices. Dodd used this free service liberally for the decoration of his home, courtesy of the taxpayers. The Senate allowance for stationery and office supplies was misused by Dodd to purchase family gifts. He would insist that he and members of his family, when traveling, be met at airports and railway stations by agents of the United States Immigration Service, who had to be shifted from their duties to act as his chauffeurs.

One abuse, allowed to pass unquestioned, led to another. Dodd quickly learned the game of taking vacation trips at Government expense, a favorite Congressional pastime. Not long after he became chairman of the Juvenile Delinquency Subcommittee, he flew off to Puerto Rico on the subcommittee's expense account for a week in the sun. As a cover, he brought along two staff members to investigate delinquency among the natives, but he confined his own investigation to the surf and the sand. This subterfuge became a pattern; he seemed more and more concerned over delinquency in sunny climes. He would contrive to hold a press conference on teenage crime or to summon members of the police juvenile squad to his hotel for a half-hour conference—a gambit that would provide him with a newspaper clipping or a police report as evidence of his hard work. Then he would devote himself to relaxing at the pleasure spots of Florida, California and the Caribbean.

For pocket money, Dodd sometimes arranged speaking engagements at the places he liked to visit. Then he hit upon the idea of billing the Government and the sponsoring organization for the same travel expenses. Thus he received double payment for trips to Philadelphia, West Palm Beach, San Francisco, Miami, Seattle, Tucson and Los Angeles. He was later to blame this double billing upon his bookkeeper, Mike O'Hare, though it developed that the practice had prevailed during the regimes of three bookkeepers.

The Senator became quite flinthearted about his fees, demanding payment from even such worthy organizations as the National Council of Juvenile Court Judges. He agreed to address the judges in San Francisco on June 30, 1961. Since delinquency would be discussed, he charged the $397.27 round-trip fare to his Juvenile Delinquency Subcommittee. Meanwhile, Judge Joseph B. Felton inquired delicately of subcommittee staff director Carl Perian, "Now we come to the subject which is rather difficult to approach. As you know, our organization has little money, but on the other hand, we do not want to appear on the cheap side. We do feel that we would like to offer Senator Dodd an honorarium of at least perhaps $100. Furthermore, do you know whether or not he intends to travel on subcommittee funds or whether our organization should provide for his transportation?" Scroogelike, Dodd accepted the $100 honorarium and charged the judges an additional $376.86 for an American Airlines ticket that had already been billed to the subcommittee.

In 1964 Dodd discovered a new source of travel money and extended this double-billing concept to his campaign fund. After a speaking engagement he would often collect travel expenses from both his Senate campaign committee and the sponsoring organization. Once he collected expenses for the same West Coast trip from three sources. Through this device he pocketed several thousand dollars.

A number of corporations also helped to solve Dodd's transportation problems by offering him free use of their private planes. Administration officials are forbidden to use these luxurious, business-owned planes, which crowd the private terminal at Washington's National Airport, because free flights are deemed to be a corrupting influence. But many legislators, Dodd among them, have no such scruples. In 1962 he began traveling free of charge in a plush Cessna Queen Air, furnished by McKesson & Robbins, Inc., the large drug firm, which at the time happened to be under investigation by the Senate Antitrust Subcommittee. As a member of the subcommittee, Dodd rode around in the plane of the company he was supposed to be investigating. He also accepted free airplane travel from RKO General, D'Addario Construction, Avco, Kaman Aircraft, United Aircraft and other companies. All the while, he used his Senate influence to seek Government favors for these companies.

Dodd became so spoiled by the Cessna Queen Air that he began to make disparaging remarks about the less luxurious D'Addario aircraft. Stung by the Senator's contempt, contractor D'Addario offered to buy a new plane. He announced to Dodd's staff that the Senator could use it any time he wished. "It is always at his disposal twenty-four hours a day," said D'Addario grandly. A staff member remarked that Dodd preferred to fly in planes with no company name on the fuselage. "The new one won't have a company label on it," the contractor promised eagerly. "We aren't interested in having people know who owns the plane as long as Dodd knows who owns it."

The Senator frequently commuted between his Washington and Hartford offices in a 32-passenger Convair, 8-passenger Jet Star, or 4-passenger King Air operated by United Aircraft. His family also used this free travel service; once he even arranged to fly his pet poodle to Connecticut via United Aircraft. The plane waited for 30 minutes while Dodd's staff struggled to box the dog. Beau by name, in a crate suitable for air travel. At last company officials, late for appointments in Connecticut, refused to waste any more time waiting for a dog. The Senator was obliged to ship Beau by American Airlines, though he did not go to the extreme of paying the bill out of his own pocket. Among his campaign expenses, a bill turned up for shipping a 52-pound "pet dog" and "a large dog kennel" on November 11, 1963, from Washington to Groton, an airfield not far from Dodd's North Stonington estate. The charge was $6.24 for the dog, $15 for the kennel.

The Senate payroll furnished another obvious opportunity for profit. Dodd was allotted an office payroll of about $120,000 annually, plus committee payrolls which topped $200,000. Since Senators are not required to account to anyone for their handling of these generous sums, Dodd took advantage of the laxity. He used his Government payrolls to pay off personal and political obligations. The wife of a political ally from Hartford's North End, Mrs. Beverly Curry, drew more than $25,000 as a Senate employee while she remained at home, bearing babies. If she ever appeared in Dodd's offices or performed a single function for the taxpayers, the other staff members were unaware of it. Beginning in 1957, George Gildea, a retired railway conductor who was proud of his acquaintance with the silvery-haired Senator, had loaned Dodd a total of $19,800. Thereafter, Gildea began collecting $7,500 a year, not from Dodd but from the Juvenile Delinquency Subcommittee. He was placed on the subcommittee payroll, though he had no educational or professional qualifications for the post and did not work for the subcommittee. Not until Dodd learned he was under investigation eight years later did he repay the Gildea loans—out of testimonial-dinner funds, as it happened. Another creditor, Albert Morano, turned up on Dodd's payroll, though he was a prominent Republican and though his appointment caused an uproar among Connecticut Democrats. Morano did no recognizable Senate staff work to earn his $5,000 to $6,000 a year, but he did lend Dodd money now and then.

Dodd loaded his Government payrolls with ailing wives, unemployable nephews, mentally disturbed sons and unqualified daughters of friends and cronies. When Dodd became Juvenile Delinquency Subcommittee chairman in 1961 on the death of Senator Thomas C. Hennings, Jr., of Missouri, he inherited a professional staff of criminologists, researchers, trained investigators, and skilled secretaries. Within a year all but 8 of 21 staff positions had been filled with Dodd appointees who performed no useful subcommittee work. The new roster ranged from Liz Knipe, the daughter of Mrs. Dodd's college roommate, to John Teale, an obscure cousin, who wanted the Government to domesticate the musk-ox. He was assigned to make a Senate study of animal delinquency after he persuaded Dodd that the musk-oxen have eliminated delinquency from their herds by ostracizing misbehaving members.

The Senator received an unexpected insight into delinquency from another appointee—the son of a friend. Put on the payroll as one of Dodd's investigators, the young man set out with uninhibited zeal to earn his Government salary. One night, while he was investigating juvenile delinquency along the Mexican border, he began banging on the door of a boardinghouse where a Mexican striptease dancer was supposed to live. The police, summoned to the scene, had to break down a bolted bathroom door to reach the young firebrand. They found a pistol taped to his leg. Undaunted, the irrepressible investigator developed a new contact whom he referred to in his confidential reports as "C-5." After he submitted her name at the top of a list of recommended witnesses, the subcommittee staff discovered she was a call girl.

Even Dodd began to get apprehensive over his new investigator after a call from the Treasury Department informing him that the fellow had tried to check two Thompson machine guns, 5,000 rounds of ammunition and a P-38 pistol through the baggage room to Hyannisport, Massachusetts, while the late President Kennedy was weekending there. This episode occurred at the same time Dodd was preparing his gun-control bill. The Juvenile Delinquency unit's parent committee, Senate Judiciary, also received an FBI report alleging that the new Dodd investigator had been picked up for impersonating an officer and wearing sidearms. Chairman James Eastland, D-Miss., notified Dodd but left it to him, as a Senatorial courtesy, whether to keep the boy on the payroll. Dodd finally decided that his recruit might be unsuited for investigating juvenile crime and gun abuses—after the young man seized a Navy flare gun from the subcommittee's exhibits and brandished it menacingly during a temper tantrum.

In another slot the Senator placed Gene Cullen, a clean-cut young man, whose principal duties were to serve as the family chauffeur, valet and handyman. He frequently drove to Connecticut, so the Senator could step from his plane into the car upon his arrival at the airport—an idea he apparently picked up from observing the President's travel arrangements. On at least one occasion, Cullen drove the Dodds' maid, Mercedes, from their Georgetown house to their North Stonington estate to do some housecleaning. Another time, Tom, Jr., left a valise in Boston, and Cullen was dispatched to Boston to pick it up.

To compensate for the inactivity of his collection of drones and incompetents, Dodd drove his functioning aides doubly hard. But even here he found ways to turn the Federal payroll to personal profit. The two writers on Dodd's staff—Boyd and Martin—were required to turn out an uninterrupted flow of magazine articles, radio scripts and lectures and at least one book, for which Dodd was paid sums amounting to more than $50,000 in six years. Another more enterprising subordinate, Jay Sourwine, wrung $2,500 out of Dodd for his literary efforts. How he managed to do this is best told by Dodd himself in his diary:

January 20, 1964: Jay Sourwine visited the office. A couple of weeks ago, he came to see me and said he knew I was attempting to write a book and that he could be helpful. He would have to do this on his own time, and if I could pay him $3,500, he could be of great assistance. I told him at that time that it was pretty expensive, and he said that he owed some money and was getting pressed to pay it. This is why he would like to earn some extra money. Some days later, he called on me again and asked if I would endorse a check of his so that he could cash it at the Senate Disbursing Office. . . . Today he said that he was worried about his check and that it had bounced at his bank in Nevada. This was very upsetting to me because I had endorsed it so that he could cash it. He said he would see what he could do about it and the matter was left at that.

January 27, 1964: Jay Sourwine came by this afternoon and told me his check had bounced. I had endorsed this check so that he could cash it at the Senate Disbursing Office. I told him what I thought about it and told him I was very put out about it. He asked if I would make it good. He said he would do some extra work to help me with the book and would do it on his own time.

January 28, 1964: Jay Sourwine came by again today to further express his regrets about the check. I gave him a check for $2,500 to make good his own check which had bounced. My check was drawn on the Hartford National Bank.

The $2,500, it should be added, did not come out of Dodd's pocket but out of his testimonial-dinner donations.

The Senator's closest confidant, who was paid $15,000 a year as a Senate employee, was grizzled, gravel-voiced Edward Sullivan, who looked after Dodd's financial and personal affairs in Hartford. He submitted regular cryptic reports, scrawled in a shaky hand on lined yellow paper, to the Senator. A typical letter, dated March 14, 1960, confided:

This morning I spent an hour with Jack —————. We had a real good talk. I know there is nothing Jack wouldn't do for you, and also I know that he can steer things your way that would easily solve all your problems. I am to see him again Thursday. We agreed that, when you are around, we will get together, and Jack promises he will come up with something. . . .

I am sure, Tom, this is the right move. Your Washington income must be added to, and you must agree on a plan that will do this. You spoke for an engineering outfit, some little attorney came to Jack for them. They got what you asked for. This is fine if you are in but no good otherwise. This is enough to let you know we covered all bases, and I hope you approve. I know such a thing can work if done right; it cannot work unless handled right. Only three of us know of this move.

In another hand-scrawled report, Sullivan suggested:

Frank is interested in an S.B.L. [small business loan]. He has not applied and intends to talk with us before making a move. He plans to give me a preview of the situation Monday, February 9. According to the papers, you will be here February 10. Maybe on the plane you can think this over: 1. Fee for procurement work; 2. Getting a share of stock, plus an arrangement that would bring a steady income. This is a good business and a lot can be done for him. He knows the business, appreciates the value of spending money in the right places and has never had enough capital to handle his growth. This [sic], of course, are my ideas. I will only try to promote them after you tell me. . . .

Harold wanted to help in getting a name Scotch. They are also looking for a warehouse in Hartford. They have no attorney in this area. On this deal, I have these thoughts: Help get a Scotch. Take a fee or become their local attorney (not you I know) on a retainer basis. Or rent them a warehouse. Or take a share of the operation in this branch with a steady income. Again, these are my ideas. I hope you can agree and let me know when you are in. Money can and will be made.

Sullivan's letters—and there were many others with the same theme—indicated that his chief Senate duty was hustling money for Dodd. For this he was paid a full-time salary by the taxpayers. Long before Tom Dodd came along, of course, there had been recurring newspaper revelations about the debauching of Congressional payrolls, but the Congress had studiously avoided any investigations. And so Dodd felt free to manipulate his annual $300,000 trust, confident that whatever he did with it was beyond questioning.

4. Senator in Hock

The double standard in Washington is nowhere more apparent than in the attitude toward gifts. The much-maligned Washington bureaucrat may not even permit himself to be taken to the cafeteria by anyone with a problem before his agency. For members of Congress, however, the only guide is the individual's conscience. Thus the wining and dining of Senators and Representatives by favor-seekers is a major industry in Washington. Although individual Senators, like Paul Douglas, D-Ill., and Stephen Young, D-Ohio, have adopted strict personal codes against the acceptance of gifts, the Congress as an institution has refused year after year to condemn this practice.

Little wonder that Tom Dodd, as he exhausted the limited opportunities for trimming his various Senate allowances, began to look upon the greener pastures of private interests who sought the help a Senator could give them. It began rather modestly· French perfumes for Mrs. Dodd from the foreign lobbyist, Julius Klein; silver plate from the International Silver Company, which has a large stake in the silver policy set by Congress; clocks from the Ingraham Company, participants in a multimillion-dollar Federal urban-renewal grant; cut-rate home furnishings from Syd Simon, a Connecticut merchant, who had pressed Dodd to obtain a Presidential pardon for a friend.

As Dodd's importance as a Senator grew, the gifts increased; among them were a portable television set from Metromedia's girl Friday, Florence Lowe, at the same time that the Juvenile Delinquency Subcommittee was investigating Metromedia's TV fare and the exclusive use of a succession of new Oldsmobiles from David Dunbar, president of a moving company Dodd was helping obtain Government contracts.

Before his first term was up, the former crime buster and Justice Department prosecutor was wallowing in a veritable deluge of gifts and favors of all descriptions, received from sources whose offerings a United States Senator should have scrupulously avoided. Dodd had persuaded himself that he was entitled to these tributes, and he felt the same way about his family, which shared in the largesse.

Grace Dodd joined her husband on pleasure jaunts to London, St. Thomas, Miami, Los Angeles, Curaçao and Aruba. She summered in Spain and made frequent winter appearances at the swank Florida and Caribbean resorts. Sapphire rings, a loaned Lincoln Continental, appliances and home furnishings poured in from her husband's benefactors. Once a simple woman, she was now seen regularly on Embassy Row in furs and jewels.

The Senator prevailed upon one wealthy backer, Patrick Frawley of Schick Electric, to provide a "scholarship" to finance the studies of his son, Tom, Jr., in Central America. Young Tom stayed as the razor maker's guest at the Casa Frawley, his estate in Managua, Nicaragua. Later Dodd leaned on the State Department until it released classified documents so that Tom, Jr., could use them for his doctoral thesis—which was typed, incidentally, by Senate secretaries. And young Tom did at least one stint on his father's Senate payroll, while vacationing in Connecticut over the year-end holidays.

For daughter Martha a $5,000 wedding party was paid for, in cash, out of testimonial-dinner funds, and the engraved wedding invitations were charged to the taxpayers through the Senate stationery account. Dodd also billed the stationery account for an expensive desk set that Martha presented as a birthday gift to her new husband.

Son Jeremy was once handed $4,900 in campaign funds

and, after dropping out of a number of schools and jobs that his influential father arranged for him, wound up on the Senate payroll at $7,500 a year. Once, while on a vacation trip in Mexico, also arranged by his dad, Jeremy discovered that his hiking boots had been left behind in Washington. It was an oversight, however, that caused him no inconvenience; Dodd arranged for the boots to be delivered overnight in a diplomatic pouch via State Department courier.

Another son, Christopher, became quite the young college man-about-town, driving around in the shiny new Oldsmobile furnished the family by the president of the Dunbar Company. While at Providence College, he was permitted to charge to his father's Senate phone allowance hundreds of dollars in long-distance calls to girl friends. And the Dodd for Senate Campaign Committee paid Christopher's gasoline bills for fun trips around the country.

The private planes that Dodd was able to command were also available to his family. Example: on August 7, 1965, RKO's Thomas O'Neil sent his private Aerojet to Washington to pick up the Senator's son, Tom, Jr., and a friend. They were flown to Westerly, Rhode Island, the closest private airport to the Dodd country home, where the plane picked up the Senator and flew him to New York City. There Dodd changed places with his daughter Carolyn, who was whisked back to Westerly.

The Dodd vacations were also financed largely by people eager to make a favorable impression upon a powerful Senator. Perhaps the most memorable was a grand tour of the Far East, arranged by the Universal Shipping Company in early 1965 for Dodd, his wife, and aide David Martin. There was an understanding that Dodd would visit Korea, for Universal Shipping was anxious to impress the Korean authorities with its Washington connections. The company delivered $6,000 in cash to Dodd to purchase the airline tickets. It must be said that Dodd put on an impressive performance in Korea. He came home loaded down with rare silks, screens, chests and other Oriental treasures heaped upon him by the Koreans. A few days after his return, he delivered a long speech on the Senate floor on "The Miracle of South Korea's Resurgence." Gratefully, Universal Shipping arranged another trip, this one to Europe, for Dodd's sons, Christopher and Nicholas. They traveled free of charge on a ship operated by the United Fruit

Company, another firm always glad to promote friendships on Capitol Hill.

For a Senator of modest means who insists on keeping up with the Harrimans and the Kennedys, Washington is a frustrating place to live. More and more, it has become a Mecca for ostentatious spending. A new Senator, suddenly thrust into the heady atmosphere upon the social heights, can find himself a constant guest of honor at lavish dinners and parties, at the country estates and oceanfront villas of the very wealthy. He also learns that many of his colleagues in the Senate were millionaires before their election, that others who arrived in modest circumstances emerged years later as wealthy men. A vain and imitative man like Tom Dodd is sorely tempted to keep up with the affluence he sees around him.

Dodd was not a poor man, by ordinary standards, during his early years in the Senate. With his $22,500 Senate salary (raised to $30,000 in 1965), plus the $40,000 that he averaged each year from legal fees, business deals, speaking honorariums and the like, his income usually topped $60,000 per annum. Most Americans could struggle along on this amount of money. But it was not enough to sustain the standard of living Dodd desired, or to meet the mounting personal indebtedness piled up by his spendthrift ways.

Many a new Senator, just arrived in Washington, will purchase a modest home in the suburbs. But Dodd insisted on living in the fashionable Georgetown neighborhood near such millionaires as G. Mennen Williams, Averell Harriman, Joseph Clark and John F. Kennedy.

For weekends and off seasons, Dodd too required his country retreat. Gradually he transformed his $10,000 farm in North Stonington into a $100,000 estate. He pumped thousands of dollars into remodeling, often changing plans in mid-construction in the manner of the eccentric rich. He even planned to build an exact replica of his office inside a cave in a rocky knoll behind his farm. Happily, he contemplated calling it the "Rath of Dodd" from an old Irish word he had discovered, meaning the stronghold of a chieftain. This project, however, never got beyond the drawing board.

Magnanimous by nature, Dodd also enjoyed throwing lavish feasts for his friends. He would disappear into the kitchen where, surrounded by an air of mystery, he would cook the lobsters and roast the corn himself. He would make a day-long spectacular out of special occasions, such as Thanksgiving or Christmas. He would take responsibility for the turkey on Thanksgiving and would trim the tree on Christmas. Staff members who had no place to go were invited to share his table. He proffered his hospitality with style and flourish, damn the expense.

Dodd alternately spoiled and oppressed his six children. Each stormy encounter was followed by exaggerated beneficence, often involving lavish expenditures. All six were sent to expensive private schools, and his oldest sons remained financially dependent on their father long after the age when young men normally begin to fend for themselves.

When campaigning among Connecticut's poor, Dodd liked to contrast his poverty with the wealth of his opponents, citing how his wife had to do the cooking and housecleaning and clothes making for their large brood. But now, Llewellyn, a cook and handyman, Clara, a housekeeper, and Mercedes, a maid, were visible reminders of the new elegance that had come to the Dodd household. The Senator also became a member of exclusive clubs—the Congressional Country Club and University Club of Washington, the Hartford Club of Hartford, the New York Athletic Club of New York City. Once a rumpled figure whom Connecticut constituents would remember with loosened tie and cigar ashes on his coat, Dodd now blossomed into an immaculate fashion plate with Italian shoes, expensive silk ties and elegantly tailored suits of the latest style. He smoked only the best cigars. He drank the finest of imported liquors and stayed at the most luxurious hotels: the Fountainebleau in Miami Beach, the Beverly Hills Hotel, the Caribe Hilton in San Juan, the Royal Hawaiian in Honolulu, Grosvenor House in London, the Crillon in Paris.

But as the cost of gracious living mounted, worry lines began to crease Dodd's handsome, sculptured face. By 1961—only two years after he took his Senate seat—his indebtedness had reached $150,000. He was later to attribute this to old campaign obligations, but the evidence was overwhelming that his personal splurging was more to blame. He could no longer obtain credit through normal commercial channels and turned, perforce, to unconventional sources.

It was a peculiar kind of indebtedness that Dodd contracted. Generally, no interest was charged. There was also no schedule of repayment, often not even a signed note. Even when years passed without repayment, few attempts were made to collect from so distinguished and influential a debtor. Most of the men who lent Dodd money had an interest in his desperation. Staff aides, who could not fathom his inexplica-New York lawyer whose firm loaned $27,500, sought and received a Presidential appointment to the board of the Government-administered General Aniline & Film Corporation. James Kelley ($5,000) gained appointment through Dodd's intervention to a post in the Commerce Department. George Gildea ($19,800) and Albert Morano ($15,000) were placed, as we have seen, on Dodd's Senate payroll. Lazarus Heyman ($13,000) wanted nothing for himself, but his son Samuel was appointed at Dodd's insistence as an Assistant United States Attorney in Connecticut. Paul McNamara ($7,500) got Dodd's backing in an unsuccessful bid for Connecticut Attorney General.

The chronic need for money sometimes reduced Dodd to desperation. Staff aides, who could not fathom his inexplica-ble tantrums, traced them at a later time back to financial worry. In his quest for funds he also became reckless. In June of 1962, for example, Dodd was in the grip of one of his re-curring financial crises. He needed $5,000, and he needed it in a hurry. He tried to get it from Sanford Bomstein, a Washing-ton nightclub owner, whom Dodd already owed $7,500. Bom-stein would not be touched for more, but he did produce a friend named Eddie Perkins, a land speculator. Dodd request-ed the money in cash, but this was too fast for Perkins. He agreed only to cosign a bank note. With Perkins' signature, Dodd obtained a $5,000 loan from the Suburban Trust Company of Hyattsville, Maryland.

Shortly thereafter Perkins began to press Dodd for assist-ance in a land zoning problem that Perkins had encountered in Prince Georges County, Maryland. Perkins had purchased a valuable tract of land adjacent to NASA's Goddard Space Flight Center. His intention was to have the land rezoned for apartment dwellings; then it could be sold to builders at a profit of hundreds of thousands of dollars. Perkins had a way with local zoning boards, and all went well until the space center objected. Its complaint was that the electrical appli-ances in the proposed apartment buildings would cause inter-ference with the delicate space instruments operated by the center.

Perkins correctly assumed that Dodd, as a member of the Senate Space Committee, which has life-and-death power over NASA's budget, had the muscle to bring about a relaxation of the space center's stand. Dodd intervened, and the space people relented. A grateful Perkins, accompanied by Bomstein, came to Dodd's office in August 1963. Perkins carried an envelope in his pocket containing $5,000 in cash. Like most Senatorial benefactors, he wanted to give the money to Dodd personally. Informed by Marjorie Carpenter that Dodd was unavailable at the moment, he agreeably sat down to wait. He was not told, of course, that Dodd was "out" on his office divan after a heavy day of drinking. For an hour Mike O'Hare tried to revive Dodd, urged on by Bomstein's protestations that Perkins was tired of waiting and might leave in a huff with his $5,000. At length O'Hare got Dodd back on his feet, and the two visitors were admitted. They emerged beaming, and Bomstein told Jim Boyd that Dodd had happily pocketed the cash.

The Perkins affair was symptomatic of the straits into which Dodd had gotten himself. He became less and less careful as to how he got the money he needed. His debts became so pressing that mere borrowing was no longer a palliative. He had to have unobligated cash, thousands in cash, and he had figured out a way to get it. He began to hold testimonial dinners, which were advertised as political fund-raising affairs.

Although prominent front men were recruited as treasurers, the donations were handled exclusively by Dodd and his trusted money hustler, Ed Sullivan. They solicited contributions from a list of businessmen whose companies had been helped by Dodd. Some dropped by his Senate office to deliver their contributions in cash; others made arrangements to meet Dodd in Connecticut. The staff members knew the purpose of the appointments, but they seldom saw the actual transfer of money. It can only be assumed, therefore, that considerable unrecorded cash changed hands. On one occasion Dodd forgot an appointment with one businessman, R. H. Blinken, who arrived at the Senate office with a sealed envelope. When two secretaries delivered the envelope to Dodd in Connecticut, he opened it, and they could see it contained cash. Senate investigators later obtained an admission from Blinken that he had donated $2,100 in cash.

Another $8,000 cash gift from the International Latex

Corporation also came in after David Martin boasted to other staff members that he had arranged it. The *quid pro quo,* he said, was that Dodd would support the board chairman, A. N. Spanel, for a major ambassadorship. Senate investigators discovered that the cash had been taken from International Latex's corporate funds.

Dodd's first $100-a-plate political dinner was held in November 1961 at the Statler Hilton Hotel in Hartford. The Senator assigned several staff members, their salaries paid by the taxpayers, to work full time selling tables. One of them, George Gildea, reported from Danbury, Connecticut, on August 14, 1961:

> The response is most encouraging and I am sure of at least several tables from Danbury. I expect to be on the road traveling after tomorrow, making contacts with people who are in a position to sponsor a table. Before my departure from Washington, I left with John O'Keefe [a Dodd crony] a typewritten list of names he is to contact in Washington; also he will add additional names of friends he wishes to participate in this dinner. . . . I also left with Jim Gartland [a Senate aide] his list of people, who he has done favors for and helped to get business through your office.

The guest speaker was Vice President Lyndon Johnson; the head-table guests were prominent Democrats. Outwardly it seemed just another in the long series of fund-raising dinners that have become common in political life. Only Dodd and his closest confidants knew that this one was to be different. The dinner raised $64,000, not counting unreported contributions; after expenses, a balance of $55,000 remained. The results were never publicly announced; the money was never turned over to any campaign committee or political organization. Neither the Connecticut press nor the Democratic party ever asked for an accounting of what was to be done with it.

All of it was deposited in Dodd's personal account at the Riggs Bank in Washington, D. C. Dodd used the entire $55,000 as his own, to pay personal debts and to meet personal expenses. For the most part, the money had come from people who had a stake in Dodd's role as a Senator—insurance officials concerned over a possible investigation of their industry by Dodd, arms-industry executives who wanted a hand in the writing of gun legislation Dodd was drafting, contractors who lived on Government appropriations, political job-seekers who wanted Dodd's aid, and persons connected with the television industry whose presence might have been prompted by Dodd's investigation into television programming. Although the dinner was a financial success, it did not satisfy Ed Sullivan, who wrote in his shaky hand to the Senator on November 25, 1961: "I was much surprised at the few leads to come from the office. I am sure that enough concerns have had favors from the office that should have given us another 25 tables."

The $55,000 was soon gone. Dodd began to plan a whole series of fund-raising affairs to be held in Connecticut, Washington, D. C., New York City and Los Angeles. They would begin in late 1963, close enough to his 1964 re-election drive to make them seem like normal campaign functions. The scheme seemed foolproof; even Dodd's top Washington aides thought the affairs were innocent political fund-raisers. If all went well, Tom Dodd would be on the path to solvency.

3

OFF THE PEDESTAL

1. The Price of Solvency

Favors are part of a politician's stock in trade. He is expected to produce Government jobs, public works projects, appointments to the military academies, and Government contracts for the people he represents. All of these Federal blessings can be arranged within the constraints of the law and ethics. To help Congressmen meet their obligations to the people back home, every Government agency maintains legislative liaison officers (lobbyists for the Government) to expedite Congressional requests. Traffic moves both ways along these arteries. The people at home are supposed to be grateful and show their thanks—and those of their relatives, friends and employees—at the ballot box. The Congressman, in his turn, can express his gratitude to the agencies by supporting their appropriations. It is sometimes a clumsy system, a throwback to the less artful days of government, but it seems to work, and both the dedicated and the venal Congressmen participate in it fully.

Tom Dodd was skilled in the intricacies of this system. He delivered the spoils for his supporters. He was not always content, however, to wait for Election Day to bask in the gratitude of the people of Connecticut. To him, money had become more important than duty, and he began trading favors for cash like a hotel bellhop. There was no set price for Dodd's benevolence. There was no direct relation between influence expended and cash extracted; nor did a petitioner's ability to pay seem to figure into any formula for pricing. Dodd simply took what he could get.

The Oldsmobiles provided for Dodd's use by David Dunbar, the president of Dunbar Transfer Company in Newington, Connecticut, cost Dunbar more than $2,700, with the company furnishing the registration and insurance. There is no doubt that Dodd appreciated the cars and wanted to keep them rolling. "I want you to know how deeply grateful I am to you for the wonderful assistance you have given us," Dodd wrote to Dunbar on July 23, 1964. "The car is just great and it sure gets me around."

Dodd got around a good bit for Dunbar, although not always by car. In June 1965, for instance, the Senator made an attempt to get Dunbar the contract for the Government Printing Office's move from downtown Washington to a new headquarters in the suburbs. There was one hitch: the printing office was not ready to move.

A month later Dodd learned from sources inside Pratt & Whitney, the West Hartford manufacturer of aircraft engines, that the Atomic Energy Commission was about to close its Connecticut Advanced Nuclear Engineering Laboratory. There would be need for an independent contractor—a deserving company, say, like Dunbar—to come in as caretaker. Dodd's knowledge of nuclear engineering may have been skimpy, but this was a case that called for political engineering, and here the Senator was at home. "This seems to be a situation which will support an award to Dunbar on an exigency basis," one of Dodd's office memos noted. "The problem at the moment is to put the Dunbar Transfer Company on the ground floor, and to cause AEC to retain jurisdiction over the work for as long as possible."

Dodd was uncommonly helpful also to a New Haven concern that billed itself, with some understatement, as the Mite Corporation. Mite, on its own resources, had developed a miniature teletype printer for military use. Robert Blinken, the company's president, began seeking Dodd's assistance early in 1964 after the Navy Department announced it would ask for competitive bids on this equipment in the future. Over the years the Department of Defense had found it could save the taxpayers approximately 25 percent on its purchases by demanding competitive bids.

To spare Mite any such troubling competition, Dodd met with an Assistant Navy Secretary, then wrote to the Deputy Defense Secretary, and finally, in late February 1964, set up an appointment for Blinken with Navy Department officials. Mite was nevertheless compelled to bid, and as the Defense Department suspected, the taxpayers benefited. Blinken whined to Dodd in a letter: "Naturally, we would have preferred not to have been subjected to the bidding process which necessitated our proposing a price on this quantity which was less than what we consider equitable."

The question of equity came up again when the two men met a short time later. Blinken thought $2,100 was equitable for Dodd's rather routine services. It was turned over in cash, and was neither reported as a campaign contribution nor deposited in Dodd's bank account. It was, apparently, just pocket change.

Not all of Dodd's constituents found it necessary to go through the Senator's office to have pressure exerted for them in Washington. Albert Morano, who lent Dodd money, provided a shortcut for the Conetta Manufacturing Company, of which he was an official. He went on Dodd's payroll at approximately $5,000 a year, so the taxpayers could help support him while he labored on Conetta's behalf. Conetta made triggers and trigger assemblies for the Army's M-14 rifle. In late 1964, the Army stopped ordering the rifles after giving its contractors ample warning. Conetta, however, kept squeezing out the triggers. When it was left without a market, Louis Conetta, of the company that bore his name, arranged through Morano for Dodd to rally to the rescue. The company would be glad, Conetta said, to sell the triggers to the Government at a discount.

Dodd went through all the familiar haggling with Defense Department officials, who assured him in a letter that the Army would not be interested in buying M-14 triggers at any price for at least two years. But Dodd declined to pass the letter back to Conetta and Morano. "The Senator decided to handle the matter himself," one staff aide noted in a memo to the file, "and did not want a copy of this letter to be sent to Conetta." The staffer was obviously puzzled by Dodd's behavior, but the picture became clearer when the Government, out of the blue, accepted the company's offer to unload the unneeded triggers.

When his dual role as an employee of Dodd and an official of Conetta was revealed, Morano told reporters that he had stopped working for Conetta when he went on the Senator's payroll. The fact is that he was still occupying an office at the Conetta plant after signing on as a Senate employee. Whenever Dodd's office staff wanted to reach Morano, they called him at Conetta. Morano may well have had difficulty, of course, separating his chores for Dodd from his work for Conetta, since they appear to have been identical. As for the unneeded triggers, the cost was high, but the taxpayers may have gotten off lightly. After all, Conetta might have been making obsolete tanks.

Dodd's membership on the Senate Aeronautical and Space Sciences Committee put him in a strategic position, particularly to promote Government contracts for Connecticut's hungry aerospace industry. He laid his Senatorial influence on the negotiating table, like up-the-sleeve aces in a poker game, for companies like United Aircraft Corporation, Kaman Aircraft and Avco which supplied the private planes that ferried Dodd around. Executives of these companies also aided Dodd financially. United Aircraft's Joe Barr worked actively to sell tickets for the Dodd testimonial dinners. Charles Kaman gave $4,000 to Dodd's campaign in 1964, which was listed as a contribution, plus another $300 which was not listed. Former West Point football coach Earl Blaik, now chairman of Avco's executive committee, helped round up the crowds for Dodd's testimonials, and introduced the Senator with a verbal 76-trombone flourish at a fund-raising dinner in 1965.

Dodd, for his part, pulled strings with Lockheed Aircraft to have Kaman selected as a subcontractor for Military Aircraft; he also set up demonstrations of United Aircraft equipment. For Avco, he intervened in its battle with General Electric over a contract in 1965 to develop a new Army helicopter engine. Avco fed favorable information on its capabilities to Dodd, who, bypassing the Defense Department, wrote a letter to his friend Lyndon Johnson at the White House. After the letter had gone out, Dodd began to feel some anxiety. Doreen Moloney, his secretary, wrote this memorandum to Gerry Zeiller, his executive assistant: "The Senator wants to know if this letter was sent to Valenti. He doesn't want it handled by Larry [Lawrence F.] O'Brien [a Kennedy-appointed Presidential aide]." It had been sent to Presidential Assistant Jack Valenti, all right, but the answer came from O'Brien. "Your comments will be called to the attention of the Department of the Army and you may be sure that they will be given all appropriate consideration," Dodd was informed by O'Brien's note.

Another copy of the letter was sent to Presidential Assistant McGeorge Bundy, whose response was more caustic:

> Your office has sent me a copy of your letter of March 25 to the President on the subject of a pending contract. Simply to avoid any misunderstanding, I think I should inform you that there are standing instructions here in the White House which forbid staff officers to concern themselves with business of this sort which is pending in any of the great departments.

Dodd, stung by the rebuke, drafted two letters in reply to Bundy. But he reconsidered and never mailed them. The Senator's spirits were revived two weeks later when the contract was awarded to Avco. Once again, Dodd felt, merit had triumphed.

When Dodd recommended men for high office, there was also usually a *quid pro quo*. He suggested three men for ambassadorships, and all had given him money.

A. N. Spanel, the president of the International Latex Corporation, gave Dodd an $8,000 cash contribution from company funds in December 1964. Dodd's assistant, David

Martin, told other staff members that, in return, the Senator would seek an appointment for Spanel as ambassador to France. By February 12, 1965, the intrigue had proceeded far enough for Spanel's Washington operative, Irving Ferman, to send Dodd a résumé about Mrs. Spanel, which noted that she was "fluent in Italian and French."

The price was cheaper for Edgar G. Parser, a diamond merchant, whose ambitions were more modest than Spanel's. Parser was not interested in matching wits or ego with Charles de Gaulle. He merely wanted to become ambassador to Luxembourg. In his letter to the President recommending Parser, Dodd declared that he had "the highest respect for him because of his outstanding character and high intelligence." The tangible signs of Parser's character and intelligence included a $1,000 political contribution to Dodd, two star-sapphire rings for Mrs. Dodd, and a $3,000 interest-free loan to the Senator.

Dodd also recommended New York attorney Joseph T. P. Sullivan for the ambassadorship to Ireland. When that failed to materialize, Sullivan came through with a $2,500 contribution to Dodd, who then suggested to the President, "Joe Sullivan is a very distinguished lawyer with a very distinguished background and, indeed, I add an ardent Democrat. Many of his friends feel that he would make an excellent ambassador to the Netherlands or Italy and I am one who thinks this is true." LBJ, apparently, did not think so.

John Mosler, the president of the Mosler Safe Company, gave Dodd only $1,000 for his 1964 campaign, but also gave yeoman's service as treasurer of the National Nonpartisan Committee for Dodd. This was enough to persuade Dodd that Mosler would make an excellent Assistant Secretary of State for African Affairs. But again Dodd did not succeed in persuading the White House, which, by return mail, sent him pleasant, noncommittal replies. His contributors were duly impressed that he had tried and that things might jell later.

These gentle billets-doux, however, would not work with the real big spenders like Mathew Manes, the New York lawyer whose firm had made two loans to Dodd without interest. The first was for $25,000, the other $2 500. If Manes was openhanded. he left his palm extended. He would accept a valuable directorship in the General Aniline & Film Corporation, which was seized as alien property after the United

States entered World War II and was run under Government supervision until it was sold in 1965. With a strong push from Dodd, Manes received his appointment to the corporation's board, and with another nudge was reappointed.

During Dodd's 1958 campaign for the Senate, Meade Alcorn, the Republican national chairman, had attempted to make an election issue of Dodd's employment as a Washington representative for Guatemala. At that time Dodd responded, "Of course, I will not represent the Government of Guatemala or any other private client if I am elected to the Senate." It was another promise that he abandoned after Election Day. While in the Senate, Dodd not only continued to represent private clients but intervened for them with the Federal Government—a definite violation of the law.

When Thomas Frouge, a Connecticut real-estate developer, decided to build 53 high-rise apartment buildings outside San Francisco, he took his problems to his lawyer, Thomas Dodd. California conservationists were complaining that the apartments would obscure the view of the Golden Gate, and these objections were echoing off the walls of the Department of the Interior in Washington. The complaints also richocheted off the executive paneling of the then Governor Edmund G. Brown's office in Sacramento.

Dodd did not inform Brown that Frouge was any more than a constituent when he telephoned, wrote and even flew to Sacramento to see the Governor. After a series of communications Dodd wrote to Brown:

> My friend, Tom Frouge, has again been in touch with me asking that I remind you of his urgent needs for his project in Marincello, particularly the use of an entry road and water supply. As I have told you, Tom is an old and good friend and a very capable businessman. You will remember that he is from Bridgeport, Connecticut.

Brown was not moved, but the Marin County Board of Supervisors eventually approved the project unanimously. Still, Frouge had problems. He wrote to Dodd: "It would be very helpful if Secretary Udall would make a statement that this site is not being considered for a park at this time or in the future." Dodd obediently contacted Udall. The Interior Secretary, who had blocked apartment houses along the Potomac, decided that his jurisdiction did not extend to San Francisco. Frouge wanted even more. "If a meeting could be arranged with President Johnson as soon as possible," he wrote to Dodd, "it would eliminate any doubt as to our intent and would bear out that we are planning our development to coincide with his discussion on planned communities under the New [*sic*] Society."

Frouge spelled out more bluntly in another letter what he had in mind: "Tom," he wrote, "I think this is a great opportunity for you and me. If we could get the Government to lease some space from us—this would mean acceptance by the business world of Marincello as a satellite city to San Francisco." Sure that "if this was brought to LBJ's attention, he would like the concept and do something to help us," Frouge concluded. "An announcement such as this would be fantastic—it would mean immediate success."

There is no record that Dodd ever spoke to the President on the subject. Possibly, the President had matters on his mind more important than the success of Frouge's apartment buildings. Dodd did, however, take the request for Government participation to the General Services Administration, which rents Government office space. The answer was polite but negative.

For other clients Dodd intervened to get a $120,000 loan from the Small Business Administration for Ford dealer Henry Nielsen and steered wholesale liquor dealer Johnny Barton to Paul V. McNamara's law firm. McNamara later sent Dodd a $3,750 check as a share in the fee.

The law office was a remunerative sideline for Dodd, but he was still dissatisfied with the income it brought him. When one of his law partners, John L. Calvocoressi, suggested that he should share in the $50,000 fee Dodd collected from the Teamsters in 1961, Dodd's temper flared. He wrote to Calvocoressi:

There will be no Teamster fee for anyone else.

In view of the long struggle I went through, borrowing and paying interest and the many sacrifices I have had to make since that time, I think it is asking too much to expect any share of that fee. I am sure you will understand when I tell you that I have made a large contribution to the firm, and actually my return has been small. It should be much larger and this is something I will have to talk about very soon.

I am sure you know as well as I do that there is a considerable amount of business that goes into the office because of me.

I do not expect to share in this because normally people do not mention their reason for bringing in business. Yet my name and association is a realistic fact which definitely has value. . . .

I am very busy with my Senate duties and I have very little time to devote to the law practice. Yet I must supplement my income in order to provide for my family. . . .

Many men who are in public life receive a steady income from their law practices because of the value of their association. I have never asked for such an arrangement, but I must increase my income from my private law practice.

To put it simply, I wish you men would sometimes think about how you can help me.

Dodd, of course, was not incapable of helping himself. With his choice committee assignments, he discovered soon after he arrived in the Senate that negativism had its rewards and that sometimes there could be big money in doing nothing. His investigation into the movie industry foundered after he was given a $500 contribution by a lobbyist for the Motion Picture Association. He accepted a $1,000 contribution from Lawrence Ehrhardt, a vice president of the huge McKesson & Robbins drug company, and frequently used the drug firm's private plane, although he was serving on both the Foreign Relations Committee and the Subcommittee on Antitrust and Monopoly, both of which were investigating the abuses of the drug industry. The latter, specifically, began probing United States drug sales to Colombia; by coincidence, the biggest wholesaler to Colombia was McKesson & Robbins.

The Juvenile Delinquency Subcommittee's investigations, meanwhile, enhanced Chairman Dodd's image as a battler against adolescent delinquency while he managed to hide his adult delinquency from the public. The hearings on sex and violence on television, in particular, projected Dodd's name into the headlines. His subcommittee staff built an interesting case against Metromedia. an entertainment octopus that owns a string of television stations and the Ice Capades. Metromedia did not subscribe to the code of the National Association of Broadcasters, and its TV fare was heavily laced with reruns of old network shoot-'em-ups. When the subcommittee staff monitored the three network stations and the Metromedia outlet in Washington for a week in January 1964, they recorded 232 acts of violence shown during prime time, of which 111 appeared on the Metromedia station.

Metromedia's president is John Kluge, a dynamic executive who left the drab mills of Holyoke, Massachusetts, to make a fortune. Part of Kluge's success is based on the strategic friendships he formed easily. His courtship of Dodd included frequent dinners and at least one fat campaign contribution in 1964. When Kluge coughed up the money, Dodd wrote to Florence Lowe, Metromedia executive in Washington: "John Kluge's check arrived and, believe me, it is mighty welcome. Many, many thanks to you and John."

Mrs. Lowe is an efficient saccharine-sweet woman whose duties ranged from the nebulous area called public relations to producing interview shows with politicians. She became friendly with the Dodds, and presented them with a portable TV set. In a note of thanks Dodd allowed, "The picture is so beautifully clear."

The staff of the Juvenile Delinquency Subcommittee was not tuned in to these particular developments until a request was made to subpoena the records of Channel 5, Washington's Metromedia station. "Channel 5 is out," Dodd told a staff aide, thus shutting off any further investigation of Metromedia. In another strange move Dodd appointed Mrs. Lowe's son Roger to the subcommittee staff.

In 1962 seniority had raised Dodd to the chairmanship of an antitrust subcommittee charged with investigating the insurance industry. Coming from Connecticut, Dodd was strategically situated to conduct a penetrating probe in the public interest. Hartford is the center of the United States insurance business, and Dodd had good contacts inside the industry. The Senate did not intend, however, that the investigation should improve Dodd's contacts.

One of his law clients, Manlio M. Liccione, had a plan to develop four buildings in Albany, New York, and offered Dodd a partnership if he could arrange the financing. "These properties look very good to me," Liccione wrote to the Senator, "and could very well stand a mortgage of $3,750,000 to $4,000,000." Dodd was delighted and told his Senate employees, "This could make me a rich man." He sent Liccione to three Connecticut insurance companies for the loans. Although the insurance people were eager to appease Dodd, they could not envision mortgages of the size Liccione wanted, and the deal fell through.

Dodd did set up a $650,000 mortgage for Liccione to construct an office building in White Plains, New York, through Aetna, and Aetna later moved its local office into Liccione's building. Liccione admitted paying Dodd's law firm no more than the standard one-percent finder's fee.

At the same time that Dodd was investigating the insurance industry, his law firm also represented (according to the list it provided to the Martindale-Hubbell legal directory) Maryland Casualty, Standard Accident Insurance, Phoenix of Hartford Insurance, American Insurance Group, American Fidelity, Reliance Insurance, Fire Association of Philadelphia, Northwestern National Casualty, Central Mutual Insurance, and Norfolk and Dedham Insurance. While Dodd showed little interest in investigating insurance companies, he increased his personal interest in the insurance business. He received $5,000 in 1962, too, for intervening with the Connecticut Insurance Commission to arrange for Bankers Life and Casualty Company to do business in the state. Jeremy, one of his sons, went to work for Aetna, and the Senator himself enjoyed the use of a Travelers Insurance Company plane. Insurance executives piled contributions into the Dodd campaign chest, and Dodd was paid to lecture to insurance groups. The Senator, curiously, also stopped paying his own premiums. From 1962 until November 1965, Dodd's bill with Charles H. McDonough Sons, a Hartford insurance broker, mounted up to $3,403.37. Indeed, the Senator made no effort to pay his bill until December 1965, when he learned that newsmen were investigating his misconduct.

In one of his speeches to insurance executives, Dodd congratulated them on their clean house. "There has been no pattern of large-scale abuses, no block-busting allegations of wrongdoing and lawbreaking of the scope we have encountered with other industries," he said. Less partial investigators came to less enthusiastic conclusions, but Dodd was happy with his role as friend of his hometown industry. He did not need an actuary to tell him that the insurance men were giving him amazing coverage.

2. The People's Choice

Few politicians can appraise themselves without seeing the people's choice. On the same afternoon that a bullet in Texas made Lyndon Johnson the President, Dodd suddenly saw himself as the people's choice for Vice President.

On that fateful day Dodd was in Hartford. His staff in Washington reached him by telephone in a bar to tell him the news. During the course of the long afternoon he called his office back a number of times, demanding, "Is Lady Bird all right?" Another notion also became lodged in Dodd's mind as several quick snorts blurred the tragic event. He became convinced, apparently, that Lyndon Johnson needed him to help run the nation. It was in response to this call to duty that he summoned a private plane from the United Aircraft Corporation's fleet to rush him to the capital.

Dodd's friendship with LBJ was more endearing and enduring in Dodd's imagination than in reality. When Johnson was running the Senate, he knew his strength was weakest among the liberals from the Northeast, and he shrewdly picked out Dodd as an easy convert. He courted Dodd with special favors and nimbly played on his ego until Dodd became convinced that he was Johnson's strong right arm. If the truth were to be told, the skillful Senate Democratic leader had more right arms than an octopus.

But Dodd became as devoted to Johnson as a toy poodle is to a woman with a large lap. At the 1960 Democratic convention in Chicago, Dodd had been the only delegate from New England who backed Johnson against John F. Kennedy. Dodd took the rostrum to second Johnson's nomination and rose to oratorical heights. But inside the Connecticut delegation, Dodd's actions made him a figure of mild amusement.

When LBJ left the Senate, his interest in Dodd diminished. It was Johnson's nature, to be sure, to hug a Senator to his bosom on occasion or to whisper intimately into his ear. But this was standard treatment for a number of Senators—not Dodd alone.

Despite his determination to be Lyndon Johnson's best friend, Dodd found himself frequently snubbed by his idol. The stories of Vice President Johnson's lavish parties at his elegant northwest Washington mansion were all over the society pages, but Dodd was almost never on the guest list. He did spend a weekend at the LBJ ranch while on a speaking engagement in Texas, but from the hospitable Johnson that was a bare formality. Political favors and their return are a way of life for Johnson, and he shared them with Dodd as he did with other Senators from both parties. The doors to Johnson's private friendship, however, were never really opened to Dodd.

Still Dodd, having no other source of power, persisted. John Bailey had become Democratic national chairman under Kennedy, and Abe Ribicoff moved from Governor of Connecticut to Secretary of Health, Education and Welfare. Then he left the Cabinet to run for the Senate while proclaiming his loyalty to Kennedy. Dodd was out of step with the party in his state, and only Johnson could bolster his sagging political stature. For a while it seemed a thin hope. Dodd was sure the Kennedys wanted to urge both him and LBJ.

In October 1963 Johnson flew to Connecticut to speak at three of Dodd's testimonials dinners, and the two men shared a car between Hartford and New Haven. The Vice President then told Dodd of his deep fears and resentments. As later recounted by Dodd to his staff, Johnson said that the Kennedy people were out to ruin him completely by making him look like a "crook" and forcing him out of the Vice Presidency in 1964. He said he had done everything he could as Vice President to carry out his end of the bargain. Johnson, Dodd said, was mystified by President Kennedy's own behavior to him. Whenever they were together, the President treated him with warmth and kindness, and he believed that President Kennedy had nothing to do with the conspiracy against him. The key to the Irish Mafia plot, as Johnson saw it, was the Bobby Baker scandal. Johnson believed it was put together "to get him," Dodd related.

Dodd, who feared a purge himself, sympathized. But he did not let this keep him from seeking a small personal gain from Baker's trouble. A few days after the irrepressible Bobby was forced to resign from his job as Secretary of the Senate. Marjorie Carpenter, Dodd's secretary, jokingly remarked this would be a good chance to acquire the ornate crystal chandelier that hung in Baker's Capitol office. Mrs. Carpenter was astounded when Dodd took the suggestion seriously and sought to have the chandelier transplanted to his own office ceiling. He made a formal request for the chandelier and refused to be put off by Gordon Harrison, the chief clerk of the Senate Rules Committee, who pleaded, tongue in cheek, that Senators are only temporary, while the building is permanent. Dodd carried on his campaign with all of the determination of Harry Truman marching against Tom Dewey in his 1948 whistle-stop campaign. Senator Everett Jordan, D-N.C., who as chairman of the Rules and Administration Committee had jurisdiction over both the Senate's property and the investigation into the Baker case, was Dodd's next target. When the badgering became a nuisance. Jordan dispatched a letter to Dodd telling him that chandeliers were in short supply and therefore Baker's could not be moved. Grudgingly, Dodd gave up.

The Vice President has an office in the Capitol resplendent with a many-splendored chandelier, and Dodd decided that if a chandelier would not come to him, he would go to the chandelier. In January 1964 the shock of the Kennedy assassination began to wear off in Washington, and the pundits began a guessing game, trying to pick the new Vice President. First it was Bobby Kennedy. then Sargent Shriver, then a host of lesser-known politicians like Representative Cornelius Gallagher of New Jersey and Senator Edmund Muskie of Maine. Dodd was somewhat annoyed to notice that his name was not among those frequently tossed up by the speculators.

Although few were aware of it, there was indeed a Dodd-for-Vice President movement, headed by a Petersburg, Virginia, restaurant owner named John Vonetes. The two men had first met in Germany after the war when Dodd was executive trial counsel for the United States at the Nuremberg war crimes trials and Vonetes was a cook for the staff. Reared in Buffalo, New York, Vonetes migrated south and went into business in Virginia.

When the Dodd boom produced only a very small pop, Vonetes went to work, pursuing Southern politicians by letter, telephone and in person. His activities were noticed, and reporters questioned Dodd about them. Dodd smiled tolerantly and shook his head. Vonetes, he said, was merely an old friend, and Dodd was doing all he could to discourage him.

Dodd's efforts to discourage Vonetes included putting his Senate staff to work preparing a long tract entitled "Several Reasons Why Senator Thomas J. Dodd Is the Most Logical Choice for the Democratic Vice Presidential Nomination." It pointed out that Dodd was an Irish Catholic from the Northeast, that he was an enthusiastic anti-Communist, that he was "the only member of the Senate who kept up a sustained attack on the [nuclear testing] moratorium," that he was "a hero of the many nationality groups in this country who honor him for his ceaseless crusade in behalf of freedom for the captive nations." Moreover, the tract proclaimed, Dodd was "a moderate."

Vonetes distributed the document widely; every delegate to the Democratic convention from the South received one. Vonetes' own record as a moderate was revealed by an incident at lunch in the Senate dining room one day. A Senator recognized Vonetes and hailed him from across the room, asking how his restaurant business was doing. "Great," Vonetes shouted. "I haven't allowed any niggers in yet, and I'm not going to, no matter what you fellows do." Vonetes' opinions embarrassed even Dodd, who tried publicly to disassociate himself from his ardent supporter while continuing to egg him on.

Dodd's campaign for the Vice Presidency turned into a sad little charade as the Democratic convention drew closer. He received no encouragement from the White House. Dodd pretended that he did not really want the job but that Johnson was begging him to take it. He would tell his staff about confidential calls and meetings he held with the President, and for a while his staff made a game out of checking the stories and proving them false, until that too became a bore.

Dodd's communications with Johnson were, in fact, almost nonexistent. Long before the convention he began lobbying with White House assistants Walter Jenkins and Mike Manatos to be named the keynote speaker. When that possibility became more and more remote, he begged to make the nominating speech for Johnson. After this brought still no positive response, he beseeched Johnson's aides to let him do a repeat performance of his 1960 seconding speech.

Democratic Chairman John Bailey, who enjoys needling

his political adversaries, shared a seat with Dodd on an Eastern Airlines flight from Hartford to Washington in the summer of 1964. Bailey knew that Dodd was ripe for his needle. Abe Ribicoff, Bailey said with a dead pan, was the leading candidate to be the convention keynoter and could probably get it if Dodd would only put in a word in his favor. Dodd, taking the bait, could hardly wait for the plane to land. As fast as he could get to a telephone he called Walter Jenkins and demanded that Ribicoff be dropped from consideration. He reminded Jenkins that Ribicoff was the New England leader of the Kennedy drive in 1960, and said that Ribicoff's selection would make him the laughingstock of Connecticut. Jenkins seemed puzzled by the call, and Dodd, still in a panic, took his problem to Senator Richard Russell of Georgia, who often serves as a father confessor for other Senators. Russell thought it was improbable that Ribicoff would be chosen, but pointed out tactfully that Ribicoff would be the speaker if the President wanted him. Dodd dejectedly abandoned his campaign to block Ribicoff's selection and phoned Jenkins to say he would support Ribicoff if that was what the President wanted. Jenkins was more mystified than ever, since the Ribicoff rumor had never been more than John Bailey's private joke. The keynote speech, of course, was assigned to razortongued Senator John Pastore of Rhode Island.

For Dodd, the convention was a nightmare. Ribicoff was picked to second Johnson's nomination, and Dodd's own brief moment on the stage was a disaster. He was called upon to read one plank of the draft platform, and it turned out to be a call for peace—a far cry from his hawk tendencies. The greatest humiliation, however, came when Senator Warren Magnuson of Washington introduced him to the crowd in Atlantic City's Convention Hall as "the Senator from Kentucky." Dodd was deeply hurt and avoided everything but the parties.

To salve his ego and save his image, however, he continued to push his candidacy for the Vice Presidency with the Southern delegates, using friends and aides as go-betweens. In the basement of Convention Hall, Vonetes stored hundreds of Dodd-for-Vice President signs, waiting for the dreams and the schemes to become a reality. Dodd knew they would not and began searching wildly for a publicity gimmick that might bolster his prestige.

Dodd ordered Marjorie Carpenter to place a succession of

calls to Ed Wiesl, who had been counsel of the Senate Preparedness Committee when Johnson was its chairman, and enjoyed a close personal relationship with the President. Dodd also called Elliott Janeway, the newspaper economics columnist, who had pipelines to the President. Dodd told them both that he was being treated shamefully, and since he was the only New Englander to support Johnson in 1960, it was a humiliation. Something had to be done, he pleaded, to make him look good.

On the day that Johnson was to end the Democratic guessing game and name his running mate, Dodd received a telephone call from Walter Jenkins, asking him to go to the Atlantic City airport and fly to the White House with Hubert Humphrey. The word spread quickly, and to the delegates at the convention and people across the country, it seemed that Johnson had narrowed his candidates to two men. At the airport, Humphrey was puzzled. He looked Dodd in the eye and questioned, "Has he asked you to be Vice President?" Dodd said no, and Humphrey told him that he had not been asked either.

The contrast between the two men was apparent on the flight to Washington. Humphrey fell asleep almost immediately, while Dodd fretted away the miles. He was still nervously pursing his lips when they arrived at the White House, and the President led them around the grounds on one of his famous tourist-watching expeditions. Dodd dropped out after one lap. When Johnson returned, he summoned Dodd into his office first, and let him be interviewed by waiting reporters while Humphrey was being told he would be the running mate.

The press conference Dodd held on the White House steps was a stroke of publicity genius. He announced solemnly that he had told the President that he would not consider the Vice Presidency and that it should go to Humphrey. It kept the reporters from asking Dodd whether the job had really been offered—which, say insiders, never entered the President's mind. LBJ was merely responding to Dodd's appeal for a moment in the spotlight. But Dodd's story grew with each retelling. Back in Atlantic City that night, he confided to Jim Boyd that Johnson had been about to offer him the Vice Presidency but that he stopped the President and insisted he was not qualified. The following day, Dodd's daughter Carolyn told the New Britain (Connecticut) *Herald,* "The President offered my father the Vice Presidency and he turned it down."

On the closing day of the convention, Dodd bragged to his staff that he had been offered the Attorney Generalship, which Bobby Kennedy had just given up. He gave out the same story in interviews with Ralph De Toledano, the right-wing columnist, and Herb Klein, the former press assistant for Richard Nixon. Dodd's "appointment" made the banner headline in the afternoon Philadelphia papers, which were widely circulated at the convention. When other reporters quizzed him, he declared he would not leave the Senate to accept the office, thus avoiding the embarrassment of having the news come from Johnson. Back in Washington, Dodd sent a letter to Johnson, disclaiming any responsibility for the Attorney General story. The convention that started as a disaster ended, by his measure, in a publicity triumph.

3. "Why Don't I See You Any More?"

The triumph was as shaky as its foundation. Through all Dodd's scheming and plotting, worrying and rejoicing, his staff began to see him in an unflattering new light. He had been skillful in concealing from his closest associates the extent to which he was betraying his oath and his office. He kept his staff divided into separate compartments, where each could see only one aspect of his many-sided operations. Now and then, staff members would chance upon something that seemed suspicious, but there was at first a tendency to view such fragments as the eccentricities of an unorthodox but essentially honest man. Ugly whispers occasionally reached their ears, but these, too. were dismissed as the rumors that inevitably circulate about any public figures. Politics also breeds a rare form of dedication. People who work closely with a candidate, particularly in the heat of a campaign, begin to think of the candidate as an extension of themselves and find themselves blinded to his flaws.

But slowly his aides began to recover their perspective, and, inevitably, they started to compare notes. It was during the year preceding the election of 1964 that Dodd's acquisitive ventures began to peak. and the staff soon recognized that something was gravely wrong. From intimate glimpses into

Dodd's political life, they began putting together a grotesque mosaic made up of the compromises, equivocations and sellouts they had seen. The Dodd they had caught lying and cheating was not the man for whom they had worked long, sleepless hours on the campaign trail.

As the weather turned cooler and the campaign warmer during the fall of 1964, some of the Dodd aides began noting the contributions blowing in like autumn leaves and wondering where all the money was going. Eventually they were struck with the realization that whereas Dodd had collected roughly $500,000 in connection with his 1964 re-election bid, he had spent less than $250,000 for legitimate campaign expenses. The deeper they dug into their boss's other dealings, the more dismaying the pattern of fraud they turned up.

Jim Boyd and Marjorie Carpenter talked together, sharing their disillusionment and searching together for an answer. Aides Mike O'Hare and Terry Golden were brought into their confidence. What should they do? Their own livelihoods and future careers were tied to the powerful and vindictive Dodd. The normal reaction of subordinates who witness corruption in Congressional offices is to sit tight, cover up and hold on to their attractive salaries. The four Dodd aides agreed that they knew too much to keep silent, but they did not know the best way to proceed. They considered going to the Department of Justice but rejected the idea. It was unlikely that the Justice Department would act against any Senator, particularly one who served on the Judiciary Committee. The FBI also made itself so much at home in Dodd's office that staff members joked about assigning the Bureau a desk. Former FBI Agent Dodd was always first on his feet to defend J. Edgar Hoover over any public slight, real or imagined. And if the FBI wanted a suspected subversive cross-examined under oath and could not convoke a grand jury for that purpose, Dodd was always willing to subpoena the suspect behind closed doors of his Internal Security Subcommittee. The Dodd aides also ruled out the idea of turning their boss in to the Senate, which —they knew—was a benevolent mutual protection society.

After considerable soul-searching, the troubled members of Dodd's staff came to the conclusion that they would turn over their evidence to Dodd's employers, the American people. First singly, then in a group, they began talking to the authors of this book, who simultaneously had started an investigation of Dodd. The evidence was quietly collected over a 12-month period. Once the first chapters of the convoluted, frightening story were made public, Dodd's aides offered to disclose all of it, with documentary proof, to all of the press.

The four staffers were well aware that their own futures were in jeopardy. They knew it would be most difficult for them to find new employment, that they would be harassed and punished socially, and that the whole course of their lives would be altered. It was a price they were willing to pay. They held the key to reform in Congress, and were morally certain they had no choice but to turn it. They did not expect, however, that their charges would be virtually ignored by the press and that they would be abused and reviled for making them—by Congress as well as the press.

As the sordid details of Dodd's machinations were presented to the public, Dodd denied the charges and called for a Senate investigation into his own conduct. The investigation soon turned into a merciless probe of his former staffers. The FBI asked for and received copies of all the Dodd documents, photostated from his files by the staff. All of these papers were revealed to Dodd by the Senate Ethics Committee so he would know how to construct his defenses. The FBI also undertook an exploration into the lives of the staffers, and of the authors who told the story of Dodd's chicanery. Throughout the investigation the FBI's activities were reminiscent of the Harding days, when the Bureau was used for political purposes.

The behavior of the Senate was no better than it usually is. Senators, who cannot be sued for their utterances on the floor of the Senate and can change their words before they appear in the *Congressional Record*, took advantage of their privileges to lambaste those who had dared to open the inner workings of the Senate to public scrutiny. As the case dragged on, the public became aroused by the reports of Dodd's behavior and by the Senate's seeming willingness to countenance it. Letters poured into the Capitol from every section of the nation, expressing the public's dismay and outrage.

The Senate Ethics Committee, formed shortly before the Dodd case exploded, reluctantly agreed to investigate. Although the committee had full access to all the evidence, it decided to ignore most of it and bring charges against Dodd on only two counts: converting campaign contributions to his private use and billing the Government for travel expenses that were paid by private organizations. It recommended that Dodd be censured by the Senate—a toothless penalty that, nevertheless, had been exercised only five previous times in history.

The rest of the evidence was swept under the rug. The impression was left that Dodd's other betrayals of public trust were acceptable conduct. The Senate did not, however, stop there. To its report, the Ethics Committee added a withering attack on the four members of Dodd's staff who had had the courage to bring the dark secrets of Dodd's office to the nation. The hypocrisy of the committee's position did not seem to bother the Senate at all.

Taking his cue from the Ethics Committee, Dodd based his defense during the Senate debate on the perfidy of his former workers. They, not Dodd, became the focal point. But unlike him, they were not given the opportunity to answer. Said Dodd, "I am telling you the truth, the whole truth, and nothing but the truth, so help me God. I am telling the truth as though I had to face my Maker in a minute. I am telling you the truth and I am concealing nothing. May the vengeance of God strike me if I am doing otherwise." He then proceeded to lie outrageously, and cynical members of the press gallery suggested that everyone following the debate wear rubber-heeled shoes.

The Senate voted 94 to 5* for censure on the misuse of campaign funds, and then, having slapped Dodd's wrist, it relaxed. The second charge, the double payment of travel expenses, failed to carry—not for lack of evidence so much as a gesture of charity toward Dodd. The other charges documented by Dodd's staff—that he accepted money and gifts from industries being investigated by committees on which he served; that he took money and loans from people for whom he obtained or attempted to obtain official appointments; that he took money and gifts from people for whom he performed official services; that he interceded for his private law clients with the Federal Government; that he charged the Government for trips that were essentially vacations; and that he padded his payroll with people who performed no official services—were not voted upon at all.

The Senate was content that it had met its obligations by its single vote of censure. When the voting was over, Dodd blandly announced that he would seek re-election in 1970. In the meanwhile he continues to hold his seat in the Senate, to investigate subversives and juvenile delinquents in the Senate's behalf, to vote on matters of vital concern to the nation and the world, and, of course, to draw his salary.

The toll, nevertheless, has been heavy. In just 100 months Dodd went from the bright headlines of his maiden address to the obscurity of a Senator whose colleagues rose almost to a man to disapprove his conduct. The action meant very little, yet it meant very much. Even with those who knew him well, the memory of the brash freshman Senator with the springing step and the pealing laughter has faded; he is now a stooped, shuffling man, old beyond his years. The crowds don't gather around Tom Dodd any more. He moves down the marble corridors slowly, his head slightly bent. Occasionally he spots a familiar face and nods. Sometimes the greeting is not returned. Sometimes Dodd stops and, in a voice barely audible, says, "You used to be around my office all the time. Why don't I see you any more?"

---

*The five Senators who voted against censuring Dodd were Abraham Ribicoff, D-Conn.; Russell Long, D-La.; John Tower, R-Texas; Strom Thurmond, R-S.C., and Dodd himself.

II

CONFLICTS
OF INTEREST

4

CROSSING THE BAR:
LAWYERS IN CONGRESS

1. *This Shingle for Hire*

Members of Congress are expected, in return for their Government pay, to serve the public interest. Behind the backs of the voters, however, many legislators do their most effective work for the powerful private interests—the oil and gas industries, business and banking combines, mining and timber operators, insurance and real-estate companies, carriers and utilities, and others with axes to grind and favors to seek.

Their influence cuts across sectional boundaries and party lines; they have established, in effect, an invisible supergovernment that shapes national policies to gratify the moneyed interests. Their friends in Congress have carved loopholes in the tax laws, squeezed subsidies out of the taxpayers, thrown open public lands for private exploitation, handed out Government patents to commercial companies. The statute books are fairly loaded with special-interest legislation. The Senators and Representatives who serve this spectral Government are paid off in campaign contributions, business opportunities, investment tips and other hidden offerings. One of the most convenient means, because of the large population of lawyers on Capitol Hill, is the legal fee. The back door to many a Congressman's office can be reached through his law practice.

Of the 535 members of Congress, more than 300 are attorneys. Few have bothered to take down their shingles. Some carry on active law practices; others are merely keeping the door ajar so they can beat a safe retreat back to their law firms in case the voters should turn them out of office. A minority never actively practiced law before coming to Congress but now draw income from flourishing legal businesses.

Many attorneys run for public office as a form of "ethical advertising" to help build up a practice. Others consider Congress a temporary watering hole and therefore feel no great ethical pull to abstain from collecting new clients or servicing old ones. Almost all have attracted clients because of their Congressional prestige. In answer to criticism, they piously contend that they keep clear of clients pressing claims against the Government or seeking favors from Federal agencies. Some legislator lawyers have gone through elaborate exercises, forming law firms within law firms, to separate themselves from their partners' Government practice. Most have at least signed agreements that they will not share in any income their law firms may collect from Federal practice.

There is nothing at all heroic about this attitude; it is the least Congressman lawyers must do to avoid Federal prosecution. For the law expressly forbids them from accepting pay for intervening with the Federal Government in behalf of law clients or anyone else. They are conspicuously less virtuous about barring clients who might benefit from legislation. Indeed, most Congressmen's law firms represent clients with considerable interest in what Congress can do for them. The authors have made a study of 50 typical law firms with partners serving in Congress. These have a remarkable similarity of clients. They represent the vested interests of America; the banks, insurance companies, gas and oil interests, great corporations.

Of the 50 law firms in the survey, 40 represent banks, 31

represent insurance companies, 11 represent gas and oil companies, 10 represent real-estate firms. Some of the biggest corporate names in America are listed as clients of Congressmen's law firms in such out-of-the-way places, say, as Nicholasville, Kentucky, and Pascagoula, Mississippi. To name just a few, there are General Motors, Ford, Standard Oil, Gulf Oil, Sinclair Refining, Aluminum Company of America, Baltimore & Ohio Railroad, Western Union, International Harvester, Seagram distillers, Coca-Cola, Equitable Life. The Travelers Corporation, for one, has retained legal counsel in such unlikely places as Piqua and Findlay, Ohio, where the company's political radar led them straight to the law firms of Representatives William McCulloch and Jackson Betts, respectively. The same insurance company was also guided unerringly to the law firms of Representatives James Harvey in Saginaw, Michigan, and Wendell Wyatt in Astoria, Oregon. Solid Republicans all, the four have always managed to find in their hearts an extraordinary sympathy for the corporate view on insurance problems. Betts has been particularly effective as a champion of the insurance industry on the tax-writing Ways and Means Committee.

There is no doubt that the vested interests have sought out and systematically engaged the services of Congressmen who are lawyers. This practice may account for the conservative bent of Congress and for the fact that the President is frequently more liberal than the Congress. Whether the predominance of corporate clients is purely accidental or a calculated tactic can never be resolved. But the situation is an ominous reminder of the days when the robber barons controlled the Senate. Why, for instance, do major corporations go all the way to Peoria, Illinois to seek the legal services of Davis, Morgan and Witherell? Could it have anything to do with the fact that Senate Republican Leader Everett Dirksen is associated with the firm?

2. Everett Dirksen:
The Voice of Righteousness

The gentle breeze caught the balloon and started it swaying. The rockaby motion made it difficult for the second lieutenant in the gondola to keep his sights fixed on the trenches, two-thirds of a mile below. The young officer in the gas balloon was Everett McKinley Dirksen, who later in politics was to rise on hot air to a greater height than he ever attained over the battlefields of France.

Although his career in France in 1918 was not particularly heroic, it made for grand conversation when the boys got together at the American Legion post in Pekin, Illinois, in the twenties. He had left the University of Minnesota's law college a year away from a degree to ride his balloon as an artillery spotter. Back in Pekin, the hours aloft were a pleasant memory to be shared as shoulders sagged and bellies blossomed. At the Legion meetings Dirksen's voice rose above the others. He had more to talk about than just the Great War. He was the one who planned the post's entertainments, and he appointed himself master of ceremonies.

"Those were the trial years," Dirksen later remembered. "I went around studying my techniques. I'd make a sally and see what kind of a response it received. Then I'd try another. I particularly watched the audiences. I learned how to appraise an audience—whether it was hostile, friendly, or indifferent. The indifferent ones, they're the worst. I learned to make contact with an audience, because if you don't make contact, only a little will be remembered and even less understood. I made a study of people, their attitudes and their foibles, what registered with them and what didn't."

While Dirksen was milking laughs from the Legionnaires, his sallies into the world of business met with indifference. His Army savings, which might have financed his senior year in college, went into a washing-machine factory that failed. He and his two brothers tried their luck as wholesale bakers, but the dough did not rise. On nights spent at home with his widowed mother, he wrote 100 short stories and five novels. "They covered every range of human activity," Dirksen said, but none of them was published. They were, he said, "rather juvenile." Dirksen's only early success came from his meetings, and he pursued them eagerly beyond the Legion halls. He joined the Veterans of Foreign Wars, the Eagles and the Elks and the Moose, the Masons and the Shriners.

There were also amateur theatricals. Dirksen wrote and directed and acted in a series of pseudo-Oriental dramas that appeased the hunger for culture in Pekin, a bobtailed namesake of the Chinese city. One of his leading ladies was Louella

Carver, whom he successfully courted on the stage and off. In 1927 she became Mrs. Everett Dirksen.

"I had an uncommon interest in drama all my life," Dirksen once admitted. "I fixed the habit in high school, and it persisted. It gave me slightly distorted ambitions. I began to make plans to pursue a theatrical existence, which I confided to my widowed mother. But she had a typical old-country, small-town, puritanistic view of the stage as a wicked domain. She demanded that I assure her right there that I would not essay it as a career. I gave her that assurance, but that, of course, did not destroy the urge. I *had* to appear before people. So I decided on politics."

Dirksen's parents were German immigrants, as unquestioning in their faith in the Republican party as they were in Calvinism. Their Sundays were spent with the church, but their saints were drawn from the party. They named their oldest son for President Benjamin Harrison; Everett McKinley got his middle name from an even less distinguished President, and his twin was named for Thomas Reed, the Speaker of the House in 1896 when they were born.

Dirksen's father, Johann, a painter, died in 1905, and his mother, Antje, moved her boys to "Beantown" on the shabby side of shabby Pekin, where vegetable gardens rather than rose beds were the foundation plantings. The Dirksens used their acre and a half for cows, pigs, chickens and enough greens to feed the boys and to sell to less ambitious neighbors. "There was a certain ruggedness about life," Dirksen has recalled.

Even in that rugged world, Dirksen established himself as an indoorsman. The happy days for him were the rainy ones. "Then he could go back out to the barn, nail a sort of platform out of some old boards, usually using nails twice too big," his brother Tom has reminisced. "Then he would get up and start speaking. Preaching to himself, that's what he did." He also preached to others. In Sunday school he was the president of Christian Endeavor, and in high school he was a member of the debating team.

His brothers were both high-school dropouts, lured away from the books by paychecks. Ev stayed in school and worked nights, first at the Corn Products Refining Company in Pekin (this early association with corn is considered symbolic by some observers) and then as an ad taker for the Minneapolis

Tribune while he was in college. He spent one summer as a traveling salesman, pushing cow cures on South Dakota farmers. His patent-medicine spiel, like his debating, helped him overcome a shyness that was so great, he has said, that "I was frightened to death to even ask a girl for a date. I had to walk around the block a couple of times to get up the nerve."

Those who knew young Dirksen recall his political style more than his political philosophy. In his first try for office in 1926, he was elected as Pekin's Commissioner of Finance. In 1930 he unsuccessfully challenged Representative William E. Hull in the Republican primary. Dirksen kept up his rounds of speeches and, by successfully painting Hull as a friend of prohibition and therefore an enemy of the district's corn farmers and distillers, won the nomination two years later.

That was in 1932—a year of hunger and despair, of bread-lines and soup kitchens, of Franklin D. Roosevelt and hope. In his fall campaign Dirksen spoke well of the Democrats, and he won in November by 23,000 votes.

Congress brought changes in Dirksen's life. For the first time since his father died, there was economic security. But he was still too poor to afford a dress suit and, by his own account, too scrupulous to accept one from his friends. "I went to Washington without a long-tailed coat and a white tie," he said sadly. "The first White House reception I attended, I had no such equipment. I made inquiry. Some thought a black tie and tuxedo was sufficient. Others thought I should have a white tie and long-tailed coat. The result was I was photographed and it went all over the country that I appeared at the first Roosevelt reception in a rented dress suit. It was a matter of frightful embarrassment, I must say, and promptly they took up a collection in Peoria. As I recall, they raised $2,700. I finally had to say to them, Divide the funds and give part of it to the Salvation Army, part to the Red Cross, part to the American Legion, and so I was left finally to buy my own formal wear."

The security of anyone in politics is, of course, fragile, and even in Dirksen's solidly Republican district, FDR was making friends. Dirksen charted a careful course, supporting the New Deal when he thought he had to, voting as a conservative when he thought it was safe, many times playing it both ways. In 1937 he bragged how he had supported FDR's programs. "I have taken a rather fine pride," he said, "that I voted for the National Recovery Act and voted for the Social Security Act, for the Agricultural Adjustment Administration and for a great many other measures that were proposed by the President in the hope of lifting this country from the slough of depression to the high road of sunshine and prosperity."

Less than a year later he protested that FDR was grabbing a stranglehold on the nation. "People humbly and willingly submitted themselves," he said, "to many sweeping bills that came into this chamber, such as the Agricultural Adjustment Act, the National Recovery Act. . . ." Before he left the House, his views on agriculture had flip-flopped 70 times. He was equally dependable on foreign affairs. During his years in the House, he changed his position 62 times on isolationism and 30 times on military preparedness. He opposed sending the United States fleet to the Pacific in 1937, then in 1940 said, "Thank God there is a national defense program under way." He swiveled again three months later to vote against the draft and lend-lease. But he'd still publicly endorsed Roosevelt's foreign policy three months before Pearl Harbor, when he told Congress that opposition "could only weaken the President's position, impair our prestige and imperil the nation."

Despite an ability to keep his balance on the reeling deck, Dirksen had anxieties about his future. Unlike most other members of Congress, he had no financial backstop at home. There was no business, no bank, no law practice, on inheritance. With some other backbenchers from the House, he enrolled in a legal cram course to prepare for the District of Columbia bar examination. Like many applicants, Dirksen was not immediately successful. "I wrote the bar exam once and failed," he said. "Six months later I was fortunate enough to write the exam again and pass." On Lincoln's Birthday, 1936, he got his insurance policy against the fickleness of the voters; he later was admitted to the Illinois bar. Like most insurance policies, this went into a drawer to be kept for an emergency.

His Congressional career continued to prosper, as the voters kept sending him back. With the end of World War II, he continued to straddle the issues. He voted against making the House Un-American Activities Committee a permanent committee, then voted for a bill, proposed by young Representative Richard Nixon, to force registration of Communists.

He voted against a long-term loan to Britain but for the Marshall Plan.

Off the House floor, meanwhile, Dirksen became a worried man. He awoke one morning in 1947 and saw what he called "cobwebs" in front of his eyes. Doctors in Washington told him he had chorioretinitis, a serious inflammation of the retina, and suggested that his right eye be removed. He went to Johns Hopkins University Hospital in Baltimore, seeking a more hopeful diagnosis, but the recommended treatment was the same. Dirksen could not go through with it. On the train to Baltimore, "I got down on my knees and uttered my prayers, whether blindness was to be my lot," he said. "I called on the Big Doctor—the Big Doctor Upstairs—and the answer was no."

The eye was cured, but not easily. Long rest was prescribed, and Dirksen was compelled to retire from the House on January 3, 1949, giving up 16 years of seniority. In their traditional farewell under such circumstances, the members of the House took the floor and showered praise upon their departing member, the Democrats joining the Republicans. "If they are going to send Republicans to Congress," said Sam Rayburn, leader of the Democratic minority, "let them send Republicans of the Everett Dirksen kind."

Home in Pekin, Dirksen rested only a little while. He was soon campaigning for Republican Presidential candidate Thomas E. Dewey in 22 states, and by the spring of 1949 was actively running again himself, this time for the Senate seat of Democratic Leader Scott Lucas. He also had exercised the privilege of his insurance policy—he joined the prosperous law firm of Davis, Morgan and Witherell in Peoria, a few miles from Pekin. "I began as a full partner, not altogether active, of course," Dirksen said. "It was firmly understood that I was not to participate in any Federal actions by my firm or to receive any remuneration for such actions. I didn't like the arrangement, though. It looked dubious even though I abstained from Federal cases."

Said Arleigh Davis, a senior member of the firm, "As soon as his eyes improved and he decided to run for the Senate, he made a definite understanding that he would take no part at all in anything relating to the Federal Government."

The agreements were, for the moment, of small importance. Dirksen won the nomination for the Senate in April

1950, and turned to the Democrats for his campaign ammunition against the Senate Majority Leader. He distributed copies of Sam Rayburn's 1948 endorsement, and in October he was handed his most valuable weapon of the campaign by a Democrat. Tennessee's Senator Estes Kefauver brought his crime investigation to Chicago and announced that the Al Capone gang was still in operation. The transcript of a closed-door hearing leaked out, revealing links between gangsters and politicians. Election Day was a bitter one for the dispirited Illinois Democrats, and Dirksen won by 294,000 votes.

Despite his 16 years in the House and his triumph over Lucas, Dirksen was still a minor figure in the Senate. He changed that at the 1952 Republican convention in Chicago, when he stood in front of the television cameras and unleashed his incredible vocal range against Tom Dewey, the prime mover in the push for Dwight Eisenhower. Dirksen, fighting for the acceptance of the pro-Taft forces, shook his right index finger in Dewey's face and thundered, "We followed you before, and you took us down the path to defeat." Dirksen mesmerized the millions watching their first political convention on TV, who were still naïve about the ways of political theatrics.

Back in the Senate, Dirksen remained a prickly personality when the programs of the Eisenhower Administration were being considered. He continued to vote on both sides of foreign aid. He was also an unyielding supporter of Senator Joseph R. McCarthy of Wisconsin, even though McCarthy had switched his tactic and was attacking Republicans as well as Democrats.

Still, Dirksen had the good political sense to keep from irritating the Establishment. It accepted him, and he defended it. "I am always delighted to think of the Senate as a club," he said, "because it seems to me the Senate functions effectively and functions earnestly if we never quite lose the 'clubby' spirit. We can become very angry and at times, I suppose, so intolerant of one another, but I remember the almost iridescent line written by the great sales manager of Christianity, the Apostle Paul, who said, 'Let your forbearance be known in the sight of all men.' Nothing can quite equal that line, since this is an area in which tolerance and forbearance are so urgently necessary."

As the Republican membership in the Senate dwindled,

Dirksen's power increased, both on Capitol Hill and in the nation. He had hoped to be handed the Vice Presidential nomination if Taft became the GOP nominee in 1952, and he waited expectantly for the political lightning to strike. The bolt out of the blue never came, so Dirksen had to be content with becoming an institution in the Senate.

Both his hair and his sentences grew longer. As he toured the country, moving from podium to podium, he found that a paragraph did not have to be particularly well constructed, either in grammar or in logic, to make a good impression on audiences. They had come to see a Senator, and Dirksen projected that image. At the suggestion of a public-relations adviser, he added a pair of lensless, black-rimmed glasses to his wardrobe, to hide the bags under his eyes from the merciless probing of the TV cameras. Some said he was a caricature of a Senator. They were wrong; he did not wear a frock coat and a string tie.

There were few other tricks, however, that escaped him. His early practice at the Legion meetings paid off. Like a fighter who has trained long and hard for a lazy opponent, Dirksen was ready for the Senate. His 16 years in the House, if not a negotiable commodity in the Senate, gave him an intimate knowledge of the background of the issues and the ways of Congress. In debate, his tongue had more the lap of an affectionate St. Bernard than the thrust of a rapier. But it could cut. In 1954 he used it to jab Wayne Morse of Oregon, who was making a brief stop as an independent on his way from the Republican to the Democratic side of the aisle. Dirksen noted ominously that Morse was wearing a rose. "I was thoroughly distressed tonight, Mr. President," Dirksen told the Senate, "when I saw that red rose in his lapel, because I have learned that when that red rose appears, it is a signal for, shall I say charitably, a rather reasonably prolonged speech, not to exceed twelve or fifteen hours. As we came in tonight and saw that symbol of love and affection and perfection, I had the idea it was also the symbol of another great rhetorical effort tonight. But better counsel has prevailed, and so, in the spirit of amity and accord, I am quite sure he will detain the Senate perhaps no longer than I shall detain it tonight.

"As I think of the spirit of amity and accord and concord, I always think, Wayne, of the two deacons, the Republican and the Democrat, who were kneeling in their supplications in a little church in a small village in Illinois. The Republican deacon was praying to the Lord and saying, 'O, Lord, make us Republicans unlike the Democrats; make us hang together in accord; make us hang together in concord.' And just then his Democratic brethern [sic] said, 'Lord, any cord will do.' "

Despite Dirksen's frequent opposition to Eisenhower legislation, Ike had no objections to Dirksen's taking over as the Senate Republican Leader in 1959 after William Knowland left to gamble away his political fortunes in a race for California's governorship. Everett Dirksen and Lyndon Johnson, then the leader of the Democratic majority, worked well together, and Dirksen learned the art of loyal opposition from the man who was one of the Senate's greatest tacticians. But Dirksen was not the least cowed by Johnson's prestige. Congress had been in session only a month before Dirksen took the floor to needle LBJ. "One of the most delightful things about the Majority Leader is that he can often persist in error," said the Minority Leader, going on and on. Eleven days later Dirksen was at it again. "The statements made by the Majority Leader on a number of occasions on the floor and in the tables he inserted in the record are quite correct, as far as they go. As I said before, however, it is like the man who fell off the twentieth floor of a building. As he passed the sixth floor, a friend of his shouted to him, 'Mike, so far you are all right.' "

The ability to tweak Johnson subtly increased Dirksen's stature. Strangely enough, he gained even more power after John F. Kennedy took over the White House and the Republicans became a minority in all areas of the Government. On many occasions Kennedy found that Dirksen was easier to work with than the Southern Democrats. Dirksen's price, however, was never cheap. He could be coaxed to support a Kennedy bill, but only after it had been modified to suit Dirksen. Kennedy paid the price with a wan smile, and a warmth developed between the sophisticated Bostonian and the cornpone Midwesterner.

"Shortly after Jack Kennedy was nominated, and while he was preparing for the hustings," Dirksen has remembered, "he came over to me and said, 'You know, Ev, there's one thing that bothers me. I'm afraid I'm going to lose my voice.' I said to him, 'Jack'—he was a fellow Senator and I could talk familiarly with him—'Jack,' I said, 'you will lose your voice.

You constantly talk off your cords. You must talk out of your diaphragm. If I were you, I'd pick up the best voice teacher in town. Three or four lessons and you'll be taught to let your voice come out of your belly.' And, by golly, that's what Jack did and he never had any trouble after that."

The familiarity between Kennedy and Dirksen persisted after the election. He once told of answering a phone call from the White House by saying, "Oh, hi, Jack." The next time they met, Dirksen offered an apology: "Mr. President, my wife thought I committed a breach of etiquette when I called you by your first name." Said JFK, "Ev, who more than you has that right?"

It took more than friendship, however, to keep Dirksen's opposition in bounds. He was willing to cooperate with the President, but he complained that every Federal appointee from Illinois came out of Adlai Stevenson's law firm. It happened that Dirksen's own law firm had a candidate for the Federal Power Commission, which regulates interstate gas and electric rates. It has make-or-break power over interstate pipelines, and one of the Peoria firm's better-paying clients was Kansas City's Panhandle Eastern Pipe Line, which does a huge business in the Southwest yet reached outside its territory all the way to Peoria, Ilinois, to retain the Dirksen law firm.

When a vacancy occurred on the FPC, Dirksen had a recommendation: Harold Woodward, a former assistant Illinois utilities commissioner. The President quickly decided Woodward was just the man for the job. Perhaps too quickly, as it turned out. A subsequent investigation disclosed that Woodward's father, a Federal judge, had been impeached for awarding bankruptcy cases to his son's firm, an adventure that had raised Harold Woodward's salary from $4,000 to $13,000 a year. In all, the firm had collected $225,889.89 in fees from these cases. At the Senate hearing, Woodward unhappily admitted that he also had continued in law practice while serving on the state commission and had passed on a rate increase for a company in which he was a stockholder. But Dirksen, putting his prestige on the line, sat loyally at Woodward's side and saw him through the Senate squall. This open backing got him confirmed.

Woodward died before he could do much good for Panhandle Eastern Pipe Line, and Dirksen rushed over to the White House with a candidate to fill the unexpired term. This was

William Dolph, reportedly a friend of the pipeline interests. By this time Lyndon Johnson was President, but Dirksen still headed the loyal opposition in the Senate. Like Kennedy, Johnson was anxious to keep the emphasis on "loyal." The new President, perhaps remembering the trouble over Harold Woodward, discreetly ordered an FBI check on Dolph. The G-men learned that Dirksen's candidate had been fired from his job as assistant in charge of land acquisition for the Illinois East-West Tollway—after he had tried to buy the land for himself that he was supposed to be buying for the state.

Dirksen went back to his list of names and came up with another candidate: Carl Bagge, also widely regarded as a sympathizer with the oil and gas interests. The opposition to him, however, centered on the fact that he had led a fight in 1959 to keep Negroes out of his fancy Chicago suburb. This was not enough to block the appointment or his confirmation.

To Dirksen's astonished dismay, Bagge voted against the big utilities on most issues. He even lined up against a tax amendment his mentor had tacked onto a flood-disaster-relief bill. The importance of the amendment was hidden behind a smoke screen of convoluted legalisms, but in essence it permitted pipeline companies to shift the taxes on their operations in a competitive area to the operations in a monopoly area. This device would have made it possible for the companies to raise rates where there was no competition and lower rates where there was competition. Bagge opposed Dirksen's amendment on the ground that it could cost customers millions of dollars in excessive gas bills.

This unexpected show of heroism, favoring the little consumers over the big companies, lost Bagge the support of his aggrieved sponsor. Feeling terribly betrayed, Dirksen pulled strings in 1967 to block the reappointment of the man he had recommended in 1965. He telephoned Senator Warren Magnuson of Washington, the Senate Commerce Committee chairman, to request that Bagge's confirmation be held up. Magnuson declined, and Dirksen's man was reconfirmed despite Dirksen.

The lineup of corporations that retained Davis, Morgan and Witherell is impressive. In addition to Panhandle Eastern Pipe Line, there are International Harvester, International Paper, Pabst Brewing, Pepsi-Cola Bottling of Peoria, Illinois, State Farm Insurance, Mid-States Steel & Wire, Keystone

Steel & Wire, Brass Foundry. National Lock and some two dozen others. They span manufacturing, oil and gas, timber, mining, utilities, and the savings-and-loan, banking and insurance industries. The fact that these corporations went all the way to Peoria to seek legal counsel may simply speak well for the talents of the firm. Yet the question of what the law firm, through Dirksen, can do for these clients is inescapable. Invariably, Dirksen has sided in the Senate with the interests that his law firm represents. He fought against the "truth-in-lending" bill, which was opposed by the banks and the savings-and-loan institutions. He was a leader in the fight to save the "right-to-work" laws, a stand that must have pleased his manufacturing and mining clients. The senior partner, Arleigh Davis, maintains that his firm's efforts for International Harvester and Pabst are mainly in labor relations. When a labor leader found fault with private insurance companies at a Senate hearing, Dirksen termed it a "stinking charge." The labor leader attempted to expand, and Dirksen, with none of the usual rosebuds in his voice, commanded, "You just keep your mouth shut!"

During the battle over highway beautification, he defended the billboards with some whimsical rhetoric about the loss to the nation's culture of the roadside Burma Shave ditties. There was an unkind suspicion that he was less concerned over Burma Shave signs than Pabst Beer and Pepsi-Cola billboards.

The big drug companies, if they didn't retain Dirksen's law firm, raised thousands of dollars for his re-election campaign in 1962. While he counted the contributions, he moved into the forefront of the drive to stop Senator Estes Kefauver from tightening Federal regulations of the drug industry. Dirksen permitted drug lobbyists to use his office, write his speeches and prepare his legislation on the subject. Indeed, he went so far as to let the drug industry's attorneys represent him in actual Senate negotiations. In 1962 he sent two lawyers for the industry—Lloyd Cutler and Marshall Hornblower—to represent him at a secret legislative meeting in the office of Judiciary Chairman James Eastland, D-Miss. Kefauver, the moving spirit behind the drug reforms, was not invited. Hornblower and Cutler brought into the meeting with them a draft of a compromise bill that Dirksen later offered, verbatim, as his own.

The ingratiating Senate Republican Leader has raised his organ voice in the cause of small as well as large clients. On August 18, 1961, he took the floor of the Senate to urge adoption of an amendment to the foreign aid bill that would block aid to countries that did not pay debts owed to American citizens. He spoke of a "contractor and an architect who, in 1953, negotiated a contract with the recipient country, which last year received $12 million in foreign aid and was hopeful that it could get $20 million. The work in question was commissioned and was accepted. The contract cost, in the first instance, was around $2,900,000. The sum of $290,000 in principal and interest remains, for which the contractor and architect are at present indebted to the bank in Illinois. But they cannot get their money. It is an amazing thing, after all the effort was made, that only token payments are made. I raised the question with the ambassador five different times. I discussed it with the former Secretary of State. I have discussed it perhaps half a dozen times with the present Secretary of the Treasury. I have discussed it with a distinguished American citizen who, in Washington, serves as general counsel for the company. There are assurances and assurances; but assurances do not pay the bill. The creditors are paying interest on the note. . . ."

Dirksen did not say that the contracting firm was Lankton, Ziegle, Terry and Associates, which has built a housing project in Haiti. Nor did he tell the Senate that Lankton, Ziegle, Terry and Associates was a client of Davis, Morgan and Witherell. Dirksen later insisted to an interviewer that his intervention for his firm's client was an act of patriotism. "I not only tried, I did prevent aid to nations that owe debts to American nationals," he said. "I felt this Government was playing footsy. Accordingly, I fashioned language for the foreign aid bill. I presented the whole case in open committee. Eventually the whole Senate and the whole House concurred with my position. We said to foreign countries, 'You pay your debts to nationals of the United States—or no aid.' "

Moved perhaps by the hot breath of the interviewer, Dirksen hurried to the Senate floor with another version of his role as bill collector for his law firm's client. "They [the authors] wanted to raise a question about my making the Government of Haiti pay its bills to American citizens," he said. "I went before an open meeting of the Committee on Foreign Relations with an amendment. There was a little modification on it, but it said no aid unless they paid their bills.

"Well, an architect friend out home went down and built 300 homes. The Government took them away, rented every one of them, was drawing the rents, and then refused to pay him. I am not going to let any country do that to us or our citizens, if I can help it. I said, 'We'll see.' I dragged the Haitian Ambassador to my office. I said, 'Mister, you better get ready to do some business. You better pay responsible American citizens their bills.' And I made him pay, including the interest on the money that had to be borrowed. . . .

"Drew Pearson is no stranger to me, and neither is Jack Anderson, who used to rib me and rifle me from cellar to breakfast when I was holding the Kefauver hearings on the drug bills. . . . That is the kind of irresponsible reporting you can get when the whole truth is not known."

In point of fact, Dirksen still did not tell the Senate the whole truth. He again failed to mention the relationship between his law firm and the housing contractor.

He also refused to discuss this subject with the interviewer. His role as a Senator lawyer, he told the interviewer in a not-so-flowery phrase, is "none of your business or anyone else's." The senior partner, Arleigh Davis, was equally tight-lipped about the firm's financial relationship with Dirksen but was willing to talk about Dirksen's contributions to the firm.

"He does come down here fairly regularly," Davis said. "Oftentimes we will contact him, since he knows the ropes so well in Washington, as to where to go or whom to see." But Davis emphasized, "We get many, many calls asking us to bring some political pressure on Mr. Dirksen. We have refused one hundred percent." The requests, he said, have come from individuals, not corporation clients.

Senator Dirksen, having reconsidered his remark to the interviewer that his law practice was no one else's business, told the Senate this much: "I went to that firm when I thought I was going blind; and I got elected to the Senate; and I said, 'The partnership is off.' Now they have my name on the door as of counsel. You will find that all over the United States. There are three names on that door—of counsel. If they want to counsel with me, I am glad to do it for free; and if there is anything Federal involved, there will be no emoluments from this law firm, I can tell you. I keep a pretty careful set of books, because I keep them in part myself, and Mrs. Dirksen, who was a professional auditor, does the rest. So, you see, I know where I stand and what I am doing."

Dirksen has made it clear that he doesn't intend to open his carefully kept books to the public. "I've been on the platform before my constituents since 1926," he thundered from the Senate floor. "Any man, any citizen, could stand up and say, 'Dirksen, what do you own?' if he wanted to know, and he would have received an answer. But I am not going to see it done by compulsion. . . . Now it is proposed that I be reduced to a Class B citizen. I did not give up my citizenship when I came to the Senate. I do not propose to do so. Public office would not be worth it." These words, or ones very close to them, have been reiterated with increasing intensity by Dirksen on almost every occasion that the financial disclosure issue has come before the Senate in the past few years—and as recently as March 1968.

From time to time Dirksen has been caught in minor embarrassments that must have strengthened his resolve not to advertise his affairs. It leaked out, for example, that Nationwide Food Services, Inc., had been footing the bill for his annual birthday ball. This event four days after the New Year has become one of Washington's most glittering extravaganzas, attended by its brightest celebrities. The role of Nationwide has added a trace of tarnish to the grand affair; for Nationwide operates the Senate restaurants, and Dirksen always champions the company at appropriations time. Thanks at least in part to his intervention, Nationwide now gets an allowance of $365,000 from the taxpayers to help feed the Senators.

In the back rooms of the Senate, Dirksen had also been one of Bobby Baker's counselors and confessors. Senate investigators, looking into Baker's dealings with Freight Forwarders, discovered that the company had picked up Dirksen's bills at Bobby's Carousel Motel in Ocean City, Maryland.

These are not the things that Dirksen, who suffers from a number of maladies including emphysema, ulcers, nerve pinches, kidney trouble and the effects of a broken hip, would like future students of American politics to remember. There are, after all, a number of contributions he has made to the nation. He began by opposing both the nuclear-weapons treaty and civil rights legislation, yet neither could have passed without his eventual massive assistance.

In the course of pushing the civil rights bill in 1963, he set a proud personal record by taking 98 words to say "I don't know" when he was asked about its status in September. Said Dirksen, "Well, what's today? The 25th? That's almost October. Which reminds me, I'd better start picking my apples. They're approaching a state of ripeness. So already you're into November. As you know so well, with November comes Thanksgiving and that takes a big chunk out of a man's life. Before you know, we're into December and then the Yuletide begins. It begins coursing through our veins. Downtown they'll be hanging wreaths and soon they'll be singing 'Hark! The Herald Angels Sing,' and after that 'O Little Town of Bethlehem.' Where are we now? Who knows? Who is to say?"

Nor does Dirksen always take his own speeches seriously. He once admitted, "My speeches have an immediate purpose. They are not intended as timeless documents. I have never confronted myself with questions on posterity."

3. Servicing the Client

Everett Dirksen, who has spent all but four of his years in Congress as a member of the political minority, can be counted with the majority in the matter of law-firm affiliations. Indeed, lawyers have dominated the legislative branch since the Continental Congress, 31 of whose 55 members came out of the law firms of the day. Moonlighting for private clients has become a cherished American tradition, which Dirksen has defended in Fourth of July phrases.

No other country has drawn so heavily on its legal profession to write its laws. This is the sort of work that logically would seem suited for attorneys. They have the technical skill to draft bills, the background in legal procedure. Yet in practice the Congressmen no longer write the bills they enact into law; the drafting is done for them. There are legislative staffs to grind out the whereas's and wherefor's. For that matter, most legislation is prepackaged by the Government agencies or private interests which advocate it. As for the procedures on Capitol Hill, they are not at all encumbered with legal niceties. Congressmen seldom bother about the right of witnesses to cross-examine their accusers, for example, or the presumption of innocence until guilt is proved. Some of the most atrocious violations have been committed, in fact, by lawyers who leave their professional credentials outside the hearing room when they begin exposing supposed wrongdoers and wrong thinkers.

Congressman lawyers whose legislative records have been checked against their law clienteles have been found to represent their clients—if not always their constituents—faithfully. They have promoted legislation that would benefit banks, utilities, airlines, railroads, oil companies, insurance firms and other corporations that have retained their law firms.

A bright young Congressman can also find other ways to serve his law clients on Capitol Hill. He can make quiet calls to regulatory agencies, arrange appointments with the people who count, apply political pressure on Government officials, and slip beneficial amendments into bills on their way to becoming law. (The average Congressman, of course, would explode with righteous wrath over the offer of a bribe. Yet the same Congressman, if he has a law practice back home, might not hesitate to accept a legal fee. Thus his influence might be for sale not merely if the price is right but if it is given the respectability of being called a retainer.) Through his contacts in Congress he can also line up law firms with the right political connections in other states. When the socially prominent Neil Firestone tried to get his son Douglas out of prison in Mississippi, for example, Senator Thomas Dodd, D-Conn., took the matter up with Senator James Eastland, D-Miss. Though Eastland has no active law practice of his own, he had definite ideas on who should get the business. Firestone was already represented by a Tupelo, Mississippi, lawyer named Sam Lumpkin, but Eastland suggested another attorney in the same city. The story is told in the correspondence between Senator Dodd and Firestone's personal attorney, Arthur Rogers Ivey of Greenwich, Connecticut. Ivey claimed afterward that Dodd was not paid a legal fee for his work on the case, though he accepted forwarding fees from other attorneys. Example: one of his campaign managers, Paul McNamara, was retained by Johnny Barton, Inc., a wholesale liquor dealer, who was anxious to save his distributorship in Connecticut. McNamara later forwarded a check for $3,750 to Dodd as his split.

Such forwarding fees are not uncommon on Capitol Hill where legislator lawyers sometimes trade in political influence. They are not the least deterred by the Canons of Professional and Judicial Ethics, which declare: "No division of fees for legal service is proper, except with another lawyer, based upon a division of services or responsibility."

Perhaps the most celebrated case of this type was that of Senator Edward Long, D-Mo., the rotund Rotarian who accepted $160,000 in forwarding fees for referring cases to St. Louis attorney Morris Shenker. Critics unkindly called attention to the coincidence that Shenker happened to represent the convicted Teamsters boss, James Hoffa, whose lobbyists had urged Long to investigate Government wiretapping. Hoffa, in an attempt to beat the rap, had hoped to develop evidence that his own wires had been tapped. The Senate Ethics Committee, after questioning 33 witnesses, found no connection between Long's Senate actions and Hoffa's approaches, but later reopened the case on receipt of more information from *Life* Magazine. *Life*'s interest appeared to be inspired by Senator Robert F. Kennedy as part of his feud with Hoffa. Whatever the motives, Long's predicament could have been avoided had he severed relations with his law firm.

Another who had discriminating taste in legal talent was Bobby Baker, the embattled ex-Senate aide. He sent the Sweet Water Development Company, in search of legal advice on amending the Helium Gas Act, to the New York law firm of Representatives Emanuel Celler, who had worked on the bill. Impressed, Sweet Water hired the Celler firm for a $10,000 yearly retainer, which shall stand forever as a testimony to Celler's political tolerance. The company was owned and controlled by Clinton W. Murchison, Jr., best known for his right-wing political activities. Congressman Celler, elected to Congress from a liberal Jewish constituency, has vigorously opposed the right wing. But clearly he was too big a man to let personal politics influence the selection of clients for his law firm.

Baker was rewarded with a $2,500 check, though one of Celler's law partners, Murray C. Spett, said no services were performed for the forwarding fee. Celler later claimed his firm had been hired to examine supermarket leases, most of them on New York property. Bedford S. Wynne, a Sweet Water director, told a different story. "We wanted an opinion regarding application of the Helium Gas Act as proposed for legislation," he said. "Cel·er had something to do with the bill when it was introduced." Postscript: the firm's first Government contract, an engineering contract for water desalinization, was approved in May 1962, for $75,000. A year later the figure for the company's Government contracts climbed to almost $1,000,000. The company promptly ran into trouble with the Army, whose audit report was highly critical of, among other things, legal expenses.

Spett shed additional light on the attorney exchange market that operates on Capitol Hill. "Whenever we have any matters in another state," he said, "we usually ask Mr. Celler to recommend a Congressman or a Senator lawyer in that particular state to handle it and, conversely, [other members] who are not permitted to practice in New York refer matters to us." Spett explained that the usual forwarding fee for referrals "is a third, anywhere up to a third. As a matter of fact, we sent some matters down to a Congressman in Alabama, and he sent us a forwarding fee of 50 percent."

Celler is one of those Congressman lawyers, incidentally, who abstain from Government practice with a great show of piety. Celler's law firm has erected an elaborate façade of separating its clients in a way that leaves the Congressman unsullied by cases directly involving the Federal Government. What the firm does in the name of ethics, of course, is required by law, which prohibits Congressmen from taking fees in Federal cases. Celler has not been the least inhibited, however, about sharing law fees from clients who have had an interest in legislation.

The door to Celler's law layout displays two signs. One identifies the firm of Weisman, Celler, Allan, Spett and Sheinberg. The other omits Celler's name. All cases involving the Government are assigned to the firm without his name. A prospective client might have difficulty, however, in distinguishing between the two firms. Both have the same telephone number; indeed, they share furniture and fixtures as well as phones. While they keep separate books and bank accounts, the same staff is used by both firms.

Few legislator lawyers will admit that they draw more than token incomes from their law firms. One of the more candid is Senator Jacob Javits, R-N.Y., who, in the spirit of disclosure now in vogue among liberals, has confessed that he lives on the income from his law practice. His entire $30,000 Senate salary, he has claimed, goes to pay for extra staff help and office expenses. He has been less open about his law clients, who are discreetly omitted from the Martindale-Hubble legal directory. Nevertheless, his blue-chip firm—Javits, Trubin, Sillcocks, Edelman and Purcell—is known to represent some of the nation's greatest real-estate trusts, including the First National Real Estate Trust of New York and the Crown Zellerbach Corporation. This does not seem to have inhibited Javits from voting on real-estate legislation.

Most Congressmen covered in our survey claimed they receive little more from their law practices than the payouts from their pre-election accounts. Presumably their nameplates, which appear on the doors of law firms across the country, are mostly ornamental. They might be more convincing, of course, if their firms would divulge the identities of all clients and the division of the spoils. The voters might like to know, too, what arrangements have been made for the Congressmen to return to full partnership and whether they will collect retroactive benefits if the next election does not turn out well.

Certainly if some clients are not paying extra for legislative favors, they must be among the most undercharged law clients in the history of jurisprudence. The Greyhound Bus Lines, for instance, retained the law firm of Kimble, Schapiro, Stevens, Harsha and Harsha in Portsmouth, Ohio, a city not renowned as a great bus center. One of the Harshas happens to be Republican Representative William H. Harsha, Jr., who on June 22, 1964, led the House fight against the Mass Transportation Act.

"Mr. Speaker," he declared, "the Mass Transportation Act is nothing more than a tool to drive private transportation systems out of existence and to establish a Federal czar over local development and planning. And, for the good not only of the transportation industry but also the welfare of this nation, Congress should reject this legislation. . . . The power of the Federal administrator to set rates, fares, schedules and modes of operation is the power to break a private transit system and force it into Government ownership."

Then he got down to cases and cited the transit systems he had in mind. "For the almost 97 percent of our transit systems that are all bus systems," he said, "the problems are supportable routes and time schedules, reservations of lanes for bus travel. . . ."

Congressman Harsha also introduced legislation to limit the importation of fuel oil, which must have pleased two other law clients, Phillips Petroleum and Ashland Oil and Refining.

Pittsburgh Plate Glass went into the West Virginia mountains for legal advice and selected the law firm of Moore and Moore in Moundsville. The firm's last surviving Moore is Representative Arch Moore, a most sophisticated hillbilly, huskily handsome, with a clean-cut, all-American look, who is also the only surviving Republican in the West Virginia delegation. He has chosen the glass industry as one of his great political causes to champion. Specifically, he has become the stirring defender of the plate-glass industry. "The American flat-glass industry," he told his colleagues in one glorious speech, "is a significant part of the total glass industry, producing approximately one-third of the entire dollar value of all manufactured glass." He quoted other statistics to dramatize the importance of plate glass in the American way of life. But the industry had come upon hard times, he lamented, because of imports. He appealed to his colleagues not to let any lesser consideration, such as international relations, stand in the way of plate-glass prosperity. "The times call for drastic measures," he thundered. "It must mean that the national interest will be put above the specious merit of international relations, where it has rightfully belonged since our national birth. It is time to raise our tariffs or other protective measures."

When Arch Moore gets on the subject of national interest, there is no sacred American institution that can inspire him quite like Pittsburgh Plate Glass. He showed up at a hearing of the House small-business committee* in high dudgeon, for example, when he heard that executives of his favorite company had been called on the carpet to explain their pricing practice. Moore kept interrupting with statements defending the company and condemning the investigation. "It would seem to me that this committee has been given another nice ride down the highway," he blustered, thus disregarding the adage about those who live in glass houses.

---

*Select Committee to Conduct a Study and Investigation of the Problems of Small Business.

But he would not want his constituents to think that he would defend Pittsburgh Plate Glass for such a crass consideration as a legal fee. It was his deep devotion to glass, he explained, that caused him to speak out in Congress. He had never represented the company "in its glass capacity," he said; his law firm merely represented the company's Columbia Southern Chemical Division. Moreover, said the Congressman, his $80,000-a-year law practice had dwindled to a mere green trickle.

To Representative Thomas Curtis, the dynamic Webster Groves, Missouri, Republican, it isn't glass so much as lumber that seems essential to the national welfare. There are no virgin forests in the St. Louis suburbs and no big-muscled, hard-swearing lumberjacks among his constituents. Yet when the domestic timber industry was threatened by Canadian imports, Curtis was even more indignant than were the Congressmen from the logging districts.

"On this specific problem of lumber," he said, "when we talk about increasing foreign trade, we have to talk about fair trade, which means reciprocity. . . . It seems quite clear in the instance of lumber that Canada in effect has a Governmental subsidy on the lumber products that are then turned over to private concerns." Curtis joined in sponsoring a bill to curtail lumber imports, an issue that would not win him any glory in St. Louis. But it should have pleased two of his law clients: J. R. Perkins Lumber Company and Egyptian Tie and Timber Company. The Congressman's law firm—Biggs, Hensley, Hughes, Curtis, and Biggs—also represents the American Urological Association, Inc., whose members were opposed to medicare. Curtis led the fight inside the House Ways and Means Committee against medicare.

Some legislator lawyers can benefit their law clients at the same time that they advance the legitimate interests of the state. For example, New Hampshire's Democratic Senator Thomas McIntyre, whose Irish eyes smile in the traditional manner, reared up in the Senate on April 10, 1963, to plead for import quotas to protect the shoe industry. "The position of the shoe industry is a matter of urgent concern to many American communities . . . ," he said. "The Administration should give urgent priority and continued attention to this problem so that the shoe industry may retain its important part in the American economy." In following years he echoed this theme again and again.

His law firm, it turned out, represents the Laconia Shoe Company. Yet it is only fair to state that New Hampshire has another 54 shoe plants, not his clients, which he is supposed to represent as Senator. These plants contribute to the livelihood of more than 18,000 of his constituents.

The state also has a large textile industry. Presumably McIntyre had this in mind when he repeatedly seized the Senate floor to decry the plight of the textile manufacturers. He neglected to mention in his speeches that his law firm—McIntyre, Normandin, Cheney and O'Neil—represents such textile producers as the Cormier Hosiery Mills, Fenwick Hosiery Mills and Belknap Sulloway Mills. Though the Senator may have been speaking also for the 130 other textile mills in his state, he would have been on more solid ethical ground if his firm had not been accepting retainers from shoe and textile companies.

McIntyre is troubled over the ethical problem. "I don't ever remember getting so much as a traffic ticket back home," he added, "but when you come down here you are suddenly suspected of every crime in the book. I'm very concerned that young people will turn their backs on politics as a career because they grow up thinking it's dirty. Of course, we all come down here with built-in biases. If you've been associated for twenty years, say, with a finance company, you naturally bring your experience and modes of thinking with you to a committee meeting. That does not mean, though, that a vote in favor of the finance companies was made because you have any financial interest in the company any more."

Similarly, Senator Alan Bible, D-Nev., whose native state is honeycombed with mines, has fought in the Senate for the mining interests at the same time that his Reno law firm represents the Sweepstake Mines, Inc. For that matter, Bible owns 13 mining claims of his own. Yet his speeches in behalf of mining clearly serve an important industry in his state. Incidentally, Bible has admitted taking a 10 percent cut in the profits of his firm—Bible, McDonald and Carano—at the same time he is supposed to be a full-time Senator. "I see nothing wrong with this," he said. "In fact, I sure hope I get a dividend this month."

Senator Gordon Allott, R-Colo., a power on the Senate Interior and Insular Affairs Committee, which deals with irrigation, admitted frankly to the Senate on April 22, 1963, "As a practicing attorney, I have represented ditch companies and water companies over a long period of time—in fact about a quarter of a century—and I think I know the intrinsic value of water." He has been unabashed about advocating irrigation benefits at the same time that his Lamar, Colorado, law firm —Allott and Rogers—still represents the Amity Mutual Irrigation Company. He has also championed oil and gas legislation, including a 27½-percent depletion allowance for mineral mined as a source for oil or gas, which would benefit another law client, Plateau National Gas Company.

Other members of Congress, who claim they would do as much for any constituent, seem to be extra helpful to constituents who are also law clients. Halifax Worsted Mill, for example, is an important constituent of Virginia's deep-drawling Representative William Tuck, who may not have fought for the Confederacy but is proud that his daddy did.

He became so worked up over the mill's economic problems in April 1961 that he wrote a letter to the then Secretary of Commerce Luther Hodges. "I respectfully recommend and urge," he wrote, "that import quotas on textiles be established by country and by category and that the same be limited in such a way as to relieve the serious and critical economic problem that exists in textile areas." Tuck also called for textile import quotas in an April 18, 1961, House speech. His concern for a constituent was exceeded only by his concern for a client. For the Halifax Worsted Mill had retained his law firm—Tuck, Bagwell, Dillard, and Mapp of South Boston, Virginia.

The venerable Virginian has set up a unique system to avoid conflicts. He simply stashes all out-of-court retainers into a separate account not available to him as long as he remains in Congress. He has now announced his retirement, at which time, presumably, he will consider it proper to collect this legal jackpot. Meanwhile, he has kept his name on the law-firm door as insurance against the uncertainty of his political future.

Another Congressman with an important constituent is Representative Sam Gibbons, of Tampa, Florida, one of the bright stars of Congress, a Southerner acceptable to the controlling clique but a man with liberal instincts. The constituent, U.S. Phosphorics, has retained the Gibbons family firm —Gibbons, Tucker, McEwen, Smith and Cofer—since Sam was a baby. Thus he has found himself representing U.S. Phosphorics not only as a constituent but as a client.

Investigators for the Federal Trade Commission have charged, in an unpublished report, that "four producers of concentrated phosphate fertilizer [among them, the Tennessee Corporation, U.S. Phosphorics' parent company] conspired, through their brokers, to divide markets and fix prices" on foreign aid procurement. Congressman Gibbons has quietly tried to discourage this investigation.

U.S. Phosphorics has also been able to hold down its own electrical costs and to keep the rates of its competitors as high as possible. To this end, the Gibbons firm helped persuade the Florida Public Utilities Commission to boost rates for residential customers so the phosphate company could get a rate cut. When the Bonneville Power Administration sought to spend $80 million in Federal funds to run transmission lines to phosphate producers in southern Idaho, Gibbons jumped into the fray. He wrote to Secretary of the Interior Stewart Udall that the transmission lines would give the Idaho phosphate companies an advantage over Florida phosphate companies. "Thousands of my constituents depend on the phosphate industry for their livelihood," he wrote. "Taxing these workers to raise monies that will subsidize a threat to them is obviously unjust and unwarrantable on its face." The Congressman claimed he merely intervened to help his constituents. What he did not say was that one of his better-paying clients had the most to gain.

A similarly confused situation occurred over the construction of a needed Veterans Hospital which Congressman Gibbons promoted for his hometown of Tampa. He personally pushed a special bill through Congress authorizing the construction. A 22.2-acre site was purchased from the Higo Corporation, which the Gibbons law firm had set up specifically for the purpose of selling the land. The site, once bought, turned out to have a soft subsurface, thus requiring additional tax dollars to pay for the additional construction costs.

Another Florida legislator who has blatantly and effectively used the privileged floor of the Senate on behalf of his law firm is George Smathers, partner in the firm of Smathers, Thompson, Maxwell and Dyer, of Miami, whose clients include Pan American World Airways and the Seaboard Coast Line Railroad. When the 1961 tax bill was before Congress, Smathers introduced an amendment that would have eliminated the 10 percent tax on railroad, airplane and bus travel, cutting $300 million from tax revenues. Earlier that year he had lashed out at the State Department for giving landing privileges to foreign airlines but failed to tell the Senate that his firm's top client, Pan American Airways, was suffering from this competition. Smathers was also the author of the 1958 Transportation Act permitting railroads to drop passenger traffic, giving them greater leeway in rate-making and extending Government guarantees to private banks making railroad loans. One year later Seaboard paid the Smathers law firm $34,290 and the year following, $62,810.

A spot check also indicates that corporations having an interest in legislation deliberately seek attorneys who serve on the relevant Congressional committees. We found that insurance companies that have received special tax benefits thanks to the benevolence of the tax-writing House Ways and Means Committee had retained the law firms of committee members. Defense contractors had hired the firms of members of the Armed Services committees. And corporations doing business in interstate commerce had shown a preference for the firms of Commerce Committee members.

Representative James Utt, the ultraconservative Republican from California, made a startling admission about Congressmen's law firms. "The greatest conflict," he stated flatly, "is in immigration cases. They will charge from $500 to $1,000 to sponsor a private bill. It's an open door." Rumors about the "sale" of private immigration bills (passed to admit a specific individual into the country) have been heard by reporters for years. The Immigration Service actually investigated charges that a New Jersey Congressman had been cashing in on immigration bills through his law firm, but the evidence was insufficient to press charges.

Through the years, Congress after Congress has rebelled against setting guidelines to govern the outside income of its lawyer members. As a result, the only guidelines are the general ones set for criminal behavior. A series of laws in Title 18 of U.S. Code make it a Federal crime for a member of Congress to receive compensation for rendering any services before a Government agency, to practice law before the court of claims, to enter into contracts with the Government, to accept payments or gifts (or campaign contributions) for any service or for any particular vote or to conspire to defraud the Government.

These statutes, however, are seldom enforced. *Congressional Quarterly,* the highly respected and impartial reporting service, has said: "The statutes have a major drawback: they concern areas in which it is difficult to obtain proof of wrongdoing and thus they were not extensively tested in the courts. In conflict of interest cases, for instance, it is often hard to show a cause-and-effect connection between a gift or a campaign contribution and service rendered or a vote cast." Among Senator Bible's many clients, for example, is the Nevada State Pharmaceutical Association. Senator Bible was one of the foremost opponents of the late Senator Estes Kefauver's drug investigations. Is there a cause-and-effect relationship?

While not binding, the American Bar Association's Canons of Professional and Judicial Ethics advises Congressmen not to represent opposing interests in the roles of lawmakers and lawyer. Also, the Bar Association decrees that a law firm should not appear before a legislative committee while a member of the firm is serving in the legislature, even though the association is disclosed and no fee is accepted. But the Canons have had little effect on Congressional behavior. Congressmen rarely if ever bother to request an opinion from the Bar Association's Committee on Professional Ethics as to what is morally expected of them in a specific instance. Writing in the *Federal Bar Journal,* Erwin G. Krasnow and former Representative Richard E. Lankford of Maryland, both attorneys, candidly reported that "although the American Bar Association's Canons of Ethics apply to lawyer members of Congress, many such members appear to continue to enjoy a robust law practice without the intervention of any professional ethics committee either of the national or local bar associations."

When the Association of the Bar of the City of New York called for a code of ethics to guide Congressman lawyers, it received polite attention but no action on Capitol Hill. In contrast, the association's suggestions on tightening up the conflicts of interest in the Federal Administration were warmly received and applauded by the Congress. Legislation followed.

In the last analysis, the Congressman lawyer, even in the broadest sense, is not a free man. He must serve two masters —his private client and his constituent. The voters generally are unaware of the conflict let alone how it is resolved.

5

LOOPHOLE LEGISLATORS: THE OIL DEPLETION ALLOWANCE

1. The Great Dry Hole Myth

The nation's tax coffers have sprung so many leaks—loopholes of all sizes—that half the money due the Government now escapes into the pockets of the privileged. Senator Paul Douglas, in his last Senate debate, pleaded that the tax rate could be cut in half, without reducing Federal revenue a single cent, if Congress would only plug the tax loopholes. "Last year," he said, his voice ringing with indignation, "a charwoman earning $55 a week paid more in income taxes than an oil company whose income was $26 million."

The seventy-five-year-old Douglas, tired after 18 years of lonely battles in the Senate, went down to defeat in the 1966 election—an event that provoked celebrations in the paneled boardrooms of the oil companies. Their joy was reflected in the headlines of the trade paper *Oil and Gas Journal*, which crowed: "OIL WINS BIG IN OFF-YEAR ELECTIONS." The story proclaimed: "The Senate's most articulate critic of percentage depletion, Senator Paul H. Douglas (D., Ill.), was defeated. . . ."

At the end, Douglas stood before a press conference, his white head held high, his Indian-chief face unflinching, to announce his return to teaching and to concede his failure to end tax favoritism. "The tax system is like a sieve," he said. His accusation was directed at the depletion allowance, a form of legalized tax evasion that permits privileged producers to deduct a percentage of their taxes. The size of the loopholes varies from 27½ percent for oil down to 5 percent for common gravel. "The depletion allowance for oil and gas," added Douglas, "has spread like a great disease."

True, the oil depletion allowance, which became law in 1926, was the loophole that started all the other loopholes. It excuses petroleum producers from taxes on 27½ percent of their income on every barrel of oil they pump out of the ground. Although the 27½ percent figure has taken on almost religious significance to oilmen, it was simply a compromise between the Senate and House figures. The House had voted for a 25-percent depletion allowance: the Senate had favored 30 percent. The figure also bears absolutely no relation to the amount of oil depleted. The producers can go on taking the tax write-off eternally, or at least until their wells dry up. For the average well, they save in taxes 19 times the original investment.

The appearance of this lovely loophole brought other lobbyists swarming over Capitol Hill like high-school students at cherry blossom time. Rather than plug the tax dike and send them all home, Congress obligingly punched dozens of new holes in the statutes. Now almost 100 minerals get some depletion allowance—among them bismuth, clam shells, clay, coal, lignite, limestone, mica, rock asphalt, sand, shale, soapstone and vermiculite. Douglas noted ruefully that "the list does not include soil, sod, dirt, turf or mosses from seawater. But I understand that there is a lawsuit now pending in an attempt to include water in the depletion allowance." But the most gaping loophole, through which an estimated $2.5 billion seeps each year, is still the old oil allowance. Almost as wondrous, however, are the drilling and development deductions —"golden gimmicks," one investor happily called them— which permit oilmen to deduct many of their intangible costs. The deductions can be taken in advance and amount to as much as 80 percent of the costs, which makes oil speculation a singularly attractive investment.

To justify these benefits, oilmen have perpetuated the great Dry Hole Myth. For years they have given anguished testimony that for every gusher there are eight dusters. This has been quietly contradicted by no less than the holy writ of the oil industry—the *Oil and Gas Journal,* which has confessed that the average is closer to two successes for every dry hole. Only the wildcatter takes the risk; and after he has bet his last borrowed dollar on a rig and a prayer, has drilled deep into the landscape and has found black gold at the bottom of a hole, then the big companies move in. Sometimes they buy their way into an oil strike; other times they simply siphon off a generous percentage of the profits, for the wildcatters must go to the oil giants to get their oil processed and marketed.

If oilmen are hard-pressed to explain the economic justification for their tax privileges, they solemnly assure doubters that the granting of such advantages is the patriotic thing to do. They can become positively lyrical over how vital oil is to national security. Such a consideration might conceivably justify a tax break for the discovery and development of domestic oil, but oilmen consider it equally patriotic to drill for oil in faraway places with strange-sounding names, especially since they are permitted to deduct against their United States taxes the royalties, disguised as "taxes," that they pay to foreign potentates.

Thus, Standard Oil of New Jersey—to take the giant— claimed tax payments of $740 million in 1966, the last year of record. Yet the real fact is that the top 22 oil refiners, combined, paid the Federal Government only $585 million in 1966—less than Standard Oil alone claimed to have paid.

The same 22 refiners, as a result of all their Federal blessings, paid only 4 percent of their gross income as United States income tax in 1964. This caterpillared up to 6.9 percent in 1965 and, breaking all records, finally hit 8.5 percent in 1966. The rate for wage earners and small businessmen was around 20 percent; for the average American corporation, it ran close to 49 percent. Some of these statistics were released by the usually humorless Internal Revenue Service in a pamphlet decorated by a rambling ranch house, swimming pool and bikini-clad bathing beauties, with oil derricks in the background. The ironic montage was removed after complaints from sensitive oil producers, who were not amused.

For more than a decade, the craggy Senator Douglas assaulted the oil depletion allowance with the same results he could have expected if he had been attacking the Declaration of Independence. His chief opponent was Robert S. Kerr, oil millionaire, uranium king, cattle baron and Senator from Oklahoma, who dominated the Senate's back rooms in the late 1950s and early 1960s. He worked his will with the finesse of one of his prize bulls. He was a one-man stampede, who simply trampled down his opposition. Five years after a heart attack felled him on New Year's Day, 1963, they were still talking about Bob Kerr on Capitol Hill.

2. Blatant Bob Kerr:
"Hell, I'm in Everything!"

Robert Kerr was born in Ada in 1896, when Oklahoma was still Indian Territory. He was the oldest of five sons (he had an older and a younger sister). Although the family had little money, the boys were encouraged to get an education and go into politics. Kerr's father was a disciple of William Jennings Bryan, and refused to let his six-foot-three son Bob play college football, saying, "I would rather have made Bryan's Cross of Gold speech than to have won every athletic contest staged on this earth since Cain and Abel ran their first footrace on the banks of the Euphrates."

Kerr passed through more than one college but never earned a degree. He started at the East Central Normal School in Ada, transferred to Oklahoma Baptist University, returned to East Central and finally enrolled at the University of Oklahoma. Even without a degree, he passed the state bar examination in 1922. He was commissioned a second lieutenant in the field artillery during World War I, and married in 1919 a few months after his discharge. His wife died five years later, and Kerr plunged into business. He tried the farm produce business, and was wiped out by fire. He was $10,000 in debt, earning just barely $3,000 a year, when he married Grayce Breene in December 1925. Bob Kerr had already resolved to go after three things: a family, a million dollars and the governorship. He was to get them exactly in that sequence, beginning with four children.

Like many others in his generation, he began his political rise in the American Legion, becoming state commander in 1926. His experience in the Legion convinced Kerr that he had the political skill to become governor. While he waited for his opportunity, he jumped feet first into the oil business.

Everyone knew there was oil under Oklahoma City, but most drillers did not have the nerve to go down after it. Tragedy had dogged the few who had tried. City Hall finally placed the downtown sections off limits, and required a $200,000 bond against accidents for each well in the residential areas. The risk seemed too great for the big companies.

Kerr did not share their timidity. It was 1932, and the depression increased his hunger. He had been in the oil-drilling business for six years, since he and his brother-in-law, James L. Anderson, had borrowed $30,000 to buy out the drilling company that had employed Anderson as its chief field man. Anderson possessed an uncanny ability to find oil, and he knew how to sink a well at lower cost than most other drillers. Kerr had abandoned his law office, and the new firm was called the Anderson-Kerr Drilling Company.

Their early ventures were modest and did not bring in nearly enough money to cover the ante for a drilling operation inside the Oklahoma City limits. Kerr solved the financing by selling Continental Oil Company a half interest. Continental Oil paid Anderson-Kerr $360,000 plus a $15,000 advance against their earnings when each hole was completed. Anderson-Kerr sank six holes, and all of them paid off. The partners cleared almost $2 million.

Kerr's reputation was enhanced as much by the deal with Continental Oil as it was by the strike itself. K. S. "Boots" Adams, the assistant to Phillips Petroleum's president, Frank Phillips, was so impressed that he put through a call for Kerr in 1935. The Anderson-Kerr strikes in Oklahoma City had emboldened the big companies, but the ordinance restricting wells to the residential areas was keeping them off land that seemed rich in deposits. Phillips Petroleum held a number of leases on downtown sites, and Adams decided Kerr was the man to charm the voters into granting downtown drilling permits through a popular referendum.

Kerr agreed to run the campaign, but refused pay for his work. All he wanted, he told Adams, was a contract to sink the wells for Phillips. Kerr successfully wooed the voters to change drilling laws, and his oil rigs moved into the high-rent district. A year later, Kerr was tapped to talk the voters into approving another referendum to open up more of the city, and shortly thereafter derricks began sucking oil from the grounds of the state capitol itself.

Brother-in-law James Anderson, satisfied with his share of the business, retired in 1937, and Kerr offered partnerships to two young men in the Phillips organization. One was Dean McGee, who at thirty-three was already making a name in the oil industry. Phillips Petroleum regarded him as the best oil geologist in the nation. In a world where everything was for sale, McGee's defection to Kerr was accepted without a quarrel, though Frank Phillips simmered over the departure. When Kerr genially approached Phillips for a donation to a Baptist orphanage, Phillips gave him $100,000 and said, "I'd rather give $500,000 and have it that you'd left those boys alone."

To repair his relationship with Phillips Petroleum, Kerr worked out a 10-year deal that gave Phillips a half interest in oil lands that McGee discovered for Kerr's company. In return, Phillips had to foot three-quarters of the cost. Under this agreement, oil was found in Alaska, Latin America, and the Louisiana tidelands.

With his Dun and Bradstreet rating as a millionaire established, Kerr turned his attention in 1941 to the governorship. First, taking into account the state's preponderance of Baptist voters, he moved his sons from a Christian Science Sunday school to a Baptist Sunday school across the street. Next, he lined up the support of Oklahoma's oilmen. He had been handling public relations for the oil industry in Oklahoma and Kansas, and when the assignment came up for renewal, he spoke of his plan to run. "I told them that if I lost the election, they wouldn't want me," he said later with a characteristic chuckle, "and if I won, they wouldn't need a man in the job."

Kerr ran under the Roosevelt banner in 1942. With massive contributions from the oilmen and his share of votes from the Baptists, he eked out victories in the primary and the general election. But his November margin of 16,500 votes was the smallest for a Democrat in Oklahoma in 28 years.

His administration was strangely quiet for a man of Bob Kerr's flamboyance. He used the wartime shortages of men and materials as an excuse to cut back state spending and to reduce state debts. Despite his failure to stir Oklahomans, he managed to attract some national attention. Roosevelt knew of Kerr's bombastic ability on the stump and picked him as the keynoter for the 1944 Democratic convention. Kerr took a speech drafted by party ghost-writers and, he claimed, completely rewrote it. "I saved one sentence from that ghost job," he said. "It was a good sentence."

Kerr was elected to the Senate easily in 1948 and quickly turned the job into a profit far beyond the modest salary. He pushed through a bill in 1950 that would have increased the price of natural gas and boosted the profits of the oil companies that owned gas wells, including Kerr-McGee Industries, Inc. President Truman had privately promised to hold his nose and sign the bill, but the outcry in the press over Kerr's blatant conflict of interest compelled Truman to kill it with a veto. It was one of Kerr's few defeats. While others might have been brooding, he went to work on the Federal Power Commission and helped extract a ruling for the price increase that the President had vetoed.

The natural-gas bill taught Kerr the virtues of subtlety. Thereafter, he found other Senators to introduce his windfall legislation, and he merely provided the push. He gave beneficial shoves to relief measures for the producers not only of gas and oil, but of beryllium, boron, helium, potash and uranium as well. To no one's particular surprise, Kerr-McGee was found to have heavy investments in all of those products.

There was nothing subtle about Kerr's attitude toward conflict of interest. His friend Bobby Baker once recalled, "Bob Kerr used to say that he was opposed to all monopolies unless he had a piece of them." And Kerr himself boasted with a chuckle, "Hell, I'm in everything."

On another occasion Kerr said, "I represent the financial institutions of Oklahoma, and I am interested in them, and they know that, and this is the reason they elect me."

Few men have worked for the financial institutions of their home state with more dedication. Kerr was always a formidable foe on the Senate floor. Standing six feet three and weighing 220 pounds, he could be both biting and bruising in debate. In later years he started wearing suspenders and would punctuate his oratory by snapping his galluses. There were few men in the Senate whom the affable Oklahoman could not reduce to jelly when he was fully aroused. But he reserved his most withering fire for those who dared challenge the oil depletion allowance—a tactic that caused critics to suggest unkindly that he was paying more attention to his own business than to the Senate's business. On issues in which he had no financial interest, he usually followed party discipline. Indeed, liberals found much in his record worthy of praise. He could stand comfortably among the populists in the Senate and harangue his colleagues on the evils of water pollution or the private power monopoly. He was in the forefront of Senators supporting President Truman after the firing of General Douglas MacArthur. The inside fact, however, was that Kerr had asked Truman to fire MacArthur when it appeared the general was going to send partially trained National Guard troops from Oklahoma into battle.

The next logical move for Robert Kerr was into the White House. At the 1952 Democratic convention in Chicago, the demonstration for him was the biggest, best financed and least sincere. Kerr had a staff of professionals, a booming band, and plenty of pretty girls passing out buttons picturing the log cabin in which he was born. All he lacked was delegates. For Kerr the convention was an exercise in futility, which he carried off with a good-natured grin. Earlier in 1952 he had actually believed he could win the nomination and had recruited professionals like Clark Clifford to plan his primary campaign. If Kerr was not humbled by defeat, he was at least able to wisecrack, "It would appear that people did not realize what a superior product was being offered them."

Nor did his demonstrated lack of national appeal make him lose interest in expanding his power. Immediately after Eisenhower's inauguration, Kerr set about consolidating his strength in the Senate. His great personal wealth and his influence with the oil industry enabled him to help other Senators out of the financial problems that so often beset them. "When people talk about big contributors to political campaigns, I always think of Kerr," one professional said. It was a good investment worth critical votes when an issue on which Kerr had an interest on his pet issues came to the floor. He was almost unbeatable on his pet issues, which invariably involved his own pocketbook. "Making money is a sickness with Bob," once remarked Senator Clinton Anderson, D-N.M., who found the disease catching.

By the end of the 1950s Kerr-McGee had cornered about 25 percent of all the known uranium reserves in the United States—worth more than $1 billion—and became the biggest supplier of uranium to the Atomic Energy Commission. Other uranium producers were so frustrated by Kerr's success in grabbing contracts (a 1958 contract with the AEC provided for the sale of more than $300 million in uranium over eight years) that they appealed to the Justice Department for an investigation of "political influence" and "certain combinations and conspiracies . . . in the production, processing and sale of uranium materials." The AEC merely spread Kerr-McGee deliveries over 10 years, with an agreement to buy still more in 1969 and 1970.

In the late 1950s, Kerr-McGee also acquired 73 percent of the biggest natural helium pool in the world at Pinto Dome, Arizona. Shortly after the purchase, Lynn Adams, the company's vice president and general counsel, came to Washington with a plan to conserve the nation's helium supply. The Government, he told Congress, should be allowed to extract helium from natural gas, with the taxpayers paying the entire cost of the processing and producers being paid for the extracted helium. The processed natural gas, according to his plan, would be sold back to the producers at the original cost. Then he suggested a legislative footnote that he said would make it fair to all producers. Since the helium extracted from the natural gas would be more expensive than natural helium, he called for a provision forbidding the sale of helium to the Government at less than the highest cost. This would entitle the owners of Pinto Dome to the higher price that was paid for extracted helium. Adams' helpful suggestion was written into the legislation, complete with several references to Pinto Dome.

The bill was steered quietly through the Senate Interior Committee by Senator Clinton Anderson. Kerr had no better friend in the Senate than Anderson, but Kerr did not bank on friendship alone. Kerr had also arranged for Anderson to get 10 percent of Pinto Dome before the bill came to a vote in June 1960.

Anderson sent the committee's report to the printer too late for other Senators to obtain copies for study. The printer's manuscript was the only copy in existence when the bill was reported to the Senate two days before Congress adjourned. Senator John Carroll, a Colorado Democrat later opposed by the oil and gas interests and retired by the voters, objected that the issue had come to a vote during the closing rush without a printed report. The Senate, however, disregarded this breach of form and passed the bill with all the features recommended by Kerr-McGee's counsel.

For Anderson, passage of this new bill completed a cycle. He had first attracted public notice in the early Twenties, when he had blown the lid off the Teapot Dome scandal as a reporter for the Albuquerque *Journal*. He had learned that some cattle and a racehorse had been delivered to the ranch of Interior Secretary Albert Fall in Three Rivers, New Mexico. More probing revealed that the animals had come from oilman Harry Sinclair, and Anderson, in hot pursuit of the facts, discovered that Fall had sold the Government's oil reserve in Teapot Dome to Sinclair.

After the first stories appeared, Fall stormed into the *Journal*'s editorial office. "Who's the son of a bitch who is writing all those lies about me?" he bellowed. Anderson, tall and lean, stood up. "I'm the son of a bitch," he said calmly, "and I don't write lies." From this crusading start, Anderson entered public service and wound up in Congress. In 1945 he was appointed Secretary of Agriculture, a position in which he withstood the demands of the whiskey and beer lobbies, backed by General Harry Vaughan, to secure grain when it was needed to feed Europe. After election to the Senate in 1948 he became one of the foremost champions of civil rights, medicare, civilian control of atomic energy and generally battled for the underprivileged. But somewhere along the way, Clinton Anderson became an apologist for the oil interests. He solemnly defended oil privileges that have cost the taxpayers more than the Teapot Dome scandal ever did. In a 1951 net-worth statement, he listed oil holdings valued at $500,000. This, of course, did not include his interest in the Pinto Dome helium, which his Senate sleight-of-hand had boosted in value and which he claims to have sold after the Government began purchasing the helium. From Teapot Dome to Pinto Dome, Anderson had come a long way.

Another erstwhile crusader profited by an alliance with Kerr. James G. Patton, blustery president of the liberal National Farmers Union, who wore a patch over one eye in the manner of a buccaneer, had been a constant irritant to the oil interests. He frequently attacked the oil depletion allowance, helped torpedo Kerr's natural-gas bill in 1950, and helped launch a national campaign to block the tidelands oil give-away. For years the oil interests had fought to have the oil-fields that lie on the continental shelf off the coasts of Louisiana, Texas and California declared the property of the states rather than the Federal Government. They eventually succeeded over the defiant protests of James Patton, thus validating state leases owned by the big oil companies.

Patton came to terms with Kerr in 1954 after the National Farmers Union borrowed money from the Prudential Insurance Company to lease 20,000 acres of newly discovered potash land in New Mexico. The NFU needed more capital to exploit the 165 million tons of potash—an agricultural fertilizer—and Kerr-McGee bought in for a half interest.

Kerr was able to spread the fertilizer around. Boots Adams, who had risen to chairman of the board of Phillips Petroleum, suggested his company might also be interested in a potash investment. As the two men ate dinner, Kerr goaded his friend. "I told him that he shouldn't get in on any deal with the Farmers Union," Kerr later recounted. "I said that he was a big businessman, and his company might not want to get in with people who go around organizing cooperatives and fighting for public power. I was just needling him, see." The merits of the 15-percent depletion allowance on potash, however, outweighed whatever reservations Adams may have felt. Kerr estimated that the 20,000 acres would net the strange consortium $100 million by 1980. Thereafter, Jim Patton was silent about oil privilege.

Kerr did not confine his manipulations to domestic matters. As a power in the Senate, he had great influence over foreign loans. Among the nations with outstretched hands in 1959 was Argentina. There was no rush to turn over the money, and there were hints on Capitol Hill that the impediment was President Arturo Frondizi's repudiation of drilling rights for American oil companies. Suddenly, in May, Argentina was granted $350 million in United States loans from Federal agencies and cooperating banks. The following July, Frondizi quietly rescued the scrapped oil agreement. One of the biggest shares went to the New York investment firm of Carl M. Loeb, Rhodes and Company, which subcontracted the Argentine oil development to Kerr-McGee.

When Robert Kerr died on January 1, 1963, no one outside his family mourned him more than Bobby Baker did. As Senate Majority Secretary, Baker had helped Kerr line up votes for his pet legislation, and Kerr, in return, had steered him into a few profitable deals. Bobby's grief intensified when he got into trouble over his deals and Kerr was not around to bail him out.

Hauled up for trial, Baker tried to persuade a Federal jury of eleven government workers and one pensioner that he had delivered $99,600 in $100 bills to Kerr. The money came from California savings-and-loan executives, whose sudden generosity coincided with Senate activity on a bill that would have increased the industry's taxes. Since the Senator was beyond questioning, the jury decided the story was too pat and convicted Baker of stealing the money.

Yet no one who knew Bob Kerr doubted that, had he been alive, he would have crashed his great bulk against the foundations of the Republic to keep Bobby out of jail. Kerr liked the boy and, naturally, wanted to make him a millionaire. It was Kerr who took Bobby up on the mountaintop and showed him a world of wealth spread out below. Baker once remarked that the death of "the kindest, nicest, warmest, most generous friend I ever had in my life cost me at least ten million dollars, if you want to measure it moneywise, because we had agreed to go into the cattle business in southwest Kansas and he'd arranged to lease eight thousand acres."

Baker's $10 million boast is believable, because Kerr had the Midas touch. With his wife and children, Kerr owned 22 percent of Kerr-McGee and its widely diversified interests; a 40,000-acre ranch in eastern Oklahoma with 3,000 head of Black Angus cattle grazing on the land and 100,000 tons of good coal under it; a $400,000, 330-foot ranch house; a $160,000 home outside Washington, and a penthouse atop the Kerr-McGee offices in Oklahoma City. His net worth was variously estimated at between $15 million and $150 million. Yet he was ever in hot pursuit of the next million. For Bob Kerr had three basic beliefs: the Baptist faith, the 27½-percent oil depletion allowance, and his divine right to make millions. He allowed nothing to stand in his way, and he had a knack for hanging beneficial tax riders on bills in the Senate Finance Committee. "Bob had a special way of explaining his 'innocent little amendments' so you'd be convinced you were just voting for simple justice," another committee member said in grudging tribute. "But after it was all over and you'd find out what you'd really voted for, he'd cackle and say, 'Well, you know me. I'm against any conspiracy I'm not in on.' "

During his years in the Senate, there were few conspiracies that escaped him.

3. Oiling the Wheels

There are few members of Congress who have not been tempted to go along with the oil industry's interests. For their favors, the oil barons offer them campaign contributions, law fees, stock tips, even cash under the table. Every year, the oilmen spend an estimated $50 million to publicize the imaginary distress of the oil industry and to subsidize its lobbying effort.

The oilmen save billions each year through tax loopholes, and the more the patricians of petroleum drain from the Government through tax loopholes, the more they slip to politicians to make the loopholes in the tax laws even bigger. And each time the corruption goes the full circle, the pockets of the oilmen are a little fuller.

Occasionally the oil bribes are turned down. In 1956 the late Senator Francis Case, R-S.D., shook with emotion as he reported an effort to buy his vote. He was offered, he said, a brown paper sack filled with $2,500 in hundred-dollar bills. He identified the bagman as John Neff, who had been authorized to make "certain expenditures" by his boss, Superior Oil lobbyist Elmer Patman. If Case had taken the money, of course, he would have been hooked for the rest of his career.

To the Senator who would bristle over a raw bribe, a campaign contribution may be nearly irresistible. It is usually channeled through a campaign committee—a device that enables the recipient to camouflage the source. He reports that the money came from the committee, thus complying with the letter of the law, without mentioning that it was earmarked for his campaign by the oil interests.

When Bobby Baker was in his heyday in the back rooms of the Senate, he once beckoned aside Senator Thomas McIntyre, D-N.H., and hinted that support for the oil depletion allowance might magically rid McIntyre of a $10,000 campaign debt. The Senator was about to accept the proposal when his Senate mentor, Estes Kefauver, heard about it and raised the money from less demanding sources to pay off McIntyre's campaign debt. Senator Frank Moss, D-Utah, had a similar proposition put to him by Washington fund-raiser Joe Miller, who offered to guide a $5,000 oil donation to his campaign through the Democratic Senatorial Campaign Committee. In the end, both Senators turned down the oil money which, no doubt, was shunted to others less scrupulous.

Those who cannot be bought may find themselves investigated. During the fight over the Kerr bill to increase natural-gas prices, *The New York Times* reported that "the gas bill lobby ran a complete genealogy on Senators," and quoted an unnamed Senator as saying he had received letters from almost forgotten relatives asking him to support the bill. One Senator was buttonholed by the son of his mother's classmate; another was pressured by one of his wife's former suitors. Commented Senator George Aiken, R-Vt., "They have checked on who you have been associated with, who are your friends, who has supported you in the past, anybody who has ever worked for you or with you. And they get them to contact you."

There are reprisals, too, for the Congressmen who don't go along. Those who fight the oil lobby find that their opponents have well-financed campaigns.

For years, the oil privileges were protected on Capitol Hill by that powerful pair from Texas, the late Sam Rayburn and his pupil Lyndon Johnson. Rayburn, as Speaker of the House, controlled appointments to the tax-writing Ways and Means Committee. No one was admitted to this select circle who couldn't give Rayburn the right answer to one question: "Do you favor the oil depletion allowance?"

Fittingly, the Rayburn Memorial Library in Bonham, Texas, was built largely with oil money. *Life* Magazine's coverage of the library dedication showed a photograph of a grinning Johnson with an arm around the late oil millionaire Sidney Richardson. A reporter who covered the affair later added, "I walked in and forgot for a moment whether it was supposed to be a Republican or Democratic gathering. I see the same men at Republican affairs."

When Rayburn was corralling Democratic votes for oil, Massachusetts' late Joseph W. Martin, Jr., then the House Republican Leader, lined up the GOP votes. Texas oil millionaires decided to show their appreciation in 1958 by helping

Martin raise campaign funds in what was then solid Democratic territory. Letters went out to oilmen, under the signature of H. J. "Jack" Porter, himself an oilman and Republican National Committeeman from Texas:

Joe Martin has always been a friend of Texas, especially of the oil and gas producing industries. He mustered two-thirds of the Republican votes in the House each time the gas bill passed. . . . As Speaker of the 83rd Congress, he led the fight for adoption of the tidelands ownership bill. It will be up to Joe Martin to muster at least 65 percent of the Republican votes in order to pass the gas bill this year. He had put Republican members from the Northern and Eastern consuming areas on the spot politically, because the bill is not popular due to the distortion of the facts by newspaper columnists and others.

The dinner was held in Houston's Rice Hotel—in the same banquet hall where many of the same oilmen had gathered a few weeks earlier to attend an appreciation dinner for Lyndon Johnson. In fact, 12 of the sponsors of the Martin dinner had also given their names to the Johnson testimonial, evidence that oil and politics not only mix but are bipartisan.

Johnson subscribed to the political doctrine that no one could get elected in Texas without oil money. Better than most men, he knew how to tap this rich campaign well. As far back as 1938, when he was merely another Representative from Texas, he had funneled oil money into Democratic campaign chests. The Democrats had expected to lose some seats in the House that year. President Roosevelt had been displeased with the efforts of the Democratic Congressional Campaign Committee and had asked Johnson to take over some of the fund-raising. LBJ had rented a room in the rear of Washington's Munsey Building and had passed out $100,000 in oil contributions to Democratic candidates. After he moved up to the Senate and became the Majority Leader, Johnson was not the ungrateful sort who would forget his rich friends. He jealously guarded the Finance Committee where the tax loopholes are enlarged after the House, in fulfillment of its Constitutional function, has initiated them.

When a Democratic vacancy occurred on this key committee in 1955, the man in line for it was Senator Douglas, the

cast-iron opponent of the depletion allowance. Johnson artful-
ly kept the vacant seat warm himself until he could turn it
over to Senator Alben Barkley, D-Ky., a former Vice President, whose prestige entitled him to his choice of committees
and whose views on depletion were more flexible. Not until
Barkley died and Douglas' seniority could no longer be overcome did the anti-depletion-allowance Senator finally force
his way onto the committee.

Johnson performed a major act of devotion to oil and gas
again after the celebrated $2,500 bribe offer to Senator Fran-
cis Case. This clumsy attempt to buy Case's vote raised demands for a Senate investigation. Without waiting for Johnson's permission, Senator Albert Gore, D-Tenn., announced
that his Elections Subcommittee would start probing. Johnson, who was relaxing at his ranch, hurried back to Washington and kept after Gore for ten days to relinquish his jurisdiction to another, less hostile committee. Gore finally did let go,
and it is one of those tantalizing coincidences that, not long
afterward, Gore quietly became a partner in a ranching
operation with Robert Kerr.

Johnson had a personal reason for sidetracking the investigation. His chief Texas political lieutenant, John B. Connally,
who later became Secretary of the Navy and Governor of
Texas, was directing the oil and gas lobbying. On the day
Case sounded off about the bribe offer, Connally sat white-
faced, for hours, in his Mayflower Hotel room. He was never
called as a witness in the probe. The Majority Leader, moving
cautiously, had maneuvered the investigation into the hands
of Senator John McClellan, D-Ark.

McClellan had a reputation as a grim and relentless investigator. The public did not know, however, that McClellan's
law firm in Little Rock, according to its listing of clients in the
Martindale-Hubbel directory, at that time represented Standard Oil of New Jersey, Seaboard Oil, Tidewater [Associated]
Oil, and Carter Oil. His investigation dribbled along unspec-
tacularly, then faded away without going beyond the Case
incident. Superior Oil's bagmen, Elmer Patman and John Neff,
pleaded guilty of failing to register as lobbyists, and received
small fines and suspended one-year jail sentences.

Elmer Patman was back in action on Capitol Hill in 1962
when Superior Oil became impatient in its quest for an oil import quota. Companies authorized to import oil paid only 50

cents a barrel for crude, which meant an immediate profit of between $1.20 and $1.60 for every barrel sold on the domestic market. This added up to a glorious $1.5 billion a year windfall. Inland refiners, who preferred to avoid the shipping problems, were able to sell their quota tickets for between $1 and $1.25 a barrel. While other companies were profiting on the imports—or the quota tickets—Superior was left in the cold.

Elmer Patman slipped around to see his cousin, Representative Wright Patman, D-Tex., then the House Small-Business Committee chairman. The Congressman, who has the benevolent look of a country pastor, has battled against the big banks and other special interests with an evangelical fervor. But in this case, blood proved thicker than oil and he rallied to the side of Cousin Elmer. First, Elmer Patman attacked the import program at an Interior Department hearing. Two weeks later, Wright Patman ordered his Small-Business Committee to investigate oil imports. The Congressman followed up his probe with a letter to President Kennedy, dated March 16, 1962, charging that "quotas are being traded for cash." He complained that Gabriel Oil Company had been able to get a quota while Superior Oil had not. He used almost the identical language in discussing the case that his cousin had used at the Interior Department hearing.

Representative Patman was not alone in looking after family oil interests. Representative Hugh Carey, D-N.Y., began phoning the Interior Department in 1967, when the Commonwealth Oil Refining Company sought to import 14,000 barrels of gasoline a day from its Puerto Rican refinery. Carey, who could speak in a demanding voice as chairman of the House Interior Subcommittee dealing with Puerto Rico, did not mention on the phone that his brother, Edward M. Carey, happened to be founder and chief stockholder of Commonwealth Oil Refining. Interior Department officials remember quite distinctly having received the Congressman's calls, though he denied making them. "I have kept strictly hands off," he said.

The oil industry's interest in foreign affairs goes beyond import quotas and tax credits for royalties paid to foreign Governments. It has a huge stake in Vietnam, where some of the overhead has found its way into strange hands. Officials returning from the war front tell a story that was as true in 1967 as it was when the United States first became involved in the bloody business of keeping South Vietnam out of Communist hands. "The safest way to drive across Vietnam," they say, "is in an oil truck." Secretary of State Dean Rusk admitted to the Senate Foreign Relations Committee that American oil companies have paid "tolls" for passage through Communist-controlled territory. Ironically, no one under the American flag puts on a greater show of patriotism than Texas oil millionaires, who have a curious affinity for right-wing causes with star-spangled names.

The Vietcong did destroy $140,000 worth of oil in Esso tanks near Danang on August 5, 1965. The chances are, however, that the guerrillas didn't see the friendly Esso sign. Saigon itself has been shelled in broad daylight, but the Vietcong never troubled the oil depot at Nhabe, 20 miles from the city, until the Tet offensive in February, 1968. An oil storage tank was hit, possibly by accident. During the same offensive, fighting raged around the Esso storage tanks at Can Tho. Yet the great tanks, which the Vietcong could have destroyed at will, miraculously escaped damage. Oil officials have tried to claim that 40 percent of their Vietnam shipments were being destroyed by the Communists. When Senator George Aiken pressed the question at a closed-door session, however, General Earle Wheeler, chairman of the Joint Chiefs of Staff, testified that oil losses had amounted to "only a fraction of one percent."

The oil barons miss Sam Rayburn and mourn Bob Kerr. And they must now deal at a different level with Lyndon Johnson, who no longer puts the oil interests ahead of the national interests. Still, they seem to find plenty of protectors who recognize how essential petroleum is to the national defense, the American economy and the welfare of the fur salons and Cadillac dealers in Dallas. As their spiritual leader in Congress, the oil boys have now turned to Senator Russell Long, the son of the late Kingfish and heir of the Long political dynasty of Louisiana.

Russell does not own as many oil wells as Bob Kerr did, but he has oil in his bloodstream from both sides of the family. His father, the fiery and flamboyant backwater demagogue, Huey Long, founded the Win-or-Lose Oil Company in the early 1930s. The company happily won more than it lost; it bought up marshy, river-bottom lands for next to nothing, then leased them to the oil giants at huge profits. Win-or-Lose was disbanded in 1938 for a tax advantage, then quietly reorganized as a family partnership. Its main activity today, apparently, is investing the royalty income from the oil lands.

On the maternal side of the family, D. B. McConnell, a brother of Russell Long's mother, began another oil operation. This has now been taken over by Russell's brother, Palmer Long. Under no special corporate name, he watches out for drilling opportunities. He explained, "I find a deal here and there. If mother or sister or brother want in, it's up to them to come along. If not, well, I just take it myself."

A portrait of Huey hangs over Russell's desk in his Senate office, and visitors are sometimes startled by the physical resemblance. Huey was assassinated in 1935 and succeeded in the Senate by his wife Rose. They were both loners who were excluded from the Senate's inner circle. Their son fought his way to the center of the circle, determined that people should look at him and say of his father, "Huey couldn't have been so bad." Then Russell, too, began to alienate his colleagues with his nest-fouling performances on the Senate floor (e.g., tying up the Senate machinery in a pointless filibuster in 1967 and spitting insults at his uncooperative colleagues).

The oilmen, noting that Russell Long was in line for the chairmanship of the Senate Finance Committee, helped him to become the Senate Democratic Whip in 1965. He was able to offer his colleagues well-oiled resources for their next campaigns at the same time he was soliciting their votes. He telephoned Connecticut Senator Thomas Dodd's office, for example, to say he had someone with him who admired Dodd's record and wanted to make a $1,500 contribution. Dodd beat it over to Long's office with unaccustomed haste.

Long, who has the appeal of an affable puppy, has candidly confessed that he passed out a few oil contributions while he was running for Whip. "Shucks," he said, "that's the name of the game." He also paid personal calls on every Democratic Senator save his two opponents—John O. Pastore, D-R.I., and A. S. Mike Monroney, D-Okla. His greatest sacrifice, he later said in recounting his campaign for Whip, was giving his father's old Senate desk to delighted Senator Olin Johnston, D-S.C. Originally the desk had belonged to Johnston's famous predecessor, John C. Calhoun. Long had previously denied the desk to Senator Strom Thurmond, R-S.C. With the Whip's job at stake, Long overcame his own nostalgia for the sake of Johnston's vote. Recalled Long, "I said to myself, 'Please forgive me, Daddy, but this time I'm going for broke.'" Olin Johnston happily voted for Long, who won on the second ballot.

Like Kerr, Russell Long does not let his personal oil holdings inhibit him from a heroic defense in the Senate of oil privileges. "Any friend of oil," he has said, "is a friend of ours." Indeed, he has contended, "Personally, I believe that the 27½-percent depletion allowance is a little small."

6

CROOKED FURROWS:
THE WASHINGTON FARMER

1. Harvesting Greenbacks

Great streams of migrant farm laborers flow through the nation like human highways, skirting the metropolitan areas and cutting through the fields. Caught up in the flow are thousands of faceless men and women and their anonymous children who move with the harvests, stopping only long enough to pick a crop and to earn enough until the next stop.

These are the people who help make America the best-fed nation in history, yet they themselves are often undernourished. Agricultural areas plead for their services when there is picking to be done, then pressure them to move on lest they tap the welfare coffers and burden the schools with their children.

The lot of the nonmigratory farm workers is sometimes not much better and often considerably worse. In the Deep South, families that have tended the fields since slave days are suddenly obsolete, replaced by tractors, automatic cotton-pickers and weed killers. Many are too poor to afford even the Government stamps to buy cut-price food, and they exist on a diet of starches and water.

Life is a little better, but only a little, for the small farmers—the traditional guardians of American values. Between 1960 and 1966, almost six million of them were driven off their land by their inability to compete against the agricultural giants. Depression-born laws to protect the small farmers are hopelessly outdated, and now serve to subsidize the giant landowners as they gobble up ever greater bites of the countryside.

As a result, the big farmers harvest their favorite crop on Capitol Hill—greenbacks. The average United States farmer reaps $831 in greenbacks each year to make up the difference between the market price and the pegged price for certain crops. This support price is based upon a complicated formula, which favors the big farms. For example, farms that gross more than $100,000 a year compose less than 2 percent of the total number of farms, yet they rake in 20 percent of the price supports.

The plight of the small farmers and farm laborers gets little attention in Congress. Many Senators and Representatives are too busy with the problems of the large planters. In some cases the Congressmen *are* the large planters. They plow the legislative fields in Washington, then partake of the financial harvest at home.

This little Congressional secret was let out of the bag by Senator Stephen Young, D-Ohio, who sometimes forgets to show the proper reverence for Senate traditions, and mentions the unmentionable. "In the field of agriculture," he has confided, "certain members of Congress, as farmers, have collected various sums from the Federal Government under the farm load and subsidy program. Some also sit on the committees which help shape agricultural legislation."

Such a Congressman is California's Charles M. Teague, who, as the number-two Republican on the House Agriculture Committee, exercises a powerful influence over farm legislation. He is not the least deterred by the fact that his family has a major interest in Limoneira Ranch, the largest lemon producer in Ventura County, California, where agriculture is big business.

Limoneira, like California's other great ranches, has prospered on the sweat of the *braceros,* Mexican stoop laborers who have provided inexpensive help, wandering from one farm to another, picking fruits and vegetables and living in medieval squalor. Special legislation was passed in 1952 to open the border to the *braceros* provided that local workers "were not willing, able or qualified to do the work for which the foreign labor was sought, and that importation of this foreign labor did not adversely affect the wages and working conditions of native labor."

As the Mexican labor flooded into the country, union, welfare and church spokesmen charged that the *braceros* provided a pool of cheap, docile foreign labor competing with domestic migrants for jobs and undermining the wages and working conditions of native Americans. The situation came to a head with the publication of a 1959 Labor Department study reporting that 60 percent of the *braceros* were used on surplus, subsidized crops and that farm wages, though rising elsewhere in the United States, tended not to go up in areas where *braceros* were used heavily. The report led to an attempt by the Kennedy Administration in 1961 to curtail the traffic in Mexican workers. The House Agriculture Committee beat down attack after attack to change the system. Leading the battle to keep the *braceros* was none other than Congressman Teague.

The story of Charles M. Teague, the Congressman from California, has a prelude and a postscript. The prelude tells of his father, Charles Collins Teague, who wore a vest with a gold watch chain stretched between the pockets until the day he died in 1950. The postscript tells of Mario Soto, who never owned a vest and could not afford a watch chain.

2. Teagueville

In the first week of May 1941 Charles Collins Teague received a singular honor from his employees. He was a founder of the California Citrus Growers Exchange, a president of the California Chamber of Commerce, a member of the Federal Farm Board under Herbert Hoover, and a man whose word was law in Ventura County, California. Still, he had never been so honored by the workers.

In a small, county-owned park north of Santa Paula, the workers pitched their drooping tents and erected a sign, proclaiming their squatters' community as "Teagueville." Teague did not appreciate the honor, and a county employee ripped the sign down. The workers put it up again. The county then placed armed guards around the camp and ordered the workers away.

The workers were attempting to organize a union, and they were picketing the citrus farms, including Teague's Limoneira Ranch. The old man was determined to beat them down. "It is easier to hold firm now than later," Teague told the other growers. "Always remember that. We must make this a fight to the finish."

The strikers and their families had been evicted from their grower-owned shacks on the edges of the groves, many of them forcibly pushed off the land. Teague himself moved against workers who occupied 358 houses on his properties. The workers and their families were herded into the tents in "Teagueville" and elsewhere in the county. When the County Board of Supervisors was finally forced to rent land from the growers for the tents, one member complained, "I feel this is selling the ranchers down the river, and they are paying a major share of the bill. I feel sorry for these Mexicans but I feel their angels should care for them instead of the county."

With the Mexican laborers evicted and camping out in their tents, the ranchers moved in strikebreakers. They had recruited hundreds of hungry dust-bowl farmers from Oklahoma and Arkansas to cross the picket lines. It was skillful exploitation of racism and human misery.

Charles Collins Teague, more than anyone else, was an embodiment of the California citrus industry. Like a slot-machine owner, he made a fortune out of lemons. The family lemon grove known as the "Teague Forty"—managed and half owned by Teague—was exceptionally successful. He became a general manager of the Limoneira Ranch when he was twenty-five, and by 1928 had expanded it from 400 acres to 3,250 acres. To prevent the profits from being squeezed out of the lemons by brokers and speculators, he helped organize the California Citrus Growers Exchange, which gave the world the famous Sunkist label, and for 30 years was its president.

With Sunkist, Teague and the other growers outmaneuvered the middlemen and defeated the laws of supply and demand. Rather than glut the market with their fruits, the growers agreed to regulate the market and keep prices up.

Although Teague's polemic for his cooperative could serve, with little alteration, as a rallying cry for the United Farm Workers Organizing Committee, Teague did not view labor in quite the same light as production. "Undoubtedly, in some instances, it has been necessary for labor to organize in order to gain fair treatment," Teague wrote, "but I do not believe that the unionization of agricultural laborers is a practical thing." Viewing it strictly from "the standpoint of the workers," he felt union affiliation would be "a distinct handicap."

Just as Teague did not wish to burden workers with the handicap of a union, he also saw little point in handicapping small farmers with Government loans. He was appointed to the Federal Farm Board by Herbert Hoover in June 1929, a few months before the depression hit Wall Street. Financial crisis was already spreading like a blight over the farms, and the small farmers lined up for loans as soon as the Farm Board opened for business. The Board, though, decided solemnly to make loans only to cooperatives "that had a good record and were fundamentally sound, financially and otherwise, or that could be reorganized to meet such qualifications," Teague said. He stalked out of a meeting when it seemed the Board might at least listen to the farmers who were desperate for loans. He demanded that the Board set up a division to "screen out" those who weren't big enough to meet the qualifications.

Charles Collins Teague died in 1950 while shooting skeet at the Rancho Sespe, another large citrus farm not far from his own Limoneira Ranch. He was known as "the grand old man of California agriculture" when he died at age seventy-seven. He had distributed much of his legacy before his death. Troubled about great estates that were dissipated by "extravagant and riotous living," he decided to pass on part of his wealth to his daughter and two sons while he could still watch them. "Thus," he wrote, "they would have a chance to demonstrate whether they could properly manage it before receiving any balance they might inherit. . . ."

Both of his sons were schooled to protect the family inheritance. The elder, Milton, became general manager, then president of Limoneira Ranch. He also moved into his father's niche as president of both Sunkist and the California Chamber of Commerce. The young son, Charles, was sent to law school.

Representative Charles M. Teague now sits in the shadow of power. It is a role to which he has long been accustomed. He is a pleasant man, the sort who can be found at any Rotary luncheon. His suits speak well of his tailor, and his colleagues speak well of him. His 14 years in the House have not been marked by either the political charisma or the dynamic intellect that propels men out of the tedium of the House to the prestige of the Senate. But Teague is a gentleman, and he does not complain. Nor does he seem to mind his relative obscurity. With the security of a safe district, he can ride the escalator to leadership. The seniority system and a Republican sweep could one day make him chairman of the House Agriculture Committee.

His career has been plodding but nevertheless well plotted. He has seldom varied in his voting from the Republican party line, and his public statements have been a mirror of conservative cant. He is a fearless champion of thrift, diligence, hard work and free enterprise. He abhors Government spending. "The poor have lost faith in the high promises of those who thought they could solve difficult problems by simply spending billions," he has said, speaking up for the poor even as his father did for the workers.

His stands are almost always applauded back home in Ventura County, as well they might be. The opinions of the people there, like Teague's own, were largely formed by Teague's father. Yet he nearly lapsed into heresy when he gave his first reaction to the John Birch Society. "In their zeal to awaken our citizens to the menace of Communism," he said, "they made statements and have taken positions that are so intemperate that they do not accomplish the objective most Americans seek." This produced mumbles from his bedrock conservative backers, who invoked the memory of his father. He got a chance to recant when Birchers were blamed for the bombing of two ministers' homes in the San Fernando Valley in February 1962. Teague rushed to their defense with this professional analysis: "While in the service during World War II, I attended a counterintelligence school conducted by the FBI. Even though the Soviet Union was at that time our ally, much of the course was devoted to the subtle terrorist techniques used so successfully by the Communists. Therefore, knowing their methods, I suggest that it is far more likely that the bombs were placed by the Communists than by members of the John Birch Society."

When Congress finally stopped the *bracero* program in 1965, Teague pointed an accusing finger at Secretary of Labor W. Willard Wirtz. The Secretary was guilty, he charged, of "rank discrimination against both our good neighbor to the south and our farmers who still need Mexican workers to keep crops from rotting in the fields." To save the crops, Teague and his fellow growers preferred to import docile, uncomplaining Mexicans and send them back when the season ended. But the California ranchers managed to surmount the crisis by recruiting native Americans—many of them Mexican Americans—to do the work. If citizen labor was less tractable than alien labor, the growers simply took precautionary measures. At Limoneira Ranch and elsewhere, patrols were organized to rove the fields and housing areas in jeeps equipped with two-way radios, searching for dissatisfied workers and other prospective troublemakers. Anyone who even looked like a union organizer was hustled away from the rest of the workers. On occasion, even ministers were captured, stripped of their clothes and held as prisoners by the patrols.

As another technique for keeping the workers down on the farm at the prevailing wages, the landowners welcomed peddlers driving station wagons piled with tacky merchandise. These credit sales could keep the laborers in financial bondage.

The abuse of farm laborers is not limited to Ventura County or to California. It is probably worse in Texas, where the fabled Texas Rangers, always the good guys who in TV westerns wear the white hats and fight for the oppressed, helped the ranchers as recently as 1967 to keep their stoop laborers stooped and submissive by breaking up minor strikes against the big ranches. Abuse can be found wherever farm laborers with little or no education try to eke out a living on meager wages. They have little voice in their destiny, and because they are uneducated and lead the lives of vagabonds, they have virtually no political power. These farm laborers come cheap and are little bother, yet they are despised by those who profit from their work, described by Teague himself as "stoop labor under the broiling sun."

On occasion the workers in Ventura County find someone who can write and send appeals in their behalf to Teague in Washington. These letters are usually in Spanish, and Teague's office answers them in Spanish, with the signature "Carlos Teague." His father would have been proud. The paternalism of "the grand old man of California agriculture" still prevails. If his attitudes seem out of date for this time in this century, even by southern California standards, it is worth recording what happened at a meeting of the trustees of the Oxnard District High School on August 4, 1965. A proposal was made—but not seconded—to apply for Federal funds to provide a little basic education for farm workers and unemployed Mexican-American adults. "If we'd starve them just a little bit, they'd find work," said John Cooley, one of the trustees. "We don't owe them anything. There is no reason why these people couldn't attend adult education classes at night. They'd be twice as productive if they had a job during the day."

The program was designed to prepare the farm workers, most of whom spoke little English and were illiterate in Spanish, for employment. The most frightening aspect of the program to many growers was the Government's plan to pay the students while they learned to read and write. The Government stipend, $75 a week, was more than many of the workers averaged while picking fruit. With the help of the state Education Department, the Oxnard program eventually got under way, but it did not win the approval of the Ventura County establishment. After all, schooling would only hamper what Charles Collins Teague called the "opportunity to enjoy life" of the farm workers.

To find labor to replace the *braceros* on the Ventura County citrus farms, the growers commissioned William H. Tolbert to round up migratory workers from around the country. Tolbert, a tough, relentless man, who later became director of the state's Employment Service Farm Placement Service under Governor Ronald Reagan, did his job well. One who responded eagerly to Tolbert's invitation to come to California was Mario Soto, a migrant worker whose last previous address had been somewhere in Texas.

3. Keeping 'Em Down on the Farm

Like Representative Charles M. Teague, Mario Soto was born on a farm. Unlike Teague, his father did not own the farm.

Soto grew up on a succession of farms, without much education or hope—just another pair of hands in the army of migrant workers who tramp the nation looking for work. Soto was recruited by the Delta Labor Agency to pick fruit for the Ventura Citrus Growers. He was given token travel-expense money, four days to reach Santa Paula, and a piece of paper entitled "Agreement to Employ." Actually, the sheet made no such agreement. At the bottom of the page, it stated: "This is not a contract for employment. The prospective employee shall be employed when he reports to the place of employment specified above." And it skimped on other promises. The document stated: "Rate of pay: prevailing piece rates of area as posted in agency office."

With his wife Anita and their 10 children, Soto got into his Chevrolet truck and headed west. They reported for work on May 22, 1965, and were assigned to the Rancho Sespe—the place where old Charles Collins Teague had died. There they were assigned to a double housing unit—a five-room shack—on the ranch. Rent was $20 a month plus utility charges. In its "housing agreement" Rancho Sespe retained the right to "cancel this license at any time even though licensee may still be working for employer. . . . Cessation of employment shall constitute termination of this license unless otherwise agreed to in writing and any occupancy by licensee after cessation of employment, during any labor dispute, or after cancellation, shall be in the capacity of licensee only." It was difficult for a man who could neither read nor write his own Spanish language, let alone English, to comprehend. Still, the Sotos had high hopes that California would turn out to be the land of milk and honey. The wages were better than those in Texas, and Mario's wife and their nineteen-year-old son, Roberto, could also work and add to the family gross.

During June, his first full month on the job, Mario Soto earned $210.97. After the deductions, including repayment of a $145 advance—the kind frequently given to workers to keep them in bondage—Soto's pay was $7.68. The family worked through the best picking months on into autumn, when the fruit still on the trees was hard to reach and the piece rates no longer reflected the effort of the job. While Anita Soto was on top of a ladder, cutting oranges off a tall tree, she slipped and injured her shoulder. A doctor told her to stop working. In September Mario switched to picking peppers on another farm where the wages were better. His son Roberto was required to sign a new housing agreement for the family; the $20 for rent and $10 for gas and other deductions came out of his check from Rancho Sespe.

If the local schools and welfare agencies did not welcome the Sotos, the draft board did. In December—a month after Mario Soto signed up for the adult education class—Roberto was drafted. Mrs. Soto asked for work in the packinghouse, where there would be no lifting, but Rancho Sespe officials refused. With Roberto training for Vietnam, there were no Sotos working on the ranch, and the housing-agreement provisions were enforced. The Sotos were ordered to move out four days before Christmas.

Appeals to the management of Rancho Sespe did no good. The general manager, Allen Lombard, simply grumbled that the Government was stealing workers off the farms. "It happened at the peak of our full harvest," Lombard growled. "We were way behind, due to the labor shortage. We had 20,000 to 30,000 boxes of lemons drop on the ground and were unable to pick our export oranges fast enough." It is not possible to verify Lombard's statement about the harvest problems. It is worth recalling, however, that Soto left the ranch in September to pick peppers because there wasn't enough work to keep his earnings up.

The eviction fight dragged on into January. One ranch official wanted to let the Sotos remain in their shack for $75 a month, but the proposal was rejected by Lombard. "We're not running a charity institution," he said.

The ranchers' suspicions of the education program were well based. As Soto began to read and write, he also learned to assert himself. Suddenly he was a proud man. After a year in school his horizons expanded, and he went looking for better work. He tried several jobs, and in March 1967 found employment at the Burmite Powder Plant in Saugus, a 60-mile round trip each day from the adequate home he had found for $45 a month in Santa Paula's Mexican ghetto. The job in the munitions factory gave him a sense of pride he had never known before. He was, after all, making things that might be used by his son Roberto in Vietnam. When friends asked him about his work, he flashed his plant badge and whispered, "You realize this is top secret."

It is no secret, however, that Mario Soto is blacklisted by

the Ventura growers for deserting the fields and cannot get work there again picking crops. He doesn't care. An American by birth, he is at last awakening to the benefits of his birthright.

Soto's escape from the perpetual poverty of the farms, unfortunately, is an isolated case. Few others have made the jump, and for many the prospects are dimmer than ever. Their living standards have been held down by the big ranchers, thus assuring their availability at low wages. From California to Texas the political power has been on the side of the ranchers, whose agricultural empires are tied into the banks, the railroads, the real-estate interests. These pressure groups have more friends in Congress than the Mario Sotos, who cannot afford the campaign contributions, law fees and other favors it seems to take to win friends and influence Congressmen.

No one has been more vociferous in championing the ranchers, for example, than California's darkly handsome Representative Burt L. Talcott, whose constituency adjoins that of Representative Charles M. Teague. Both Republicans, Talcott and Teague have always stood together, crying out in angry duet against any infringement upon the feudal rule of the ranchers.

Unlike Teague, Talcott is not himself a rancher. But his law firm—Pioda, Leach, Stave, Bryan and Ames—represents the packing and processing houses that do business with the ranches. Among them are Martin Produce Company, Salinas Lettuce and Farmers Co-op, Valley Packing Company and Admiral Packing Company. Ranchers and packinghouses alike appreciated the legislation, for example, that Talcott introduced to impose import limits on meat products.

Deprived and depressed as the migrant workers may be, they are probably better off than the Negro tenant farmers way down south in the land of cotton. There the industrial revolution has come to the plantations of Mississippi, Louisiana and Alabama. The reasons for the mechanization of the farms are partly economic, partly racial. The upkeep of a few machines is cheaper than the cost of hand labor. The Federal Government is also putting the heat on the white farm owners, who have controlled the courthouses for generations, to allow their Negro farmhands to vote and to share in other rights of citizenship. This has produced an undercover campaign to push the Negroes northward. Every day more Negro families are evicted from the shacks on Southern farms. They are hurled into a world for which they are not prepared. In the swelling slums of Southern hamlets, according to Senate testimony taken in 1967, Negro women and children endure the gnawing pains of hunger while they pray for help and hope for death. The stronger ones move northward to fill up the ghettos of the big cities.

The story is repeated over and over again throughout the South. Families who have tilled the land since slavery times are no longer wanted, and now they sit on creaking porches with distended stomachs, shriveled limbs and running sores. Even while looking at these victims of greed and bigotry, the mind rejects the knowledge that this is the United States.

4. The Good Earth

Not far away from this misery, laughter comes out of the window of a big white house, and ice tinkles in highball glasses. It is the plantation house in Sunflower County of Democratic Senator James O. Eastland of Mississippi. He is back from Washington, and the politicians, the big planters and the big segregationists have come to the farm outside Doddsville to pay homage to "Ol' Jim."

Like the starving Negroes, Eastland was born on this rich black soil. His grandfather bought it for $1 an acre, and today the Eastland plantation's 5,800 acres are valued at more than $3 million. The yearly crop alone grosses more than half a million dollars. Over the years Eastland has been a vocal opponent of what his set likes to call "big Government spending" and "creeping socialism." His prejudices in this area, however, do not apply to his own farming interests.

In 1965 Eastland, a member of the Senate Agriculture and Forestry Committee, joined forces with the chairman, Allen Ellender, D-La., in an attempt to rewrite the price-support laws on cotton. Under the Eastland-Ellender scheme, big cotton farmers would make more than ever, the nation's cotton surplus would pile higher, and the cost to the taxpayers would be more staggering. The plan was defeated, and cotton price supports were offered only to farmers taking part of their land out of cultivation. Eastland obligingly went along with the law. In 1966 he received $129,997 for cotton he didn't plant.

From his vast acreage, and from his Senate vantage point, Eastland feels he knows what is happening in Mississippi. He didn't blink when he stood up before the Senate subcommittee on manpower, employment and labor, took a dead cigar butt from his mouth and told his fellow Senators, "I deny there is mass malnutrition in the Mississippi delta." The charges of famine among the Negroes, he said, were a "libel."

In the same Senate hearing room was Dr. Raymond Wheeler, a physician from Charlotte, North Carolina, who had personally investigated the famine in the midst of plenty. He had told of the conditions and described Mississippi as "a kind of prison" for the unemployed farm workers. "It is not a medical emergency, it is a national disaster," he said.

Dr. Wheeler listened to Eastland's denial, then he spoke in a voice filled with emotion: "I invite Senator Eastland and Senator Stennis [also of Mississippi] to come with me to the vast farmlands of the delta. I will show them the children with their shriveled arms and swollen bellies, their hunger and pain, and the terror and misery of their parents."

Jim Eastland is a man who is seldom intimidated, but he had no answer for Dr. Wheeler. He did not accept the invitation to tour the delta and see it, possibly for the first time, as it really is. Perhaps he didn't care. It has been his political dogma, expressed on the Senate floor, that "The Negro race is an inferior race." The Senator has the facts on his side. He can prove that no Negro farmer anywhere in this country has received $129,997 in Government price supports.

Jim Eastland was appointed a temporary Senator in 1941. He successfully bottled up an OPA attempt to put a ceiling on cottonseed oil and made this his platform for election in 1943. Now he reigns as head of the Judiciary Committee, which, counting private bills, handles 60 percent of all Senate legislation. The committee has jurisdiction over Federal courts and judges, civil rights, civil liberties, Constitutional amendments, interstate compacts, patent claims and immigration and naturalization.

Eastland is against most of the legislation that passes over his desk. He uses his power to kill laws, stall appointments and bog down the Senate when it tries to override him. Senate Majority Leader Mike Mansfield, D-Mont., has said of Eastland, "He has proved almost impossible to move and indeed it requires really the entire Senate to budge him."

Round-faced and close-mouthed, blinking through glasses, Eastland has the knowing look of a stuffed owl. He likes to make speeches in flowing generalities about the dangers of Communism, the evils of sin and the rewards of virtue. As he talks, he often rubs perfume across his pudgy fingers, now and then dabbing a little on his chin. He has the relaxed air of a man who has power and knows how to use it.

There is disagreement over the plight of the 84 sharecroppers who work the Senator's own farm outside the sleepy town of Doddsville, Mississippi. They appear to be better off than Negro tenant farmers elsewhere in the delta region. Those who could be interviewed gave the impression that Eastland is a paternal plantation owner. But Andrew Hawkins, a forty-five-year-old former cotton chopper, now chairman of the Mississippi Freedom Labor Union, has told a different story. When he was waging strikes for higher wages for farm workers in the area where Eastland cotton is grown, Hawkins claimed that some field workers were paid 30 cents an hour for a 10-hour day, that some tractor drivers earned no more than 60 cents an hour. Workers on the Eastland farm, he said, were so poor that they sold moonshine to supplement their pay.

Allen Ellender was picked for political advancement by Huey Long when the Kingfish was fighting the big interests and his word was law in Louisiana. Today Allen Ellender's word is law in the Senate Agriculture Committee. He has abandoned the populist philosophy of his political mentor, however, and has switched from the little farmer to the big farmer. Nor is he averse to fighting in an inconspicuous way for his own interests.

His interests coincided with those of the big sugar cane plantation owners in 1955 when the Senate was struggling to pass a bill changing the quotas for sugar imports into the United States. Though a full year remained before the sugar quota act expired, the lobbyists had already mobilized on Capitol Hill. Senator Ellender naturally was anxious to protect Louisiana cane sugar growers from an avalanche of sugar from abroad. He pushed a bill, restricting sugar imports, with unaccustomed vigor one year in advance and even threatened retaliation against farm price supports if House Agriculture Committee Chairman Harold Cooley, D-N.C., did not accept the sugar import restrictions. Thus Ellender demonstrated more interest in helping the cane and beet sugar companies than in helping the farmers.

A possible reason for Ellender's interest became evident after the subsequent disclosure that he had been permitted to buy four acres of choice land outside his home town of Houma for only $10,000. It was so potentially rich in oil that adjacent lots sold for around $4,000 an acre. Yet Ellender was able to buy his land for only $2,500 an acre. The company that sold the land to the Senate Agriculture Committee chairman was the South Downs Sugar Company, an organization exceedingly interested in passing the new sugar bill. The company president, Wallace Kemper, was active in the sugar lobby and testified before Ellender's committee for a change in quotas.

Immediately after the purchase, a neighboring businessman offered to buy another adjacent four acres from the South Downs Sugar Company for the same $2,500-an-acre price paid by Ellender. He was turned down. The company was not willing to make the same offer to others that was available to its friend Senator Ellender at a time when he was urging sugar quotas favorable to the company.

Senator Ellender was not ungrateful. As the debate over sugar quotas reached a climax before his committee, and as the sugar bill was ready to be written up, Ellender took two lobbyists representing the sugar interests into an executive session of his committee. This is a serious violation of Senate ethics. On a previous occasion Senator Hiram Bingham, R-Conn., was officially censured by the Senate for similar conduct. Yet Ellender invited Robert Shields of the American Sugar Beet Industry Policy Committee and Josiah Ferris of the American Sugar Cane League into secret sessions of the Agriculture Committee, from which the public and the press were barred. Though Ellender's conduct was subsequently exposed in the press, his colleagues in the Senate took no notice. They had censured Senator Bingham a quarter of a century earlier, but the morals of Congress had deteriorated.

In the matter of conflicts of interest, the cotton and sugar Senators were outdone on at least one occasion by the chicken Congressmen. Representatives Phil Landrum, D-Ga., and Prentiss Walker, R-Miss., led the opposition to Government loans for a Pennsylvania chicken production business in 1965.

The Greater New Castle Development Corporation and Lipman Brothers, Inc., sought $2,600,000 from the Economic Development Administration for the project.

"I am concerned," protested Landrum, "because we are dealing with a prospective competitor for my area." Walker agreed: "Such a loan should have been disapproved months ago. . . . If the loan is approved, it reportedly will create three hundred new poultry farms." Both Congressmen owned chicken farms and were eager to hold down competition.

Another farmer, House Agriculture Committee Chairman Cooley, also had difficulty keeping his own farm interests out of farm legislation. His interest ran more to tobacco than to poultry. He was one of the architects of the controversial tobacco subsidy, which pays rigid price supports and imposes severe production controls, making it almost impossible for new growers to enter the field. He pushed through this subsidy program, protecting existing tobacco farmers, at the same time that he owned rich tobacco land in Nash County, North Carolina. He was the absentee owner of two farms near his hometown of Nashville. The Agriculture Department, which had to go before Cooley's committee with hat in hand for legislation, had granted his farms a tobacco allotment of 44.98 acres. Tobacco allotments were then selling for about $2,000 an acre, making the Congressman's allotment worth nearly $90,000.

While the migrant farm workers and the sharecroppers and small family farmers are denied a voice in their own destiny by the agricultural powers, the big landowners maintain their hold over Congress. Two sons of famous fathers hold seats on the Senate Agriculture Committee. Herman E. Talmadge, D-Ga., and Harry F. Byrd, Jr., D-Va., inherited their fathers' farms along with their Senate offices. The Talmadge farm produces, among other things, hams that are sold widely throughout the state, even in the Atlanta airport. Byrd's fortune grows on trees—the Byrd apple orchards in the Shenandoah Valley are the most extensive in the world, and at one time the late Senator Byrd, Senior, though an almost rabid opponent of government in business, pulled Senate wires to continue government subsidies to a non-profitable steamship line because it carried his apples to the British market.

The farmer legislators, like Teague and Talmadge, Eastland and Byrd, pretend to protect the farmer through legislation that actually increases their own profits and gouges the consumers. Their legislative efforts have produced little to improve the lot of the impoverished farm worker or to aid the small farmer. In a very real sense their Congressional power enables them to wage class warfare upon the poor. It is not merely a question of dollars. It is an issue of human misery.

7

CURBING WATCHDOGS:
CONGRESS AND THE
REGULATORY AGENCIES

1. Powerful Antennas

The double standard in Washington ethics is nowhere more evident than in the relationship between the regulatory agencies and the agencies' regulators. In the Constitutional scheme of government, the watchdogs are watched by the people most in need of watching. Congress oversees the regulatory agencies, though the greater need is for someone to oversee Congress.

These quasi-judicial agencies wield tremendous power. The Interstate Commerce Commission, for instance, can authorize billion-dollar mergers between great railroads, such as the Pennsylvania and New York Central. The Civil Aeronautics Board decides which airlines will get the choice routes. The Federal Trade Commission hands down antitrust rulings that, theoretically at least, could divorce Chevrolet, say, from General Motors. The Federal Power Commission fixes the rates that millions of consumers pay for electricity and natural gas. The Securities and Exchange Commission can put a stockbroker out of business or compel a corporation to withdraw from the stock exchange. And the Federal Communications Commission allocates wave lengths for radio and television that have become so valuable that, in 1966, station WIIC-TV in

Pittsburgh was sold to the Cox Broadcasting Company for $20,600,000 though its tangible assets added up to only $3,800,000.

These are merely a few of the powers of the commissions, which are supposed to protect the public from airplane accidents, dangerous drugs, misleading advertising, excessive utility rates, fraudulent stocks and such predatory promoters as may prey across state lines. If one company gains a monopoly on bubble-gum baseball cards, the Federal Trade Commission will save the gum-chewers from exploitation. Or if an airline pilot tries to fly his plane with a pretty stewardess on his lap, the Federal Aviation Agency will sternly admonish him. Indeed, the regulatory agencies are supposed to be watching benevolently over the innocent citizen every time he picks up the phone, switches on TV, reaches for an aspirin or boards a bus, train or plane.

Yet the citizen pays scant attention to these public guardians who are besieged instead by the lawyers and lobbyists of the corporations that are supposed to be regulated. Congress has imposed a strict code of ethics upon the agencies to make sure they are not improperly influenced by these corporate pressures. But there is a complete absence of regulation to prevent Congressional pressures.

The result has been that Congressmen have access to the commissions through back doors that are closed to lobbyists. A pipeline company seeking a rate reduction or a Wall Street firm accused of stock irregularities will usually seek a powerful Senator or Congressman to put in a word with the right commissioner. When, for example, the staunchly Republican Boston *Herald-Traveler* sought to purchase Channel 5, publisher Robert Choate induced Senator Leverett Saltonstall, R-Mass., to apply political pressure on the FCC. And when the Channel 5 case came under Congressional review, Representative John Heselton, R-Mass., sought to stop the House Commerce Committee on which he sat from investigating the case. Some committee chairmen wield as much power and influence in regulatory bodies as the commissioners themselves.

The antennas of most commissioners are sensitive to the faintest signals from Capitol Hill, particularly if these should come from the Congressional committees with jurisdiction over them. A mild complaint from House Interstate and Foreign Commerce Committee Chairman Harley Staggers about the long walk at the Washington National Airport to board Lake Central planes bound for his native West Virginia, for example, was all the hint the FAA needed to move Lake Central Airlines up to a front gate.

There are few officials in the regulatory commissions who are unable to recognize the names of the powers on Capitol Hill. There are even fewer who are willing to risk antagonizing important members of Congress. Thus it is unnecessary for a Senator to shout to be heard inside the commissions. A whisper will usually do.

Of all the watchdogs, the Federal Communications Commission seems the most eager to sit up and beg or roll over and play dead at the command of Congress. The politicians on Capitol Hill have tamed the FCC until it has become little more than a retriever for the networks. The network executives soothingly stroke its fur, confident that Congress will keep the watchdog from biting. The Congressmen, who will sit up and beg themselves for a chance to appear on stations in their constituencies, are only too happy to oblige. Observed Michigan State University's Walter B. Emery in a 1963 study of broadcasting and government, "This agency that regulates all broadcasting and a vast portion of the telephone and telegraph industries in the country, since its birth in 1934, has been viewed more or less continually by its progenitors on Capitol Hill as a delinquent child—congenitally weak and depraved, and requiring frequent discipline."

The owners of radio and television stations are given licenses to enter their neighbors' homes to peddle cigarettes, toothpaste, deodorants, laxatives, tinned soup, and what have you. Just as a door-to-door salesman can have his permit revoked if he becomes offensive, the broadcaster theoretically can lose his license. In practice, the licenses are routinely renewed every three years, with rare, rare exceptions. The station owner, if he gets into trouble with his friendly regulators, need merely cry to his Congressman. When the FCC tried to curb the merciless torrent of commercials on the public broadcast bands, for example, the House voted overwhelmingly, 317 to 43, to stop the FCC from protecting the public against this commercial abuse.

Some members of Congress, taking advantage of the FCC's timidity, have joined in applications for radio and television licenses. They are aware that strategically placed Congressmen have accumulated vast wealth from radio and television licenses, which have been awarded almost as the kings of yore awarded colonies to regal favorites.

2. The Next Voice You Hear

KTBC wasn't anyone's favorite spot on the radio dial in 1939. The Austin, Texas, station had a low-power transmitter suitable for its low-quality programs. It was a loser, and the three businessmen who owned it were running out of patience.

No one faulted the owners for the station's history of failure. One was Robert B. Anderson, who was later to demonstrate his knowledge of high finance when he became President Eisenhower's Secretary of the Treasury. He knew how to reap a fortune from his big investments, but he couldn't put the little radio station in the black. There were too many obstacles. KTBC was a sundowner; its broadcast day was limited by the Federal Communications Commission to the daylight hours. Part of its programming time was taken by Texas A&M University's campus station, which shared the wavelength.

Anderson and his partners began trying to unload the station, but they had no more luck in finding a buyer than in selling broadcast advertising. They finally received an offer from J. M. West, publisher of the Austin *Tribune,* who bid $50,000—nearly twice the investment in KTBC equipment. He was promptly given an option to buy, provided the FCC would grant him a license.

West received a new option when the station went back on the air in 1940 after a temporary shutdown. The new price, reflecting KTBC's distress, was down to $20,000, with West also promising to pay off $12,000 of the station's debts. Unhappily, a new FCC policy withheld broadcasting licenses from newspaper publishers. West and the station owners waited for two years while KTBC slipped further into debt like a dinosaur in a tar pit. They were still waiting when West died in 1942.

That was the year Lyndon Johnson went to war as a Navy lieutenant commander, and came home again, unscathed, with a Silver Star pinned on him by General Douglas MacArthur. Johnson had left his seat in the House of Representatives to go to the Pacific, but returned dutifully to Washington after President Roosevelt decided the best war work for Congressmen was in Congress. While Johnson was still in the Pacific, he was nominated for a fourth term in the House, and there was no opposition. So he came home, after a brief military career, to a promising political career. The sting of a 1,511-vote defeat in the special 1941 election for the Senate was gone. He was the protégé of both Franklin Roosevelt and Sam Rayburn, and his post on the Naval Affairs Committee gave him an opportunity to make his voice heard on the war.

Young Congressmen are usually as obscure as file clerks, but Johnson already had power. He had the backing of the Texas oil crowd, who not only provided the wherewithal for his own campaigns but also used him to funnel campaign cash to other worthy Democrats. Still, his personal bank account was modest, and politics is an uncertain profession. He was insecure. "We never really faced up to what would happen if I was defeated in politics," Johnson told friends. "My wife had a degree in journalism from the University of Texas. She always thought she could get a job on a newspaper if she had to. I had taught school a little while but I wasn't competent to go back to that. When I thought about it at all, I figured I could make a living as a salesman."

Then suddenly the Johnsons had money to invest. Lady Bird collected an inheritance that the Johnsons hoped would buy the security politics could not give. "Daddy had made about three forays to me about paying me off—that is, pay me my share of my mother's estate," Mrs. Johnson explained. "He had remarried, and I think he didn't like to have it hanging over his head." They looked over investment possibilities, with particular interest in newspapers. "I figured that my wife could be the editor, and I could sell the advertising," LBJ said. But they could not find a paper to suit them.

Johnson, regrouping after his defeat in the Senate race, had become more parochial in his outlook. Although his Washington activities were global in scope, his Texas horizons were limited for the moment to the parched hill country of the 10th Congressional District. The only Texas papers that were for sale were too far from his political base. Lyndon and Lady Bird continued their shopping.

After the death of J. M. West, another Austin businessman indicated an interest in buying KTBC. He was E. G. Kingsbury, who had the amiable, ambling personality of the slow-drawling, fast-drawing Texans in the old cowboy novels. He had approached West with an offer for the option on the station shortly before the publisher died. After the funeral, Kingsbury continued his negotiations with the executor of West's estate. On the morning of December 23, 1942, Austin's postmaster, who owed his appointment to Lyndon Johnson, telephoned Kingsbury and told him that Johnson was eager to speak to him. There was little that Kingsbury wouldn't do for his Congressman. After all, Johnson had appointed Kingsbury's son to the Naval Academy.

Kingsbury dropped by Johnson's Austin office that afternoon, and the two men chatted amicably as they sipped eggnog that LBJ whipped up. It was a pleasant, relaxed meeting. When the conversation got around to KTBC, Johnson was firm about wanting to buy it for Lady Bird. Kingsbury was not only agreeable, but he offered to help. He called to set up an appointment for Johnson with the executor of West's estate.

Even before talking to Kingsbury, Johnson made certain that his ownership of the station would not be a political liability. He wrote to the owners of Austin's two daily newspapers and asked whether they had any objections to his purchasing the station. They gave the transaction their blessing.

During Christmas week the owners of KTBC agreed to sell their station to Lady Bird. Some sources say that Johnson himself took part in the negotiations, dickering over the details at the West ranch on Christmas Day. Others claim that all the details of the sale were handled by a trusted Johnson friend, attorney Alvin J. Wirtz. FCC records show that the purchase price was $17,500 with an agreement that Mrs. Johnson would pay off the station's debts, which had risen to between $40,000 and $50,000. The station's losses in 1942 alone were $7,231 after gross revenues of $26,795.

Mrs. Johnson made her formal application for a license to the FCC on January 23, 1943, listing her net financial worth at $64,332.50 and promising "full-time and energetic efforts to engage new accounts." The application was approved in mid-February. What happened after the acquisition has been investigated and exposed in two Presidential campaigns. Reporters and politicians have sifted through FCC files in vain for evidence of hanky-panky. Yet the growth of the Johnson radio-TV empire stands as a classic case of how a power in Congress was enriched by the decisions of a regulatory agency that he, in turn, helped to regulate.

Lady Bird began her operation literally with a new broom. She looked in the corners and under the rugs and at the dirty windowpanes in the second-floor offices of KTBC. "I don't know much about radio, but I do know about cleaning house," she said as she started one of her first beautification projects. Jesse Kellam, who worked for Johnson while he headed the Texas office of the National Youth Administration and campaigned for him when LBJ turned to elective politics, came to the station as its manager. Kellam marveled at Lady Bird's industry. "She bought a pair of coveralls, a bunch of brooms and mops and some soap, and for a solid week she worked in that little walk-up, two-room radio station until it fairly sparkled," he said. "It was my job to go around town and pay the bills that had piled up in the name of KTBC. The bankers were glad to see me coming."

When her cleaning was done, Mrs. Johnson displayed other talents that were to help revive the station. She was able to master an accountant's balance sheet faster than most women can fathom a cookbook. She did not need experts to tell her that radio stations made money by selling advertising and that advertisers came to stations with the most listeners. KTBC was not in a competitive position; Lady Bird set out to make it so. "She worked eighteen hours a day for five months before we brought the station into the black," Jesse Kellam remembered. By the end of August, KTBC earned a profit—$18. Although she was already two months pregnant with Lynda, Lady Bird kept trying to improve the station's ratings. She applied to the FCC for unlimited broadcasting hours—necessitating a wavelength change—and an upgrading of its transmitter power from 250 to 1,000 watts. The previous owners had found their relations with the FCC difficult, but for the wife of an influential Congressman the regulatory body seemed most understanding. Both requests were granted.

During the war years radio was gaining stature in a new dimension. It was already established as a family entertainment medium, but now names like Elmer Davis, Edward R. Murrow, Morgan Beatty, H. V. Kaltenborn and Lowell Thomas, describing the latest moves of the Allied armies, suddenly became as popular as Ma Perkins and Fred Allen. The big news, like the big entertainment, came from the networks, and the big advertisers flocked to the network affiliates. KTBC went searching for affiliation. NBC at first agreed, then backed out with regrets after its outlet in San Antonio objected. But CBS, seeing no harm in improving its Congressional relations, gladly accepted KTBC as part of its network. For KTBC, affiliation with any network meant more advertising and more profits.

The ad revenue expanded like a Texan's boast. With the end of the war, KTBC was able to hire young salesmen to fill its time schedules with commercials. Among them were two Navy veterans who had campaigned for Johnson in his 1941 bid for the Senate—John Connally, later to become Governor of Texas, and James J. (Jake) Pickle, who worked in LBJ's Washington office while Johnson was away in the Navy, and eventually was elected 10th District Representative himself. Walter Jenkins, Johnson's administrative assistant in Washington, doubled as the station treasurer.

The change in KTBC's fortunes was symbolized by changes in its corporate structure. Its old corporation disappeared in 1945 and ownership was vested in Lady Bird's name. Two years later there was another change and the stock was transferred to a new corporation, the Texas Broadcasting Company, expanding upon the station's call letters. Johnson signed the transfer agreement as phrased by Lady Bird's lawyers, "joined by her husband . . . as required," since Texas community property laws gave him a half interest in Lady Bird's profits.

Booth Mooney, who worked in Johnson's Washington office before and after he produced the biography *The Lyndon Johnson Story,* wrote that Johnson grew "restless" while Lady Bird's station prospered. "He wanted to make money, which he knew he would never be able to do in politics," Mooney said. "Johnson felt that, with the inhibition of his official position removed to give him a free hand at promoting the station, he could help with its continued development. He was thinking about a television station, too. He wanted to get in on the material possibilities of the new world he had predicted was going to open up once the war was finished."

The material as well as the political possibilities of the new world did indeed quickly open up for him. After some hesitation, he ran for the Senate again in 1948; this time he won the primary by 87 votes, squeaked through the state Democratic convention, and was elected in November. In the Senate, he was appointed at his own request to the Commerce Committee, which has authority over the FCC. His enormous abilities were quickly recognized, and in 1951 he became the Senate Democratic Whip, a demanding job that made him a powerful national figure.

Not long after his rise to eminence, his hope of acquiring a television station became a reality. The FCC declared a freeze on new TV stations between 1948 and 1952, while it studied the saturation pattern of existing television coverage. On April 14, 1952, the ban was lifted and Austin was assigned three TV channels. Only one was to be very-high-frequency—VHF—the kind that could be picked up on most TV sets. The VHF station would be Channel 7.

Anticipating the end of the ban, Lady Bird applied for a television license a month in advance. Her application included a financial statement showing the assets of KTBC at $488,116 with net profits in 1951 of $57,983. In those days, TV stations were not the gold mines they have become today. Perhaps this was the reason that other Austin applicants did not fight for the VHF channel. One of them, however, later explained, "Lyndon was in a favorable position to get that station even if somebody had contested it. Politics is politics."

In the middle of 1952 the FCC began processing the flood of applications from across the country. On July 11 it announced approval of several new licenses. Two were for ultra-high-frequency stations in Austin. Another was for KTBC-TV, Channel 7. It began broadcasting in October with the network facilities of NBC, CBS and ABC, a market area of 45,000 to 50,000 homes, and no competition. The UHF channel, lacking both networks and audience, couldn't get going.

LBJ surged ahead in politics as well as broadcasting. In 1953, the first year of the Eisenhower Administration, the Republicans had a one-vote majority in the Senate, and the Democrats elected Johnson the Minority Leader. He won a reputation—often to the dismay of liberals—of being able to get along with the Eisenhower Administration better than the Republican leadership could. The balance of power in the Senate shifted two years later, and Johnson, at forty-six, became the youngest Majority Leader in history. He was one of the most powerful men in government.

Four weeks after the election turned control of the Senate over to the Democrats, the FCC granted Lady Bird Johnson's Texas Broadcasting Company permission to purchase KANG, a TV station in Waco, about 100 miles north of Austin. The price was $134,000, with $109,000 of it earmarked to pay off the station's creditors.

Just like KTBC when the Johnsons purchased it in 1943, KANG was a station with seemingly impossible problems. It was a UHF station, and few of Waco's citizens had TV sets equipped to receive UHF pictures, nor did they have much reason to do so. A standard-wave station in Temple, 30 miles away, was beaming NBC's programs into Waco, and another standard-wave station was planned for Temple.

Johnson had personal knowledge of Waco's TV picture. Ironically, his office had received a letter from a group in Waco seeking a VHF franchise. The letter was forwarded to the FCC with a printed "buck slip," requesting a reply for the constituents. A second letter was also referred to the FCC with a routine request that the commission give "serious consideration to the problem, based on its merits." The FCC heeded Johnson's suggestion and finally licensed the new station—KWTX-TV—on the same day, it turned out, that Mrs. Johnson received the go-ahead to buy the older, impoverished KANG.

The promoters of KWTX-TV felt confident that they could make their station pay. They had already been dickering with CBS and expected to become the network affiliate. With their license in hand, the KWTX owners were ready for serious negotiations with CBS, but learned to their chagrin that CBS had decided to make KANG its link for Waco. ABC made the same decision, even though it would have to share KANG's uncertain charms with CBS. Not long afterward, in March 1955, the Johnson station in Austin was given FCC permission to increase its power and beam programs into part of the Waco market.

Realizing that their apparent gold mine was producing only gravel, the KWTX-TV owners complained to the Justice Department's Antitrust Division, as well as to the FCC, about the competition of the Johnson-owned stations. Its lawyers were also instructed to prepare a civil antitrust suit.

Suddenly, on May 15, 1955, KWTX-TV's proprietors changed their minds, explained to the FCC that they had learned "certain facts," and withdrew their complaints. Simultaneously, ABC let it be known that it was switching its allegiance from KANG to KWTX, effective in September.

The maneuvering that led to these decisions was as long and convoluted as some of the compromises Johnson effected in the Senate. Wilfred Naman, one of the KWTX owners and its attorney, said that Johnson appeared personally in the settlement of the TV dispute. "I visited with him both in his office at the Capitol and at his home in Washington," Naman said. "I also recall once during these negotiations, I had a conference with him down on his ranch. I believe that his lawyer first suggested that I talk with Mr. Johnson." The evidence is that the conversations leading to the settlement were amicable, if afflictive. Texas Broadcasting wanted the antitrust action dropped, and it wanted a controlling interest in the KWTX corporation. This included an established radio station besides the unestablished TV station. "One of us was offering less, the other was asking more. Each of us was sparring for position," Naman said.

The conversations between the rival TV operations were at an impasse when Johnson had a heart attack in July 1955. Later that year the talks were resumed, and an agreement was finally reached. On New Year's Eve, Waco viewers could watch the mobs in Times Square only on KWTX-TV. Besides "Auld Lang Syne," KWTX-TV picked up KANG's CBS affiliation and physical assets. In return, Texas Broadcasting Company received 29 percent of the KWTX television and radio stock.

No new competitors have been licensed on the Waco scene, and the enterprise has prospered. It has expanded its holdings to include 78.9 percent of a radio station in Victoria, 75 percent of a TV station in Sherman and half of a TV station in Bryan. The Bryan station was originally set aside by the FCC as an educational channel; it was allowed to change to commercial programming, which both the CBS and ABC networks happily provided.

"I know it looks bad in the circumstances," one of the KWTX stockholders admitted. "But I'm sure that Mr. Johnson had nothing to do with it, at least I'm as sure as I can be. We were just lucky. Actually, the Johnson people were against the Bryan station. They thought it might threaten their station in Austin."

Lyndon Johnson, meanwhile, thrived on the therapy of the relaxed but opulent life at his ranch. His heart recovered; he was back in Washington when Congress met in January 1956. He resumed his duties as Majority Leader, and if his pace slackened, it was not noticeable in his performance. It was a Presidential election year, and a busy one for politicians.

The bustle at KTBC continued, too. Its corporate name was changed, in keeping with the Johnson custom, to the LBJ Company. Thus branded, it became the Austin supplier of Muzak and discovered another foundering Texas TV station. Lady Bird put in her bid for the station, KRGV-TV in Weslaco, a dusty southern Texas border village between the Gulf of Mexico and the Rio Grande. KRGV-TV had started broadcasting in 1954, but its income had not justified the investment of its owner, O. L. Taylor. Nor had its prospects sufficiently intrigued businessman H. L. Cockburn, who since 1953 had held an option to buy 25 percent of the station for $100,000 but had never exercised his privilege.

When the LBJ Company made its intentions known, Cockburn suddenly evidenced renewed interest and sought to block the sale with a complaint to the FCC. His claim was disallowed, and Lady Bird purchased 50 percent of KRGV-TV for $5,000 plus a loan of $140,000 to the station at 7-percent interest and another loan of $100,000 to a radio station owned by Taylor.

The professionals from the LBJ Company quickly revamped the Weslaco station. With FCC permission, its broadcasting power was also more than tripled, and the station affiliated with both NBC and ABC. Advertising increased, and Taylor merged his radio station with the television company. In 1957 he sold his share of the venture outright to the LBJ Company for $100,000. Taylor said this price did not reflect Mrs. Johnson's total investment, which—with loans forgiven, debts assumed and a consulting fee—totaled nearly $600,000. Three years later the Weslaco TV-radio operation was sold for $1.4 million.

The Federal Communications Commission was uncommonly generous to Lady Bird's prospering interests in other ways. On two occasions it turned down competitors' proposals that the Bryan station be moved closer to Austin. This would have put LBJ-brand stations in competition with one another.

FCC rulings also helped the LBJ television station to fight

off the only serious challenge ever made against its monopoly status. In the early 1950s Community Antenna (CATV) operations began to bring network programs to small isolated towns across the nation. CATV outlets built high antennas to trap television signals from distant cities, then piped them into homes for a subscription fee, much like Muzak. CATV quickly outgrew the original purpose of bringing television to areas without their own facilities, and began invading the sacrosanct territories of TV broadcasters.

Early stirrings were heard in Austin, where the city council began receiving requests in 1957 for a CATV franchise to bring competing broadcasts into KTBC's exclusive area. One of the applicants was KTBC itself, which thereby sought to join a trend that might be too big to fight. Another was Midwest Video Company, a Little Rock, Arkansas, corporation that had already organized CATV outlets in New Mexico, Mississippi and elsewhere in Texas. One of the Midwest Video stockholders was none other than Arkansas's fiercely stern Senator John McClellan, who had built a reputation in Washington as a racket buster. Two other stockholders were his son and son-in-law, who were also law partners of the late C. Hamilton Moses, the president of Midwest Video.

There were conferences between the competitors, and both applications were withdrawn, to be replaced by a combined offer by a new corporation, Capital Cable. If this had the ear-marks of a Lyndon Johnson compromise, there was no record of a summit meeting between the two Senators. Midwest Video's late president, Ham Moses, said only that the merger was initiated "by the mayor and some prominent citizens." The mayor was the late Tom Miller, an ally and friend of Johnson's.

The deal was complicated. Midwest Video agreed to pay the costs of bringing Austin into the world of CATV, also to pay KTBC $1,000 a month rental for use of its broadcasting antenna atop Mt. Barker to intercept the four stations in San Antonio. Without raising any funds whatsoever, KTBC was granted an option to buy 50 percent of Capital Cable within three years of the date it began its transmissions. KTBC was in no rush to have the programs from San Antonio cutting into its market, so the bid for the Austin CATV franchise languished. By 1962, however, other bidders had come on the scene, and voters began pressuring the city council for the broader range of programs offered by CATV. The decision was finally announced on January 28, 1963, amid the hoots and jeers of the losers. To no one's great surprise, Capital Cable was the council's choice.

The anger of the losers continued to swell until the mayor, at the next city council meeting on February 9, told them that it was not the city's intent to increase the power of a monopoly. To prove his sincerity, he said a second CATV franchise had been awarded to an outfit known as TV Channel of Austin. This would make Austin the first city in America to authorize CATV competition.

Both operations filed applications with the FCC to use microwave transmissions from their interceptor antennas to their distribution points, the most practical manner of feeding the captured TV signals to the city. A stumbling block for both CATV firms was a notice published by the FCC the previous December. It was planning a rule to compel CATV firms to black out programs that local stations intended to use in the future. In a broadcasting situation such as KTBC enjoyed, there is not time enough to show all the fare offered by the three affiliated networks. Many programs are taped for delayed broadcast. To protect the local broadcaster, the FCC wanted CATV stations to hold up the relayed programs for up to 15 days.

TV Channel of Austin agreed in its application to comply with the FCC's request. Capital Cable refused, causing an agonizing review inside the FCC. Both applications gathered dust while the FCC screwed up its courage. The verdict was finally handed down in July 1963, against Capital Cable and the LBJ interests. Capital immediately spent an extra $100,000 and brought its programs into Austin by wire—a strategy that put it, for the moment, beyond the clutches of the FCC. Unlike its competition, Capital was not using the airwaves, so it was immune from the blackout. It was able to relay network programs into Austin at the same time they were being shown in San Antonio and Waco.

TV Channel, though it had a two-month head start in signing up subscribers, realized it was selling second-class merchandise. It appealed to the FCC for relief from the blackout. This brought a warning from Capital Cable's parent, Midwest Video, that it would be compelled "to enlist the aid of our delegation in Congress, if TV Channel received a favorable ruling." The FCC needed no reminding of Capital Cable's political connections, certainly not after the consolidation of the Johnson-McClellan interests. The commission turned down TV Channel, whose position continued to worsen. Perhaps unfairly, and certainly unwisely, its newspaper ads contained thinly veiled attacks on Johnson. Despite the ads, TV Channel went out of business in 1965. During these encounters, the Johnson interests held no actual stock in Capital Cable, which was run by the Little Rock crowd.

Not until the following year did KTBC exercise its option, gaining half of the surviving Capital Cable. Although the company's books showed a loss of $881,824 for its operations in Austin, most of which came from equipment purchases, the business was valued at $3.5 million as of August 1966. With TV Channel out of the way, Capital Cable was bringing in $766,260 a year and continuing to gain new subscribers.

Meanwhile the LBJ broadcasting empire had to face competition in February 1965 from still another source in Austin. One of the allocated UHF stations, KHFI-TV, began broadcasting on the ultrahigh band. A year after KHFI-TV went on the air, the American Broadcasting Company agreed to switch its affiliation to the new station, then flip-flopped the next day. "It was all highly questionable," said Dan Love, the manager of KHFI. "They were unable to give me details when I asked why. They only said some problems had arisen." KHFI did wangle the right to show programs from the three networks that KTBC wasn't interested in screening. It was still left in an impossible marketing position, however, by Capital Cable's piped-in programs from other cities. KHFI asked the FCC to compel the CATV firm to black out programs it intended to use. The station charged it was "being whipsawed in a crudely transparent attempt to undercut any degree of effective competition in the Austin television market. . . . We've tried to be gentlemen for the last two and a half years, but it's been a study in frustration," said Love in mid-1967. "Being a decent, honest competitor doesn't do the job when you're dealing with the LBJ people."

The LBJ people have pushed up the market value of the Johnson broadcast holdings from $17,500 in 1943 to an estimated $10 million today. This growth process has been nourished by the frequent consent of the FCC, an agency beholden to Congress and subject to the Senate Commerce

Committee. There is no evidence that Johnson, while he was a power on Capitol Hill and a member of the Commerce Committee, ever applied the slightest pressure on the FCC to benefit his family holdings. There is not a single recorded instance when KTBC invoked Johnson's name to get special consideration. Once it asked the FCC to expedite a move of its radio transmitter site because its lease was about to expire, but the FCC refused to consider the KTBC application out of turn. The LBJ interests, clearly, benefitted from a fantastic growth in the radio-TV industry. They got into TV in its infancy and rode the crest of the wave. They also had smart lawyers who knew their way around the FCC.

Said a top FCC official, "I've never once had anybody pressure me in behalf of Lyndon Johnson. The pressure there is an obvious one, though. It simply stems from the position occupied, particularly when you have a company named the LBJ Company." No one is more aware than Johnson that political pressure can be exerted more safely, but just as surely, by being exerted subtly.

As President, Johnson now has the power to reject or reappoint the FCC commissioners. He has followed the precedent of past Presidents of putting the family holdings into trusteeship. The First Family, in theory at least, is completely divorced from dealings with their broadcasting interests. When special telephone lines were installed, linking the White House and the LBJ ranch with the ranch of the trustee for the Johnson broadcasting empire—A. W. Moursand—the Secret Service took responsibility for ordering the direct lines because of the President's frequent visits to the Moursand ranch.

And apparently somebody in the white House still had enough influence with the LBJ Company to arrange a job at KTBC for a young man named Patrick Nugent after he married the President's daughter.

3. In and Out of Commission

The contrast between Congress's own lax rules and the strict standards it sets for the regulatory agencies was vividly illustrated during Senate hearings in 1960 on Edward K. Mills, a New Jersey lawyer nominated by President Eisenhower to the Federal Communications Commission. As required, the nomination was sent to the Senate Commerce Committee for an investigation before the Senate gave its consent. Mills had previously served in Government with distinction, and his qualifications were beyond question. Despite this, he was obliged to request that his nomination be withdrawn. He said it was impossible for him to comply with Federal standards; there was a potential conflict between his private investments and his public responsibilities as an FCC commissioner. The regulations prohibit commissioners from having financial interest not only in broadcast companies but even in companies that manufacture or sell communications equipment. The law is rigid, explicit, enforced.

Mills explained that his father had established a small, irrevocable trust fund for his two sons, which was managed by trustees outside the family. Soon after the trust was established, the trustees bought stock in an electrical firm that, among other things, manufactured communications equipment. Over the years the stock had increased in value, and the trustees said they could not justify its sale. Although Mills was willing to get rid of the stock, he had no control over the trustees.

No one doubted that Mills was an ethical, honest man, and his inability to arrange the sale was the best evidence that he was completely divorced from financial control of the trust and could not influence the trustees. Yet the Senate committee felt so strongly about the ethics involved that it agreed with the nominee that he should not serve.

While enforcing this high standard on Presidential nominees, Congress places no such restraints on itself. For example, the Senate Commerce Committee that agreed to hold the FCC nominee to the letter of the law has as its chairman Warren G. Magnuson, D-Wash. Like Mills, the able and affable Magnuson is a man of unchallenged integrity.

Yet during most of his term as chairman his far-reaching investments included 10,000 shares—about 4 percent—in the Queen City Broadcasting Company which operated KIRO, its TV, AM and FM stations in Seattle, Washington.* This did not deter him from participating actively in overseeing the FCC. Indeed, in his official role Magnuson has launched in-

---

*The Senator began selling his KIRO shares in 1964 and was no longer a stockholder in the station by the end of 1966.

vestigations into the workings of the FCC. One of them was raked by criticism for its failure to produce "startling revelations," and was generally considered to be a mild probing.

The station in which Magnuson held valuable stock was one of three competitors for the lucrative Seattle license. No one will ever know just how much Magnuson's presence on the list of stockholders influenced the FCC. Nor will the public learn whether Magnuson's influence was responsible for the decision by CBS Television to switch its precious affiliation from a Tacoma station to KIRO-TV shortly after the Senator became involved. The Senate Commerce Committee also serves as a watchdog of the networks.

On the House side, the Commerce Committee chairman, until he resigned to become a Federal judge in 1966, was dry, laconic Oren Harris, the Representative from Arkansas. Almost immediately after he became the chairman in 1957, he bought 25 percent of television station KRBB in El Dorado, Arkansas. He paid $500 in cash and gave a promissory note for $4,500. At that time FCC records showed the station's net capitalization at $150,000. The station cost an estimated $110,000 alone to build. Clearly Harris had found a bargain.

KRBB applied to the FCC in 1957 for permission to increase its transmitter power from 24,000 to 316,000 watts—from almost minimum to maximum power. The increased output, it was estimated, would also increase the station's value to more than $350,000. At the time, KRBB was the only TV station in southern Arkansas, and reached 325,000 sets with an estimated audience of 800,000. The FCC authorized the expansion the following year when KRBB also changed its call letters to KTVE.

Meanwhile Dr. Bernard Schwartz, a New York University law professor whom Harris had retained to conduct a scholarly study of the regulatory agencies, broke out of his ivory tower. He unearthed evidence of favoritism and fraternizing between the regulators and the regulated. At the top of the compost pile were some smelly FCC cases. When Harris tried to suppress the investigation, the indignant professor tipped off the press, which raised an almighty clamor. This put the unhappy Harris on the spot; he had to decide whether to ignore the clamor or submit to the demands for an investigation. While he was deep in the decision process, a mimeograph machine at the FCC started churning out a news release. The FCC had decided to approve the expansion of KRBB, the station in which Harris had acquired an unpublicized interest, without waiting for formal hearings.

Harris did not spend much time investigating the FCC. He got rid of Schwartz, returned to his scholarly approach toward the regulatory agencies and found other causes to occupy his committee. One was the pressing cause of CATV, which sought to plant its community antennas throughout the country with minimum interference from the FCC. To further this end, it was whispered, certain CATV companies had offered investment opportunities to key members of Congress. The only admission came from Representative John Moss, a powerful Democrat on the House Commerce Committee, who said he had turned down an offer to participate in a CATV venture in his hometown of Sacramento, California. Although he had heard rumors that similar offers had been made to other committee members, he refused to conclude that the CATV people were trying to influence the committee.

If Chairman Harris or his family had any CATV holdings —one of the more persistent whispers—the evidence has never been produced. There was no question, however, that he was close to Midwest Video, the Arkansas firm whose CATV outlets were mushrooming all over the country. When it was threatened with the loss of seven relay-station licenses in South Dakota, Ham Moses, the venerable president of Midwest Video, appealed to Harris for a little political pressure. "We greatly need your help in this matter and the time is urgent," Moses wrote on October 12, 1962. Mrs. Harris had received regular gifts of nylon stockings from Moses when stockings were scarce during the war. Harris immediately fired off a letter to the FCC, requesting a report on the situation. The hearing examiner ruled against Midwest Video, but the more prudent commissioners overruled their examiner.

It was accepted in the capitol's corridors, cloakrooms and cocktail lounges that the FCC might show a political preference for stations with the right Congressional contacts. But no one had been rash enough to say so openly until a 1960 dispute over the award of a TV license to Capital Cities Television Corporation of Albany, New York. FCC examiner J. D. Bond took public notice of the fact that some of the stockholders were Congressmen. "Some of these individuals," he said, "have achieved civic and political prominence which denotes in them an ability to discern and be responsive to the interests of the people of their community; to be elected and re-elected as a member of the House of Representatives is such a manifestation. The aggregate civic backgrounds of each applicant are good, but Capital Cities' locally acquired familiarity with civic affairs of the Albany area is manifestly superior."

The Congressmen's political, if not civic, credentials were unquestionably superior. The applicants included Representative Leo O'Brien, D-N.Y., a member of the House Commerce Committee; Representative Eugene Keogh, D-N.Y., a member of the House's ruling clique; Representative Dean Taylor, R-N.Y., a former state Republican chairman; Representative James Delaney, D-N.Y., a member of the powerful House Rules Committee, and Representative Peter Rodino, D-N.J., who belonged to the Judiciary Committee. The lineup was too formidable for Frederick Ford, then the FCC chairman, to buck. He hastily agreed that "civic participation" was an appropriate yardstick for granting licenses.

Frank Fletcher, attorney for the Veterans Broadcasting Company, which was denied the channel, pleaded in vain that the presence of five Congressmen on the rival company's list of stockholders "should not be a factor in awarding a preference to that organization." The victory, of course, meant millions for Capital Cities. Commented David Wise, writing in the New York *Herald Tribune:* "This should be good news for Congressmen who are in a position to allow or disallow funds for the FCC and who can pass laws affecting the agency's operations."

The award brought demands for reform, and in Congress the voice of Senator William Proxmire, D-Wis., was raised in an appeal for legislation to prohibit such favoritism. "These television and radio awards are worth literally millions of dollars," he said. "It is especially unfortunate that a criterion of membership in Congress should be used by the FCC, as it admittedly is being used, to give preference in these enormously valuable awards. . . . Specifically favoring an applicant because it has a Congressman participating could turn into a form of payola. We in Congress benefit from the practice. It is up to us to end it."

Congress listened politely to Proxmire, but it did not act. And William Henry, a successor to Ford, contended that the policy of favoritism did not apply and that each case was to be judged on its merits. (Ford, by the way, maintained his interest in both broadcasting and Congress when he left the FCC by becoming a lobbyist for the CATV industry.) Legislation proposed by Proxmire would not prohibit members of Congress from having financial interests in stations but would only prevent this ownership from influencing the FCC. It is, perhaps, too much to expect that a bureaucrat or a commissioner, dependent upon Congress for survival, will ignore a Congressional call. Few applicants for licenses have the ready access to regulatory agencies that is as much a part of a Congressman's existence as his high-backed leather chair.

This easy access to the inner workings of government certainly has not deterred Congressmen from their pursuit of broadcasting licenses. In 1963 at least 33 Congressmen or their relatives had radio or television interests. In 1967 the number had decreased to 15. The fluctuations are not a measure of Congressional morality, but rather of the normal change in personalities.

Those on the list, naturally, saw nothing improper about their radio-TV holdings. A few were merely trustees for colleges that owned radio or television stations. Others claimed they had no connection with stations that their relatives owned. Mrs. Jane Morton Norton, Jr.—the sister of Senator Thruston Morton, R-Ky.—is the principal owner of WAVE-TV and AM in Louisville, Kentucky, WFRV-TV in Green Bay, Wisconsin, and WFIE-TV in Evansville, Indiana. Although the Senator insisted he had no connection with the stations, he had sufficient influence to arrange a job for his son, Thruston, Jr. As president of WAVE-AM-TV, the Senator took the precaution of resigning from the Senate Communications Subcommittee. He did not resign, however, from the Senate Commerce Committee, which also has jurisdiction over the FCC. Across the Capitol, Representative Clarence Brown, Jr., R-Ohio, has not bothered to resign even from the House Communications Subcommittee despite his 75 percent ownership of WCOM-FM of Urbana, Ohio.

Senator Stuart Symington, D-Mo., explained that his brother James was blind and got his entertainment from radio. This led James to purchase WAGE in Leesburg, Virginia. Jennings Randolph, Jr., son of the Senator, was a professional broadcaster who invested in WKLP of Keyser, West Virginia. Perhaps the most unique explanation came from Senator John

Sparkman, D-Ala. He was driving around his state with his wife, he said, when they reached a spot where the car radio could pick up nothing but static. They agreed this would be a good location for a radio station and promptly applied for a license. Ivo Sparkman, the Senator's wife, was listed as a partner in WAVU-AM and FM in Albertville, Alabama, until late 1967.

The issue should be clear to Congressmen. Representative Theodore R. Kupferman, R-N.Y., sold his interest in three radio stations after he was elected to Congress in 1966 to replace New York's Mayor John V. Lindsay. Kupferman, who was once an attorney for NBC, explained, "I don't think I should be involved in any matter concerning Federal regulation while I am a Congressmen." Others do not feel similar moral restraint. Representative Paul Jones, D-Mo., whose family until recently owned KBOA-AM and FM at Kennett, Missouri, was not the least inhibited about discussing FCC matters on the House floor. "I have had a recent experience with the Federal Communications Commission and have been the victim, so to speak, of rulings made by incompetent employees who have been given too much authority, with no supervision and no responsibility," he grumped to colleagues on February 27, 1964. "I am not saying that the commission members themselves were directly responsible for that because frankly I do not think they know what is going on in some of their departments, or what some of their hired hands are doing with the authority that has been relegated to them. When you try to talk to some of the commissioners, you are usually referred to some subordinate who under the law should not be clothed with the authority they apparently have."

It is perfectly legal—and ethical by the standards Congress sets for itself—for Congressmen to own stations whose destinies they help guide. They continue to apply pressure to bodies such as the Civil Aeronautics Board, the Federal Trade Commission and the Securities and Exchange Commission while they cash in on their own investments. Indeed, Congressmen have become the chief water carriers for the corporate interests that are regulated by the commissions.

Few have been more energetic in hounding the commissions on behalf of Wall Street and Madison Avenue than Walter Rogers, D-Tex., who gave up his House seat in January 1967, to cash in on his connections through a Washington law practice. During his sixteen years in Congress, he was supposed to represent the hard-grubbing folk of the Texas Panhandle, not the gentlemen in pin stripes who inhabit the executive suites in the New York skyscrapers. Yet he repeatedly seemed more devoted to the interests of the Madison Avenue moguls than the interests of the Panhandle. He became the champion of the advertising, airline, broadcasting, oil, railroad and other interests who appeared before the House Commerce Committee. As second in seniority, he was a power on the committee when he decided it was time to capitalize on past favors and friendships.

Despite his Texas upbringing, Walter Rogers was never much for ostentation during his years in Congress. The gray walls of his inner office were never defiled by decoration because, the Congressman said, "I hated to mar it with a lot of pictures." He could not resist displaying a couple of Lone Star emblems and a plaque from a broadcasters' organization. But instead of hanging them on the walls, he simply put them on the floor, tilted against the baseboard. "I'm a great admirer of appropriate plainness," he explained a few days after the 89th Congress closed. "I don't like flamboyancy."

As Congressman from Texas' 18th District, the bald and ruddy Rogers was anything but flamboyant. Few tourists would have picked him out of the throng of House members or, for that matter, out of the three Representatives named Rogers in the House. Like many another Texan under the benign regime of Speaker Sam Rayburn, however, Walter Rogers somehow seemed to gravitate toward two of their choicer committee assignments—Commerce and Interior. From behind the barricades of the Commerce Committee, he bombarded the regulatory commissions, it sometimes seemed, every time they tried to regulate.

The folks back home in the twenty-eight Panhandle counties were satisfied to keep sending him back to Washington every two years. His constituency was sharply divided between the urban workers of Amarillo and the wheat farmers of the surrounding countryside. Throughout the district, the strident voice of the John Birch Society was heard preaching gloom and Communist plots. While Rogers did not exactly hold this district in the palm of his hand after eight terms in

Congress, he had a pretty good grip on it. Yet he decided not to run for re-election in 1966. Why?

"A lot of reasons," said Rogers, sitting back at his desk and fiddling with his reading glasses. "I think the primary one is you feel like you have a certain debt to your family that you ought to pay." Rogers and his wife have six children, the two oldest already in college. It costs as much to keep two youths in college these days, Rogers said, as it used to cost for half a dozen. How can a Congressman raise six children on a $30,000 salary? "Well," concluded Rogers, "you can't." By his own calculation, he went into the hole about $3,000 a year while he was in Congress for a dismaying total of $50,000 over his sixteen-year tenure on Capitol Hill. If he had stayed home in Pampa and practiced law, he felt, he might have been worth half a million dollars. Instead, he said, his savings were just about depleted. While it is true he kept a law office at home, Rogers insisted he could not solicit new clients because "I thought that would be a definite conflict of interest."

His scruples did not prevent him, however, from running interference both on Capitol Hill and inside the regulatory agencies for the special interests. He introduced legislation to block the Federal Trade Commission from carrying out its duty to regulate cigarette advertising, went to bat for the Madison Avenue advertising empires when their practices came under Congressional fire, pushed a crippling amendment to stymie auto-safety legislation, helped lead the drive in the House to kill the truth-in-labeling bill, tongue-lashed FCC commissioners who wanted to regulate the CATV companies, and, of course, pushed oil and gas benefits at every opportunity. He could use withering language to devastate anyone who dared to stand up against the great corporate interests. When Dr. Luther Terry, then United States Surgeon General, testified that excessive cigarette smoking was injurious to health and a probable cause of cancer, for example, Rogers accused him of trying to "brainwash" the public and "destroy" the tobacco industry. He charged the Federal Trade Commission with trying "to run this country" because the commissioners felt they should restrict cigarette advertising.

Now that Rogers is off the public payroll, he has a new outlook. He is confident that he will find plenty of clients, although he was reluctant to discuss who they might be. He acknowledged only that he expected to have "several" oil and gas clients, at least one in communications, and perhaps one in merchandising. The railroad and trucking interest could not be ruled out. "All of these people, you understand, are interested in tax situations that develop," Rogers explained carefully. And a few of them, presumably, are likely to forget his past services on Capitol Hill.

Congressional pressure upon the top of the regulatory agencies is all too often magnified as it spreads to the lower levels. Insecure bureaucrats tend to overreact to outside pressures. Commented Harvard Professor Louis L. Jaffe, "It has been a stereotype of political wisdom that the bureaucrat is ever ready to exercise authority arbitrarily. But there is the far greater danger that the second-rate, insecure personality who often finds his way into bureaucracy will become uncomfortable at having to exercise authority and will anxiously seek to placate as many interests as possible. This fear to offend, complaisance, and readiness to listen and be 'fair' and 'reasonable' clog the muscles of the will, and what begins in amiability can end in corruption."

The flagrant behavior of some legislators not only corrodes public trust in Congress but erodes public faith in the regulatory agencies. And doubt in the integrity of administrative action poisons the wellsprings of government. For the good of the nation, the regulatory agencies need to function with the independence of courts. For its own good, Congress needs legislation to make it illegal for Congressmen to involve themselves in regulated industries.

8

ADDED DIVIDENDS:
BANKERS IN THE CLOAKROOM

1. Capitol Gains

The love affair between Congress and business has been an open secret for almost two centuries. They began to eye one another before the first asphalt went down on Wall Street. Members of Congress were not content, however, to carry on a flirtation from afar. They became businessmen as well as Congressmen. This dual role of theirs has made it difficult to sort out the motives of those who vote for business benefits. Among Congressmen with corporate investments, any comparison of personal holdings against voting records would reveal a number of conflicts. The unresolved question is: do they vote the business viewpoint out of conviction or for a profit?

In the best American tradition of worshiping financial success, many Senators and Representatives can be found in zestful pursuit of the capital gains. A few own businesses whose profits and dividends are affected by legislation. Many others of corporations whose prosperity they influence and whose conduct they help to regulate. Some purchase stocks in their own names; others find it more discreet to use the maiden names of their wives or the names of intimates. The more cautious buy their stock in a "street" name, whereby the broker makes the purchase and keeps the stock in his company's portfolio.

Members of Congress also receive advance notice of almost trade actively on the stock market, buying and selling shares all contracts awarded by the Government in their states. These contracts often go to publicly held corporations whose stock can be launched into orbit by a multimillion-dollar Government announcement. Thus advance knowledge can mean quick profits.

Consider what happened in late 1965 when Senator Richard Russell, D-Ga., hinted to Atlanta newsmen that the Lockheed plant at Marietta, Georgia, would get the $2-billion contract to build the new C-5A jet transport. The distinguished Senator was careful not to say he had inside information. But he was, after all, the Senate Armed Services Committee chairman with direct pipelines into the Pentagon. His careful hint was enough; the stock soared. As he predicted (though there is no evidence that he profited personally from the knowledge), the bonanza later went to the Georgia plant.

Senator John Williams, R-Del., the cockspur of the Senate, has protested to Secretary of Defense Robert McNamara against the "policy under which the Defense Department permits members of Congress to make the first announcement of all defense contracts that are being awarded in their respective states." He warned this could develop into "the greatest era of influence peddling we have ever seen." One reason for his concern, he said, "is the misunderstanding which is rapidly developing on the part of many contractors and the American people in general that the way to get a Government contract is to see their members of Congress."

A favorite sideline for Congressmen has been savings and loan, an industry that has benefitted from special legislation. Research for this book disclosed 26 members of the Ninetieth Congress with extensive holdings in savings and loan companies. But of all beckoning businesses, banking seems to hold the greatest attraction for Congressmen. The records at the Federal Reserve Board, listing the top 20 stockholders of each national bank, contain the names of dozens of Congressmen and their relatives.

Thus, on Capitol Hill, bank interest has become more than just the percentage of loans paid to the nation's financial institutions. It has become an almost constant preoccupation of a number of legislators who make it their business to see that the banks are not deprived. And those who have championed banking legislation have been known, on occasion, to turn up with bank stock.

Banks are regulated by Federal agencies that, in turn, are supervised by Congress. Banking legislation is handled by the

Banking and Currency committees of the Senate and House, which also process all housing legislation and hold power over price controls. It was through the Senate Banking and Currency Committee that the late Robert Wagner, Sr., D-N.Y., churned out key legislation for Franklin Roosevelt's New Deal. Through the same committee, the 80th Congress scuttled the Office of Price Stabilization. And through the Banking and Currency committees of both houses, the banking lobby gains favorable legislation in almost every session of Congress. In theory, the committees are set up to protect the public. In practice, they seem to work for the bankers as some of the Congressmen turn handsome profits from their own investments. Those who oppose the banking lobby find that the enormous resources of the nation's financial institutions are turned against them on Election Day. Those who play along sometimes find unexpected dividends.

One of the few who have thumbed their noses at the banks is that grizzled old populist, House Banking Committee Chairman Wright Patman, D-Tex. Distressed, the bankers for years turned for solace to the number-two Democrat on the committee, New York's Representative Abraham Multer, pressed and pomaded, who looks, quite appropriately, like a banker.

2. *Abraham Multer: Up from Coney Island*

On a blustery autumn day along the Hudson River, people paused to watch the churning tugs inch the S.S. *Rotterdam* into its berth at Pier 40. Some of the spectators were reporters, and as the first passengers disembarked, the bluster of the day increased perceptibly. The passengers included Senator John Tower, R-Tex., and two Representatives, Congressmen Eugene Keogh and Abraham Multer, both of Brooklyn. The gentlemen were accompanied by their wives. It was unusual for the debarking passengers to be so unhappy after a carefree seven days floating in the Caribbean.

The unhappiness first became evident when the reporters had the bad manners to ask the voyagers who paid for their trips. The Congressmen turned on the innocent charm that is an automatic defense mechanism for politicians. When that failed to work, they admitted that they had been the guests of the New York State Savings Bank Association, which had been holding its convention aboard the ship. One of the statesmen wavered in his confession. Representative Multer, biting his lower lip, insisted to newsmen, "I have always paid my own way." Several months later, in a 1967 interview, Multer made this amendment: "This was one of the few bankers' functions I attended at which I was not a speaker, in which case I think it would have been proper to have them pay my expenses." The reporters on the Hudson River pier, unaware of such subtleties, asked Multer how much he had spent for his seven days of floating luxury. "That," snapped the Congressman, "is none of your business."

Multer rather resembles the American eagle, bald and bold, with hungry eyes and clutching talons. From his perch near the top of the seniority pyramid, he could make his shrill cry heard on three House committees—Banking and Currency, Small Business, and District of Columbia. He also sat on the Joint Committee on Defense Production. Following his election to the House of Representatives in 1947, Multer drew a fine line between his personal business and the public's business that was not always easy for others to distinguish. As a lawyer, banker, businessman, lottery lord, real-estate developer, and House member, Multer often was too busy to specify exactly whom he was working for. The bankers, however, seldom had a reason to doubt his allegiance.

The spark that set Multer burning for power in the world of high finance may well have been struck one day in 1911. His father, a tailor, had been longing to move his seven children away from New York's crowded streets and build a better life for them. He saved his money and searched for an opportunity. He found it on Coney Island.

Coney Island, in those days, was not quite the crowded, noisy, dirty, slum-by-the-sea that it is today. Then it was a spa where middle-class New Yorkers went on family outings, where Manhattan children pedaled on their bicycles, and where Tammany Hall pols held forth in the Half Moon Hotel. In those uncomplicated days, before the subway reached Coney Island, Multer's father withdrew his life savings and laid them on the line as payment of a year's rent on a hotel. The tailor, his wife—who was expecting her eighth child —and the seven children moved with high expectations into the big wooden hotel. It seemed to them to be a prime location, almost next door to Dreamland ("the playground of the world") with its roller coaster, games of chance, freak show and calliope.

Two days later Dreamland and the four city blocks surrounding it—Multer's hotel included—went up in a spectacular blaze. "We weren't even unpacked yet when the fire struck," Multer said. "We literally left the premises with nothing but the nightshirts on our backs. Then something happened which my mother never tired of retelling and which left a deep impression on me. An Italian family in the neighborhood took us in, all nine and a half of us. We had nothing, and they gave us everything. The mother even bought us new pots, pans and dishes so we could have a semblance of a kosher kitchen. We were very touched. Two months later my mother had the eighth child, and my father went back to tailoring."

As the family struggled to get back on its feet, Multer was hard at work himself, putting in 72 hours a week as an errand boy for a Coney Island dairy shop. His work didn't bring much —only $3 a week—but it was enough to keep him in high school. With college, there were new jobs that kept him busy days while he went to classes at night, first at City College of New York, then at the Brooklyn College of Law. He was a railway mail clerk, then a runner for a Wall Street bank, and finally a bank clerk. He arranged to make time payments on his tuition and paid the last installment to his law school a month after he was graduated.

Somehow, in this crowded schedule, Multer found time to devote to other activities. He worked for the Young Men's Hebrew Association, also as a volunteer for the Jewish National Fund. The Italian family's kindness to his family, he said, motivated him toward a public life.

He was able to give up his job in the bank when he passed the New York State Bar examination in 1923, but he continued his interest in banking. One of his first law clients was a bank, and by the time he was elected to the House, his knowledge of the banking industry uniquely qualified him for an appointment to the Banking and Currency Committee. His committee work, of course, vastly increased his intimacy with banking. By 1963 he was able to boast, "Because of my background as a Congressman, I can tell anyone how to organize a bank just about anywhere in the world." It was not an idle boast.

Through his law firm, Multer was called upon in 1960 to exercise his bank-organizing ability in the Bahamas, where he set up the Guarantee Trust Company, a Swiss-style bank with secret accounts, and became its president. "Nassau is a tax haven," Multer explained. "That was the principal reason for establishing a bank there. The Swiss-type banking was a most incidental feature."

The element of secrecy apparently was not so incidental to Gene San Soucie, a Teamsters official and a confidant of Jimmy Hoffa's. San Soucie found Multer's bank in Nassau a convenient place to stash $266,000 worth of negotiable Ohio Turnpike bonds that he was eager to sell. They were delivered to the bank by Sam Marroso, a henchman of San Soucie's. Marroso was escorted from Miami to Nassau by Hyman Green, a respected official of the bank, who figured in other interesting deals with Multer.

Green had asked the Bank of Miami Beach to check the bonds. The bank examined one and ruled that it was genuine; then Green and Marroso flew to Nassau, with Green in good faith shepherding the bonds through customs. They were sold through a Nassau broker to Cutter-Bennett, a New York securities dealer, which turned them over to Grace National Bank. At Grace National, the bonds received a more thorough scrutiny and were pronounced counterfeit. Payment to the Guarantee Trust Company was stopped and San Soucie never got his cash. No one will ever know where San Soucie got the bonds, or why he decided to send them to Multer's bank in the Bahamas. Shortly after the thwarted transactions, San Soucie was killed in a mysterious crash while flying his own airplane.

There is nothing to link Multer directly to the San Soucie deal. But it was the Congressman from New York who set up the bank under circumstances that would not be permitted in the United States. The Swiss-style secrecy of the accounts may have been "incidental," as Multer asserted, but it was most inviting for people like San Soucie. Multer claimed he sold his interest in the bank on November 23, 1960. "I got ten percent over what I paid," he said. In August of 1961, however, his partners still insisted that Multer was involved in the bank. "An agreement was executed but it was never carried out," said Irving Wolff, a Miami lawyer who served as secretary of the bank. "Multer has not been paid off yet and still remains president of the bank in name." The bank eventually closed up.

"I filed to liquidate because of some questionable dealings, including the solicitation of funds by some officers of the bank," Multer now tells questioners. "My law firm and I did participate, as lawyers, in the organizing of the bank. It was totally offshore and out of the territory of the United States, so there could not possibly be any conflict."

Those who stop to consider that Multer helped write the nation's banking laws and in theory, at least, had an interest in preserving them might have a different view. And they might also raise an eyebrow at Multer's introduction of a lottery, the Bermuda-based Medical Award, into the Bahamas through his bank. "They asked me to organize it in Nassau," he explained. "They came to me as an attorney." Asked why a Bermuda lottery would go to a Brooklyn Congressman to organize lottery ticket sales in the Bahamas, Multer said, "A lot of people come to a U.S. Congressman."

Later a Federal grand jury tried unsuccessfully to find out how the lottery tickets, printed in Ohio, could be transported to the Bahamas without violating the United States law against transporting gambling paraphernalia across state lines. At least two witnesses gave testimony implicating Multer, but the grand jury evidently did not believe them.

Multer had less success with some of his domestic ventures. He and Adam Clayton Powell, D-N.Y., organized a small group that attempted to start a savings-and-loan association in Rockville, Maryland, in 1962. They were (perhaps rashly, considering the political consequences) turned down by Joseph P. McMurray, then chairman of the Federal Home Loan Bank Board. McMurray, who is at least as expert as Multer on banking and mortgages, received a number of phone calls from Multer, who sought to rescue his savings-and-loan charter. McMurray made it clear that he would not change his mind. Shortly thereafter he was summoned to appear before an unpublicized hearing of the House Subcommittee on Bank Supervision and Insurance, which was headed by none other than Abraham Multer. The Congressman badgered McMurray about the Rockville S&L, and challenged the Board's decision on "legal grounds." McMurray, refusing to be bullied, replied that Multer's loan association failed to safeguard the public, since less than 5 percent of its stockholders were Maryland residents. FHLBB regulations required that at least 75 percent of a savings-and-loan organization's stock be held locally. The stock for Multer's savings-and-loan project, Mc-Murray said, was controlled by "a few men from New York. . . . If a small group controls the capital of an association, there can be manipulation. For the long-run benefit of the community, it might not be good to have a few, especially outsiders, operating."

Defeated in his own hearing, Multer at least wanted the record to show that his conduct was proper. He asked McMurray, "Did I do any twisting of any arms?" McMurray retorted wryly, "Now, sir, as you know, I ran around in a sling for a long time. That was due to slipping on the ice."

Multer's worst luck came when his wife, or someone using her name, invested in the District of Columbia National Bank. D. C. National opened in the fall of 1962, the first bank chartered in Washington in 29 years. Unfortunately for Multer, the names of stockholders eventually became news. All over the capital, people who considered themselves insiders were trying to get on the inside with D. C. National. The demand for the new bank's stock far outstripped the issue. Purchasers included Bobby Baker, then still entrenched as secretary of the Senate; Senator John J. Sparkman, D-Ala., the 1952 Democratic Vice Presidential nominee, then second in command and now chairman of the Senate Banking and Currency Committee; seven Representatives from Alabama; and Bertha L. Multer, wife of the Brooklyn Representative.

When the Baker case hit the headlines, some critics charged that the high-powered stockholders influenced Comptroller of the Currency James Saxon to grant D. C. National a charter. They offered little proof to support their claim. It was demonstrated only that Baker was able to get an unsecured loan for $125,000 from the bank, that Sparkman borrowed money to buy his shares, and that the note on his loan was held by D. C. National. Saxon denied, however, that any influence was brought to bear on him.

"I had nothing to do, directly or indirectly, with the bank's organization nor did my law firm," Multer said in 1967. "After the charter had been approved, members of Congress were approached about buying stock. It was all open and proper. It was bought in my wife's name because her money was used. This was strictly for purposes of estate planning—tax purposes—and not to hide anything." The stock was sold, Multer maintained, after the storm involving Bobby Baker broke on the nation's front pages and Mrs. Multer's investment became known. Multer insisted that there was nothing improper about the purchase. Nor about his own ownership at one time of stock in New York's Morgan Guaranty Trust Company.

There is no evidence that Multer ever considered his public trust a bar to private advantage. Many interesting clients found their way to Multer's New York law firm—Multer, Nova and Seymour—which adopted the *nom de guerre* of Nova and Seymour when it operated on cases involving the Government. It did not, however, change its address or its phone number.

It was as a lawyer that Multer became involved in 1961 in the Honeymoon Isle Development Corporation, a resort development near Tampa, Florida. Multer invested $12,500 in Honeymoon Isle, and Hyman Green (the man who brought Sam Marroso and the $266,000 in counterfeit bonds to the Swiss-style bank in the Bahamas) arranged for loans from the Teamsters Brotherhood. Multer was to be paid $50,000 in legal fees for 10 years, but the partners began squabbling before the Congressman was able to collect. Multer sold his shares for $97,500, a profit of $85,000 in less than 18 months. As usual, Multer had a ready explanation. "This was a completely private real-estate transaction," he said. "I was trustee for a group investing in the deal. . . . There was absolutely no Teamster involvement in any aspect of the deal."

The Teamsters did have a slight involvement. They put up a $4-million mortgage while Multer was an investor in Honeymoon Isle. The conflicts become even more glaring in light of the Banking and Currency Committee's obligation to supervise public and private housing.

In Washington, meanwhile, Multer sponsored several curious pieces of legislation that had no apparent profit motive for him. One was an attempt to hand over the proposed Washington subway to financier O. Roy Chalk, although it had already been decided that private development was not practical. Another Multer legislative ploy was an attempt to change the Washington liquor laws. It was opposed by all three Washington newspapers and defeated in Congress, according to Multer, "because it contained a provision prohibiting false advertising." Actually, Multer's bill made it illegal for liquor stores to advertise prices, a move most observers believed would increase liquor prices substantially. Not everyone, of course, was against Multer's bill. It received strong support from Milton Kronheim, Washington's biggest liquor wholesaler.

Such expeditions into the dark forests of private enterprise were merely diversions for Multer. His main effort was devoted to the Banking and Currency Committee. Chairman Wright Patman, because of his independence from the banks, had his authority cut out from under him by the pro-banking majority on the committee. This made Multer, as second in seniority, the *de facto* chairman until he abandoned Washington in November 1967, after running successfully for election to the New York State Supreme Court. His devotion to the committee was, to his way of thinking, a pure "community service." "My position is that my conduct has always been perfectly legal, moral, proper and ethical," he has said. "Any number of Congressmen have participated in the organization of banks and savings and loans. There is nothing wrong with this. I have no stock in savings and loans or banks. I have repeatedly refused to be a director of any bank, although, again, I don't see conflict with my colleagues who have done so, even if they are on the Banking and Currency Committee."

Like his speech on the dock, after the boat ride with the New York bankers, Multer must have added mental footnotes to his disclaimer. "People don't understand," he protested, "that banking bills don't affect just one bank. If a man is a director or a partner in a single bank, that certainly does not disqualify him to pass on legislation affecting the whole banking industry."

3. Mutually Beneficial

The great legislative push by bank-connected members of Congress for the whole banking industry is exactly the point of conflict. In the forefront of this push, until he was retired by the voters in 1966, was Senator A. Willis Robertson, D-Va. He pushed through a bill in 1964, legalizing six bank mergers that had been blocked by the Justice Department as blatant violations of the antitrust laws. Robertson's legislation nullified Supreme Court rulings against two of the mergers and prevented prosecution of the other four.

The Senator claimed that his bill was drafted "with a view to giving appropriate relief to banks which I felt had been subjected to treatment that was too harsh, and specifically to three of them that had merged in good faith under the provision of the 1960 Merger Act and before the Supreme Court had announced a different rule." All of the banks concerned had, in fact, been warned by the Justice Department that the mergers would be contested despite their "good faith" and Senator Robertson's sympathy.

Robertson, an archconservative, faced the toughest campaign of his career in the 1966 Democratic primary, when he was challenged by William Spong, Jr., an able and articulate moderate. In Robertson's hour of need the bankers rallied to his aid, just as he had rallied to theirs. New York's Manufacturers Hanover Trust Company, one of the banks whose mergers had been ruled illegal in court before Robertson came to the rescue, sent letters to more than 44,000 stockholders all over the country. "We believe that Senator Robertson, Senate Office Building, Washington, D.C., would like to know you appreciated his attitude and efforts," the letter, signed by the bank's chairman of the board, hinted pointedly. Another letter, from the president of a bank in Quantico, Virginia, reminded other Virginia bank presidents that "Senator Robertson has supported us in all banking legislation." They were urged to pressure their employees to contribute to the Robertson campaign and vote for him. The specific recommendations: "Your bank cannot make a contribution, but individuals in the bank can make a personal contribution. . . . It has been suggested that each of our banks raise $10 per million of resources to this fund. . . . It has also been suggested that each person in your bank be permitted to contribute to this fund so that he may be a part of it and that he and his family be urged to vote for Senator Robertson." The bankers were also told: "Urge your officers, who have large departments under them, to wear Robertson buttons and speak in behalf of their candidates. Talk Robertson."

The letters brought in at least $30,000 for the bankers' chosen candidate. When the texts leaked to the press, however, they handed Spong the kind of campaign issue for which most candidates would gladly suffer a week of laryngitis. He issued a statement pointing out that the Corrupt Practices Act makes it illegal for banks to give political contributions. "Although the people involved," he declared, "may claim that the banks themselves are not technically involved, it is difficult for me to follow this argument."

Robertson, brought to bay by reporters, said he did not know about the $30,000 raised for him by bankers and promised to disclose all his campaign income at the proper time. He also professed not to know that Charles Emmett Lucey, the man he had hired as a researcher three months before the primary, was a registered lobbyist for banking interests. He knew Lucey only as "a splendid lawyer," the Senator said. Although he was a key member of Virginia's powerful Byrd machine, Robertson was swept out of office. Now, at eighty-one, he is employed by the bankers as a consultant.

The bankers had more trouble battering Robertson's bank-merger bill through the House, but they managed it just the same—through some highly questionable methods. Banking Committee Chairman Wright Patman, who distrusts bankers instinctively, had set out to block the bill. His worst suspicions were confirmed on an October day in 1965 when a majority of his committee—all the Republicans and a handful of Democrats—met in a rump session to approve the bill. The rebels, led by Representative Thomas Ashley, R-Ohio, waited until Patman had left to take his wife to the hospital, then summoned their forces to the committee room where, for secrecy's sake, they worked without lights. They had already shouted out unanimous approval before Patman returned and found them. He impounded the stenographic transcript. "I am really saddened by this disgraceful performance," he told the House that afternoon.

The participants in the rump session showed no inclination to repent. Until they seized control of the committee, it had appeared that Patman had managed to block the bill. Confronted with mutiny, however, Patman was compelled to accept a face-saving compromise in January 1966, and the bankers' mergers were saved. It is worth recording that Ashley's legislative assistant was Kathleen Lucey, sister of the same banking lobbyist, Charles Emmett Lucey, whom Robertson planted on the Senate payroll.

Like Robertson, Congressman Ashley found the bankers

most appreciative. During his 1966 re-election campaign, O. B. Anderson, executive manager of the Ohio Bankers Association, wrote to bank presidents in the state, urging them to support the Congressman "in every possible way." He listed Ashley as one of seven legislators who "have shown an understanding of banking matters and a willingness to help develop sound laws on these subjects." Unlike Robertson, Ashley was returned to Congress by a comfortable margin.

The defeat of Robertson left Senator John McClellan, D-Ark., one of the twenty largest stockholders in the First National Bank of Little Rock, as the banking industry's most obedient champion in the Senate. He offered a sympathetic ear to bankers who had worked themselves into a state of apoplexy over Comptroller of the Currency Saxon's policy of breaking up banking monopolies in many cities by chartering new national banks. Not long after his appointment in 1961, he was granting new charters at the rate of fifteen a month against an average of two a month during the previous ten years. The grim McClellan, the embodiment of righteous wrath, soon opened up his Senate artillery upon Saxon. As chairman of the Senate Investigating Committee, he held headline hearings into the failures of three newly chartered banks. He also appeared before the American Bankers Association convention to charge that "too many national banks are being unwisely chartered too fast and too freely" by Saxon. The Senator did not, of course, mention that among the charters he was particularly anxious to block were three for the Little Rock area. One would have been in direct competition with McClellan's First National Bank. Another would have brought competition to a suburb where McClellan also had an interest in the existing Bank of West Memphis, Arkansas. He was joined in his opposition, incidentally, by Representative Wilbur Mills, D-Ark., the House Ways and Means Committee chairman, who owned stock in Little Rock's Worthen Bank and Trust.

After McClellan made his headlines, he abruptly adjourned his investigation. An intra-office memo, circulated inside the office of the Comptroller of the Currency, summarized the results:

McClellan looked into the failures of three national banks, one organized in 1892, another approved by Saxon's predecessor and the third approved by Saxon. McClellan did not pursue his announced intention of looking into any of the failures of state-chartered banks. In the last three years, there have been sixteen state bank failures versus three national bank failures.

Now, [House Banking Chairman] Patman has launched his own investigation, leading off with one of the state bank failure cases. A significant sidelight to the Patman investigation—and one that has escaped attention—is Patman's action in obtaining an executive order giving his House Banking and Currency Committee authority to inspect federal income tax, estate tax, or gift tax returns for 1956 through this year "if the inspection of these records is connected with the investigation." Republican minority members of the committee are up in arms over this as they see far-reaching implications. Some believe that Patman, with this power, could look at tax records of almost anyone in the banking industry, including even Congressmen who are bank directors.

This was a frightening prospect, indeed.

One of Patman's investigators, Ray Cole, called upon Comptroller Saxon and subsequently prepared this confidential report of the conversation, dated March 4, 1966:

> Relative to Saxon's testimony before the McClellan Committee [March 1965] and the Senate investigation, Mr. Saxon stated that in the San Francisco Bank case they had provided for the Committee their complete file. Further in the hands of the McClellan people, the context of the files was exaggerated, twisted and blown all out of proportion for publicity purposes. Mr. Saxon stated that copies of their files were even printed and sold on the West Coast by a public relations figure (not otherwise identified). Mr. Saxon stated that because of his unhappy experience with the San Francisco file and the McClellan Committee, he would not again provide such service to a Congressional committee. . . . During the discussion, Saxon, appearing the aggrieved public servant, told of Senator McClellan's banking interest, his membership on the board of the Little Rock bank, his association with the West Memphis bank, and efforts McClellan had made to [oppose] three charters.

If Saxon was indignant over McClellan's banking ties, he showed more tolerance toward a Congressman who overnight got into the banking business. On August 7, 1963, the Comptroller rejected an application for a national charter to establish a new bank in Silsbee, Texas, the Neches National Bank, which had only one state-chartered bank to serve some 9,000 people. Seven months later he approved a charter for the same bank. He also wasted no time in granting the approval. A charter application usually lingers in Washington at least sixty to ninety days before a decision is handed down from the Comptroller's office. The Silsbee papers arrived in Washington on February 2; in a record twenty days the application was as good as gold.

The only significant difference between the two charter applications was that the name of Jack Brooks appeared on the second application as the bank's majority stockholder and board chairman. Brooks happens to be the Representative from that section of Texas, a power in the House and a close confidant of President Johnson. When newsmen started to ask questions, Brooks described his interest in the Neches National Bank as "a perfectly valid business venture." Indeed, he added, the bank's prospects were so good that "I borrowed all the money I could get my hands on to buy the stock." It is illegal, of course, to borrow money from a bank to purchase its stock. Brooks did not say whether another bank had been openhanded enough to lend him money so he could get a national charter for a competitor. He just mourned, "I'll probably be an old man before I get it all paid back." He was a spry forty-one at the time.

In all, nearly forty Senators and Representatives are linked by stock or directorships to national banks. More are investors in the state banks and in savings-and-loan associations. The relatives of at least 100 members of Congress have also been identified on the lists of bank stockholders. In addition, the law firms of many other Congressmen collect legal fees from banks.

Patman described how the seduction sometimes takes place. "One clever means of anti-public action by the banking lobby," he said, "is as subtle as a wart on a movie actress's nose. It takes the form of offering a Congressman bank stock either free or at a cost greatly under the market value. A member of my committee was approached and offered $14,000 worth of bank stock as a gift. I am proud to report that he is of such caliber that he told the would-be donors to get out of his office and stay out."

The Congressman was Representative Henry Gonzales, D-Tex., who was obviously embarrassed at the disclosure. He acknowledged that the attempted bribe came in a conversation with a well-known businessman-banker from San Antonio, his home town, on a summer day in 1963. "You are very popular in the part of town where we are going to have the bank," Gonzales paraphrased the businessman's pitch. "It would be very helpful to have you in a serious business enterprise. In fact, we would like you to be chairman of the board."

The businessman reached for his briefcase and started to open it. "We have prepared some papers," he said. "We think it would be a mutually profitable arrangement. We know you don't have any side interests, and your name would be helpful to us. It would give you a chance to be in a serious, dignified business."

"Surely," said Gonzales, "you know I am a member of the Committee on Banking and Currency of the House." The businessman looked at him quite innocently and replied, "No, I didn't know that." The Congressman continued his account: "I felt a swelling up within me of a little anger. I got a little mad. I said to him, 'You are not going to tell me you were not aware of my committee standing.'" Undaunted, the man from the bank repeated his offer: "Well, I have these papers here, and we are going to let you have $14,000 in stock." The money, he suggested, could be paid back "in time." Gonzales showed his visitor to the door. Only the refusal by Gonzales, apparently, made the incident unique.

Representative George E. Brown, Jr., D.-Calif., gave another account of the process of corruption: "I have stock holdings in both a savings-and-loan company and a nationally chartered bank. I'm a director of the S&L, and I am an organizer of the bank in my district. Politicians are generally offered stock opportunities to purchase stock at opening price. In California it's a stock bribe equal generally to double the amount of the original cost. It is a commonly held myth by people interested in forming these things that there is heavy political involvement. In order to protect themselves, they will ask a Congressman to intervene. However, I honestly don't think there is much a Congressman can do.

"In California people bought stock after World War II for, say, $10 a share and sold it ten years later for $1,000 a share. In other words, you could divest yourself for a hundred times more profit. So $1,000 worth of stock became worth $100,000. This is not so true today. The state and Federal regulation agencies have reduced this unearned increment in two ways—first, by increasing the capital required to charter, and, second, by increasing the number of charters." Though the benefits have been drastically reduced, permitting Congressmen merely to double the value of their stock, they can apparently still get in on the ground floor.

Brown is a vice president and director of Monarch Savings and Loan of Los Angeles. Three other Los Angeles Congressmen have a financial interest in local savings and loan companies: Chet Holifield, D-Calif., Pacific Savings and Loan; Glenard Lipscomb, R-Calif., Lincoln Savings and Loan; and Edward Roybal, D-Calif., Eastland Savings and Loan. Senator Everett Dirksen, the wooly-haired Senate Republican leader, owned shares in Chicago's First Federal Savings and Loan at the same time that he served on the Senate Banking and Currency Committee. He left this committee to accept a seat on the Senate Finance Committee. Both groups process legislation affecting the savings and loan industry. Another Finance Committee member, Senator Herman Talmadge, D-Ga., is a leading stockholder in the Clayton County Savings and Loan Association of Jonesboro, Ga. On the House side, Representative Tom Curtis, D-Mo., who influences savings-and-loan legislation as a member of the Ways and Means and Joint Economic Committees, is affiliated with St. Louis' Lafayette Savings and Loan.

Congressmen caught with a little financial stock stuffed into their safe-deposit boxes generally excused themselves by pointing to the example of their elders. One who was repeatedly cited was Representative Howard Smith, D-Va., the wily House Rules Committee chairman until his defeat in 1966 by a less ancient candidate. Congressman Brooks, for instance, blurted upon the discovery of his banking interests, "Why, Judge Smith was a stockholder of a bank in Alexandria before I was born!"

For that matter, Judge Smith (he retained the title throughout his Congressional days although he forsook the bench for the Hill in 1930) had a number of outside interests. He raised dairy cows at Cedar Hill, his 170-year-old place in Broad Run, as well as on two other spreads in Fauquier and Prince William counties. The milk from the judge's Guernseys and Holsteins ended up on many a Washington breakfast table.

Judge Smith's tailoring had an antebellum cut, but he was not entirely impervious to change. He did not go back to wing collars, for instance, after the style changes and shortages of World War II made them impossible to get. He also progressed from pince-nez on a black ribbon to gold-rimmed bifocals during his Congressional days. But he had old-fashioned ideas about taking care of his kinfolk. During the 89th Congress, for example, he quietly pushed through the House a bill that would have changed Washington's zoning regulations to allow the use of a 17-room Washington town house as a chancery by Niger's diplomatic mission. This uncommon interest in the housing problems of an African mission by a diehard opponent of Negro integration was stimulated, it developed, by one Robert B. Norris, who had sought unsuccessfully to obtain a variance from Washington's ban on diplomatic chanceries in certain residential areas. Having no Congressman of his own, he went to Judge Smith, who happened to be his uncle by marriage. The judge also was acquainted with the house's owner, Mrs. Leo B. Norris, who happened to be his son's mother-in-law. Judge Smith got their bill through the House all right, but it ran aground in the Senate.

It was also quite true, as Congressman Brooks suggested, that Judge Smith was a bank stockholder. He held 1,340 of 100,000 shares issued by the Alexandria National Bank, with assets of more than $36 million. Indeed, he was chairman of the bank's board of directors, and his son, Howard W. Smith, Jr., was attorney for the bank. Banking, in fact, seems to be the favorite sideline of the Virginia delegation. While Senator Robertson was being defeated, in part because of his backing by the banks, Senator Harry F. Byrd, Jr., was elected to a full term with the less blatant support of the bankers. He is the second biggest stockholder in Winchester's Shenandoah Valley National Bank and sits on its board of directors. His late father, whose seat young Harry inherited, was chairman of the Senate Finance Committee.

Representative Watkins M. Abbitt is a director of the Farmers National Bank of Appomattox. Ex-Representative W. Pat Jennings, who sat on the House Ways and Means Committee until his defeat in 1966, was a director of the Bank of Marion. And, as befits a former governor of the Old Dominion, Representative William M. Tuck sits on the board of not one but two banks: the Citizens Bank of South Boston, Virginia, in his home district, and the State-Planters Bank of Commerce and Trusts in Richmond, which is far enough away not to be in direct competition. Tuck also finds time to handle an occasional legal matter, though he claims he does not keep up with his old law firm the way he used to. "When I left my law firm," he said in his office, nervously relighting a cigar butt and tossing the snuffed-out match on the rug behind his desk, "I told the boys I would like to remain a limited partner of the firm. I have never taken any Government subsidy. I feel I should not draw money from the Government other than my salary." But this does not mean a man who goes to Congress should give up all his outside sources of income, according to Tuck. "I feel a man who doesn't have anything isn't worth being here," he said forthrightly. "He's just another one of those relief-eaters."

Another Virginia Congressman who has been able to get by without relief is Representative Joel T. Broyhill, who is a stockholder in two banks, the First National Bank of Arlington and the Arlington Trust Company, plus the United Savings and Loan Company in nearby Alexandria. He has voted down the line with the bankers, and at a closed meeting of the House Ways and Means Committee, he argued mightily for an exemption from the Bank Holding Company Act for the huge Financial General Corporation. Both his banks happen to belong to the 27-bank empire of Financial General. Broyhill has also been a stockholder in another lending institution, the Federal Services Finance Corporation, which went out of business in 1966 after it was exposed for gyping American soldiers on auto loans. It started by practicing simple usury—lending soldiers money to buy cars with interest rates as high as 100 percent. Then the company developed some original methods of wringing more money out of unsuspecting GIs. There was the hidden $30 charge, for example, for maritime insurance on cars shipped home from overseas and automatically insured by the Government. Dummy corporations were also set up to bid on repossessed cars after the GIs could not keep up with the company's outrageous interest payments. Federal Services Finance would accept low "competitive" bids from its own phony corporations, file suit in court for the rest of the money supposedly owed on the car by the hapless buyer, then take over the car from the dummy corporation and resell it at a generous profit. One Army legal officer who investigated the scheme described it as "extortion pure and simple." Broyhill was down for 315 shares on the company's list of stockholders.

Not that Broyhill is primarily a banker; he is really a real-estate man, though he claims no longer to be "actively associated" with the firm of M. T. Broyhill and Sons. It should not be difficult for him to keep up with the company, however, since his brother Marvin is president, and a cousin, Thomas Broyhill, is executive vice president. The Congressman has been repeatedly re-elected because of his reputation as a man who can do something for his constituents. Yet when he sponsored a $28-million sewer line from Dulles International Airport, he did not bother to route it through his district. Instead, he arranged for the line to be routed hard by the suburban Sterling Park real-estate development, owned by M. T. Broyhill and Sons.

4. Mind Your Own Business

Some legislators' business involvements can be traced through the meager records available to reporters, and occasionally these provide a clue to what is going on behind the legislative scenes. Year after year, for example, the "truth-in-lending" legislation was bottled up in a Senate Banking and Currency subcommittee. The law would require lending institutions to disclose in advance the actual amount of a borrower's commitment and the precise rate of interest he must pay. The bill was introduced following exposés of widespread overcharging, particularly by retailers who sold cheap merchandise on credit to the poor. Opposition to the legislation came, in general, from bankers, loan companies and retail merchants. The votes that repeatedly blocked action on the bill were cast by Senators A. Willis Robertson, D-Va., Wallace F. Bennett, R-Utah, Peter Dominick, R-Colo., Edward Long, D-Mo.,

Thomas J. McIntyre, D-N.H., Milward L. Simpson, R-Wyo., John J. Sparkman, D-Ala., and John G. Tower, R-Tex. Although all the Senators may have voted their conviction, some stood to reap a personal gain from suppressing the legislation.

Long and Bennett, for example, are investors in businesses in which interest rates contribute heavily to their profits. Senator Bennett, a former president of the National Association of Manufacturers, is head of an automobile distributorship and director of a fire insurance company. Long is a director of a St. Louis bank. Senator McIntyre's law firm represents both banks and insurance companies. Senator Dominick's former law firm represented the Colorado Bankers Association. The strategic votes were cast in the quiet confines of the committee room, where the heavy wooden doors shut out the public. Would the votes have been different if the voters were aware of the possible conflicts?

Another businessman in the Senate, B. Everett Jordan, the Senator from Saxapahaw, N.C., conducted the Bobby Baker hearings. Whenever the name of a Congressional colleague entered the discussion, he looked the other way. "We're not investigating Senators," he said. He was, it developed, in no position to investigate Senators, for he happens to be the wealthy owner of a textile plant as well as an officer and director of Sellers Manufacturing Company at Saxapahaw. On several occasions he has argued in the Senate against increases in foreign textile imports, thus tending his company's cash register from the Senate floor.

Some Congressmen help finance their businesses with Government contracts. One, Representative William "Clean Sheets" Cramer, R-Fla., has managed a small subsidy for his St. Petersburg laundry by using his administrative assistant, Jack Insco, to oversee the laundry operations. Although Cramer voted against the war on poverty, or perhaps for that reason, his laundry was granted an exclusive contract, without competitive bidding, to supply clean linen and do the dry cleaning for the Women's Job Corps camp in St. Petersburg. The contract, worth approximately $24,000 a year, was awarded by the contractor who runs the camp for the Government. Cramer's laundry also provides laundry services for MacDill Air Force Base, though the contracts—good for approximately $80,000 a year—were subject to competitive bidding. Jack Insco runs the laundry, though his salary as

Cramer's administrative assistant is paid by the taxpayers. The enterprising Representative has also paid some of his past printing bills by putting Caroline Baron, wife of his printer, on the Government's payroll. A year after he hired her, he arranged for the owner of the Art Press, Carl Baron, to draw a Government salary.

There was also the case of Representative H. Allen Smith, R-Calif., who sought to kill Congressman Wright Patman's investigation of tax-exempt foundations and hoped to pick up a little personal business from the grateful foundation heads. Smith challenged Patman's right to subpoena foundation records. "I do not think," declared Smith in a House speech, "we should pester some of these good foundations and get all their records, more records and more records." He rose on the House floor at the same time that the trustees of the Irvine Foundation, one of the biggest in California, were refusing to submit any more records to the Patman committee. The Irvine Foundation owns 93,000 acres of land in southern California's suburban Orange County. At least 13 miles of this choice real estate extends down the Pacific Coast. Thus the Irvine Ranch, now chiefly devoted to growing oranges, constitutes one of the most important prospects for suburban real-estate development in California, and a number of real-estate men have wanted to get part of it. Congressman Smith is one of those realtors.

Smith's personal interest was revealed when he wrote to Mrs. Thurmond Clarke, mother of Joan Irvine Smith, largest stockholder in the Irvine Ranch:

> On another subject, for the past year or two, I have been trying to get started at Irvine, maybe building an office building, apartments or other facilities. A very excellent builder friend of mine, named Frank Howard, and another close friend, Lou Lewis, have moved to Irvine Terrace and are anxious to move their building facilities into the area and try to get started and grow along with the development of the Irvine Ranch. We have had a number of conversations with Charlie Thomas and Mr. Porter and others who have certainly been most cooperative. I simply wanted to mention this because I know that we could build in accordance with the regulations in a very outstanding manner, and if some opportunity opens up, we would certainly be

interested. Of course we're not in the million-dollar category of large developments but could do a very good job on what we're able to do.

What the Congressman did not know was that Mrs. Clarke and her daughter Joan, unlike the other trustees, were not opposed to the investigation, and Joan Smith cooperated fully with the Patman committee. They did not respond to the Congressman's brazen proposal.

Even when a law exists to constrict Congressional misbehavior, it is seldom invoked. Take the case of ex-Representative William Miller, R-N.Y., who ran as Barry Goldwater's Vice Presidential candidate in 1964. Representative Don Edwards, a freshman from San Jose, California, sought to apply House Rule VIII against Miller. The rule states that "every member . . . shall vote on each question unless he has a direct personal or pecuniary interest in . . . such a question." Edwards had learned that Congressman Miller had made speeches and voted to reduce the tariff on the raw materials of felt at the same time he was receiving a $7,500 retainer from the Lockport Felt Company, and was a major stockholder in Lockport Holdings, a wholly owned affiliate of Lockport Felt. He owned one-fourth of the company. Miller's law firm, in which he was the senior partner, also represented Lockport Felt before the Federal Trade Commission in an antitrust case.

When Edwards gave public warning that he would debate the conduct of Congressman Miller, however, House leaders had no intention of permitting him to lift the lid off Pandora's box. To proceed, Edwards asked for a special order to conduct the debate. Under the special order he could not get the floor until the close of all legislative business, and he waited patiently all day. When he rose to speak, however, he was blocked by Representative Charles Halleck, R-Ind., who incorrectly charged that Miller had not been notified. Then Halleck suggested the absence of a quorum, and the House was abruptly adjourned. The next day Congressman Edwards tried again. But by then the pressure began to mount. A Democratic Representative from Brooklyn cautioned that Edwards would be blackballed on committee assignments. When he would try to get his private bills passed, he was told, both Democrats and Republicans would gang up on him. A California Democrat told Edwards he was upsetting the understanding between Democrats and Republicans. The Congressman was also warned that he would be called to order the minute he got on his feet. He gave up. He could not buck the system.

He was not the first to be frustrated in an attempt to reform the Congress. As John Fischer has explained in *Harper's Magazine,* nearly all Congressmen "faithfully observe one of the most ancient rules of politics: never squeal on a colleague. This great principle transcends party lines. It links Democrats and Republicans alike in a silent brotherhood, The Politicians' Mutual Benevolent and Protective Association."

Mr. Fischer, who covered Capitol Hill before becoming editor of *Harper's,* wrote that one Senator (whom he privately identified as the late Senator Pat McCarran, D-Nev.,) "was notorious in Washington for his close relationship with a certain large corporation. He looked after its interests assiduously, both in the handling of legislation and in its dealings with the agency which regulated its affairs. Every member of the Senate knew this. Many of them detested him, politically and personally. Yet no senator ever mentioned this curious symbiosis in open debate when reporters suggested—as several of us did— that it might make an interesting subject for Senatorial investigation, his colleagues either laughed or looked appalled."

The situation hasn't changed in the years since Pat McCarran. Vested interests still have their way while many of the good men turn their heads and hold their noses, explaining to themselves that politics must be this way and never acknowledging that they make it this way.

III

THE ABUSES
OF PRIVILEGE

9
THE FINE ART OF JUNKETING

1. *Wide Wide World*

Each year, Senators and Congressmen crawl like army ants over the world, kissing the Blarney stone, intruding into King Faisal's harem, sipping rum-and-Coca-Cola at Bimini's End of the World Bar, poking their legislative noses into every place from the back alleys of Paris to the front lines in Vietnam. Many of the trips are of unquestionable value to the nation. Contacts are made, understanding is reached, legislation is born. Many of the trips, however, are all-expenses-paid vacations in official guise.

Congressional junkets cost the taxpayers $695,671 in 1965 and $718,278 in 1966 (the latest available totals) if the official audits are to be believed. But each Congressman makes his own audit, and for every dollar of record, legislators on the loose spend several unreported and uncounted dollars.

These are discreetly hidden from the taxpayers' view in the budgets of U.S. agencies and embassies, which feel this is the least they can do for the Congressmen who pass upon their appropriations. All together, millions of dollars are squandered overseas by men who preach Government economy at home.

Embassy staffs are sometimes able to render valuable assistance to touring legislators by providing information, making appointments and expediting arrangements. But all too often embassy personnel are treated as lackeys, luggage carriers and pimps by the tourists from Capitol Hill. Grumps a former member of the VIP section of the Madrid embassy, responsible for the care and feeding of Congressional visitors, "Almost invariably Congressmen talk too loudly, drink too heavily, spend too much and stay too long."

Congressmen have found at least half a dozen ways to charge the public for their travel:

Appropriated Funds—Money is authorized by Congress to pay the expenses, travel included, of its committees. Some committees also have confidential funds, which the chairmen spend without giving the taxpayers any specific accounting. Out of these funds, for example, Representative John J. Rooney, D-N.Y., takes at least one trip abroad each year. Under the Reorganization Act, each committee is eligible for an additional $10,000 annually for miscellaneous expenses, and travel seems to be a favorite miscellaneous activity.

Counterpart Funds—Local currencies held by our embassies are available to touring Congressmen. These funds could be spent without an accounting until repeated embarrassments forced Congress in 1964 to limit spending to $50 a day plus transportation costs. Some fast-moving Congressmen have managed, however, to collect their full per diem allotments twice or more in the same day by arranging stopovers in more than one country. And in Ceylon, the Democratic Republic of the Congo, Egypt, Ghana, India, Israel, Pakistan, Poland, Tunisia and Yugoslavia—where the supply of counterpart funds seems limited—Congressmen can still help themselves to all the local currencies they can stuff into their pockets. This is how some do their Christmas shopping.

Representational Funds—Almost a million dollars a year are distributed among embassies for official entertaining. This helps lighten the burden for diplomats who are called upon to pick up the checks for Congressional high jinks abroad. Usually the social demands upon an embassy exceed the entertainment budget. Once the Dublin embassy, its liquor allowance low, faithfully followed the custom of stocking the hotel rooms of visiting Senators with liquor, then handed the bill to a flabbergasted Darrell St. Claire, the accompanying clerk.

Contingency Funds—Emergency money is provided embassies and consulates to help out stranded American travelers, such as seamen and students. These funds sometimes are tapped, according to insiders, by non-stranded Congressmen, too.

Agency Funds—Among Congressmen who like to cover up their overseas bills, the favorite arrangement is to travel as guests of Government agencies. The State and Defense departments offer the best Congressional tours; no more de luxe service is available anywhere. There is no bother over schedules, accommodations, baggage and the other travel nuisances. For a worthy Congressional group the Air Force will provide a plane from Special Air Mission—complete with escort officers, pretty stewardesses, baggage handlers, sometimes even a doctor with a first-aid kit full of bicarbonate. The military escorts, boon companions all, pick up the tab for everything.

Ex-Secretary of Defense Robert McNamara, torn between his passion for economy and his desire to influence the right people on Capitol Hill, set up a point system to limit this free-travel plan. Each of the armed services is charged one point for each day it is host to a Congressman. The limit is 300 points a year for each service, and freshmen Congressmen are excluded from the fun.

The Congressmen who really count, of course, receive point-free travel. House Armed Services Committee Chairman L. Mendel Rivers, the doughty Democrat from South Carolina, for one, seems to regard the Air Force as his own private airline. The Air Force will have a jet warmed up and waiting for him any time he feels the urge to travel, whether he wants to fly home to Charleston for the weekend or take a brief fling in Paris. A pilot, chatting with a visitor at Andrews Air Force Base before taking off for Madrid in an empty Boeing 707, said he had been ordered to pick up Rivers and fly him home. Similar travel privileges are available to key members of the Armed Services Committees, the Defense Appropriations Subcommittees, and the Government Operations Subcommittees. Still other Congressmen get around the point system by junketing while on "duty" as reserve officers taking their annual "training."

The idea behind Congressional travel, justifying the taxpayers' considerable investment, is that Congressmen should learn more about the world whose destiny they help to shape. The wider they wander, so the theory goes, the better they will understand world problems. This theory has been shattered by two compulsive travelers from Louisiana, whose views have narrowed as their horizons have broadened. They are Senator Allen J. Ellender and Representative Otto E. Passman, both Democrats.

2. Allen Ellender: Ambassador of Ill Will

For the reporters, it was to be just another tedious interview with a self-important visiting American. For Senator Allen Ellender, it was another chance to tell foreigners how to manage their own affairs. They sat facing each other in the cool recesses of the American Library Auditorium in Salisbury, Southern Rhodesia. It took him only a few moments to damage years of patient American diplomacy aimed at winning the confidence of the emerging nations of Africa.

Ellender cleared his throat and told the white-supremacist Salisbury press, "If there is any part of Africa in which the natives have built up a community of their own, I have yet to see that area. The average African is incapable of leadership except through the assistance of Europeans." His words spread like a chain reaction across Africa and to the world beyond. Allen J. Ellender, whose career in the United States Senate is distinguished largely by his ability to outlive Senators with more seniority, was suddenly, that day late in 1962, on the front pages of the world.

When his commandeered Air Force plane touched down at his next stop, Dar es Salaam in Tanganyika, a crowd awaited him at the terminal. Ellender beamed as he surveyed the scene, squared his ancient shoulders, and brushed aside U.S. Ambassador William Leonhart, who had sprinted up the ramp to warn that the crowd was hostile. "Wait a minute," the Senator directed the ambassador; then he flashed a toothy smile at the photographers who swirled around the plane. "Come on," he told them happily, "take some more, boys."

He was still grinning when a Tanganyikan official elbowed his way up the ramp and handed Ellender a document. The Senator squinted to minimize the glare of the hot sun against his prescription sunglasses, and read the Government's words of greeting: "To Mr. Allen Ellender, of Louisiana, U.S. Take notice, that you are a prohibited immigrant on the grounds that you have no pass or permit to enter Tanganyika. You are hereby ordered to leave the country immediately."

Comprehension dawned slowly on the Senator, who fruitlessly protested that he did have a visa. The bewildered Ellender turned to Ambassador Leonhart who volunteered more bad news. Uganda, where an advanced civilization flourished at the headwaters of the White Nile long before the depredations of the white man, had also closed its borders to the sight-seeing Senator. He was the first person to be so exalted. Other African nations, the ambassador warned, would probably do the same.

Before he could leave Dar es Salaam, Ellender endured yet another indignity. He was not allowed to leave the sweltering cabin while his plane was refueled. He put his two hours of quarantine to good use. He summoned the chiefs of the local Peace Corps, U.S. Information Service, and Agency for International Development to join the ambassador, then lectured them all on how to get along with Africans.

It is doubtful that Ellender ever recognized his *faux pas*. An editorial in the New York *Herald Tribune* failed to enlighten him. "Every American possesses among other freedoms the freedom to make a fool of himself," it commented. "Among the distinguished citizens who have recently availed themselves of that right is Senator Ellender." The Senator, taking note of the editorial, scribbled savagely in his black notebook, "The pipsqueak who wrote that is uninformed. If by telling the truth I have made a fool of myself, then I am compelled to plead guilty."

Allen Ellender's election to the Senate was in itself something of an accident. Like many Southern political accidents, nothing has been done to remedy it. He began his elective career as a foe of Louisiana's then political czar Huey Long. When Ellender was elected to the state legislature from Terrebonne Parish in 1924, he was still against Long. By 1929 he had changed sides. The Kingfish had been indicted by the state legislature for impeachment, and Ellender was the defense attorney.

"I do not want you to do anything that is not right, but I want you to help me carry out my program," is the way Ellender remembers the Kingfish's proposition. Ellender did not hesitate over the call. His answer, as he later repeated it, was, "If that is what you want, I am with you. I would be glad to do that."

Long, of course, was cleared by the legislature, and Ellender's career began a rapid ascendancy. He became the floor leader, then the speaker. The Kingfish ran the state, and Ellender was his happy helper. They developed such a rapport, that, in 1936, Long offered to back Ellender for governor. "It was all set, but Huey's assassination—one day before putting me up for nomination—ended it," said Ellender. His chance for immediate power was gone, but he had collected some political IOUs that were still negotiable. "The incumbent, Governor Allen, blocked my nomination at the caucus, and they offered, instead, to put me on the national ticket as candidate for Senator." Thus began a tenure in the Senate exceeded at present only by Carl Hayden of Arizona and Richard Russell of Georgia.

It had been a long struggle to the top for Ellender. He was born in 1890 on a run-down family plantation, named—with more candor than charm—Hard Scrabble. It clung to a bayou on the delta, near Montegut. As a boy, he stayed home from school to help his parents scratch a living from the earth. "We had 300 acres all together, but it was encumbered and there was only about 125 acres of good, hardscrabble earth," he said.

A cousin tutored him in single-entry bookkeeping, and by the time he was thirteen, he was keeping the accounts for Hard Scrabble. It was lonely work for a small boy. He remembered later, "In the winters when the other children were attending school, I was in the scale house of the plantation, weighing sugar cane and keeping the books. I managed to get about four or five months of schooling a year."

When he finally started school full time in Montegut at fourteen, riding the distance on an old mule, he was something of a prodigy. In just four years his teacher thought Ellender was ready for college, and took him to New Orleans 54 miles away. At St. Aloysius College he was tested in science and math. "I made the grade, and they told me they would enter me in the senior class," he said. "Strange to say, the only thing I was deficient in was the one thing I had worked at— bookkeeping. I knew single- but not double-entry. Professor Arthur offered to teach me double-entry on Saturdays and Sundays. And I learned it all right!"

He worked to pay his expenses at St. Aloysius and at Tulane University Law School. With a law degree as his passport to fortune, he left Hard Scrabble for the bright lights of Houma, the Terrebonne Parish seat. He quickly found it was easier to earn a living from the law than from the land.

He had little difficulty becoming a part of Houma. From his mother, whose maiden name was Javaux, he had learned Cajun French, and he was accepted by the people from the bayous and the swamps. He made his first mark as Houma's City Attorney; by 1915 he was District Attorney for Terrebonne Parish. He began investing in land and bought several potato farms. Soon he became known along the Gulf as "King Potatus I," a tribute to his spectacular ability to harvest 347 bushels of potatoes from land that had previously produced only 80. He was thirty-four when he was elected to the state legislature, forty-six when he came to Washington.

He settled happily into the easygoing, Southern-paced, Jim Crow life that dominated Washington in the 1930s. Whether his reputation with potatoes had preceded him or it was merely a matter of political fortune, he was appointed to the Senate Agriculture Committee. Minding the advice of his Southern peers, he sat back in the Senate and let the seniority system bring him quietly toward the top. While time worked its erosion on Senators with more tenure, Ellender watched the world map on his office wall, and his imagination jammed pins into places like Paris and Beirut, Hong Kong and Moscow.

With the end of World War II, real pins started appearing on the wall map. He hurried from nation to nation in an effort to keep up with the map as fast as it was subdivided. By the beginning of his sixth term in 1967, his travels had taken him around the globe seven times and deep into many of its remote areas. It is something of a testament to his character that the world did not look much different close up from the way it did in the bayous of Terrebonne Parish. Like the map on his wall, the world that Ellender viewed was flat.

Still he keeps traveling, and only tiny Albania has been able to keep its borders inviolate. Elsewhere he has come and he has seen and he has written incredible masses of words about all the exotic sights. His reports, each of which runs hundreds of pages, are printed at taxpayers' expense by authority of the Senate Appropriation Committee on the presses of the Government Printing Office. His reports are not, however, reportage. His bland prose has had the impact of a detailed account of a garden club lecture on the petunia.

A random example, from his 1961 tour of Russia:

> After a most restful night I was up at 8 A.M. for breakfast which was served in my room. At about 9 o'clock I was on the streets taking a few movies. There were not many people to be seen. Nakhodka is a city that covers quite a few miles along a fine inland harbor, and is surrounded on the other side by government buildings, the hotel where I stayed and a movie theater. There were a number of small fishing boats in the harbor. No large ships were in the port, as far as I could see. There are many fishing industries here. Herring, in particular, is pickled and packed in barrels. I saw hundreds of locally made barrels piled at the wharf.

Such enlightenment is packed like herring into every page of his travelogues. On rare occasions his wanderings have turned up mildly sensational discoveries, which are treated with the same attention to detail as those barrels on the wharf. During a stop in Moscow on his 1957 world junket, Ellender learned from Anastas Mikoyan some details of Russia's sixth five-year plan, which had been kept secret from the Russian people and the American embassy. Ellender began his explanation of his greatest triumph:

> Ambassador Thompson told me he had not been able to find out why the plan's adoption had not been announced. Well, I went to see Mikoyan the next day and, while I was talking to him about past plans, I got around to asking him about the new plan. Without hesitation, Mr. Mikoyan told me that the reason why the sixth Five-Year Plan was not adopted as scheduled. . . .

True to his literary style, Ellender submerged his scoop under 2,000 words of trivia in his report of that day's activities. Mikoyan's answer yielded precedence to such information as the population of Moscow (seven million), the number of private autos in the city (100,000), the Senator's lunch, a description of Mikoyan ("an Armenian by birth with coal-black hair and dark eyes, a tan complexion, standing about 5 feet 3 inches in height . . .") and a discussion of Russian agricultural problems.

Unfortunately, Ellender was not always so circumspect. Although he has managed not to offend the Russians, he has been a disaster for American diplomacy at other ports of call. On a 1958 junket around the Caribbean, for instance, he praised the Dominican Republic's dictator, Trujillo. Then he moved on to Havana, where he asked reporters at his press conference, two weeks before Castro's victory, "Has there been any fighting?" He informed embassy officials that he didn't want their opinions and volunteered his own murky thoughts, with the appendage: "Of course, I don't know anything about this."

On a junket to Nepal in 1961, he kept the king and queen waiting impatiently at a reception in his honor while he lectured the Cabinet. He wrote on his return: "The streets were filled with people. Apparently the citizens do not work very much." The same year, he was disappointed by his stop in Hong Kong and commented, "Very few changes have been effected since my visit last year, notwithstanding the good advice I attempted to give." In Singapore he presented the caricature of the American tourist by waving a fistful of dollar bills, while haggling with a huckster, and shouting, "I don't have any of this funny money [of yours]. I'm here with good money—dollars."

His comments on his 1962 trip through Africa took on more opprobrium with each stop. "The only black man I know of with the stuff it takes to be a United States Senator was Booker T. Washington, but he had a white mother and is dead now," he said before Senator Edward Brooke's election to the Senate by the voters of Massachusetts. He complained that "Egypt hasn't achieved anything great since the pharaohs began practicing desegregation with their slaves." And Ethiopia, he said, "would have nothing if it weren't for the Italians." None of these goodwill messages, however, came close to creating the kind of anger abroad and dismay at home that was touched off by his comments at the press conference in Southern Rhodesia.

While the storms of protest rolled over his head and American prestige in the emerging African nations faded like a bookkeeper's smile, Ellender's sycophants in Washington attempted to spread the word that the Senator was actually performing a vital service for his country. He was, they whispered, gathering intelligence at every stop. "That's why," they said, "he always carries his movie camera with him on his trips. Over the years he has been an enormous help to military intelligence."

For that matter, if Ellender was indeed snooping for the Government, he can only be congratulated on his disguise. No more unlikely James Bond ever played the secret-agent role. And the photo analysis experts who supposedly pondered over his films can only be pitied. Consider these consecutive paragraphs from Ellender's report on Russia:

I spent the whole day again visiting various parts of Moscow and I took many pictures of people on the streets, at Red Square and in GUM, the largest department store in Russia. I am particularly anxious for the film taken on the inside of GUM to come out all right. They will demonstrate the tremendous size of this store as well as show the thousands of people who trade there.

I visited Gorki Park, a large playground, and talked to many people. I took numerous pictures of people at play. Many consented to permit me to take closeup photographs of them. The doorman at the restaurant where I ate insisted that I photograph him, as well as a woman whose job was to gather dishes and beer glasses. One of the waiters and a young girl who sold oranges, cigarettes, and sweets, consented to be photographed.

That is a new turn of affairs here. I was not so successful during my visit last year. At the famous fairgrounds, I met in much success in photographing groups, as well as two young girls. I photographed crowds without any difficulty, and with no objection on the part of anyone.

James Bond might have been interested in the two young girls at the fairgrounds, but not even he would have been bold enough to pass it off as a significant peek behind the Iron Curtain.

On his travels Ellender has been known to communicate in his almost unbreakable code, known back in Louisiana as Cajun French. It is said to be the tongue brought to the bayous by the Acadians, the French Canadians who were deported to Louisiana. Some claim it is acceptable sixteenth-century French; others allow that even by these archaic standards it is provincial dialect. It is, at any rate, beyond the comprehension of most of today's Parisians. Ellender proudly practices it upon the French-speaking peoples he encounters on his travels.

On a visit to Mali, a former French colony, Ellender was a guest of President Keita, and launched into a prolonged discourse on communications satellites in his Cajun code. President Keita sat through it all with glazed eyes. Ellender, in his report to the Senate, bragged, "Most of those present were surprised to hear me talk French. I believe the Ambassador was pleased." Ambassador William Handley, in a confidential message to the State Department, commented, "The Senator speaks an adequate and at times impenetrable French."

If Ellender's lecture on space communications, like Telstar, was over President Keita's head, the Mali leader had the courtesy to feign interest. This nearly encouraged the Senator, in a flush of Gallic garrulity, to offer Mali the United States aid he had come there to oppose. Ambassador Handley reported that Ellender "almost—to the surprise of the Americans present—promised some aid." Ellender was less generous to those who lacked Keita's patience. On another trip the Senator said of a group of Mali students, "Their French is very poor."

Wherever he goes—Africa, Asia or an Appropriations hearing—Ellender is a missionary for economy, and his sermons have a certain sameness. He has complained about the salaries of State Department officials in hardship posts, about aid to countries that compete with Louisiana in cotton sales, about Peace Corpsmen living a notch above complete deprivation. But nothing seems to arouse Ellender's wrath quite the way *Time* Magazine and the U.S. Information Service do. It may be merely a coincidence that Ellender's erstwhile committee aide, Grace Johnson, once sued *Time* for its unflattering account of a round-the-world junket she had made to investigate the USIS. Her trip had been taken at the taxpayers' expense, of course, courtesy of Senator Ellender. Thereafter the Senator could not look at *Time* or pass a USIS library without blowing a fuse. Here are some typical reactions collected from one of his tours.

From Madrid, he wrote:

> The Ambassador lives in a rented house notwithstanding the fact that a spacious residence for our ambassadors was built here several years ago at a tremendous cost. This spacious residence is now being occupied by USIS. What a crying shame!

From Chad, U.S. Chargé d'Affaires Robert Redington cabled the State Department:

> He [Ellender] appeared to doubt the desirability of the U.S. Government giving free subscriptions to U.S. magazines to local persons and thought it a mistake to include among those officially distributed publications such a magazine as *Time* which gave distorted impressions of current developments.

And from Gabon, this confidential message from Ambassador Charles Darlington:

> The Senator delivered a very strong criticism of *Time* magazine and *Newsweek*. He was particularly scathing in his criticism of *Time* and went so far as to say that it ought not to be put on the library shelves.

Ellender was inclined to lecture his hosts on any subject that might flit through his mind. Reported Darlington in the same confidential cable:

> The Senator cautioned the AID director on the difficulty of raising chickens in hot, wet climates. But on being informed that chickens were being successfully raised in this climate, the Senator indicated that it was "probably" worth a try.

Everywhere he went, Ellender looked upon himself as the protector of the dollar, a fiscal prophet whose self-appointed mission was to go wherever the dollar is spent and cry out against Government extravagance. He descended upon embassy after embassy, like a cranky old uncle who expected to be pampered but who wound up scolding his hosts for their profligateness. His standard sermon, as summarized by Ambassador Darlington, was that "the purse of the United States was not bottomless, that [the embassy staff] should economize wherever possible and that before any recommendation is made to Washington for the expenditure of American funds, the Senator requested each member of the mission to consider the effect such a request would have on the American economy."

In Pakistan Ellender's outrage over Government spending was intensified by his discovery of Pakistan cotton piled in bales on the docks. It happened to be short-staple cotton not in demand for export, but Ellender viewed it as a threat to Louisiana cotton. He rounded up the embassy staff and, with sleeves rolled up, proceeded to excoriate them. "I appeal to you as Americans," he said passionately, "to stop giving our taxpayers' money away to these foreigners."

One USIS aide, more brash than bright, broke in: "But, Senator, in USIS we don't give money away. We give ideas away." Ellender slapped the table and roared, "I don't care what you give away! I want it stopped!"

The Senator is more lenient over his own use of the taxpayers' money. Wherever he wanders, he demands—and usually gets—transportation in military planes assigned to embassy air attachés, although it would cost the taxpayers far less to have him fly on commercial airlines. He shuns hotels and expects to be put up in the homes of embassy officials. When he does end up in a hotel, he can be depended upon to complain about the accommodations.

The embassies on Ellender's itinerary customarily receive advance warning from the State Department. A typical notice, signed by Secretary of State Dean Rusk, advised that the Senator "will travel for most part by Air Attaché C-47 planes. Posts requested to furnish transportation. Will require usual briefing by Ambassador and staff, and will be interested in meeting top officials of other governments. If convenient, Senator prefers to stay with staff member. If not, obtain single room with bath at each location. Assign control officer meet assist through customs in any way possible. CTF 19FT561 [counterpart funds] authorized."

In recent years, after the public outcry about his travels penetrated even his sensibilities, Ellender has taken to sending questionnaires to the embassies he plans to visit. These documents, which can run as long as 16 pages demanding nearly 600 answers, could be expected to give him a reasonable picture of American activities abroad. As one embassy official put it, "With all this information, there was no good reason for him to bother bringing himself along."

Yet he continues to make his trips, and American diplomats continue to be perplexed by his performances. In 1966 he traipsed through 20 Latin American nations in two months, insulting Americans and Latins as he went. Explained one embassy official, "Although the American staff had spent weeks preparing answers to Ellender's questionnaire, he paid no attention to it or to them. He arrived on a Saturday, insisted on a Saturday night embassy briefing, then, as ever, paid no attention to what the staff told him. He was especially picky about—and curt to—the military staff, barking about how they were taking up space but apparently doing nothing. He did commandeer several junior officers on Sunday to drive him around to housing projects, get him into local schools, and show him what the natives were doing to relieve their revolutionary restlessness and to merit U.S. aid.

"Despite having sent this long questionnaire, Ellender proved he knew nothing of substance about the country. He repeatedly alienated embassy men and some Latins with questions that betrayed his small mind and ignorance of facts. He was much more interested in justifying the expenses of keeping up the embassy bathrooms than in understanding what were the aspirations and problems of the Latin people in whose behalf the money was ultimately being spent. When officers would try to suggest politely that there *were* other factors Ellender might consider, he would say, 'Aw, you don't know what you're talking about. Don't give me that; just give me plain common sense.' "

If Ellender learned little about the foreign service from the endless briefings and questionnaires, the foreign service learned a lot about him. Ambassador John H. Ferguson, after a few hours' exposure to Ellender in Morocco, sent this confidential report to the State Department:

During and subsequent to the visit of Senator Ellender to Morocco, escort control officers learned that Senator is a widower, a grandfather, that he neither drinks nor smokes, that he does not eat shellfish, that he drinks only tea at breakfast, that his relevant hobby is color movie photography, that he insists on going to his room no later than 10 P.M. no matter what program is in progress, that he speaks 'Cajun' French, that he likes early-morning starts, that he started his political career under the auspices of the late Huey Long.

Meanwhile the Senator's wordage has kept pace with his mileage. Nothing is too trivial to be omitted from his official reports to the Senate. Future historians, studying the Senate of the 1960s, will discover, for example, that Senator Allen Ellender ate a delicacy he recorded as "Coush-Coush" in Mauritania. He has recorded for posterity, "I ate more than I should and much more than I expected." On the same trip Ellender purchased "a fig leaf worn by native women" in Cameroon and sampled fresh lichee nuts in Madagascar. "I ate some of the nuts, and they were delicious," he has officially informed the Senate. "They taste like a sweet rose smells." He had such a busy day in the Central African Republic that his feet began to hurt. "I was not really tired," he has explained, "but had been on my feet too long." And in Nigeria he got a haircut. So that history would not overlook this event, he has recorded in an official Senate report: "My next appointment was with a barber. Barbers are scarce in this part of the world. This one was an elderly man and he did a fine job of relieving me of a bushy head of hair."

Such are the profound observations which the Senate has made available to historians and scholars—at no small expense to the taxpayers—in each great volume of *Ellender's Travels*.

3. *The Mysterious Travels of Otto Passman*

Another lawmaker from Louisiana, Representative Otto Passman, shares many traits with Ellender, including a passion for economy and a desire to see the world. In the cause of saving the taxpayers' money, Passman, too, has lavishly spent the same for round-the-world travel.

Passman's youth was even bleaker than Ellender's. He was born at the turn of the century to tenant farmers, and his early memories are of meals of unseasoned corn bread and clabbered milk. In the summers in backward Washington Parish, his feet were as bare as the table, and at ten he was hired out to a neighboring farmer for $5 a month. Still, he claims, he was happy. He says with a straight face, "I spent a good deal of time walking through the woods, walking among the honeysuckle, whistling, maybe just humming a hymn I'd heard. I was much happier without wealth than with it. The happiest people are the ones who can carve out a living for themselves."

Passman decided to carve out his own living after he turned fourteen. He dropped out of the fourth grade, worked on a cotton and rice farm for a while, then made his way to Covington, about 25 miles away in St. Tammany Parish, where he was hired by a grocer. He received his keep and a small salary, which he hoarded jealously. But perhaps more valuable, he was given tutoring by the store owner's wife, a schoolteacher. Among other subjects, he learned bookkeeping as Ellender had done—a talent that was to become his ladder to power.

By 1919 Passman was married and running his own grocery business while he took a business administration course. Three years later he was on the road again, as a salesman for what he has identified only as "a Louisville, Kentucky, corporation." With the depression, Passman braced for the economic storm in Monroe in northern Louisiana. The memory of his grim childhood had developed in him a fierce attachment for every dollar he had earned. While other businessmen went under, Passman survived and invested in more businesses. He owned part of a restaurant and tavern, half of a jewelry store. His Passman Wholesale Equipment Company, a commercial refrigeration firm, and Passman Investment Company thrived under his tight fist.

While he treated every dollar with tenderness, he was not unmindful of those less blessed. He tithed to the church and became an active Mason. When friends were down on their luck, he was available for a loan and lecture on economy and

Christian living. He left Monroe temporarily for the Navy, which, despite his lack of formal education, gave him a commission as a supply officer during World War II.

Otto Passman was successful, and in Monroe, Louisiana, he was admired. He put that admiration to the test in 1946 by trying for Congress. His campaign literature, a Horatio Alger tract, was signed by Passman's "faithful employees," including his nephew, Stanley Passman. He won by 455 votes.

In the House, Passman attracted more attention for his wardrobe than his legislative contributions. He is a lean six-footer, and his tailor-made suits fit him as easily as his drawl. He has several hanging in his Congressional closet and is delighted to exhibit them to the most casual visitor. His political stands were the conventional ones for a Southern Congressman. He was against socialism, Government spending and foreign aid; he was for white supremacy.

As a member of the Appropriations Committee, he learned happily that he could take VIP tours throughout the world—all the better to denounce foreign aid. Over the years it became a tradition for Passman to disappear when Congress recessed for Easter. He was usually seen next in a posh hotel in Paris or Beirut or Hong Kong.

Unlike Louisiana's great wandering Senator, Congressman Passman has no interest in publishing his findings, and the results of his foreign investigations go largely unrecorded. He likes to cast an air of mystery about his knowledge of foreign aid, springing an obscure fact on a Government official before his Foreign Operations Subcommittee.

It was, in fact, a mystery to many how Passman became chairman of the subcommittee. In his book, *House Out of Order*, Representative Richard Bolling of Missouri tells the story:

> . . . Clarence Cannon of Missouri, chairman of the House Appropriations Committee late in the 1950's . . . was unfriendly to the foreign-assistance program. Representative Vaughn Gary of Virginia, chairman of the subcommittee handling budgets on foreign aid, was critical but not hostile. One day Cannon simply replaced Gary, selecting in his stead Otto Passman of Louisiana, a vociferous opponent of foreign-assistance programs . . .

With the arbitrary power that Congress invests in its chairman, Passman has been able to lop off large amounts of foreign-aid funds that Presidents and thoughtful legislators believed necessary to maintain the strength of the free world. He denies that he is solely responsible for the aid cuts. "I have never done anything," he says in solemn innocence. "It has always been the fine committee I've had the honor to be chairman of."

He runs his subcommittee by whim, scheduling and canceling hearings as the mood suits him. He once summoned G. Mennen Williams, then Assistant Secretary of State for African Affairs, from a conference on Cyprus for a hearing that was not held. During the formative days of the Peace Corps he ordered Sargent Shriver to appear for an extraordinary Saturday night session, then lost interest at the last moment and canceled the meeting.

The Peace Corps, despite its remarkable accomplishments at economy prices, has been a frequent target of Passman's. He has an enduring personal interest in leprosy and makes a point of frequently visiting America's only leprosarium, located in his Louisiana district. On his Asian junkets Passman goes out of his way to inspect leper colonies and makes private donations to them. One picture on his office wall shows him putting a $10 bill into the clutching hand of a young leper in Asia. Yet when the Peace Corps tried to get funds to work with lepers in Asia in 1964, Passman did his best to ravage that part of the appropriations bill.

That was the year when Passman suffered an unusual indignity from his colleagues. His committee broke tradition and restored the foreign aid budget to a figure that almost everyone but Passman thought reasonable. Then, to add insult to indignity, Passman was ordered to submit his travel plans in advance for approval before his annual 1964 junket was funded. On most other occasions, however, Passman has kept his members under tight control.

He once bragged, "My first rule to the subcommittee during foreign trips is no tuxedos. I don't smoke or drink. We hold our hearings in detail and get away from the big shots who would like to take us on tour. We know the heads of missions are told to show us as little as possible, and we move independently. We duck cocktail parties to look at projects the missions may not even know about. When they think we're in bed, we're out making interviews. We talk a lot to private citizens of the countries we visit, asking reactions to U.S. programs, about U.S. popularity and the like. We also have private sources of information from American businessmen, missionaries, and so forth who live in foreign countries and send us reports."

His knowledge of the tiny details of foreign aid is unparalleled. Another Congressman once said in exasperation, "He knows the number of coat hangers they have in Khartoum, but not what the AID program is doing in the Sudan." Unquestionably, the Agency for International Development is Passman's number-one whipping boy. He badgers AID at every opportunity, and in return AID provides the funds to take him on many of his junkets. There is no public accounting of these expenses, and Passman's dividend to AID is more abuse and, of course, more trips.

In his Washington office, Passman is light years away from the boy who was rented out to a farmer for $5 a month. Some of his critics believe he has obliterated poverty from his memory. People who have met him know better. On his neat desk among neat stacks of neatly typed memoranda, a visitor once noted an inventory of Passman's wardrobe that began:

Suits: 36
Shoes: 30 pair
Shirts: 48
Ties: 48

"It's just as easy to keep things in detail as not," he tells his visitors, although he can recite the items without looking at the list. And should the inventory need checking, Passman needs only to walk a few paces from his desk to a closet filled with his silk and camel's-hair clothes.

He runs his business back in Monroe with the same devotion to detail. When he is in Washington, the telephone on the desk rings each morning at 10, and Passman jots down the dollars and the pennies that have changed hands since the preceding morning.

A few years ago he set up his favorite nephew, Stanley Passman, in business. When the young man squandered his money, Uncle Otto wrote him a stern seven-page letter, recounting his misdeeds, offering some paternal advice and announcing a painful decision. The displeased and disappointed uncle, who had retained title to the business location, brusquely sold the building out from under the business, called in a $25,000 note that Stanley owed and cut off his lines of credit. The effect was to put poor Stanley out of business.

Later, relenting a little, Passman gave his nephew $10,000. An entry on the canceled check, however, identified it as a commission for the sale of the building. Asked about this, the Congressman snorted, "Stanley had no more to do with selling my building than you did!" Then why was the $10,000 recorded as a commission? Was it that Passman would have been compelled to pay taxes on a gift but could have deducted a commission as a business expense? The Congressman hastily explained that he had cleared the whole transaction with Internal Revenue.

On at least one occasion, he also had to do some clearing with United States Customs. When he goes abroad junketing, he is an almost compulsive barterer and buyer at jewelry stores from Geneva to Hong Kong. On his return to the United States, he demands that Customs pass his luggage unopened. He blusters for equal treatment for his assistant, Frank Merrell, who often travels with him.

His friends are always delighted to welcome him home from a junket, since he usually showers them with gifts of jewelry. His administrative assistant, Martha Williams, began wearing an expensive ruby and sapphire necklace after Passman returned from a trip to Thailand in the early 1960s. He keeps a hoard of gold watches, diamond-studded gold cuff links and other glitter in the bottom drawer of a file cabinet in his office. And on many Saturdays he has been seen to linger around Livingston's, a jewelry and pawn shop in downtown Washington.

Customs officers visited his Capitol office in 1964 to quiz him about bringing in undeclared jewelry. Passman admitted he had brought some jewelry home with him from Hong Kong, but he insisted it was just on consignment. Since he was planning to return much of it, he didn't feel a need to clear it through Customs. The Customs agents left without further argument. It should be noted that Passman serves on the subcommittee that passed on Customs Bureau appropriations in 1964. The story he told the Customs men differs from his answers to reporters. Asked about evading duty on his jewelry imports, he thundered, "Hell, no! I've declared and paid duty on every item I've ever brought into the country."

While Passman does not chronicle his overseas adventures in the manner of Ellender, he can be just as undiplomatic. On a six-week tour of Europe and Asia in 1959, Passman stayed in the luxurious, Government-owned Asoka Hotel in New Delhi, where he lounged around, loudly denouncing Indian Prime Minister Nehru for "inefficiency." On another occasion, while contemplating a trip to Spain, he nagged State Department officials about his desire to confer with Generalissimo Franco. Passman was so insistent that our embassy in Madrid finally had to charter a special plane to take him to Franco, who was on vacation. Although he is a pious Mason, Passman has cooperated closely with two Brooklyn Catholics, Representatives John Rooney and Eugene Keogh, in earmarking aid to Catholic Spain. No other country has had its aid specifically earmarked. The reason, Keogh has declared to friends, is to keep "those Masons down at the State Department" from eliminating aid to Spain.

Even in Washington, Passman displays little concern for the sensitivities of others. During one of his subcommittee meetings a Negro messenger arrived with a dispatch, and Passman stopped his session to shout jovially at the man, "We're going to cut you a piece of land out there in Africa, and we're going to make you king—put you on a throne. Then you can qualify for foreign aid. How much do you want?"

Passman was invited by President Eisenhower to join a few other Congressional leaders at a White House meeting on foreign aid in 1957. The session had scarcely begun before Passman made it clear he wasn't interested in what anyone else had to say. He began one of his bookkeeper lectures to Eisenhower, John Foster Dulles and the assembled Congressmen. Eisenhower, a patient man, listened for a while, then nudged an aide and said, "Remind me never to invite that fellow down here again."

Although he is an expert on the details of foreign aid, Passman has a grotesque idea of its purposes. He told a group of doctors back home in Monroe in 1967, "Giving away our wealth to secure friends is a new concept in foreign policy; it has contributed to bringing about a world of confusion and turmoil with America actually having fewer friends now than when we started the program. . . . The foreign aid program was created and is being continued because of the scares and claims of the one-worlders, liberals, schemers, dreamers and personnel in our State Department and embassies in 98 countries of the world. . . ."

Still, Passman continues to breeze around the world at the taxpayers' expense. In 1964, for instance, the travel expenses he charged to Congress—$5,468—were the highest on Capitol Hill. And this sum did not include the amounts that were picked up by other Government agencies or otherwise shielded from public view. His answer to his critics is a disarming one. Says Passman simply, "Believe me, I'm not holier than thou."

4. The Road to Timbuktu

If Ellender and Passman have outdistanced their footloose colleagues, they certainly cannot afford to slow their pace— not if they are to keep ahead of the world's most determined travelers. For each tourist season, Senators and Representatives set out from Capitol Hill in droves to explore the world. Such is the scope of the great migration that it can be said the sun never sets on Congress while it is out of session.

By the latest available count, 243 of the 535 members embarked upon 337 foreign trips at Government expense in 1966. This did not include those who escaped the survey-takers by slipping off on unrecorded junkets. Still others arranged to charge their travel to foreign Governments and private groups. The junketeer of the year was Representative Wayne Hays, D-Ohio, who took six trips and ran up a bill of $6,585 on the taxpayers' cuff. He interrupted an investigation into the travel abuses of Adam Clayton Powell, D-N.Y., in November 1966 to take a final swing through France, Italy, Germany and England. (It should be noted, though, that Hays has been chief sparkplug in the North Atlantic Conference, an organization of NATO leaders, which holds important sessions abroad.)

Not all the wandering legislators are glorified sightseers. Some seek out the Quai d'Orsay instead of the Folies-Bergère. In the world outside, where two-thirds of the United States budget is being spent, Congressional committees have uncovered and remedied waste and bumbling. They have learned firsthand of needed reforms and have written appropriate legislation. They have talked directly to the people of the world. Such trips, with split-second schedules and heavy work loads, are anything but glamorous.

But most junketeers contrive to arrange their overseas business at the world's pleasure spots. The Interparliamentary Union, for example, selected sun-blessed, palm-studded Mallorca off the Spanish coast as the site for its 1967 conference. The 41 Americans who represented Congress at the meeting stayed at the Victoria Hotel, which has colorful flamingos in its tropical gardens, black swans floating in a pool off the lobby and a telephone in every bathroom. Indeed, the lure of the sun, surf and sand is so powerful that for the past few years the busiest man in the Pacific, after the first breath of winter chills Washington, has been Lieutenant Robert F. Blume, chief of the Army Visitors Bureau in Hawaii. He has been kept in a frenzy meeting planeloads of legislators, arranging hotel reservations and answering questions about bathing beaches and nightclubs.

Many of Lieutenant Blume's Congressional clients, after preparing themselves at Waikiki for the ordeal, have gone on to South Vietnam long enough to pose for pictures with our fighting men. That they spent more time in Honolulu and Hong Kong did not detract from the publicity value of their Vietnam visits. These visitors became such a hindrance to the war effort that the Washington *Post* felt constrained to plead: "Since it is impossible to accommodate all the Congressional candidates who want to go to Vietnam in the interests of their political prestige, the best course would be a complete suspension of such junkets during the campaigns."

The golden age of Congressional junketing began in the late 1940s, when Senators happily discovered the need to check on Marshall Plan aid. The late Senator Elmer Thomas, D-Okla., and Senator John McClellan, D-Ark., set the standard for future visitors by threatening to cut off Marshall Plan funds to Sweden when the Swedes failed to roll out the red carpet for them on a 1949 tour. By the time their party got to Norway, their hosts had taken the hint. Mrs. Norma McClellan, the Senator's late wife, wrote home, "These people over here stand in awe of us. Each country that we visit seems to be trying to outdo the one we have just left in entertaining us." One evening, Mrs. McClellan reported breathlessly, "the Prime Minister of Norway opened one of the oldest castles in Europe and gave a state dinner in our honor. . . . Our way to the castle after entering the gate . . . was lighted by flaming torches like those used in ancient time and sentries stationed every few feet." Arkansas was never like this, Mrs. McClellan added, home-style: "I have to pinch myself to believe all this could be happening to 'little ole me.' "

Although the bill for flaming torches was picked up by the Norwegian taxpayers, the folks back home paid for the Senator's Air Force plane and five escorts, including a doctor in case the high living disagreed with anyone. Wrote Mrs. McClellan, "John is truly relaxing and having the time of his life, and he and I are having a long-delayed honeymoon."

While the golden age lasted, junketing members of Congress were allowed to draw as much in counterpart funds as they thought they could spend—with no questions asked and no accounting given. It was left to the State Department to keep track of the totals, which were kept secret. Once in a while, however, a few details leaked out and the taxpayers got a glimpse of the standard of living they were subsidizing in foreign currencies of all shapes, colors and sizes. For one party headed by the late Senator Dennis Chavez, D-N.M., the American embassy in Rome advanced three million Italian lire. The junketeers managed to spend more than 2.4 million lire in just six days of the good life in and around Naples. Among the itemized expenses: whiskey, 45,000 lire; Kleenex, toilet tissue, soap, 5,625; cigars, 6,250; taxis on Capri, 10,000; Blue Grotto excursion, 2,000; cigarettes, 2,500; trips to Pompeii (destroyed by a volcanic eruption in 79 A.D.), 10,000; Coca-Cola, 400; coffee, 800; car rentals, 570,000 (almost $1,000).

The Senators left some unpaid bills that the American embassy dutifully picked up. This chore was left to John G. Bacon, an embassy aide, who gave an accounting to Edward B. Wilber, a deputy assistant secretary. "Dear Ed," wrote Bacon, "I have enclosed a copy of the 455 [authorization form] by which you drew the last L. 1,000,000 of the counterpart funds. From this L. 1,000,000 I paid all expenses up to date, including the rental of vehicles, whiskey, Kleenex, etc., for the hotel rooms. . . ." This was followed a week later by another "Dear Ed" letter, reporting:

Your letter to the Ambassador stated that "unusual costs incurred by reason of entertainment or other activities resulting from the visit of this group" would be reimbursed on your approval. The Ambassador has now presented me with an itemized statement of the cocktail party held at Villa Taverna on October 5th, and I have been requested to forward this to you for approval. The breakdown in the expenses is as follows:

Cook	Lire	80,425
Butler		6,700
Extra help servants		9,000
Liquors		23,030
	Total Lire	119,155

Thus the taxpayers, who never left home, became substantial spenders at Europe's fun spots. One who happily scattered the taxpayers' money around the world was Representative Adam Clayton Powell, the Harlem globetrotter. He indulged openly in pleasures avoided by the righteous and practiced by the prudent only when they thought nobody was looking. This typical cable clattered out one summer day in 1962 from the State Department headquarters in Washington's Foggy Bottom to United States embassies in London, Paris, Rome and Athens:

CONGRESSMAN ADAM C. POWELL, CHAIRMAN COMMITTEE EDUCATION AND LABOR ACCOMPANIED BY MRS. TAMARA J. WALL AND MISS CORRINE HUFF STAFF MEMBERS TRAVELING WESTERN EUROPE ACCORDANCE FOLLOWING ITINERARY:

AUGUST 8 SAILING QUEEN MARY ARRIVING SOUTHAMPTON 8/13; PARIS 8/16; VENICE 8/20; ROME 8/23; ATHENS 8/27; DELPHI 8/30; SAILING LEONARDO DA VINCI 9/15 FROM GIBRALTAR. ARRIVAL TIMES AND FLIGHTS FORWARDED WHEN FIRM.

PROVISIONS HANDBOOK CONGRESSIONAL TRAVEL APPLY. CODEL AND PARTY AUTHORIZED USE LOCAL CURRENCIES 19FT561 FUNDS. MEET ASSIST APPOINT CONTROL OFFICERS.

Translated from cablese, this meant that Powell and two of his most attractive employees—Mrs. Wall, a shapely young divorcee, and Miss Huff, first Negro to win the Miss Ohio beauty contest—were planning a five-week grand tour at the height of the travel season. The Congressional delegation ("Codel" in State Department jargon) could collect foreign currency every time it got to a new country and use the money for shopping, tips or nightclubbing. The cable went on:

> REQUEST ONE SINGLE AND ONE DOUBLE WITH BATH AS FOLLOWS: LONDON CUMBERLAND MARBLE ARCH HOTEL; PARIS HOTEL SAN REGIS; VENICE ROYAL DANIELI; ROME (1) EXCELSIOR (2) FLORA (3) VICTORIA WHICHEVER HAS SPECIAL EMBASSY RATES; ATHENS BEACHHOUSE AT ASTIR HOTEL; DELPHI NEW GOVERNMENT HOTEL NAME UNKNOWN. CONFIRM DEPARTMENT SOONEST.

The hotels were all plush. No matter where the embassy billeted him in Rome, Powell could be sure of de luxe accommodations.

> LONDON—REQUEST THREE TICKETS 8/14, 15 BEST SHOWS PLAYING, EXCEPT BROADWAY PLAYS.

The Congressman didn't want to take a chance on going to a show in London that he'd already seen in New York.

> PARIS—CODEL DESIRES USE U.S. ARMY CAR AND CHAUFFEUR. RESERVE THREE FOR FIRST SHOW AND DINNER BEST TABLE LIDO 8/16.

The Lido is a Champs-Élysées nightclub famous for its bare-bosomed lovelies. The pastor of the Abyssinian Baptist Church did not inform the embassy whether he was planning, in his role as chairman of the House Labor Committee, to study the girls' working conditions.

> VENICE—IF THE FILM FESTIVAL GOING ON REQUEST THREE TICKETS 8/20 OR 21. CODEL ALSO REQUESTS USE CONSULATE'S MOTORBOAT.

If you need an Army car and chauffeur to get around in the Paris traffic, obviously you need a consular motorboat to chug down the Grand Canal to the Venice Film Festival.

ATHENS—ARRANGE USE RENTAL CAR TRIP TO DELPHI PAYABLE 19FT561 FUNDS 8/30.

DELPHI—CODEL INQUIRES WHETHER BOAT TRIP ABOUT 6 DAYS AROUND ISLANDS POSSIBILITY. POSSIBLE VISIT RHODES.

And finally, after using the State Department as a travel agent for the five-week junket, the Powell party had one more favor to ask:

SOUTHAMPTON—CODEL REQUESTS BE MET AT QUEEN MARY CHERBOURG WITH $100 U.S. EQUIVALENT IN LOCAL CURRENCIES FOR EACH MEMBER PARTY.

In other words, the busy embassy in London was supposed to send a "boodle boy" to Cherbourg for the day with a wad of British pounds so the Congressman and his traveling companions wouldn't have to stand in line to change their dollars when they got off the boat in Southampton.

If the 1962 European junket was spectacular, it certainly wasn't isolated. With Miss Huff, the Congressman visited Switzerland in 1963 and Hawaii in 1964. His itinerary over the past few years has included a week-long Caribbean cruise aboard the *Sea Rose,* a yacht provided by the Teamsters Brotherhood, and a trip to Acapulco, Mexico, where he pulled thirteen sailfish and eight marlin out of the Pacific. Although he has a home in Puerto Rico on a choice beach-front property outside San Juan, these days he prefers the fishing at Bimini in the Bahamas.

The House Administration Committee, showing a belated righteousness over Powell's travel abuses, invalidated all 22 of the airline credit cards held by his staff and started an investigation in late 1966. In the first 20 months of the 89th Congress, according to the committee, Powell or his employees made 65 round trips to San Juan or Miami. The investigators found that on October 22, 1965, 18 round-trip tickets worth $2,118 were charged on the credit card of C. Sumner Stone, Powell's chief lieutenant. But apparently it was Powell, not Stone, who did the traveling.

The committee also discovered that Powell was guilty of cheating on the expense accounts from his foreign travels. He claimed that he had spent only $6,902.29 in counterpart funds while gallivanting around the globe between 1961 and 1964. The investigators found records that $13,615.43 in local currencies had been turned over to him.

The Powell investigation fell to a special subcommittee headed by Representative Wayne Hays of Ohio. Earlier a couple of Washington reporters had made another discovery in the higgledy-piggledy House travel records. The vouchers showed that Hays charged the House NATO delegation for five one-way auto trips between Washington and his Ohio district, plus a total of 47 one-way fares between Washington and the two airports nearest his home.

Hays was assisted in his investigation of travel abuses by Representative Omar Burleson, D-Tex., who, as chairman of the Administration Committee, is the stern guardian of all House expenditures. The vouchers showed he had collected $12 per diem for committee business on 84 of 88 days between October 1 and December 27, 1958. He spent most of this time campaigning for re-election in Texas, but he also pocketed per diem on Thanksgiving and Christmas. He also billed the taxpayers for 1,128 miles of travel by car at 10 cents a mile during the campaign. He justified the charge by claiming he was investigating "election matters" in his home district.

Another choice set of vouchers revealed that 15 members of the House Public Works Committee, 10 of their wives and a committee counsel had laid out more than $900 in Government money one June weekend in New York City for a study of "Long Island beach erosion." The vouchers did not indicate how much of the money had been spent for suntan lotion. They did show that someone had carefully inked out "Mrs." on the hotel bills of Congressmen who brought their wives.

These revelations spurred the Administration Committee to take hasty action requiring all House committees to report their spending in the *Congressional Record* periodically. But it also discreetly locked up the individual vouchers from any more embarrassing inspections. The committee also neglected to clamp a ceiling on Congressmen's living expenses abroad. On one European trip, Powell submitted a report showing total expenses of slightly more than $3,000, including

$1,117.07 for "miscellaneous." After mulling it over for a few more years, the committee finally gave House members a choice between the standard Government per diem rate plus $10 a day, no questions asked, or up to $50 a day if the member wanted to submit an accounting.

Of course the new rules failed to stop Congressional junketing, or even slow it down noticeably. One arid noontime in 1964, a Congressional delegation even dropped in on Timbuktu, long a byword for the end of the earth. Four members of a House Agriculture subcommittee, headed by Representative W. R. Poage, D-Tex., in a broad-brimmed Texas hat, swooped down in the middle of a junket that covered 14 countries in 15 days. They presented a Kennedy half dollar to the regional governor who met them at the airport, then chugged into town for date cookies and lemonade at the home of American missionaries. The Congressmen decided to skip the camel ride, but sampled Timbuktu's other tourist attractions: a visit to the 600-year-old mosque and a drink at the only hotel in town. Then, after improving Mali's balance of payments by buying an assortment of tribal swords, lances, daggers and decorated ostrich eggs, they climbed back into their plane and took off for Bamako. Total elapsed time in Timbuktu: three hours.

What the Congressmen were doing there in the first place was not easy to determine. The subcommittee was supposed to be studying the distribution of American surplus food, but Mali wasn't getting any. The Congressmen were also looking into African agriculture, but Timbuktu had none. And one of the four Congressmen in the party, Representative Charles B. Hoeven, R-Iowa, wasn't even returning to Capitol Hill for the 89th Congress. Being a lame duck, however, has never stopped a member of Congress from taking a junket.

The law forbids airlines, railroads and steamship companies from providing free rides for public officials. This doesn't apply, however, to Government transport agencies like MATS and MSTS. For such privileged and powerful legislators as Senate Armed Services Chairman Richard Russell, D-Ga., the Air Force will place planes at their beck and call. Most others can hitch a ride at least with a MATS transport plane from time to time. Or for those who prefer sea travel, they can arrange passage on an MSTS ship.

A favorite Congressional excursion is a Caribbean cruise to the Canal Zone aboard the Panama Canal Company's own S.S. *Cristobal*. The company, of course, is owned by the taxpayers and operated by the Army. All the cruising Congressman needs is a letter from his committee chairman. Explains the company's secretary in Washington, W. M. Whitman, "Presumably he will be traveling on official business, but we don't ask any questions." The company does draw the line at Congressmen's families; the wife and kids have to pay a reduced fare of $150 for a round trip—still an attractive bargain considering that a swimming pool goes with it. "It's in everyone's interest," says Whitman, "to get Congressmen down there and see what we have."

But for careful, minute-by-minute planning that would put a cruise director to shame, nothing tops the armed forces. A few years ago the Army and the Air Force jointly invited selected members of the House Armed Services and Appropriations committees to the Army-Air Force football game in Chicago. The schedule for that junket elaborated the VIP treatment for the Congressional guests in detail worthy of an invasion plan:

0830 EST Guests arrive Andrews AFB and are met and escorted to aircraft.

0850 All members of party on board aircraft. Seating as desired.

0900 Wheels up. Flying time: 2 hours, 55 minutes. Light luncheon served in flight.

1055 CST Arrive Midway Airport, Chicago. Met by CG [Commanding General] Fifth US Army.

1105 Board charter buses for Soldier Field. Seating as desired. Buses will be marked by Army Mule and Air Force Falcon.

1200 Arrive Soldier Field. Escorted to seats by Army or Air Force escorts.

After the game, it was the same drill in reverse, with dinner served on the return flight. The services not only furnished cars to bring their guests to Andrews Air Force Base and take them home again; they provided blankets and rain gear at Soldier Field in case any of them forgot to wear their galoshes. The schedule didn't say anything about Government-issue hip flasks—or about the effect of this junket on the Congressmen who vote for military appropriations.

After the Cuban missile crisis was safely over, the Navy ran a series of Congressional specials to its huge base at Guantanamo Bay. Congressmen who didn't necessarily want to be where the action was could see where the action might have been and still feel they were living dangerously. If they also happened to be Naval Reserve officers, they could collect active-duty pay for the junket. Guantanamo was so fashionable in the spring of 1963 that at least 33 Congressmen were flown in and out again by the Navy over a period of less than two months.

The Reservists in these boarding parties didn't wear their uniforms, but they got the kind of treatment the Navy usually saves up for its shiniest brass. The four escort officers sent along from the real Navy outranked many of the Congressional sailors, but they dutifully hustled the Congressmen's baggage and made sure they were safely tucked in at night. Among them was James E. Van Zandt, a former Republican Representative from Pennsylvania, who came along for old times' sake. Although the voters had retired him from Congress a year earlier, he found it hard to shake the junketing habit.

There was a time when the railroads gave so many free passes to members of Congress that it became a national scandal. The press and public became so indignant that Congress finally passed a law making it illegal for a railroad to give free transportation to any Congressman or Government official; the rule was later extended to include airline and steamship companies.

There is no law, however, to restrict Congressmen from flying on corporate or Government planes—though such a law is long overdue. How Congressmen take advantage of this loophole and how it may influence their voting and, perhaps, the award of Government contracts, is another chapter in the story of Congressional travel.

Texans can always hitch a ride, for example, in Ling-Temco-Vought's 10-seater, which takes off from Washington's National Airport almost every Thursday evening for Dallas. Perhaps the most frequent Congressional passenger on this run has been Representative Earle Cabell, D-Tex., who resigned as mayor of Dallas to run for Congress a few months after

President Kennedy's assassination. Mrs. Cabell often accompanies the Congressman, thus saving the $181.13 that a round-trip commercial flight would cost. It is a bargain, too, for Ling-Temco-Vought, which can use Congressional support to improve its competitive position at the Pentagon. The company was the sixteenth largest contractor with the Defense Department in 1965, with billings of $249.3 million. Less frequently, Representatives Bob Casey of Houston, Olin Teague of College Station, Joe Pool of Dallas, Ray Roberts of McKinney and Graham Purcell of Wichita Falls climb aboard L-T-V's $300,000 Lear Star. Sometimes, of course, there is no room for Congressmen because the plane is filled up by company officials. When that happens, however, the Texans may be able to find an empty seat on a plane owned by Tennessee Gas Transmission Company (known now less formally as Tenneco) going to Houston. Casey, Pool and Purcell have all flown as "courtesy" passengers at one time or another with Tenneco, whose natural gas production and pipelines are regulated by the Federal Power Commission.

The White House says it wouldn't allow staff members to hitch free rides in private planes. Texas Senators Ralph Yarborough, a Democrat, and John Tower, a Republican, won't fly with L-T-V or Tenneco. Ex-Representative Charles Weltner, the Georgia Democrat who quit Congress in 1966 rather than support segregationist Lester Maddox for governor, stated his policy very bluntly: "I don't take private plane rides." But Bob Casey just doesn't see any conflict of interest involved. "If I were standing on a street corner in Houston," he said, "and the President of Tennessee Gas Transmission rode by in his car and offered me a ride, I'd take it. I feel the same way about the Tennessee Gas plane. If they operated a plane just to haul Congressmen, that would be different. I'd frown on it. But they operate this plane for their convenience, not mine."

United Aircraft Corporation, Senator Tom Dodd's favorite carrier between Washington and Hartford, Connecticut, feels the same way about courtesy passengers. As befits an aircraft company, United keeps a lot of planes in the air—everything from an elderly DC-3 and a 32-seat Convair down to an 8-passenger Jet Star and a 4-passenger King Air. Practically every Connecticut Congressman—including Democratic Senator Abraham Ribicoff—has flown in at least one of them.

But United says it isn't trying to buy influence with free rides. "We are an old New England company with a well-developed conscience on things of this sort," says J. R. Patterson, the company's public relations chief. "It would be improper if we provided air transportation as a service to people in government. We don't do that. It is a service to our own people. We are very careful about these relationships." Certainly no one can deny that United Aircraft has a lot of business in Washington. In 1965 its space and defense contracts were worth $939.5 million.

United's position is that the Congressmen are going to help the company if they can anyway, ride or no ride. And the Congressmen themselves agree. Connecticut Representative Emilio Daddario's administrative assistant, Thomas E. J. Kenna, explains it this way: "United Aircraft is in our district. It employs 60,000 people. It's our job to help them get business and to help the economy of the district. We'd do it whether they had airplanes or not and whether we'd ever ridden with them."

Perhaps more eloquent is a memo, dated May 12, 1965, from Gerry Zeiller to his boss, Senator Dodd:

> Joe Barr of United Aircraft visited the office yesterday and had with him Bill Dell of United Technology, a subsidiary of United Aircraft, and a lawyer named Bob Pyle who used to be AA to ex-Congressman Perkins Bass and is now practicing law in Washington.
>
> You will recall that we arranged for a demonstration for United Technology of their snap-on 120-inch solid fuel booster rockets some months ago with Jim Gehrig and the Space Committee staff.
>
> Barr and his associates would now like to see some general language incorporated into the Space Committee report such as I have attached with this memo, similar language is included on page 121 of the House Space Committee authorized report.
>
> I talked with Jim Gehrig about the possibility of including this language in the final report, and he informed me that it would be almost impossible to include similar language in the Senate report as the report is already at the printers and ready to be put into final form . . . I believe we

can get the language inserted if we go directly to Chairman Anderson.

When Congressmen talk about going to the ends of the earth to help their constituents, they are being all too literal.

10

PADDED PAYROLLS

1. Relatively Speaking

Congressional salaries, keeping pace with inflation, have steadily risen to the present pinnacle of $30,000 a year. This is considered ample in most constituencies to keep the wolf from the door. Not one Congressman, of more than 100 interviewed for this book, thought his official emolument inadequate. Yet every time the Congressional payroll is shaken, a number of relatives fall out like overripe fruit from a tree.

Throughout history, apparently, legislators have bolstered their family finances by putting relatives on the public payroll. This hoary practice is called nepotism, and it has been practiced in the best of families. The late John F. Kennedy, while he was a member of the Senate's Select Committee on Improper Activities, voted to place his brother Bobby on the committee payroll. Lyndon Johnson, during his Senate days, helped out his less affluent brother, Sam Houston Johnson, by putting both Sam and Sam's wife on the Senate payroll. No fewer than five of the present House Committee chairmen have hired kinfolk to do the taxpayers' work. The number-three Democrat in the House leadership, Majority Whip Hale Boggs of Louisiana, has been ably assisted for years by his wife Corinne, whose services cost the taxpayers $10,000 a year. Son Tommy also turned up for a while on the payroll of the Joint Economic Committee.

Most working relatives, it should be noted, earn their pay. Having a personal interest in the boss, they often work longer and harder than others on the staff. But the public has no check on those who abuse their payroll privileges. A Congressman need not say what his employees do or how many hours they put in. A 1964 Federal law does stipulate that they must work in Washington or in the Congressman's home state. But Congressmen paid no heed to the law—which they helped to pass—until newspapers repeatedly reminded them in 1966 that Yvette Powell spent her time and drew her pay in Puerto Rico, a long way from husband Adam Clayton Powell's Harlem district and Washington office.

Others have continued to ignore the law without attracting publicity. For several months Representative Thomas Ashley, D-Ohio, carried his sister, Mary Edwards, on the House Banking Committee's payroll at $15,500 a year while she lived in Boston. Asked about this, he explained that she was doing research for the committee at Harvard. He did not explain why it was necessary to send her to Harvard for information that was more accessible at the Library of Congress across the street from the Capitol.

Though House payrolls have been open to public inspection since 1932, the names of Congressional relatives are often buried deep in the small print. Even the most diligent search of the records may fail to show that some obscure clerk on a committee staff is kin to a committee member, especially if the employee is a cousin or in-law with a different name. The name of Yvette Powell, for example, was nowhere to be found in the House records. She was listed under her maiden name of Y. Marjorie Flores. The two names most likely to identify her, "Yvette" and "Powell," were discreetly omitted.

It is even more difficult to identify relatives in the scrambled-egg reports issued twice a year by the Secretary of the Senate. These green-bound volumes list the names and salaries of employees—who's working for whom in the Senate—in what seems to be almost intentionally deliberate disorder.

A House member draws a base payroll allowance of $25,000 annually for a maximum of 10 employees if he represents fewer than 500,000 people, or $27,500 for eleven helpers if he represents a larger constituency. But in practice he can triple this figure, provided that he utilizes what the House Disbursing Office calls "most favorable disposition of the base." A rough translation of this might be: getting the most for your payroll.

The size of a Senator's staff also depends upon the size of his constituency, though the ratio may be somewhat lopsided. For example, Senator Charles Percy, R-Ill., representing over 10 million people, has a staff barely twice the number as that of Senator Howard Cannon, D-Nev., representing only 250,000 people. All told, the 100 Senators hire more clerks than do all 435 Representatives.

If the names of relatives are difficult to locate on the clerk-hire lists, their salaries are even more difficult to compute. Some observers have been uncharitable enough to suggest that the salary tables are purposely constructed in a way that the public cannot readily understand. Why else would Congress trouble with a formula that originated in 1919, the last year that a $5,000-a-year man earned only $5,000 a year?

In essence, the formula works this way: Mary Smith, who is carried on a Congressman's payroll for one year, is listed in the "Salary Tables" as making an annual base pay of $2,000. Considering her Radcliffe education and indispensability in the office, the "Salary Tables" appear severe indeed. But slide a finger crosswise from the "base" to "gross" pay column of this document, and you will find Mary commanding a more enviable $5,470 a year. Her final salary, based upon the 1919 formula amended frequently by Congress, is calculated as follows: (1) Add 20 percent increase for first $1,200, 10 percent additional from $1,200 to $4,600, 5 percent further from $4,600 to $7,500. (2) Add 14 percent or a flat $250, whichever is greater, but not to exceed 25 percent. (3) Add 10 percent in lieu of overtime. (4) Add $350. (5) Add 5 percent. (6) Add 10 percent but not more than $800 or less than $300. (7) Add 7½ percent. (8) Add 10 percent. (9) Add 7½ percent. (10) Add 7 percent. (11) Add 3½ percent plus 1 percent for every $500 or part of $500 basic salary or a straight 5 percent, whichever is greater. For the bookkeepers, this may produce complications; but as a camouflage, it definitely has merit.

When the House payrolls were first made public, just about half of the members had relatives drawing Government pay. The spotlight of publicity has sent most of them scurrying for other jobs. The latest payroll search produced barely fifty relatives—including fourteen wives, eight sisters, four brothers, three daughters, two sisters-in-law, two mothers-in-law and one each father-in-law, brother-in-law, father, son, uncle, aunt, cousin and grandniece in the House; plus five sons and one each brother, niece, brother-in-law, granddaughter and grandnephew in the Senate.

Even some of these, too uncomfortable in the white glare, are now leaving the public trough. Theoretically at least, they cannot be replaced. Congress, under the spur of public opinion, grudgingly approved a law in December 1967, barring any more relatives from the Congressional payroll. For this blessing the voters can thank the man who, more than any other, attracted the spotlight: Adam Clayton Powell.

2. *Adam Clayton Powell:*
Goodbye to Uncle Tom

In Harlem's Carver Ballroom, Adam Clayton Powell sipped a Scotch and grinned as the well-wishers swarmed around him, pressing in to shake hands and offer congratulations. They had come to pay him homage, and even in the mob scene Powell managed to appear regal. He stood above the crowd, tall, handsome, supremely confident. His height and his haughtiness seemed to insulate him from the sweltering August evening.

He could afford to be cool, for he had scored his greatest triumph. He had beaten Earl Brown in the 1958 Democratic primary, and with Brown's downfall, Adam had defeated Carmine DeSapio and the Tammany Hall organization. The Democratic regulars had been out to punish Powell for abandoning Adlai Stevenson for President Eisenhower in the 1956 election. In Earl Brown they had found an attractive, if reluctant, candidate. Brown, also a Negro, was a Harvard graduate, an associate editor of *Life* magazine, and the city councilman from Harlem.

Powell had been compelled to work in the campaign, the only time he had been seriously challenged for the nomination since Harlem had been awarded a Congressional seat in the 1944 redistricting. Powell put on a show; he set out not only to beat the Democratic machine but to humiliate it. It was a novelty in Harlem to see Powell on the campaign stump, and those who came to watch were quickly caught up in the fervor of Adam's crusade against the "downtown [white] bosses" and their "Uncle Toms"—the organization Negroes opposing Powell, including the powerful Manhattan Borough President Hulan Jack.

Powell played all the instruments. He called for racial pride. He claimed, "I am being purged by Carmine DeSapio because I am a Negro and a Negro should stay on the plantation." He pointed to his record, to his position as the next in line for the chairmanship of the House Labor Committee. "I appeal to your manhood," he thundered. "Harlem is on the march."

Indeed, more people from Harlem marched to the polls than ever before in a primary, and they voted for Powell over Brown by three to one. Powell made it look easy; he always did.

Now that it was over, admiring crowds pressed around him in the Carver Ballroom, seeking his blessing. It was a moment when he could afford to be gracious, but he could not resist giving the knife a twist. "This is the end of Hulan Jack," he said, his voice reaching the fervor it contained when it battled against sin in his Sunday sermons. "We will drive the Uncle Toms from Harlem."

His gaze shifted to bigger targets, and he pronounced the words that were already in the minds of his listeners. "Carmine will have to pay the price. They will have to treat us like the Irish and the Italians." The Democratic leaders had blundered badly in their assault on Powell. They had suspected that he was losing his control over the ghetto, that voters were tired of Adam's promises and shamed by his activities. They had forgotten that Powell *was* Harlem.

Adam Clayton Powell was a home-grown product; he grew up with Harlem. Adam was fifteen when his father, the Reverend Adam Clayton Powell, Sr., moved the Abyssinian Baptist Church from West 40th to 135th Street—from a slum to a bright, almost new neighborhood. That was in 1923, when Harlem still could offer the Negro decent housing (at higher rates than whites were paying, of course) and hope still accompanied the inescapable discrimination. It was a world where celebrities came to see the shows in speakeasies and nightclubs like the Cotton Club, where Marcus Garvey wore a red-and-green uniform and a cocked hat while he preached black nationalism, where groceries were expensive and life was cheap, where Adam Clayton Powell, Sr., was the pastor of what he called "the largest Protestant church in the world with the world's most beautiful marble pulpit."

Young Adam was different from those around him. He shared in the dreams but never in the poverty. It surrounded him but did not touch him. He was the pastor's son, whose greatest tribulations were a white Sunday suit, a sheltering mother and fawning parishioners. "I was in church with my mama the day Mattie Powell carried him in," one of the parishioners remembered years later. "Oh, what a pretty baby. We were crazy about him from that minute on. We always let him do as he pleased, that Adam."

In poor Harlem, Adam lived in affluence. In the matriarchal society of the ghetto, he was in the house of the patriarch. Adam Clayton Powell, Sr., spoke, and Adam Clayton Powell, Jr., obeyed, although not always willingly.

Like most American Negroes, Powell knew little about his ancestors. He believed his paternal grandmother was a Choctaw Indian; he knew his paternal grandfather had been a slave. Their son, Adam, was born on a farm in Franklin County, Virginia. He drifted westward to Paint Creek, West Virginia, where he met and married Mattie Schaffer. She was said to be the love child of a mulatto woman and a white man. One story has it that the father was a wealthy New York brewer. But old-timers in what is now Pratt, West Virginia, swear that Mattie was fathered by one of the community's leading lights. They also recall that Adam, Sr., hastily departed West Virginia after he fired upon a white man while guarding a melon patch too zealously.

Adam, Jr., once recounted the day when, at age ten, he was called into his father's bedroom to see his visiting grandfather. The letter "P" was branded in the old man's back. "I stood on a chair," Adam said, "and traced down his brown back with my finger that P of seared human flesh. I swore to God that I would not rest until I had wiped that brand from my memory and from the conscience of white America."

Young Adam went to public schools, then to the City College of New York, where his interest in the girls outstripped his interest in the books. He flunked out in his freshman year. The Reverend Mr. Powell was upset, and Adam, Jr., started all over again at Colgate, where there were fewer distractions. Adam went to Colgate with the desire to be a doctor. Then the patriarch spoke, and Adam switched to theology. Still, he had a surgeon's hands—long, light, thin, graceful. Later he would use them well—a finger puncturing the air at the right moment in a speech; three fingers stroking his chin to cast a thoughtful mood for photographers; a fist pummeling a lectern or a pulpit as he shouted defiance. They were different hands for Harlem, not callused and gnarled by menial labor. They were hands that would reach out to grasp the world.

Adam made his first inspection of that world on a tour of Europe and the Middle East—a present from his father after Adam received his A.B. from Colgate in 1930. Even in hungry Harlem in the first year of the depression, rank had its privileges.

Adam was back in three months ready to work. Pastor Powell set up a soup kitchen in the church basement—he called it "the largest relief bureau ever set up by colored people"— and put Adam in charge. On some days a thousand meals were served. Pastor Powell charged that "preachers have robbed people under the guise of religion and should return the loot." He put up $1,000 to get the center started, and asked his parishioners who were still employed to contribute 20 percent of their pay.

It was bleak, tiring work, but somehow Adam managed to slip away from the shuffling lines of the poor long enough each day to earn a master's degree at Columbia University. This was followed by other honors. His father's church was filled with well-wishers—including 200 ministers from other churches—on the April day in 1931 when Adam, Jr., was installed as Abyssinian Baptist's assistant minister.

But there was disapproval, too, from the patriarch and from the church's deacons when it became known he was planning to marry Cotton Club dancer Isabel Washington, a divorcee. Adam met the objections head on. He would marry Isabel, he said, even if he had to leave his post at the church. Pastor Powell relented and performed the ceremony in his church on March 8, 1933. Thousands stood outside in the rain to cheer them.

There were more cheers as Adam went on to more meaningful battles. In a day when involvement of the clergy in the struggles of their church members was not as fashionable as it was to become 30 years later, the young Reverend Powell took the cloth to the front lines. He led a protest demonstration over the firing of five Negro doctors from Harlem

Hospital—called "the butcher shop" by those who had been subjected to its care. Adam's followers marched on City Hall, were rebuffed by the acting mayor, but forced a hearing from the Board of Aldermen. The doctors were reinstated.

He was in the forefront of a coalition that picketed and boycotted and browbeat the 125th Street merchants into hiring Negroes. Consolidated Edison, New York's principal supplier of power, and the telephone company also buckled under Powell's pressure. They promised to hire more Negroes, and kept the promise by hiring a few. Powell's pickets forced the World's Fair organizers to open a handful of white-collar jobs to Negroes. He took on the New York City Omnibus Company and Mike Quill's Transport Workers Union, and won an agreement for 210 jobs for Negroes as drivers and mechanics.

And Adam flirted. He kissed the ladies on the cheek as they came out of church on Sunday mornings. "He was a form of escapism for those old colored lady domestics and a sexual attraction for the young women," one of his church members confessed. "They didn't come to worship God. They came to worship Adam." Later these women would campaign for him when he ran for office.

He flirted with the Communists and, like many of his generation, had second thoughts when the blood of Stalin's purges stained the headlines. "You know I lean left when it comes to the Soviet," he wrote in his weekly column in *The Amsterdam News*. "It can sin far greater than any other nation and yet there's always an understanding. But the recent bloody purges have been unable to gain a hearing for even my calmer moments. I don't know what it is, but the Soviet Union seems to have gone berserk."

He flirted with power. With the help of his father he fought off the objections of the conservative church elders and became pastor in 1937. Adam made no concessions. In his acceptance speech he told the church leaders, "I have never played politics with any so-called controlling group in the church. In the future I promise to preserve at all costs my individual integrity and to champion liberation in the church."

He also embraced politics wholeheartedly. In 1941 New York City adopted a new charter, and the Board of Aldermen was abandoned for a city council. Adam entered the race for councilman as an independent, then talked the Negro candidates representing the three major parties into withdrawing. He went on to win endorsements from labor, including Quill's Transport Workers. He proclaimed, "I am not seeking a political job. I am fighting for the chance to give my people the best representation in the affairs of their city, to help make Harlem the number-one community of New York."

On Election Day the pattern was one that would become familiar in Powell's political career. He polled the third highest number of votes, city-wide, and was elected easily.

Other patterns that would characterize his political career also became apparent. He set out to goad whites on the injustices of discrimination, and he was a successful irritant. He railed against job discrimination, against the lack of employment opportunity for Negroes in war plants, against the lily-white facilities of the four city-supported colleges, and against segregated housing. It was an impressive start, but in Harlem occasional grumbles were heard that he lost interest in his fights when they stopped producing headlines.

Powell's long, graceful fingers reached higher. Negro leaders and Tammany Hall politicians had been pushing to give Harlem its own Congressional district. In the 1944 state reapportionment, the gerrymander's silhouette shifted, creating an almost entirely Negro district. Powell announced that he would run for the seat. He was endorsed by the Democrats, the Republicans, the American Labor Party and had Communist support as well. "The man who gets into Congress from this district can stay in there for the rest of his life," he prophesied. One of the few who looked upon his campaign with less than enthusiasm was his wife Isabel, who had thrown herself into the activities of Adam's church and thought he should stay there.

Life was changing rapidly for the first Negro Congressman ever elected from the East. He had new interests, among them twenty-four-year-old Hazel Scott, a jazz pianist from Haiti. Hazel had everything; she was young and pretty and she earned $1,500 a week. They were frequently seen together.

"He has visited her at the nightclub in which she performs," Isabel charged in her suit for separation. "He has met her at the Roxy Theater where she had an engagement. He has visited her home in White Plains and his association with this woman is a matter of common knowledge."

The Harlem minister loftily filed a countersuit, which

claimed that Isabel tried to make him "live the cloistered life of a monk." As eyebrows rose at the young minister Congressman, he added, "I fear I just outgrew her. . . . Ministers' wives frequently plunge into church work up to their eyes, invariably to the annoyance and discomfort of their husbands."

Commented Miss Scott, "If and when he's free someday, I'd think myself an extremely lucky young lady to be his wife. He is one of the great men of our time. Really, he is the finest man I know."

She went to Washington on a blustery January day to see Adam take his oath of office—and watch him fume at Washington's subservience to Jim Crow. They could not stay at any of the downtown hotels or eat in the restaurants or go to the theaters. Powell described their problem: "Hazel had a starring role in the George Gershwin film biography, *Rhapsody in Blue,* and we went to a downtown theater to see it. The manager told her, 'I'm sorry, Miss Scott, but I can't admit you.' Can you imagine that? She could not get in to see a picture in which she was one of the stars!"

Even on Capitol Hill Congressman Powell was treated as a second-class citizen. There was an unwritten rule—observed by Representative William Dawson, D-Ill., the only other Negro in Congress—that Negroes would not offend the Southerners by using the Congressional swimming pool and the barber shops and the restaurants. Powell not only used them; he gave orders to his staff to follow his precedent. "When I heard that the dining room for Representatives' staffs was off limits to Negroes," he said, "I told my secretary and clerks to go down there and eat whether they were hungry or not."

He made his displeasure heard on the House floor, where he spoke against segregation in the armed forces, attacked Senator Robert Taft's motion for a voluntary Fair Employment Practices Commission, and called Representative John Rankin, D-Miss., "the leader of American Fascism."

"I won't sit by Powell," fumed Rankin.

"I'm happy that Rankin won't sit by me because that makes it mutual," Powell retorted. "The only people with whom he is qualified to sit are Hitler and Mussolini."

By August 1, 1945, Powell's divorce decree was final; he and Hazel Scott were married—a newsworthy event in itself. Thousands lined up for the reception at the Café Society Uptown, on 58th Street, where Miss Scott had been star of the show. Adam refused to pose for news photographers—he had sold the picture rights to a magazine—and when a disgruntled cameraman threw a punch, the bride fainted. Adam had a flair for making the front pages.

There was another furor, in October, when the Daughters of the American Revolution refused to allow Miss Scott to appear in Washington's Constitution Hall, the same auditorium where Negro soprano Marian Anderson had been barred in 1939. There was a flurry of speeches in Congress condemning the DAR, and President Truman noted a comparison with Nazi oppression. Bess Truman went to a DAR tea, and Powell, remembering that Eleanor Roosevelt had resigned from the DAR over the Marian Anderson incident, called Mrs. Truman "the Last Lady of the Land." Harry Truman said nothing more in public, but swore volubly in private. He would tolerate almost any attack on himself but considered his family above politics.

Powell kept his family in politics. Hazel gave birth to Adam Clayton Powell III in July 1946. Among the natal gifts was a gold spoon from a parishioner who said he had always wanted to see a Negro baby born with a gold spoon in his mouth. The child's first words, according to his father, were "Vote for Daddy."

Life continued at a giddy pace: parties with Broadway's big names, trips to Europe and the Caribbean—and, always, headlines exploding in his wake. Representative Powell was already earning a reputation at the Capitol for absenteeism. But the pace took its toll; he had two heart attacks in 1947. There was a scramble among those who considered themselves his likely successors, but Adam recovered quickly, chuckling over a story that 15 undertakers had offered to bury him free.

He supported Harry Truman for re-election in 1948—the year of the Dixiecrat rebellion—but their personal relationship did not sweeten. Powell had been dropped from the White House guest list, and he shouted his familiar battle cry: discrimination. The White House noted that other Negro Congressmen remained on the list.

In 1952, Truman's last year in office, the Internal Revenue Service moved against Powell. It claimed he owed the Government $2,749 on his 1945 taxes. Powell settled for $1,193, but investigation continued. In 1954, a Senate committee heard that Powell had received $3,000 from David Kent, a

New York builder, who claimed it was a loan. Kent had also sent another $3,000 to the Tenants Protective Association, a nonprofit corporation, which had Powell as its president. That, said Kent, was payment for the services of two of Powell's secretaries, Acy Lennon and William Hampton. They had been lent to him by Powell, he said, to help sell cooperative apartments in Kent's interracial housing development. The money had stayed in the bank account of the Tenants Protective Association for precisely three days; then another check was written to Paul Klein, a friend of Powell's. Klein said he could not remember receiving it, and the association treasurer denied signing the check. Powell claimed that the money had been paid to Klein for previous services. When asked to produce records, the Congressman testified that some of his records had been stolen, the rest destroyed by a fire in his church.

More intriguing still was the trial of another Powell secretary, Mrs. Hattie Freeman Dodson, an official of the Abyssinian Baptist Church and the wife of its choirmaster. The Government charged that Mrs. Dodson evaded $5,000 in taxes and had received $2,000 in illegal refunds between 1948 and 1952. She had gone to Washington with Powell in 1945, the Government said, and had stayed on the payroll after she returned to Harlem. Joseph E. Ford, Powell's 1946 campaign manager who ran a tax consulting service in the church, appeared as a prosecution witness. He testified that Mrs. Dodson had kicked back her salary to Powell from 1948 to 1952, but had been allowed to keep the tax refunds. Powell attacked Ford by calling him a man "who cannot be trusted, a man who indulged in sharp practices."

The unhappy Mrs. Dodson was unable to tell what she had done to earn the money from Powell's office or what had happened to it. She was convicted, fined $1,000 and given seven months in jail. A grand jury looked into Ford's kickback testimony, but refused to indict Powell. Adam claimed that it was all a plot to thwart his campaign against the White Citizens Councils.

In Congress, meanwhile, Powell learned to rankle the left as well as the right. Liberals accused him of sabotage when he tacked his "Powell Amendment"—a provision to keep Federal funds from going to segregated states—on such progressive legislation as housing and education bills. This did as much damage, they protested, as the Republican-Dixiecrat coalition. "I am an irritant," Powell admitted. "I rub until something gives. All my strength, all my money, comes from Negroes, and therefore I cannot be controlled by whites."

There were, however, times when Powell rose to statesmanship. He went as an unofficial observer to the Bandung conference of emerging Asian and African nations in 1955, and stole the spotlight away from Chinese Communist Premier Chou En-lai by telling of Negro progress in the United States. His performance won him praise in both houses of Congress.

Acy Lennon was convicted of tax evasion in 1956, causing Adam concern about his own case, as he returned from a three-month European vacation. Powell had missed the Democratic convention that had nominated Adlai Stevenson for a second try against President Eisenhower. Intimates later said that Powell feared the Justice Department, under the Republicans, might go after him for alleged tax violations. Perhaps with this in mind, he came ashore attacking the civil rights plank of the Democratic platform. On October 12 he spent half an hour with President Eisenhower at the White House. He left by the door of the West Wing that adjoins the press room, accompanied by press secretary Jim Hagerty. Powell stopped in front of the microphones and announced he would support Eisenhower for a second term. Not mentioned was that three of Ike's aides had arranged to deliver $50,000 to Powell to pay his "campaign expenses." There had also been discussion with White House aides of dropping the tax case against Powell.

Democratic leaders across the country—white and Negro —accused Powell of a sellout. Powell responded by endorsing Republican Jacob Javits in his Senate race against New York City's Mayor Robert Wagner. Governor Averell Harriman, a Democrat, thought it "sort of strange that a man whose associates are known to be having difficulties with the Department of Justice should come out, as he left the White House, with a statement of this kind."

Representative Emanuel Celler, D-N.Y., demanded that Powell be stripped of his seniority rights and added, "He was always unreliable, and furthermore ran out on his own people. When the Celler civil rights bill was called up for debate, he went to Europe on a pleasure jaunt." It was not the only time Powell missed voting on the issues he preached about.

On Election Day the Republicans made deep inroads into the normal Democratic voting pattern in Harlem. Javits became New York's new Senator, and Powell won re-election by better than three to one. A few weeks later the grand jury investigating Powell recessed, and Thomas A. Bolan, the Assistant U.S. Attorney in charge of the probe, was given other duties.

Late in 1957 Bolan went to William F. Buckley, the arch-conservative editor of the *National Review*, with the claim that he had enough evidence to convict Powell. In its December 14, 1957, issue *National Review* published an article titled "Death of an Investigation: The Wheels of Justice Stop for Adam Clayton Powell, Jr." Copies were sent to members of the grand jury.

In April the grand jury received another mailing of the December article, with a covering letter that said: ". . . *National Review* is not interested in persecuting Adam Clayton Powell, Jr., but is interested in the integrity of the judicial process." After talks with Buckley and Bolan, the grand jury met, and Powell was indicted on three counts.

The Government's prosecution of Powell was less vigorous. Two counts against him were dropped when prosecutor Morton Robson, brought into the case the last minute before the start of the trial, could present no evidence to substantiate them. The third charge, that Powell had taken improper deductions on his wife's return, was overwhelmed by defense attorney Edward Bennett Williams. Williams demonstrated that the Congressman had overstated her income. The jury failed to reach a decision, voting 10–2 for acquittal.

"It seemed clear to me," Williams wrote in his book *One Man's Freedom*, "that without the external pressures and without the passion aroused in the grand jurors, Adam Powell would never have been indicted and would never have been forced into a long, expensive and politically damaging trial. If the grand jurors had been left to reach their decision in the calm, careful manner in which grand juries are intended to function, no indictment would have resulted."

Powell's domestic problems were less easily solved. Hazel was immersed in her career, and after his victory in the 1958 primary, Powell had to plunge into Democratic politics to recover his prestige in the party. With Governor Harriman and challenger Nelson Rockefeller both pleading for his endorsement, Powell hesitated until Tammany Hall put up $100,000 for his "campaign expenses." Then he joined the Harriman camp. His secretary in the campaign was a pretty young Puerto Rican divorcee, Yvette Marjorie Flores Diago, whom he had met on a blind date in San Juan. When he had arrived to pick her up, he had bowed from the waist, clicked his heels—and swept her off her feet.

From New York Mrs. Flores followed Powell to Washington and went on his payroll for $3,074 a year. She comes from a prominent and affluent San Juan family, although not in the island's top financial or social bracket. Her father, Oscar Diago, is director of the Commonwealth Sports and Recreation Department, an imposing title for the supervision of the cockfight arenas. Her grandfather had been San Juan's last elected Republican mayor.

Powell's interest in Puerto Rico heightened as Puerto Ricans pushed their way into his Harlem district, and Yvette led him on hand-holding tours of the island. They were married in Puerto Rico on December 15, 1960, a month after his divorce from Hazel Scott was final. This time there were no crowds and no photographers, but Adam made the headlines again by eloping. The ceremony before a juvenile court judge was restricted to himself, his bride and 150 of her relatives.

They came back to Washington, tanned and happy, moved into a white stucco house in southeast Washington and toasted their good fortune. Yvette's salary was immediately raised to $12,974. She stayed on the payroll after she returned home to San Juan to have her baby, a boy, born on July 17, 1962.

Like Adam's son by Hazel Scott, the infant was named Adam Clayton Powell—his father apparently was fond of the name. "I'll stay here for a week after the birth, and then return to Washington," Mrs. Powell told reporters. But the call she had expected from her husband never came. She never returned to the white stucco house.

Adam, meanwhile, was finding other interests in Washington. He had become chairman of the House Education and Labor Committee through the inexorable operation of the seniority system. With President John Kennedy setting a course for social legislation, it was a busy committee. In the early months of the New Frontier, the Powell committee performed well, and its chairman reaped unusual praise from the Washington press. He still went to Puerto Rico on many weekends and sat in the sun on the beach in front of the lavish home at Cerro Gordo, built for the Powells by Yvette's contractor uncle, Gonzalo (Baby) Diago. Yvette told reporters that she earned her pay by answering letters in Spanish from her husband's Puerto Rican constituents, usually handling between 20 and 25 a day. "It is very hard to work," she said. On one occasion, she asked his Congressional office to send her instructions, in Spanish, on how to play dominoes—the Congressman's favorite pastime.

With his wife in Puerto Rico and his heavy work load in Washington, Powell found less and less time to spend in New York. He also developed less inclination to go there. In March 1960 Senator Hubert Humphrey, then a stalking horse for the Democratic Presidential nomination, was scheduled to appear on a televised interview program, *Between the Lines*. His plane was canceled by bad weather, and Powell appeared as a last-minute substitute. His conversation was wide-ranging, and at one point he repeated a charge he had made a month earlier in the House. The New York Police Department was graft-ridden, he said, and, apparently to make his attacks more convincing and specific, he named Esther James, an elderly Negro woman, as a "bag woman for the Police Department."

In the following days Mrs. James demanded an apology, but Powell ignored her. In July she hired Raymond Rubin, an attorney, to represent her in a suit against Powell. Mrs. James charged defamation of character and asked for $1 million. The case came to trial in the New York Supreme Court after a long series of postponements. But Powell, supremely confident, never appeared. On April 3, 1963, the jury found for Mrs. James and awarded her $211,500. "The king is dead," Mrs. James said over and over again outside the courtroom.

The victor, however, still had to collect her money. The Appellate Court upheld the jury's finding but reduced the judgment to $46,500. The verdict stood through challenges to the state Court of Appeals and the U.S. Supreme Court. Mrs. James threw more suits into the legal turmoil, asserting that Powell was illegally transferring his property in New York and in Puerto Rico to hide assets. Rubin sent subpoena servers looking for Powell, who stayed out of New York except to preach on Sundays, when civil subpoenas could not be served. The case dragged on through 10 separate courts and came before 80 different judges.

Behind the courtroom drama, Mrs. James was besieged with death threats and seldom left her Amsterdam Avenue apartment. From time to time she requested and received police protection. She went out alone on October 20, 1964, and was standing near her apartment when a gunman walked up behind a small-time gambler near her and put a bullet through his head. In 1966 Mrs. James retreated to Jamaica, her birthplace. Her suits continued their way through the tangle of the courts, and by the end of 1966 the judgment against Powell had grown to $164,000, counting penalties and accrued interest.

For Powell, the rosy life at Cerro Gordo was losing its glow. In the summer of 1962 Adam sailed for Europe in his capacity as House Labor Committee chairman to investigate employment opportunities for women. Liberals fumed because a vote to abolish the poll tax was scheduled in the House during his absence. They would have fumed more had they known that the State Department, at Adam's request, had sent a telegram to American embassies in London, Paris, and Rome, asking for special treatment for the Congressman, his receptionist, Miss Corrine Huff, and Mrs. Tamara Wall, the pretty divorcee who earned $194 a week as an attorney on the staff of Powell's committee.

Powell's grand tour of Europe, thanks to the State Department's considerate preparations, proceeded joyously—with only one small hindrance. He had forgotten his back brace, a sort of corset support that he wears, and his party had to cable his Washington office to air-express the brace immediately. The trip, as it turned out, was cut short somewhat when an irreverent columnist published the State Department cable making the original arrangements. The news aroused Powell's wife, who was sitting in San Juan, supposedly answering mail. She sent him a hot cable. Powell hastened home.

When the ripples from the Washington tempest over his junket reached Adam, he blustered, "What was all the fuss about? Did they want me to take an all-black staff?" But he was upset enough to cut his vacation short, leave Corrine Huff in Madrid and fly back to Puerto Rico to see Yvette and little "Adamcito." He barged off the airplane all smiles and smothered Yvette in his embrace as the flash bulbs exploded. Months afterward she remarked ruefully, "Adam Clayton

Powell is surely one of the most persuasive men on earth. To this day, despite all our troubles, I believe that if I were looking at a white wall and he assured me it was red, I would look again and be half convinced that it was indeed red."

In Congress there was talk of stripping Powell of his committee chairmanship and of a move to chop the committee in half. "They're trying to split the Adam," Powell said cheerfully. Negroes across the country closed ranks behind him, and civil rights leaders stepped in to save him. An assault on Powell's power could be motivated only by racial prejudice, they said.

Through it all, Adam never lost his aplomb. The Teamsters' chief lobbyist, the late Sid Zagri, recalled discussing legislation with him over a glass of Bourbon when President Johnson phoned from the White House. Powell leaned back in his great leather chair, feet propped upon his desk, a drink in one hand and the telephone snuggled against his shoulder. "Hello, baby!" Powell greeted the President of the United States.

Powell's committee requested a 1963–64 budget of $697,000 —$64,000 more than the allotment for the preceding two years. It was turned down. The committee was given $200,000 in 1963, and was instructed to come back for more in 1964. Powell did not bother to appear at the hearings before the House Administration Committee. California's Representative James Roosevelt explained that his chairman had the Asian flu, and the audience laughed. In Puerto Rico, Adam clarified his illness. "Afro-Asian flu," he said.

While Adam junketed, other Negroes at home kept busy. At schools, lunch counters, hotels, theaters, and churches across the South, thousands of young Negroes were following other leaders at sit-ins, freedom rides and trips to jail. It was a grueling battle, but racial barriers were falling. In Mississippi, Chief U.S. Marshal J. P. McShane led a force of marshals and installed James Meredith as a student in the University of Mississippi. In Birmingham, Alabama, Bull Connor, the police commissioner, ordered police dogs and fire hoses against demonstrators. In small communities across the South, night riders terrorized the countryside and Negro churches were burned.

Powell picked this time in history to strike an alliance with the Black Muslims. He appeared at a street rally on Seventh Avenue with Malcolm X, who was as firmly committed to apartheid as Bull Connor. On the Harlem streets Powell praised the Muslims and Malcolm, then launched an attack on white leadership in the civil rights movement. "Unless we can seize completely the administration and the policy-making of our national Negro organizations, then we must say there is no hope for us," Powell told his 3,000 listeners. "And I include the NAACP, Urban League, CORE and Southern Christian Leadership Conference under Martin Luther King."

Reaction from the Negro leaders was swift and derisive; it seemed that events were sweeping past Powell. When more than 200,000 Negroes and whites marched from the Washington Monument to the Lincoln Memorial on August 28, 1963, in a demonstration for racial equality, Powell stayed away, unwanted.

But Powell's committee kept busy turning out bills to build John Kennedy's New Frontier and Lyndon Johnson's Great Society. While he pushed War-on-Poverty legislation, Powell carved out a niche for himself. Haryou-Act, the nation's largest anti-poverty project, was put under the leadership of Powell's henchman, Livingston Wingate. In two years Haryou-Act, which was funded for $13.4 million, went $1 million in the red, through overspending and bad administration.

The nation's press continued to train its fire on Adam. Reporters discovered the identity of Y. Marjorie Flores, who was still in Puerto Rico with her son, but now drawing $20,578 on Adam's payroll. Simultaneously Miss Huff's earning power also had increased to $19,300, and she continued to travel with Adam.

Many people who had excused Powell's peccadilloes in the past became upset, however, by his continued flaunting of the courts. By the end of 1966 the court papers formed a stack 20 feet high, and Powell was under three citations for civil contempt and one for criminal contempt. He could no longer go to New York, even on Sundays.

Powell got one piece of good news as 1966 drew to a close. There was a letter from President Johnson, praising Adam and his committee for pushing through "49 pieces of bedrock legislation. . . . The passage of every one of these bills attests to your ability to get things done." But the letter was lost in the flood of unfavorable headlines. The House Administration Committee, probing Powell's unorthodox conduct, found that his wife's employment was a violation of the 1964 law allowing Congressional help to work only in Washington or the home state. It also found that Powell had used the names of employees of his committee on airline tickets—charged to the taxpayers—for trips with Miss Huff to Bimini, a Bahama island 60 miles off the coast of Florida. The investigators also learned about Sylvia J. Givens.

Miss Givens testified that she had been interviewed for a job on the Labor Committee by Miss Huff, and later by Chairman Powell himself. She started work on August 1, 1966, and, six days later, left for Bimini with the Congressman and his favorite secretary. There, she said, she worked as a live-in maid and cook in the two-bedroom house owned by Huff Enterprises, Inc. She returned to Washington when Powell and Miss Huff came back two weeks later. She returned to the committee, performed a few office chores, and was dismissed early in September. Her ticket back to Washington had been charged to the committee.

Another of Powell's pretty receptionists, Emma Swann, was listed as having taken thirty trips between New York, Miami and Buffalo during 1965–1966, but she acknowledged under oath that she had used her airline tickets only three times. On each occasion she had traveled with Powell. Subcommittee Chairman Wayne Hays, D-Ohio, examined Mrs. Swann closely.

"Did you do any work—like dictation or anything like that?" asked Chairman Hays.

"No, I didn't. I had no business. I was just going."

"Could you tell us how these trips came about, what discussions you had with Mr. Powell?"

"There was no discussion," replied Mrs. Swann. "Mr. Powell gave me the tickets."

"Well, there had to be some arrangement as to your being away from the office."

"Well, he did give me a vacation time."

"Did you ask him for the travel ticket or did he voluntarily give you a ticket?"

"No. I did not ask him for the tickets," said Mrs. Swann. "They were given to me."

"Did he tell you why he was giving them to you?"

"No, there was no discussion as to why. I was to use them."

"There had to be some reason for this gift of a ticket to Miami," pressed Representative William Dickinson, the Montgomery, Alabama, Republican. "What was the reason for this? I couldn't just walk up and give one of my employees a ticket and not say anything."

"He gave me the ticket to go to Miami with time off included and that is all," persisted Mrs. Swann.

"There was no purpose to it?"

"No purpose," replied Powell's receptionist.

When Congress opened in January 1967, and its members stood to be sworn in, Powell was challenged and asked to stand aside. Another special panel, headed by Emanuel Celler, was appointed to look into Powell's conduct. Among the witnesses who appeared, timidly, was Yvette Powell. In a soft sad voice she told the Congressmen about her life as Adam's wife and $20,578-a-year secretary.

"At the beginning, after our son was born, he kept sending me mail and work to do back in Puerto Rico, and it was, well, I felt it was a full-time job at that time with the amount of work he would send." She translated letters, she said, from Spanish to English "so he could understand them." It usually took her four or five hours a day, she said, until January 1963; then her work load dwindled to two hours a day. By the middle of 1965 she had stopped receiving work in the mail; Adam had also stopped visiting her.

Only four of her Government paychecks ever reached Mrs. Powell during her six years on the payroll. The rest were endorsed and deposited in Powell's account at the Swiss-style bank that the House operates for members, although Mrs. Powell testified that she had never given anyone authority to sign her name. "I'll take care of the finances," Powell had announced after their marriage. In November 1966 she wrote to the House of Representatives, asking that her checks be sent to her in Puerto Rico. "I had been trying to get Adam either to bring me back to Washington to work, or get me off the payroll, which to me was a very embarrassing situation back home with the papers and everything, and I just could never —most of the time I could never get an answer. . . . Aside from that, I had lots of bills that were his bills, but the pressure was on me because I am the one who is back there, and I thought I could pay some of them."

Mrs. Powell had come to Washington on August 4, 1966, a year earlier, and had registered at the Sheraton Park Hotel for the specific purpose of seeing her husband. She telephoned his office. He refused to see her. Although Mrs. Powell had brought her three-year-old son to see his father, Powell would not relent. He even sent the manager of the Sheraton Park Hotel a warning that he would not be responsible for his wife's hotel bills beyond August 6. Weary of trying to see her husband, Mrs. Powell finally checked out of the hotel with her child on August 8.

Powell was fishing and playing dominoes in sun-blessed Bimini with Miss Huff while his wife testified in Washington, but there were many in the Capitol who remembered Adam's defense on an earlier occasion: "I do not do any more than any other member of Congress, and by the grace of God, I'll not do less." Nevertheless, he was not permitted to take his House seat. Harlem voters promptly re-elected him for his own vacant seat, but the mood of the House was such that he went to Bimini instead of Washington. He turned to the courts, which he had spurned in the matter of his unpaid judgment, to rescue his House seat. But the courts refused to interfere with Congress. He declared that he would run again in 1968 for his empty seat, but somehow his announcement lacked the old savoir-faire.

It certainly had been no revelation to most House members that Adam Clayton Powell's wife Yvette had been drawing $20,578 a year in Puerto Rico from the taxpayers. Not until the public uproar grew too loud to ignore, however, did the House belatedly cut her off the payroll. For there were few things Adam did that were not accepted practice on Capitol Hill.

3. Family Planning

The House Administration Committee, which launched the investigation into Powell's activities, is headed by Chairman Omar Burleson, D-Tex., who has been known to pad his own payroll (see page 241). Another intrepid investigator, Chairman William Dawson of Illinois, whose House Government Operations Committee is supposed to crack down on the misuse of the taxpayers' money, would have trouble accounting for a few dollars of his own House payroll. His married daughter, Barbara Morgan, is listed at $514.52 a month, and below her name appears that of her husband John, for another $104.53 a month. Dawson's Washington and Chicago offices decline to indicate if either of them has performed any particular service for the taxpayers.

Probably no one was more pious in his criticism of Powell than Representative James Utt, R-Calif., a fearless crusader against Federal spending, who adds $8,166 a year to the Federal deficit by keeping his wife on the payroll. Mrs. Elmer Holland, wife of the Pennsylvania Representative, is the best-paid wife at $14,378 a year for performing secretarial chores.

Newcomers to Congress quickly learn the game. One of the most celebrated freshmen, swept in by the 1958 Democratic tide, was a beefy tool-and-die maker named Randall Harmon. He had been running for the House in Indiana's 10th District since 1942, five times as a Republican, the rest as a Democrat. He had spent five weeks of his campaign in the hospital, had made exactly one speech and had spent, by his own account, $162 to get elected. It didn't take him long to get his money back.

The first thing Harmon did, after installing a time clock in his Washington office, was to put his wife on the payroll at $344.10 a month. The next thing he did was to take down the screens from his front porch back in Muncie, replace them with glass, and rent the porch to the Government for $100 a month as his hometown office. He put his wife in charge of it. What the reporters wrote didn't bother Harmon. Fingering his black frontier tie, he dismissed them: "I don't care what they say about me because I don't read the newspaper. I don't read anything but the funnies and *The Saturday Evening Post.*"

Not long after Representative Robert N. C. Nix arrived on Capitol Hill from Philadelphia, his son, Robert, Jr., turned up on the House payroll. Eight raises in less than three years brought his salary above $20,000 a year. Yet Robert, Jr., a successful attorney, had nothing to do with the Washington office and was a ward leader, in fact, of a different Philadelphia district. Reporters who tried to discover how he earned his $20,000 found him too busy in court to answer questions. He adjusted his camel's-hair coat and offered an outstretched hand. The stone in his ring flashed a sun spark. "I'm terribly sorry about this," he apologized. "There just isn't enough time, and I don't know when there will be." Then he barged out of the door and disappeared.

Reporters had trouble merely identifying Lovie Diggs, who collected $2,500 in four months, through the office of Representative Charles C. Diggs, Jr., D-Mich. After Lovie disappeared from the payroll in September 1966, a new beneficiary turned up at $1,205.52 a month. The new name was that of Anna Johnston Diggs, the Congressman's wife.

Other Congressmen talked freely, if not always convincingly, about their tax-supported relatives. Representative William R. Anderson, D-Tenn., commander of the first atomic submarine and a conscientious Congressman, had to find something to occupy his mother-in-law. So he put her to work at home clipping newspapers. She scans 25 newspapers from 18 home counties, he said. For this the taxpayers paid Mrs. Cecilia Etzel $788.85 a month until September 1966, when Anderson raised her salary to $985.06 a month. Representative Thomas G. Morris, D-N.M., solved his mother-in-law problem by putting Mrs. Ethelwyne Stevens in charge of his office back home in Tucumcari, New Mexico. On the payroll for $703.72 a month, mother-in-law Stevens at least does answer the phone at the Tucumcari office.

The examples could fill a book: Esther Miller, wife of seventy-six-year-old Representative George P. Miller, D-Calif., draws $705.83 a month from the taxpayers. She used to put in long hours in his House office, but a friend, sitting in Esther's empty office, confided that she now spends most of her time visiting her grandchildren in California. Rowena Brown, wife of Representative George E. Brown, Jr., D-Calif., insisted that she earns twice her $750-a-month public pay, and friends of the family swear this is true. Robert T. Hall, thirty-one-year-old lawyer whose mother in 1962 married widowed Senator Winston L. Prouty, R-Vt., went to work in his stepfather's office at $700 a month, then transferred to the staff of the District of Columbia Committee at $1,300 a month. Late in 1966 he left Capitol Hill and opened a law office in downtown Washington.

Beginning in 1962, Representative Neal Smith, D-Iowa, introduced a bill each session to outlaw family-plan payrolls. In 1964 he tried to tack an anti-nepotism amendment to the pay-raise bill. Up leaped Representative James H. Morrison, D-La. "This has never been taken up by our [Post Office and Civil Service] Committee for a vote," he protested. He did not mention that, as vice chairman, he had been instrumental in blocking a hearing. Thus he raised his own obstruction as the reason for asking the House to reject the amendment.

"Frankly," he added, "I believe this amendment would do harm instead of good." It would have done harm, certainly, to Morrison's family budget. His wife Marjorie was drawing $1,009.97 a month from the taxpayers for helping around the office.

Smith offered his amendment again during the pay-bill debate in 1967. Only a handful of bored Representatives were on hand for the debate. Before they realized what had happened, they were confronted with a vote on nepotism. Unhappily, they accepted Smith's amendment rather than be recorded in favor of family payroll padding. The issue was bucked to the Senate where Senator Ralph Yarborough, D-Tex., invoked the memory of George Washington, who had appointed a stepson to his staff at Yorktown. Following Washington's example, Yarborough had appointed son Richard to his staff at $22,000 per annum—the highest pay for a relative in Congress. But Senators, like their colleagues in the House, could not afford to vote for nepotism. Petulantly, they accepted the House bill barring relatives from the public payroll. The new law went into effect immediately after it was signed in December, 1967. But relatives already on the payroll were charitably exempted.

The Congressional payrolls, of course, don't tell the full story. Enterprising legislators have discovered that they can slip their relatives on the payrolls of Federal agencies with less risk of publicity. Hiram L. Fong, R-Hawaii, the Senate millionaire and foe of Government spending, requested the Post Office to give his son and his niece summer jobs that were available for poverty-stricken youths. When the news leaked out, Senator Fong claimed he didn't know the program was supposed to be for poor people. Honolulu Postmaster George Hara said the purpose of the program had been widely advertised. He received orders from his Post Office Department superiors to put the Senator's niece on the payroll, he said, "after I had first hired the wrong Carolyn Fong." Confided Hara, "Poor parents came to me and I had to say I was sorry but I couldn't help their children. I couldn't sleep nights worrying about it." Representatives Richard Fulton, D-Tenn., and Henry B. Gonzalez, D-Tex., also took advantage of the program to get post-office jobs for their sons.

Nepotism is only one side of the payroll picture on Capitol Hill. More insidious is the practice of paying personal bills by putting a creditor on the public payroll. A leading House expert on this dodge is Representative Arch A. Moore, R-W.Va., who arranged for the taxpayers to pay part of his printing bill and to provide him with a private pilot. His pilot, Floyd Graham, appeared on Moore's payroll from September 1960 to May 1962 at an annual salary ranging from $2,950 to $4,756. Meanwhile, Graham was supposedly employed full time by Ohio Valley Aviation, Inc., in Wheeling, West Virginia. While Moore was winging around West Virginia by plane, Representative Cleveland M. Bailey—his 1962 opponent under a West Virginia redrawing of Congressional district lines—was trying to keep up in a battered old car.

Like several other Congressmen, Moore sent his private printing business to the Art Press in Washington and worked out a neat scheme for paying the bills without cost to himself. He simply put the printshop's owner, Carl Baron, on the public payroll. The printer did no work for the taxpayers and credited Government paychecks against Moore's personal printing bill. Representative Robert J. McIntosh, R-Mich., used to do the same thing before he left Congress in 1959, with the minor difference that it was Baron's brother Paul who went on the payroll. His salary was not sufficient to pay the Congressman's bill, though. McIntosh went back to Michigan owing Art Press $451.

The Baron brothers figured in the payrolls of at least two other Congressmen, Representatives E. Y. Berry, R-S.D., and William C. Cramer, R-Fla. Paul Baron never even dropped by Berry's office—not even to pick up his paycheck—but he collected $11,840 by mail as a member of Berry's staff. Carl Baron went on Cramer's payroll for a modest $74.26 per month at about the same time; his wife Caroline was previously listed as a Cramer employee (see page 209).

Both Berry and Cramer kept other interesting people on their payrolls. The ultraconservative Berry, a bitter foe of Federal subsidies, did not mind a little subsidy for himself. He stuck the taxpayers with bonus money for L. G. Parkinson, editor of a hometown weekly called the McLaughlin *Messenger,* which is owned by the Congressman's wife. Over a six-year period the $4,500 Berry paid Parkinson looked like a tidy subsidy to the Congressman's family paper.

The work of Congress, if it weren't for the pressure of the press, would likely become more and more a family affair.

Perhaps none of today's Congressional practitioners of nepotism quite measures up to the standards set by Adam Clayton Powell, but it could happen again. To get around the new law, Congressmen simply might hire one another's relatives. This cozy arrangement has already been suggested by some legislators who don't let go of a government pay envelope easily.

11

THE SENILITY SYSTEM

1. Unrepresentatives

John F. Kennedy spoke boldly at his inauguration of the torch of leadership being passed to a new generation. The Congressional hierarchy, grouped in an arc behind him according to their seniority, applauded tolerantly. But his words had no effect upon them. Congress has continued to be a council of elders, dominated by tired old men whose only claim to power is their good fortune in seldom facing serious opposition.

The Congressional seniority system hands command of the committees of the Senate and House to these men, regardless of their ability, their honesty or their possible senility. The system has produced chairmen who are not representative of the country's geography, its desires, its politics or its people. They are out of step with the times and, often, with both the national Administration and the majority of their own members.

Committee chairmen have the power—and use it—to appoint subcommittees, to decide when and whether committee meetings will be held, to hire committee staffs, to set hearings, to choose the witnesses who will appear, to call up the bills for floor action, to have the first and last words in debate.

Finally the chairmen select the conference groups that resolve the differences between Senate and House versions of a bill.

However the ballots may be cast in future elections, the voters are likely to exercise only a limited influence on legislation. For the Congress will be dominated by old men who march in slow cadence behind the nation. The committee chairmen of both the Senate and House average more than sixty-seven years of age, most of them come from small towns or rural areas, and most are Southerners. In the Senate, 10 of the 16 chairmen are from the South, the rest from the West. Although sixty-five is often the mandatory retirement age in private industry, 10 of the Senate chairmen are past that age; 6 of these are past seventy. The situation is much the same in the House, with 14 of the 20 chairmanships held by Representatives from Southern and Southwestern states; 11 past sixty-five, 7 over seventy and only 3 under sixty.

Over the years the seniority system has produced some committee chairmen who have been exceptional leaders. It has also propelled some appalling misfits into positions of awesome responsibility. Two who belong in the latter category were foisted upon the nation by the voters of rural South Carolina.

2. *The Collected Works of Mendel Rivers*

On Friday evening, the solemn solon with the flowing white hair can fly home on the Government plane that stands ready at his whim. It is a pleasant flight, with attendants in the cabin to cater to his wants. The real fun begins, however, when the great silver jet comes to a halt on the airport apron and a ramp is pushed to the door.

Then the principal passenger bounds down the steps and climbs into a waiting auto. The car will take him through an airport gate bearing his name.

Then down a highway named after him, past a seven-foot granite shaft holding aloft a heroic bust of himself.

Then around a military housing development that bears an abbreviation of his name.

And if his ego is not satiated, he can stop the car and gaze at a post office named in his honor.

This may sound like the dream of a banana-republic dictator. It is not. It happens all too frequently in that haven of homespun American virtues, Charleston, South Carolina. The beneficiary of all these petty flatteries is Charleston's Congressman, L. Mendel Rivers.

Democratic Representative Rivers, because of his ability to outlive men of more talent and his foresight in being born in an area that still treasures the one-party system, has risen to the chairmanship of the House Armed Services Committee. He is also living proof that all good things come to those in Congress who wait for the seniority system to elevate them to the pinnacle of power.

The monuments to him that dot the Charleston area like liver spots on an old man's hand are unique on the American political scene. They are as much a measure of Rivers' exaltation as are the jewels proffered Oriental monarchs. And, as might be expected, most of these public tributes paid to Rivers are financed by the American people.

The plane, like L. Mendel Rivers Field and, of course, the airport gate, belong to the U.S. Air Force. The L. Mendel Rivers Postal Annex is also the property of the Government, which refuses to honor any living men on its stamps. The housing development, Men-Riv Park, provides split-level shelter for Navy families. The highway was once Route 52; now it is Rivers Avenue. The statue that watches over it was erected by grateful Charleston businessmen in 1965, as a token of their appreciation for all the Government dollars that Rivers has funneled into his home town. Their gratitude did, however, have its limits. When the fund-raising to pay for the bust fell short of the goal, the remainder of the cost was picked up by Lockheed Aircraft, a major defense contractor. Lesser Southern heroes, such as Robert E. Lee and Pierre Beauregard, were obliged to wait until they were dead and gone to be immortalized in granite and metal.

On the scale of values upon which statesmen are usually judged, Rivers might appear to be overrated by his admirers. This does not necessarily mean, however, that he is undeserving of the homage he receives from the Government he has claimed is out to betray America; or from local businessmen who have benefited from Uncle Sam's beneficence; or from the manufacturers of U.S. armaments. In many ways Mendel Rivers is the biggest thing to happen to Charleston since Mad Dog Ruffin yanked the lanyard that sent the first cannon shot of the Civil War arching across the harbor toward Fort Sumter.

Life began humbly enough for the man with all this power. Rivers was born on September 28, 1905, in Gumville, South Carolina, on the edge of the Hell Hole Swamp. His father Lucius, who ran a small farm and a turpentine still, died when Mendel was eight, and the family soon lost its land. Rivers' mother moved to North Charleston, a drab, tired industrial suburb, hidden away behind bustling, very proper Charleston.

Life was hard for the widow and her boy. Even after her remarriage, the dollars were still scarce, and Mendel began bringing home money while he was still in grammar school. He was up before dawn every morning, to milk his cows and deliver papers before the school bell tolled.

As he grew older, the demands on him became even harsher. North Charleston did not have its own high school, and he had to take a trolley to his classes in Charleston; he had to get up even earlier to do his chores. He was not exactly a brilliant student, although he slid by after repeating his freshman year. He frequently tells interviewers, in jargon that brings embarrassment to neither the speaker nor the listener in North Charleston, "I don't think the lightning of intellect struck the taproot of my family tree."

"I had to work for everything I got," he has said, and he can still recall in detail the summers he spent working as a laborer—at the Charleston Navy Yard, in a sheet-metal shop for Standard Oil, and in the furnace heat of an asbestos mill. That last job did have some advantages, however. It was while working in the mill that he got his first taste of public acclaim, and he found that he enjoyed it. In those days of simple pleasures, sandlot baseball was a popular amusement—sometimes thousands crowded along the foul lines—and Rivers was a fleet-footed outfielder for the mill's semipro team. Then as now, sports opened a door for poor Southern boys to escape the tedium and poverty that surround them in the mills, but Rivers was not quite good enough at bat to interest the big-league scouts who watched him play. Another way out was more education, and although his taproots still didn't need lightning rods, Rivers was willing to make the sacrifice for more acclaim. He was twenty-one when he entered the College of Charleston, and after his junior year he was accepted at the University of South Carolina Law School. "I went to college just long enough to get into law school," he explained, "and I went to law school just long enough to get my degree."

He finished law school in 1931 and he passed the bar examination a year later. That year he also launched himself in politics, and won election to the state legislature. His term in the state capitol was marked by some achievement for his constituents; he was co-sponsor of the state workmen's compensation law. In 1936 he left the legislature to become a special—though largely anonymous—Justice Department attorney under Thurman Arnold. Again the cheers of the crowd had eluded him.

Rivers began his political blast-off on a steaming summer day in 1940. It was a zippety-doo-daw day in Easthill, South Carolina. The annual Watermelon Festival was in full festoonery, and many of the village's 2,000 inhabitants had turned out for the fun. The white farmers stood in knots where they could find shade under the trees, and they talked in monosyllables as they kept wary eyes on their daughters and on the city people who had come to the festival. From Rivers, at least, the farmers had little to fear. He smiled at the winsome young ladies, but he courted their parents. He walked from group to group, offering his thin, smooth hand to the hard, calloused grasp of the farmers. And he drawled, "Mah name is Mendel Rivers, an' Ah wanna be your Congress-man."

The seat was vacant. Rivers, like most political aspirants in the South, knew better than to buck the system and run against an incumbent. But the incumbent had died, and Rivers had a once-in-a-lifetime opportunity. As the summer wore on and Rivers' campaign expanded, he never abandoned his friends-and-neighbors approach, but he added a bite. Besides the handshake and the earnest appeal, he carried an attack on his opponent sharpened by sarcasm broad enough to penetrate the most isolated voters.

His opponent for the Democratic nomination was Alfred E. Von Kulnitz, a successful businessman who was backed by the courthouse regulars. As Rivers stumped the cow crossings and the turpentine farms, he talked of his own background of poverty and his possession of that political essential in these parts, patriotism. By mid-1940 the news of the war in Europe was known even in the backwoods of South Carolina, and Rivers won approving nods with his references to "Fritz Von

Kulnitz." Rivers painted the ethnic background of his opponent in strokes as broad as a cotton patch, and the patriots of the 1st District could see their duty. They knew that Rivers was an American, even if his hair did hang down over his collar like Andrew Jackson's. He triumphed on Election Day, and despite the coming of the Republican party to the South, he has never since had serious opposition.

Calculated on the basis of plain dollars and cents, Rivers may well deserve having his name etched upon the public places of Charleston. His district has prospered from his service on the military committees like a tick on a fat dog. Charleston's fine port facilities made it the site for a naval base before Rivers was born, thereby saving him the problem of creating it. The Navy listed it as expendable not long after Herbert Hoover entered the White House in 1929, but it narrowly survived the economy ax and became a naval hub during World War II. When Rivers came to Congress, he got himself appointed to a strategic position on the Naval Affairs Committee, later merged into the Armed Services Committee. As he advanced in seniority, the military brass became progressively more aware of the strategic location of the Charleston area.

Besides the naval base, the new Congressman's district also possessed an Army depot, the Marine boot camp at Parris Island, and a national cemetery at Berkeley. With World War II came a Navy degaussing station—a facility to demagnetize ships—plus a weapons station at Berkeley and an air base at Charleston. Both the air base and the degaussing station were closed after the war, and the Government payroll took a temporary dip in Charleston. But by 1949 the money was flowing back again. Rivers, through the seniority system, became vice chairman of a regular subcommittee and chairman of a special subcommittee investigating military hospitals. By the wildest of coincidences, the Navy picked that year to decide on Charleston as the site for a hospital.

In the next years the pyramiding military installations reflected Rivers' increasing power. The Air Force reopened its base in Charleston in 1950; Rivers' magnetism drew the Navy's degaussing station out of mothballs in 1951, and an Air Force tank farm sprouted in 1952. When Rivers became vice chairman of a subcommittee looking into military land transfers in 1955, then took command of a special subcommittee probing property acquisitions, the Pentagon promptly started acquiring property for more installations in Rivers' district. In rapid succession, the Navy established a Marine Corps air station in Beaufort, and the Air Force built a recreation center at Berkeley. This still left some gaps to be filled in the proliferation of military installations, and the Air Force opened a gap filler annex—an unmanned radar site—at Parris Island in 1959.

The Army, which had hardly been contributing its share to the economic development of the 1st District of South Carolina, finally leased three buildings for its activities—a National Guard office in Hampton in 1959, an Army Reserve installation in Charleston in 1960, and another National Guard office in Charleston in 1965. "If he puts anything else in Charleston," commented Representative Robert L. F. Sikes, D-Fla., referring to Rivers' empire-building, "the whole place will sink completely from sight from the sheer weight of the military installations."

Rivers is not worried about his district's sinking into its swamps. When then Secretary of Defense Robert McNamara launched his austerity program in 1965 and provoked outraged howls from Congressmen for closing bases in their district, he and Rivers celebrated one of their rare periods of good feeling. Rivers' district was not entirely spared from the swing of the economy ax. One installation was shut down; a Marine transportation shed that employed three men. To soften the blow, a Polaris submarine squadron, with 2,200 men, was hastily attached to Charleston.

Rivers has never blushed over the armed forces' blatant attempts to win his favor. "Naturally," he once confessed, "I take all the credit I can get."

For Rivers, the climb up the ladder of seniority was more arduous than it is for many other Congressmen. For much of the time that he served on the committee, its chairman was Representative Carl Vinson, D-Ga., an autocrat who ran the committee as though it were his private feudal fief. Vinson, known on the Hill as "Uncle Carl," was never anxious to share either the labor or the prerogatives of the committee with his underlings. He was a man who loved power and held it jealously.

Rivers became cozier with his chairman than most other members, sidling up to Vinson whenever the opportunity presented itself. Other Congressmen watched Rivers with astonishment. "He courted Uncle Carl something fierce," one said. If Vinson was busy in his office at lunchtime, Rivers would bring him sandwiches and snacks. If Vinson's ego needed propping up, Rivers would bolster it, either in private or in a House speech. In one speech he compared Vinson with all his heroes. Uncle Carl, he said, had reached the heights of John C. Calhoun. In Rivers' estimation, a man really could go no higher, but Rivers kept on, anyway, comparing Vinson also to Henry Clay, George Washington, Robert E. Lee, Stonewall Jackson, Abe Lincoln, Daniel Webster, Jefferson Davis, Stephen Decatur, John Paul Jones, Thomas Edison, Theodore and Franklin Roosevelt, John Pershing, William Halsey, George Marshall and Sam Rayburn. Mendel was not even content to rest his parallels on this litany of the saints. With customary understatement he added, "As St. Paul sat at the feet of our Master, it has been my privilege to sit at the feet of Mr. Vinson." There are some who criticized Rivers for going overboard, but Capitol observers noted that he never likened his chairman to Booker T. Washington.

Vinson finally stepped down in the fall of 1965, at the age of eighty-one. The mantle at last settled upon Mendel, but he was not one to forget Vinson. A sign hangs over the door of the Armed Services Committee's elegant quarters in the new Rayburn Office Building, proclaiming it as the Carl Vinson Room.

Unlike Vinson, Rivers has been willing to share some of his authority. He meets regularly with the seven top-ranking members of his committee—known in Washington as "the Junta"—and they share his knowledge of America's secrets. Not all of them, however, share his use of the military as personal lackeys. But when his primacy is challenged, Rivers can be as authoritarian as Vinson ever was. He commands his committee from the center of a double horseshoe of desks, with two small American flags flanking his place and blue velvet drapes behind him to set off his flowing white hair. From his chair he can see on a table a bronze plaque citing Article I, Section 8, of the Constitution, which gives Congress the power to raise, support and regulate the armed forces.

Aside from his power, derived from the seniority system, Rivers has left marks during all his years in Congress. In his voting he has wavered only occasionally from the blind faith of Southern obstructionism. He has backed social-security improvements and public housing, and he was a supporter of foreign aid in its early days. Over the years he has been a constant champion of military pay raises; when President Johnson recommended a 5 percent raise for the troops in 1965, Rivers demanded and got a 10 percent boost for them. On one occasion he became the unflinching champion of the consumer. It was Rivers who led the fight in 1948 to end the tax on colored oleomargarine. The dairy lobby had been able to maintain the sales of butter only because of a prohibitive tax on artificially colored margarine, leaving consumers with a choice: they could either pay the premium price for butter or buy margarine that looked like lard and color it themselves. On the House floor Rivers became so altruistic that the high-priced spread wouldn't melt in his mouth. He thundered without much lightning, "You do not get Bang's disease from oleomargarine; you do not get tuberculosis. Butter will kill you deader than Job's turkey, but eat a little margarine and you will look like a million dollars."

Across the nation—except in the big dairy areas—people rallied behind Rivers, and the bitter butter battle was won. The nation's press named him "Oleo Rivers," and back home in South Carolina the housewives were almost as pleased as the cottonseed farmers who supplied the basic components of margarine. The margarine maneuver added stature to Rivers' claim that "I am the representative of the workingman." Despite his forays into social legislation, Rivers does not often vary from the stereotype of the Southern conservative. His votes against civil rights and labor unions are as automatic as his drawl. In 1948 and again in 1953, he voted against admitting large numbers of refugees to the United States following the cant that these victims of war and Communist takeovers would somehow pollute the ethnic purity of America. He is also, of course, against Communism. He voted to make membership in the Communist party a crime in 1954, a year after he introduced a bill to expel Government employees from their jobs if they took refuge in the Constitution while being quizzed on Communist connections by a Congressional committee. And in 1961 he took the House floor to heap praise on Robert Welch, the founder of the John Birch Society. Welch, he said, is "courageous and perceptive." Lest there be any doubt concerning his position, he later told interviewers, "There's a lot more reason to say something good about them [the Birchers] than for CORE or some of these other outfits."

In his years in Congress, the seniority system has pushed Rivers from an obscure position on a back bench to a post that affects every American. The fate of approximately 100 bills a year hangs on his whim. He is privy to the deepest secrets of American security. Not only has he the power that turned the remote and listless community of his youth—North Charleston—into a more populous area than Charleston itself, but he has the authority to help guide military expenditures and policy for the whole nation. It is a frightening burden, and many in Congress believe it is too heavy for him.

Rivers seldom hesitates to embrace courses that could lead to world destruction. In 1950, for instance, he publicly demanded that President Truman threaten North Korea with atomic bombardment. Ten years later he was urging President Eisenhower to invade Cuba. In 1965 he wanted the United States to prepare for an attack on China's nuclear laboratories. In each instance the best military and diplomatic intelligence and painstaking analysis available to the nation had warned that Rivers' course would precipitate a nuclear holocaust. Rivers' far-out suggestions on international policy did not reflect national policy, and however frightening to the American people and however disconcerting to American leaders, they could still be dismissed. It was much harder to overlook others of his actions. For long before Rivers won his reputation as the economic guardian of the Charleston area, he was known in Washington as one of the capital's swingers. When the pols got together for Bourbon and branch water, Rivers was often among them, and when the rest of the boys weren't drinking, Rivers did pretty well on his own. On occasion his binges lasted for days. He has been found lying on the floor of his office on Monday mornings, surrounded by empty bottles, after a weekend of drinking. Sometimes he has been found by his staff in this state with his office safe wide-open. His staff members have had to rescue him from such places as Washington's Mayflower Hotel, where, according to a former employee, "His shirt was smeared with lipstick and he was too drunk to know what he was doing." Sometimes he was taken home by his employees to recuperate, but they found the drying-out process difficult. "We went to bed but left the bottle on the table, and the light was left on so he could get his drinks," one aide remembered. On occasion Rivers was sent to a private clinic in Washington to get over his bouts with the bottle. More often an ambulance was summoned from the Bethesda Naval Hospital, and Rivers was carried off to recover at taxpayers' expense.

Still, the military does all it can to protect him and serve him. There was one occasion when Rivers' aides were summoned to the airport to meet him on his return from a trip; they found not Rivers but several cases of Scotch whiskey he had purchased at cut rate overseas—the souvenirs of his journey. Rivers, they were told, was ill and unable to make the flight himself. Another time, an Air Force plane was dispatched from Bermuda to Charleston to carry 40 cases of whiskey to Rivers.

When Rivers became Armed Services committee chairman in 1965, he told his friends on the committee that his drinking days were over. His intention may have been the best, but his follow-through was not. The most famous of his benders occurred in 1966, when the Armed Services Committee was summoned five times to vote on a massive military construction bill. The meetings, as well as a House debate on an $18 billion military weapons procurement bill, had to be postponed. Rivers was in Bethesda Naval Hospital, recovering from another drunk.

Unfortunately, Mendel Rivers' behavior, because of his knowledge of the top secrets of both the armed forces and the Central Intelligence Agency, makes him America's top security risk.

In a conversation about his drinking in 1967, Rivers told a reporter that Drew Pearson and Jack Anderson were "Goddamn liars and sons of bitches." He admitted he once drank, although he did not admit it was a problem, and said, "Most committee chairmen find they can't do a lot of what they maybe once did. There's more work, more responsibility—phone calls regularly from the President, the Secretary of Defense, the Speaker. . . ." In the course of the conversation Rivers also said, "I don't drink." A little later he told the interviewer, "I can't recall having a single drink this year." Later still he said, "I don't think I had one last year." Then he told his listener, "Let me make this clear. If I wanted to drink, it's nobody's goddamn business. Fifty million people in Washington drink more than I ever did."

The fact is, however, that few people hold a drink as badly as Rivers does. And no other problem drinker anywhere in the world is exposed to the intricate military, nuclear and CIA secrets that are confided almost daily to Rivers. In the executive branch of government, a man with Rivers' history would be relieved of his responsibilities at once as a security risk. Under the seniority system that prevails in Congress, Rivers can be removed only by the will of the voters in his backwater district or by a revolution of the members of the House. Neither of these alternatives is a probability.

As long as Rivers remains Armed Services Committee chairman, it is unlikely that his power will be diminished. There are many who hope it will increase. Among them is his close associate and former law partner, T. E. Pederson, who does a big business representing defense contractors. He has admitted that he started working for the munitions lords while he and Rivers were still law partners. Pederson said, however, that "the Congressman did not participate in any fees that I received from them."

Rivers himself has gone to bat for defense contractors under unusual circumstances. The Power Equipment Corporation of Brooklyn bid $142,860 to repair a Navy transport, the U.S.S. *Randall,* and was awarded the contract on March 3, 1959. Three days later Power Equipment's chief stockholder, Joe Kelly, told the Navy he would need more money to perform "extra work." At one point, Kelly's demands for "extra work" reached $173,150.61. Navy officials ordered rebidding, but Kelly tried to circumvent them by visiting Rivers. A Federal grand jury, later convoked by then Attorney General Robert Kennedy, was told that $25,000 was passed under the table, but the evidence was not clear as to who received it.

In the fall of 1953 Rivers placed the wife of one of his assistants on the House payroll for two months. She never got the money. "My husband explained to me that my salary would be turned over to the Congressman," she swore in an affidavit. "I signed the checks and turned them over to my husband, who delivered them to the Congressman. On one occasion I remember, my husband was hospitalized, and Congressman Rivers drove from Charleston to Beaufort for the sole purpose of picking up my check."

Kickbacks such as this are, of course, against the law.

To keep his political base secure, Rivers believes in giving the home folks circuses as well as bread. When the bronze bust of him on Charleston's Rivers Avenue was dedicated in 1965, he had planeloads of top Pentagon brass and Congressmen fly to South Carolina at taxpayers' expense to participate in his veneration. He brought an equally glittering assemblage to the tiny South Carolina town of St. Stephens the previous year to help celebrate "L. Mendel Rivers Day." The following summer he brought James E. Webb, head of the National Aeronautics and Space Administration, with astronauts Virgil "Gus" Grissom and John Young, to the place where he began his first campaign for Congress. Rivers was no longer the humble handshaker looking for votes, and he toured the Watermelon Festival at Easthill in a car. It was the sort of stunt that impressed the melon farmers. "Hoo-ray, Mendel," they shouted as the car rolled past. Said Rivers, "If these people are for you, brother, nothing else matters."

At sixty-three, Rivers is not one of the old men of the House; 12 committee chairmen are older than he is. Still, he is typical of the system—an aging, ailing, bucolic Congressman who, because of his ability to outlive his colleagues, has been elevated to a position of power. It is unlikely that Rivers could have won the chairmanship under any test but that of longevity. He is not alone. One of his colleagues, also from South Carolina, provides an even more dramatic example of how the seniority system sometimes bestows authority like an oversized hat on an undersized head.

3. Restricting the District

The people who vote for him will tell you that Representative John L. McMillan "is a good ol' boy." It is a term of affection and respect. He has been in Washington since 1923, first as an assistant to the Congressman from South Carolina's 6th District and, since 1938, as the Congressman himself. By the measure that the good people of the 6th District apply to such things, McMillan's contribution to the democratic process has been an unqualified success. As a member of the House Agriculture Committee, he has done what he could to help the tobacco farmers; and as chairman of the House District of Columbia Committee, he has labored hard to keep the Negroes down. This proves, his constituents will tell you, that he is an anti-Communist and, hence, a good American.

These are the values in Mullins, South Carolina, where McMillan was raised, and in Florence, where he now has his official residence. There the Negroes know their place. Should they forget, there are reminders in varying degrees of severity. After all, there have not been any race riots in Mullins, South Carolina.

Mullins is a sleepy village that rises out of the tobacco fields and quickly slumps back into them. The only activity takes place along the one main street that bisects the town, or along the railroad tracks, which cut across the main street like a cross hair on a gunsight. The intersection explains why Mullins exists; there is a tobacco shed along the tracks. Down the street are a few shops and offices. It is an area where higher education is still beyond the aspiration of most of the people, and success is having enough money to pay the bills at the end of the month. Here the McMillans have done well. Carl McMillan, M.D., has an office looking out on the main street. Another brother, who died recently, was one of the richest farmers in the area. Still another, Claude, was the state highway commissioner for a quarter of a century. None of them, however, quite measured up to John.

Sometimes in the late summer evenings, when the call of the crickets rises and falls like the hum of a cotton gin, and the boys are talking about the prospects of their football team, the old-timers remind them about McMillan. "There never was a football player around here like ol' Johnny," they say, and his prowess grows with each retelling. The memory of his football career is something that still makes McMillan smile, and he sucks in his stomach when people mention it. The biography he submitted for the Congressional Directory boasts: "Educated Mullins High School, University of North Carolina, and South Carolina University Law School; selected on All-State College Football Team for 4 years, All-Southern for 1 year, and a member of the All-Time Star Football Team of South Carolina." He is less explicit about other biographical details, like his birth date, which he omits. He was born in April, 1898.

These are the credentials of the man who has virtually ruled the city of Washington and its 800,000 voteless citizens for the past 22 years. The city government was reorganized by President Johnson in 1967, placing many of the day-to-day decisions in the hands of a nine-member, appointed city council. Previously the city administration was supervised by three appointed commissioners. Under either form of government, the real power lies in the District committees of the Senate and the House. Membership on these committees is hardly a prize. Appointment to the House District of Columbia Committee, indeed, is resisted by even the most junior Congressmen, and its members usually escape to more interesting committees as soon as an opportunity opens.

McMillan's rise to power is largely a memento to Congress's distaste for governing Washington. He was a member of Congress for only eight years when the seniority system in 1946 lifted him to his chairmanship. But McMillan cherishes his post. It gives him authority that most residents of Mullins would never dream of, though his exercise of authority has been most notable for its negativism—McMillan makes his power felt by being against things. His sturdy opposition to progress over the years has stunted the development of Washington as a real metropolis. But this does not affect McMillan, for the "mayor" of Washington makes his home across the Potomac, in the white suburban neighborhood of Arlington, Virginia.

Over the years, bills to give home rule to the District of Columbia win approval with monotonous regularity in the Senate District Committee, pass by enormous margins on the Senate floor, and end up in a pigeonhole in the House District Committee. To get around McMillan, President Johnson's 1967 reorganization of the city was engineered so it would go into effect automatically unless Congress voted to block it. For the first time, McMillan was powerless to prevent the issue from reaching the House floor. But he did all he could to muster the negative votes. On the day the House made its decision, McMillan boasted of his stewardship and warned his colleagues that they might have to buy Washington license plates for their cars if his power were abridged. His plea for the *status quo*, however, was voted down.

Even as the Congressmen cast their votes, many of them suspected it was not power alone or the trappings of authority that had kept McMillan wedded to an archaic and inefficient form of government for the nation's capital. The way McMillan has played it since he became chairman in 1946, the chairmanship of the House District Committee was also important to his private interests.

With his choke hold on the city, McMillan has been able to exert pressures in many ways. He appears to be a man who is always willing to help his friends, and he makes friends easily when there is a dollar involved. The Capitol Vending Company, for instance, hit the jackpot after its coin-operated machines came under the leverage of McMillan's pull. The company was founded by Ralph Hill, who came out of the Army in 1952 and wangled a job through McMillan as an attendant in the air-conditioning department of the Capitol power plant. Sensing a real opportunity, McMillan lent Hill $3,000 to start Capitol Vending. When the company was incorporated, Clayton Gasque was identified as its secretary-treasurer. Gasque is a tall, lean man with a face so wrinkled that it seems perpetually pressed against a window screen. Officially, he is staff director of the House District Committee. With McMillan's money, Gasque's bookkeeping, and Hill's initiative, Capitol Vending prospered. Strangely enough, it won contracts to place its machines in the House Office Buildings and in the two hubs of Washington's local government, the District Building and the Municipal Center. Stranger still, the contracts were noncompetitive. As the coins came clinking down the slot, the corporation's stockholders became more greedy. Even a concession operated by blind persons in the District Building was replaced by the automatic click of Capitol Vending's machines.

Gasque stayed on as secretary-treasurer until his moonlighting was revealed in the press. He protested that he had resigned and had made no profit on his stocks. When he was asked whether the car he was driving belonged to Capitol Vending, he blurted, "I drove it yesterday, but I won't be driving it today." Capitol Vending's deals later figured prominently in the investigation of Bobby Baker, another stockholder.

McMillan stood at the center of a little clique of bright young men from South Carolina who liked to make a fast buck. This tight little circle included almost the entire cast of characters of the Bobby Baker hearings—the irrepressible Bobby himself, from Pickens, South Carolina; his original accuser, Ralph Hill, of Green Sea, South Carolina; and the star witness against Baker, insurance man Don Reynolds of Lamar, South Carolina. They became entangled in various deals together, and McMillan always seemed to be in the center of the web. Many of McMillan's dealings seemed to involve automobiles. The Congressman's own household has a rich taste in transportation; in 1961, for example, he was driving a Cadillac, and John Jr., was piloting a Corvette. McMillan's automotive interest moved farther afield that same year as he demanded that a car dealer's license be renewed for Ross Rosenberg, whose application had been rejected by city officials who viewed with distaste the 18 formal complaints against him from dissatisfied customers. The litigation against Rosenberg reached such proportions that one Washington lawyer specialized in suits brought by Rosenberg's customers. They charged that they had been bilked and swindled and that their purchase contracts had been altered to increase drastically the prices of the cars they bought. One customer, for instance, paid cash for a car, drove it away, and later received demands for payment of $500 still "owed"—his name allegedly had been forged on a loan form. Many of Rosenberg's customers who received this kind of treatment were servicemen.

McMillan's defense of Rosenberg was not encumbered by the facts. The dealer, he said in a letter to the appeals board, was no worse than many other dealers, and McMillan was sure Rosenberg would turn over a new leaf if only he were given a second chance. The "Mayor" of Washington carried a threat to back up his entreaty. Unless Rosenberg was given a license, he warned, "we are going to find it necessary to increase taxes again in the very near future."

In a second letter, sent a week after the first, McMillan said that he had instructed Hayden Garber, the counsel of his House District Committee, to examine Rosenberg's record, and that Garber could find no reason to block Rosenberg's dealer's license. "I know," McMillan wrote, "that after talking to you on the phone and receiving your letter you will see that this company [Rosenberg's] is treated justly and fairly and given his license, unless there is something on the record that I have failed to locate."

In a short time there was considerable new evidence that McMillan had not located. Six more witnesses came forward with complaints about Rosenberg's car business. But the most intriguing transaction involved the high-powered Corvette that John McMillan, Jr., was driving; it came from a car lot where Rosenberg was working after he lost his own car lot. Although the temporary District of Columbia tags issued for the car indicated that it had been sold, no payments had been made by McMillan, who insisted his son had it only on a "tryout."

Then there was the matter of McMillan's big black Cadillac. The car, list-priced at $5,700, was purchased for $5,100 in April 1961 by Don Reynolds. He turned it over to McMillan on the same day he bought it. When the transaction was investigated by the Washington *Post* late in July, McMillan insisted that he had paid Reynolds in full for the car with checks—one for $2,000 on April 14, the other for $3,100 on April 18. The second check was indeed dated April 18, but the bank cancellation stamp on the back showed it was cashed in mid-August, several weeks after the *Post* began digging into the deal.

McMillan claimed that he had asked Reynolds to buy the Cadillac for him so it would not seem that he had "used the influence of the Chairman of the House District Committee" in shopping for a bargain. "I have known him since he was knee-high," McMillan said of Reynolds. "His daddy is one of my closest friends." McMillan's friendship with Reynolds was, indeed, curiously close. The Congressman appointed Reynolds to West Point, but Reynolds flunked out. After World War II, McMillan got Reynolds an appointment to the Foreign Service, which was relieved to get rid of him after a series of complaints. Back in Washington, Reynolds, expecting shortages, bought three cars during the Korean War and unloaded a flashy Ford convertible on McMillan. He also unloaded a girl whom he had spirited illegally out of Germany. A secret State Department report on this affair states that Reynolds "made unauthorized use of his Berlin consulate's standing to obtain an exit visa for his mistress. His action was discovered and an effort made to stop the visa, but Congressional pressure on the State Department was great. The girl's destination was Congressman McMillan's home in South Carolina." There the girl worked as a maid until Mrs. McMillan ordered her out of the house.

Shortly before the Cadillac transaction, McMillan introduced Reynolds to James F. Reilly, then chairman of the board of the new $20-million sports stadium that was about to open in Washington. Reynolds' interest was simple; he wanted to write the insurance on the park. Reilly later denied that McMillan used any pressure, and McMillan insisted his aid to Reynolds was no more than he would offer any constituent seeking help. There was, however, one slight flaw in this explanation: Reynolds since 1956 had been a registered voter in Maryland, not South Carolina.

The construction of the stadium gave McMillan an opportunity to do favors for other Washington businessmen. For instance, two of Washington's parking-lot czars, Harry Swaggart and Leonard "Bud" Doggett, who had reaped fortunes from the city's traffic jams, won McMillan's favor. "I personally would like to see Mr. Swaggart and Mr. Doggett have an opportunity to work out the parking program in the new stadium," he wrote to the board. Parking in Washington has long been one of McMillan's major interests. He has blocked a number of proposals to help ease the traffic squeeze through the construction of municipally operated parking lots; he even destroyed the effectiveness of the Motor Vehicle Parking Agency, which had accumulated $4 million in parking-meter fees to buy land for parking. The money, under legislation pushed by McMillan, was passed out to the highway department for other uses, to the cheers of the private parking interests.

Another bit of McMillan legislation was tailored to protect an antiquated gas station in a swank neighborhood, although the station had been zoned out of existence to protect the view of the towers and flying buttresses of the national cathedral across the street. McMillan's bill slipped through Congress, but was vetoed by President Eisenhower. In an even more bizarre legislative offering, the House District Committee Chairman added an amendment to a high-priority bill for Washington's freeways. This amendment dealt with another kind of free way; it provided a $4,000 tax break for Jess Larsen, the former General Services Administrator, on a stock sale.

Such steps followed a constant pattern in McMillan's activities. Time and again he has used the power of his office to keep the taxes down for those who can most afford to pay them. Real-estate taxes in Washington are considerably lower than in the Maryland and Virginia suburbs, and the taxes on liquor in the District are so low that it has become a mecca for quantity buyers. One standard argument of Washington businessmen against home rule has been the specter of increased taxes to pay for schools and educational equipment. Meanwhile, Washington students suffer in antique, overcrowded schools with insufficient funds for books, while the better teachers are constantly drained away by affluent suburbs that pay higher salaries.

McMillan has his own reasons for blocking home rule; Washington was the first big city in the nation to have a Negro majority. He has done everything in his power to prevent Negroes from achieving equality in the city he controls. When Commissioner Joseph "Jiggs" Donahue ordered the city's fire department desegregated in 1952, McMillan summoned the three District commissioners to his office for a chat with himself and Representatives Howard W. Smith, D-Va., and James C. Davis, D-Ga. The commissioners were tongue-lashed as "sellouts" and "Commies." Finally the other two commissioners capitulated; Donahue's desegregation move was outvoted, 2 to 1. In 1962 McMillan torpedoed a plan for fair housing in Washington by threatening to cut off funds for schools, libraries and other facilities in the city.

It is little wonder that McMillan once went on a network television program and complained that his efforts for Washington were not appreciated. Some people are just ingrates.

4. The Rewards of Survival

The careers of those two cracker-barrel Congressmen from South Carolina, Mendel Rivers and John McMillan, suggest that age does not necessarily make a sage. Yet, like Sindbad the Sailor with the Old Man of the Sea around his neck, Congress is staggering along under a burden of age. The seniority system holds back the brightest young men, whose leadership is needed in these swift-moving times, while the legislative process is subjected to the prideful whims and prejudices of old men, many of them out of touch with the problems and perils of today's world.

These old men, honorably though they may have served in the past, are placing an intolerable brake on the creaking and cumbersome law-making machinery of the national Government, already in desperate need of overhaul. On more than one occasion the old men have nearly brought Congress to a grinding halt out of sheer pettiness. There was the time, for instance, that the ancient Senate Appropriations Committee chairman, Carl Hayden, D-Ariz., and the late House Appropriations Committee chairman, Clarence Cannon, D-Mo., held up all the money bills for several months, thus denying the Government the funds it vitally needed, because they could not agree which of them should walk the short distance across the Capitol building for joint conferences. Congress is the only Federal law-making body in the world that still chooses its leaders by seniority. "Even the law of the jungle," New York City's Mayor John Lindsay has said, "operates on a higher level than the law of seniority; the first at least works to assure survival of the fittest; the latter operates only to assure survival of the oldest." An ex-Congressman, Lindsay has departed Capitol Hill and now feels less constrained about airing his views.

The best rebuttal the defenders of seniority can offer is that it produces experience. After the slow escalator ride to the top, the Congressional leader gains a certain acquaintance with his political environment, a certain knack for parliamentary maneuvering. There is no guarantee, however, that the men promoted to power by seniority have kept abreast of the world whose destiny they are helping to guide. More often than not, they tend to hold new ideas in horror and hark back to "the good old days." Nobody wishes to blame or dishonor an aging man for wanting to return to the simpler world of his youth. He becomes culpable, however, when his toga becomes a shroud for the hopes and ambitions of a new generation.

The old men who run Congress have all but lost touch with the half of the American population who are now under twenty-five. From the most casual reading of the *Congressional Record*, it is clear that most Congressmen distrust the younger generation. They visualize it as a conglomeration of bearded beatniks, long-haired guitarists, immoral co-eds, Vietnam picketers, draft-card burners and civil rights protesters. Communications between the codgers in Congress and their young constituents have virtually broken down. To the young, the John McCormacks and Everett Dirksens are musty, misty characters who already belong to history. The postwar generation, raised in affluence with the H-bomb for a baby-sitter, identifies more easily with the brothers Kennedy. But those Congressman young enough to understand the new generation have little to say on Capitol Hill. They stand at the bottom of the seniority escalator; by the time they reach the top, they too will be old men.

The four men who moved up to chairmanships in 1967, for example, had 90 years of Congressional experience among them. They were Carl Perkins, D-Ky., who replaced Adam Clayton Powell as House Education and Labor Committee chairman; W. R. Poage, D-Tex., who became House Agriculture Committee chairman; William Colmer, D-Miss., House Rules Committee chairman, and Thaddeus Dulski, D-N.Y., House Post Office and Civil Service Committee chairman. Colmer had to wait 34 years to reach the top; Dulski made it in the rare speed of 8 years. The average: 22 years.

Even with good men in power, the seniority system betrays the nation by perpetuating them in office after their mental reflexes have been slowed by time. Few men retain their vigor and vision, their receptiveness to new ideas, past seventy. The oldest member of Congress is kindly Senator Carl Hayden, now ninety-one, who has represented Arizona on Capitol Hill since it became a state in 1912. Hayden slept under Indian blankets and served as sheriff of Maricopa County when Arizona was still a territory. He has had a productive career, but age has now slowed him to a shuffle and has given him a positively cadaverous look.*

Yet Hayden is President pro Tempore of the Senate, which puts him third in line for the Presidency. It is patently inconceivable that any man of his years could cope with the crushing burdens of the White House. He is also chairman of the all-powerful Senate Appropriations Committee. He is the ranking Democrat on the Rules and Administration Committee and holds a seat on the Democratic Policy Committee, which largely guides the Senate from behind the scenes. Meanwhile, he is still supposed to have the time and energy to direct the Senate Democratic Patronage Committee and the Joint Committee on Printing.

---

*In May 1968, Senator Hayden announced that, after serving on Capitol Hill for forty-six years, he would not seek re-election in the fall.

Inevitably, Hayden's immense power must fall upon assistants and advisers, who have never run for office and whose jobs depend upon perpetuating the myth that the old man is still mentally alert. They say he sleeps well, takes no pills, drinks diluted coffee, and writes with a steady enough hand to rewrite unsatisfactory memos in longhand. They admit cautiously that Hayden wears a hearing aid, complains of circulation problems and uses a cane to propel himself down the long Capitol corridors. He is impatient with the cane and insists to colleagues, "I may have to use this thing for a while, but I am going to get rid of it."

Nobody questions Carl Hayden's indomitable spirit or broad outlook on life. But if he should become obsessed by some whim, as old men often do, he could at any moment throw a spanner into the works of vital legislation. Sometimes he takes direction from his trusted assistants; other times he simply goes along with Senators who are old friends or who butter him up. Not long ago he claimed his right to preside during some confusion over the rules. It was up to him to rule for or against an anti-filibuster motion. The Senate parliamentarian tried to explain the situation to him, but Hayden would not listen. "I want to go with Russell," he insisted, "I want to go with Russell." He referred to Senator Richard Russell, D-Ga., now turned seventy, who is leader of the Southern bloc. Hayden impatiently banged his gavel, mumbled a ruling and shuffled out of the chamber, leaving the Senate in chaos. Several Senators rushed after him and begged him to return to the chamber to clarify his ruling. "No," he said, "I'm not going back." His refusal kept his colleagues up in the air for the next 24 hours.

Also faltering is Speaker John McCormack, gray and gaunt, who stands ahead of Hayden in Presidential succession. The assassination of President Kennedy was such a shock to the Speaker, who was seated in the House restaurant when reporters and Congressmen rushed up to him with the first reports, that he suffered a severe attack of dizziness. He started to rise, reeled, and began to lose consciousness. He raised a hand to his eyes, sank back in his seat and sat trembling.

If the assassination was a shock to McCormack, however, the realization that he was next in line for the Presidency was a far greater shock to Washington officials. The plane flying Cabinet officers to Japan banked around and jetted for home after the first assassination bulletins. One of the early rumors —that Lyndon Johnson might also have been shot—raised the prospect of McCormack's or Hayden's taking over the White House. The Cabinet members blanched visibly at the thought. Secret Service men, incidentally, raced to McCormack's Washington hotel suite during the afternoon of the assassination to protect the man who was now next in line for the White House. The Speaker, apparently fully recovered from his dizzy spell, pushed them out. "This is an intolerable intrusion in my private life and Mrs. McCormack's, and I won't have it," he protested. From that moment, he flatly refused Secret Service protection. President Johnson, anxious to placate the powerful Speaker, agreed to ignore the security provisions of the law.

More in sorrow than in anger, Democratic Congressmen began whispering in 1966 and 1967 that the Speaker was losing his grasp. They said he made blunder after blunder; they spoke in the cloakrooms about his "lack of awareness" and "seeming indifference" to the serious issues. His greatest concern after the 90th Congress convened in January 1967 seemed to be over the remodeling of the west front of the Capitol building. In a Congress beset by challenges and complexities, McCormack's only message to fellow Congressmen during the first weeks was a letter urging them to inspect a model of the architect's plan. He also put up a hopeless battle behind closed doors to save Adam Clayton Powell from losing his committee chairmanship. When colleagues warned that Powell not only would be stripped of his authority but probably would be voted out of Congress, McCormack refused to believe it. "You don't think for a moment," he scoffed, "that a majority of the House would vote to unseat a duly elected member, do you?" When it happened, he could not understand.

5. "Let's Build This Ditch for Mike!"

Some Congressmen whose seniority has carried them to the top are merely incompetent; others systematically abuse the power that old age has thrust upon them. One who uses his power as a club is that roughhewn Irish curmudgeon, Representative Michael J. Kirwan, D-Ohio, who has risen to such heights during his 30 years in the House that few members dare to cross him. As chairman of the House Appropriations Subcommittee on Public Works, he has veto power over the pork-barrel projects so dear to the hearts of Congressmen. Explained the Cleveland *Plain Dealer*: "Kirwan is almost a dictator when it comes to dispensing favors and funds for Congressmen's pet projects." He also runs the Democratic Congressional Campaign Committee, which raises hundreds of thousands of dollars every election year to finance the Congressional campaigns of "deserving Democrats." It is left pretty much to Kirwan to decide who is "deserving."

When Kirwan encountered opposition in his own Democratic primary for the first time in over 20 years, he herded 64 Congressmen upon the House floor to make flowery speeches endorsing him. Some of these same Congressmen had bitterly criticized the late President Franklin D. Roosevelt for intervening in Democratic primaries. "In forty years of public service," President Johnson has declared, "I have never supported anyone in a primary except myself." Yet 64 Congressmen, prodded by the eighty-year-old Kirwan, ignored this time-honored rule. One after another, they rose to eulogize one of their fellow members. Their lofty language made it sound like a funeral service. Not even the late, beloved Speaker Sam Rayburn received so many tributes after his death. The object of their praise, however, was not dead. He sat on the House floor listening to the tributes, apparently keeping score on how many Congressmen delivered appropriate encomiums. What no one mentioned in all the rosy oratory was that every one of the 64 Congressmen had pork-barrel projects before Kirwan's Appropriations Subcommittee.

One of the first on his feet was Representative Carl Albert, D-Okla., who perhaps unwittingly gave away his motive for singing Kirwan's praises. "Mike Kirwan has had an important influence upon countless reclamation and public works projects funded during the last two decades," declared Albert in admiration. "These have run the gamut from power and flood-control dams to fish hatcheries and game preserves. Name a project, and you can be sure that Mike Kirwan had a hand in its development." Albert neglected to add that he hoped to get $3.5 million out of Kirwan as down payment on his pet $13.3 million Arbuckle reclamation project in Oklahoma. The loudest praise, indeed, seemed to come from those who sought the most money from Kirwan to spend on vote-getting projects at home. Representative Edward P. Boland, D-Mass., called him "understanding, compassionate, kind, and sympathetic." But most of all, Boland hoped Kirwan would be generous in providing Federal funds to complete the $16 million Cape Cod National Seashore. Cried Representative Al Ullman, D-Ore., "Mike Kirwan is made of the stuff that built America." What Ullman really wanted Kirwan to help build, of course, was the Mason Dam a few miles up the Powder River from Ullman's hometown of Baker, Oregon.

Even Republican Congressmen, who are no less eager for pork-barrel projects, joined in providing campaign ammunition for this encrusted Democrat. Representative Seymour Halpern, R-N.Y., described Kirwan as "humble, forthright, honest, good, understanding, and a fine gentleman"—words Halpern hoped would be worth an appropriation from Kirwan's subcommittee to establish Bowne House in Flushing, New York, as a national religious shrine. Amid all the hearts and flowers, perhaps the true sentiment was best summed up by Representative Martha W. Griffiths, D-Mich., who wanted Kirwan to grant money for a national cemetery at Fort Custer, Michigan. "In this century," she said solemnly, "the Nineteenth District of Ohio will never again be represented by a man who has reached the power that Mike Kirwan has."

As Proprietor of the Pork, Kirwan has bequeathed public works projects to favored Congressmen more for their political good than the national good. The $4 billion public works budget is loaded with projects, according to Senator William Proxmire, the Joint Economic Committee chairman, "that serve to re-elect members of Congress but at a tragically high cost to the taxpayer." A Grinnell College study of 147 water-resource projects approved by Congress found that 63 were absolutely indefensible from the standpoint of sound economics.

On one notable occasion Kirwan stood up, at least temporarily, for sound economics. He opposed dredging the Delaware River to a 40-foot depth up to the U.S. Steel's Fairless Plant. Witnesses had testified that only one company, U.S. Steel, would benefit from this $91 million expenditure of the taxpayers' money. In a voice of righteous indignation, Kirwan urged the House not to pass the legislation. "Let the Congress prove to the country that they are not going to give them

[U.S. Steel] that $100 million to do something that is not worth it," he declared.

Then, quite mysteriously, Congressman Kirwan had a change of heart. This manifestation occurred shortly after he was visited by Benjamin Fairless, the man for whom the plant was named, then head of U.S. Steel. The visit was followed by another, perhaps unrelated, event; Michael Kirwan, Jr., the Congressman's son, went to work for U.S. Steel as a salesman in Pittsburgh and is still on the payroll. Thereafter the Congressman suddenly saw the merits of dredging the Delaware. At his word, the House voted for the $91-million dredging project just as cavalierly as it had taken his word and had voted against the same project the previous year.

In passing out the pork, Kirwan did not, of course, neglect his own pet projects. One of the most controversial was a $10-million aquarium for Washington, D.C. This quickly became known as Kirwan's "fish hotel," and opposition to it developed in the Senate. "It's a luxury the capital cannot afford while there is an acute shortage of classrooms here," declared Senator Wayne Morse, D-Ore. Furious, Kirwan threatened to block public works for Oregon unless Morse changed his mind. In a joint Senate-House conference, the old curmudgeon kept his word and chopped almost a million dollars of Oregon projects out of the Rivers and Harbors bill. "Morse was the cause of it," he grumped. "I'll hold up all of Oregon's water projects until Morse learns something about fish." But the Senator from Oregon is not easily bullied. He took his case to the then President Kennedy. "I intend to make a motion for the expulsion of Kirwan from the Congress on the grounds of corruption," Morse announced to the President. "I shall make this motion on the grounds of legislative blackmail." The threat worked, and the projects eventually were restored. The adjournment of Congress was delayed a week while the bitter battle was resolved.

Kirwan was more effective in punishing Representative John R. Foley, D-Md., a mere freshman, who dared to push an innocuous public works bill without clearing it with the Proprietor of Pork. All Foley wanted to do was make the old Chesapeake and Ohio Canal into a national monument. Piqued over Foley's persistence, Kirwan wearily objected. "I come from an area where we had a canal," he said laconically, referring to the old Erie Canal. "Two young boys rode the mules on that canal. Both became President; both got shot [Garfield and McKinley]. We don't want any more canal bills." When Foley remained unpersuaded by this curious logic, Kirwan simply waved his finger and killed the bill on the House floor. Then he short-changed Congressman Foley in the division of re-election funds. Politically and financially deprived, Foley was defeated in 1960.

Kirwan showed more tolerance for canal bills, however, after a canal was proposed in his own backyard linking Lake Erie and the Ohio River. The plan was pushed by a few Youngstown industrialists who wanted the taxpayers to build them a waterway capable of carrying low-rate freight. The idea was also favored by the Army Engineers, who, if unleashed, would happily turn the United States into a gigantic Venice. No one else wanted the canal. The mayors of Cleveland and Pittsburgh said it would be economically disastrous. The Governor of Pennsylvania called it "utterly worthless." The New York State Power Authority warned that the proposed canal would lower the level of Lake Erie and cause "very substantial injury to power users in the United States and Canada." But Mike Kirwan, despite his despair over the tragic end of the two boys who rode mules on the old Erie Canal, decided he wanted the new Erie Canal. What was good for his industrialist friends, he concluded, was good for America. And in the matter of canals, Kirwan is a majority in the United States.

First he rammed through a feasibility study that, to no one's surprise, agreed with Kirwan. Its conclusion: the 120-mile canal, which would require a 35-mile-long reservoir and would flood 90,000 acres including some of the nation's finest dairy farms, was economically feasible. This was disputed by Representative Joseph P. Vigorito, D-Pa., another brash freshman, who had been a professor of economics before coming to Congress. From his study of the figures, he announced, "Costs are systematically underestimated, benefits fantastically exaggerated. . . . The favorable benefit-cost ratio is obtained through the use of three and one-eighth percent interest rate. There is absolutely no way the Government can borrow money that cheaply." He charged that "cynically juggled figures" had been used "to justify an indefensible boondoggle." For his interest in saving the taxpayers from a billion-dollar boondoggle, Vigorito was rewarded with another short count when Kirwan divided up the campaign contributions in 1966. Other freshman Democrats, who had not crossed Kirwan, received three to five times larger allotments. Unlike Foley, however, Vigorito survived at the polls.

When the down payment on the canal came up for House approval, Kirwan had his claque ready. Representative Chet Holifield, D-Calif., started off by reminding the House, "How many hundreds of millions, how many billions of dollars of projects have Mike Kirwan and his committee members brought to the floor of this House over the past three decades for the people of America?" Others, eager for a share in the millions worth of projects Kirwan would approve in the decade to come, joined in the chorus for Kirwan. But it was Representative John Bell Williams, D-Miss.—before he left Congress to become governor of Mississippi—who delivered the rousing finale. "Yesterday," he shouted, "we voted $3.5 or $3.6 billion to throw away (on foreign aid)." Then, fastening an affectionate gaze upon Kirwan, the Mississippi firebrand roared, "Let's build this ditch for Mike!" The House approved Mike's ditch by a clamorous voice vote, and the preliminary planning has begun.

Such is the power of a cantankerous, eighty-one-year-old Congressman in the House where the god seniority is worshiped.

6. The Roster

There are older, even more cantankerous Congressmen than Mike Kirwan. For instance, eighty-six-year-old Representative Barratt O'Hara, D-Ill., though venerated by his colleagues, has a short fuse and more than once has threatened to settle an argument with his fists. During an argument with another Congressman over the State Department budget, O'Hara challenged his colleague: "Let the gentleman come out and argue with our fists. I am willing to revert to fisticuffs even at my age on the issue that no dining room in the State Department is worth $250,000 of taxpayers' money to impress foreign diplomats." More recently O'Hara, angry over his hotel bill, slapped a manager at Washington's Congressional Hotel in the face.

Some men hold their ages, of course, better than others.

The late Senator Theodore F. Green, D-R.I., for example, was sixty-nine before he was elected to the Senate. When he retired at ninety-three, he was still remarkably alert. He played a stiff set of tennis on his seventieth birthday, continued diving off the high board until his mid-eighties and walked the 16 blocks to his Senate office until the day he retired. At his ninety-second birthday party he was still keen enough, when asked how it felt to be ninety-two, to quip, "Not bad considering the alternative." He never smoked; he drank moderately, did nothing to excess, had no heart attacks. He was alert enough, however, to realize that old men ought to step aside when their age slows them down. Accordingly, he resigned the chairmanship of the Foreign Relations Committee when his eyes and ears began to fail him.

Sadly, most of the old men do not know when to quit. Most are more like the late beloved Speaker Joseph Martin, R-Mass., who at eighty-two was so infirm that he needed canes and aids simply to move around. He had a short attention span and muffled powers of sight and sound. Yet he still ran for re-election. In his case, the voters regretfully retired him.

The seniority system not only places the biggest burdens on the frailest shoulders; it also confers power on legislators who come from safe rural districts. Nine of the 16 Senate chairmen come from cities or towns with populations of less than 100,000; only five of the 20 House chairmen come from sizable cities. Men like fifty-six-year-old Representative Carl Perkins of Hindman, Kentucky, and seventy-four-year-old Senator Lister Hill of Montgomery, Alabama, are responsible for finding a solution to the crisis in our cities. The seniority system has placed Senator James Eastland, a Mississippi segregationist, in charge of civil-rights legislation. Indeed, seniority has given Southerners a domination over Congress, which thus operates not unlike a Union Army led by Confederate generals.

The following complete list of standing-committee chairmen sums up the problems:

SENATE

COMMITTEE	CHAIRMAN	HOME TOWN	AGE*
Aeronautical and Space Sciences	Clinton P. Anderson	Albuquerque, New Mexico	73
Agriculture and Forestry	Allen J. Ellender	Houma, Louisiana	77
Appropriations	Carl Hayden	Phoenix, Arizona	91
Armed Services	Richard B. Russell	Winder, Georgia	71
Banking and Currency	John J. Sparkman	Huntsville Alabama	68
Commerce	Warren G. Magnuson	Seattle, Washington	63
District of Columbia	Alan Bible	Reno, Nevada	58
Finance	Russell B. Long	Baton Rouge, Louisiana	50
Foreign Relations	J. William Fulbright	Fayetteville, Arkansas	63
Government Operations	John L. McClellan	Camden, Arkansas	72
Interior and Insular Affairs	Henry M. Jackson	Everett, Washington	56
Judiciary	James O. Eastland	Doddsville, Mississippi	63
Labor and Public Welfare	Lister Hill	Montgomery, Alabama	74
Post Office and Civil Service	A. S. Mike Monroney	Oklahoma City, Oklahoma	66
Public Works	Jennings Randolph	Elkins, West Virginia	66
Rules and Administration	B. Everett Jordan	Saxapahaw, North Carolina	72

* Ages as of 1968 elections.

HOUSE

COMMITTEE	CHAIRMAN	HOME TOWN	AGE*
Agriculture	W. R. Poage	Waco, Texas	68
Appropriations	George H. Mahon	Lubbock, Texas	68
Armed Services	L. Mendel Rivers	Charleston, South Carolina	63
Banking and Currency	Wright Patman	Texarkana, Texas	75
District of Columbia	John L. McMillan	Florence, South Carolina	70
Education and Labor	Carl D. Perkins	Hindman, Kentucky	56
Foreign Affairs	Thomas E. Morgan	Fredericktown, Pennsylvania	62
Government Operations	William L. Dawson	Chicago, Illinois	82
House Administration	Omar Burleson	Anson, Texas	62
Interior and Insular Affairs	Wayne N. Aspinall	Palisade, Colorado	72
Interstate and Foreign Commerce	Harley O. Staggers	Keyser, West Virginia	61
Judiciary	Emanuel Cellar	Brooklyn, New York	80
Merchant Marine and Fisheries	Edward A. Garmatz	Baltimore, Maryland	65
Post Office and Civil Service	Thaddeus J. Dulski	Buffalo, New York	53
Public Works	George H. Fallon	Baltimore, Maryland	66
Rules	William M. Colmer	Pascagoula, Mississippi	78
Science and Astronautics	George P. Miller	Alameda, California	77

* Ages as of 1968 elections.

HOUSE

COMMITTEE	CHAIRMAN	HOME TOWN	AGE*
Un-American Activities	Edwin E. Willis	St. Martinville, Louisiana	64
Veterans Affairs	Olin E. Teague	College Station, Texas	58
Ways and Means	Wilbur D. Mills	Kensett, Arkansas	59

Most Congressmen do not continue to serve for the money. Most could retire on the pensions they have built up over the years. They stay on in the tenacious belief that they can last longer and serve better than the young upstarts who challenge them. They feel that the country needs them. It will take severe public pressure, indeed, to overcome the seniority system.

---

* Ages as of 1968 elections.

IV

POTOMAC PITCHMEN

12
LOBBYISTS: DOMESTIC

1. The Right to Petition

The delicate art of influencing legislation—popularly known as lobbying, named for the Capitol lobbies where the backstage persuasion often occurs—has moved a great distance from the days when votes were bought with black satchels full of money and nights on the town with painted ladies. The methods have become refined since the nineteenth-century railroad mogul, Collis Huntington, wrote his three Southern Pacific partners that it would cost only $200,000 to highball a pet bill of theirs through Congress. "This coming session," he explained, "will be composed of the hungriest set of men that ever got together." No lobbyist today would openly boast, as Huntington did, "I stayed in Washington to fix up the Railroad Committee in the Senate."

Today's successful lobbyists are more likely to be smooth

professionals, skilled in the "soft sell." They seldom engage in blatant currying of favor. Well-tailored and turned out, they will make their pitches subtly over martinis at the posh Metropolitan Club or over golf balls at the exclusive Burning Tree course. But they can also retain a Senator's law firm or deliver cash in a paper sack to those who prefer that sort of gross transaction.

If lobbying techniques have been sophisticated, the name of the game is still the same: special interest. Lobbyists may call themselves legislative counsels or Washington representatives. They may organize write-your-Congressman pitches and spend their money on selective campaign contributions instead of outright bribes. They may discourse at length on the valuable services they provide to overworked Congressmen who would not be able to vote intelligently on complicated bills without their expertise. But they are still hired, in the final analysis, to be salesmen for their clients' special interests.

The lobbyists' role in government, to hear them tell it, is sorely misunderstood. They merely exercise their Constitutional right of petition, albeit with special vigor. The First Amendment guarantees "the right of the people peaceably to assemble, and to petition the Government for a redress of grievances." Apparently the founding fathers did not foresee that professional petitioners would bring such heavy axes to grind.

In the nineteenth century the first feeble attempts were made to control lobbying. A House rule in 1852 barred from the floor any newspaperman who was pushing a claim against the Government. Fifteen years later the House withdrew floor privileges from ex-Congressmen if they had a financial interest in any bill. Not until the New Deal were restrictions placed on lobbyists by law, then only in public utilities and merchant shipping. Foreign agents were also required to register and report who was paying them. Finally in 1946 Congress passed a law that was intended to require all lobbyists to register and to give yearly reports of their spending. These regulations are so full of loopholes, though, that they are more of a tennis racket than a club over the heads of the lobbyists.

The most effective lobbyists seldom register at all. They may be lawyers who devote most of their time to guiding corporations through the trackless wastes of government, or corporate "Washington representatives" who merely follow the progress of special bills. When a little pressure is needed, they will point out the Senators and bring big names from their home states to make the personal contacts.

There are intelligent men in Washington who are convinced that lobbyists exercise little power, because opposing lobbies cancel each other out on major issues, leaving the public interest as the determining factor. It is true that lobbyists come from all spectra of the American scene; they represent industries, unions, farm organizations, veterans' groups, trade associations. When Big Labor clashes with Big Business, they may indeed produce a stalemate. But this would hardly be true of tax reforms, for instance, because every group lobbies for its own tax loophole unmindful of the others. The evidence is more persuasive that legislation is shaped as much by the hidden influences as by the public debates. These less visible forces are constantly applied by lawyers and lobbyists, Washington representatives and public-relations men, fixers and expediters, who are dedicated to the proposition that the national interest is identical with their particular interest. They do not like to call themselves lobbyists. "It just isn't sophisticated to call yourself a lobbyist in Washington any more," explained Dale Miller, one of the most successful whatchamacallits in Washington.

Certainly, the effective operators no longer hang around the Capitol lobbies. They remain above the battle, cool, convivial, and, if possible, invisible. But few ever treaded with a softer foot or dealt on the inside with more effectiveness than did Clark Clifford.

2. Clark Clifford: St. Louis Smoothy

The society pages of the Washington newspapers are often more revealing than the front pages. The ladies display remarkable enterprise in pursuing their angles on the day's top stories—the bons mots, the pouts, the whims, the blunders of the social moths who nibble hors d'oeuvre as they flutter around the flame of power. In Washington's politically oriented superstructure, social acceptance is as fragile as a crystal champagne glass. The names dropped at the posh parties reflect the rise and fall of the power-seekers far more accurately than do the opinion polls. Over the years, few men in Washington have been as durable a commodity on the social pages as Clark Clifford. He is always charming, always able to put together the tame pun and bland epigram that pass as wit at Washington parties, always gracious to the press, always self-assured. It is his confidence, plus his ability to deliver, that has helped him endure through the administrations of four Presidents—nearly a quarter century at the pinnacle.

Unlike many of the guests at Washington parties, Clifford was at ease in social circles before he came to Washington. His father, an auditor for the Missouri Pacific Railroad, provided his family with a home in the best neighborhood of St. Louis. He also passed on an affection for the businessman's point of view. His father's influence was balanced by his mother's love of the language. She was a storyteller and platform performer with a local following. She attained prominence, too, as the sister of Clark McAdams, a brilliant editorial writer for the St. Louis *Post-Dispatch*. Another brother, William Douglas McAdams, was the founder of an enormously successful New York advertising firm.

In 1921, though Clifford was only seventeen, he enrolled in Washington University. For the most part, his interest in extracurricular activities outweighed his devotion to the classroom. He went out for the football team but quickly retired after four of his top front teeth were smashed in a scrimmage—an accident that remains unrecorded by the society reporters, who continue to be dazzled by the glitter of his smile. That smile and his wavy blond hair have always brought him attention. He played the romantic lead in his university musicals, and his performances made him a campus hero with the co-eds. Even after his graduation from law school, he maintained his interest in the stage.

For an extroverted man, Clifford has been unusually careful to avoid controversy. He developed a rare talent for remaining in the background of the news, directing politicians as though they were actors on his stage and allowing them to take the bows or the boos. In 1959, when the battle lines were forming for the 1960 Democratic convention, Clifford was in his accustomed role as a campaign adviser. A close friend from St. Louis, Senator Stuart Symington, felt the time had come to offer his services to the nation. His first open discussion on the subject was with Clifford, who became his chief strategist.

A little later, Clifford's political talent was sought by another Senator who had his eye on the White House. Since this Senator was also a law client, Clifford wound up simultaneously on the brain trust of John F. Kennedy. When a report was published that *Profiles in Courage* had been ghost-written for Kennedy, for example, the polished and persuasive Clifford was appointed the instrument of refutation. Still another candidate for the Democratic nomination, Senator Lyndon B. Johnson, also recruited Clifford. As the campaign progressed, Clifford was in constant contact with Johnson's campaign manager, James Rowe. For that matter, Clifford quietly advised a dark-horse prospect, Senator Robert Kerr, who was available in case the convention should become deadlocked and should want an oil millionaire for its candidate.

Clifford told each of the candidates that he was advising the others, but his counsel was considered so sound that his performance in 1960 has never been duplicated in political annals. Clifford sat solemnly on the strategy councils of the three leading Presidential contenders, advising each how to wrest the nomination from the other two. The three were veteran politicians, not easily conned and quite aware of his divided friendship. Looking back, Clifford insists that he remained loyal to his first commitment. He explained to both Kennedy and Johnson, he says, that Symington had approached him first. Not only did they understand, but he recalls Kennedy's comment to him: "If I'd known you for twenty-five years and you'd not gone with me, I'd think you weren't much of a friend."

Clifford was the go-between who approached Symington with Kennedy's offer of the Vice Presidential nomination; in return Symington was asked to board the Kennedy bandwagon before the first roll call. The Senator from Missouri, hoping for a deadlocked convention and a switch of Kennedy and Johnson delegates to himself as second choice, declined the offer. This put Clifford in the bizarre role of helping to direct the stop-Kennedy movement.

How effectively he worked against Kennedy might be measured by his role after the convention. He not only continued to sit on Kennedy's strategy council, but he was asked by Kennedy to prepare suggestions for setting up a Democratic administration in case of victory. On the morning after the election, Kennedy phoned Clifford from Hyannis Port and asked whether the transition document was completed. It was. That same day, the Secret Service carried 15 copies of the 200-page report to Kennedy headquarters at Cape Cod. Another—and some say superior—document was prepared by Professor Richard Neustadt, then at Columbia, but he was shuffled off to perform a chore for the Democratic National Committee, and the Washington *Post* was able to announce in a page-one banner that Clifford would head the transition.

It was not an entirely unfamiliar chore for Clark Clifford. After the 1952 election, he directed the changing of the guard from the Truman to the Eisenhower forces. It did not go smoothly, largely because Eisenhower was in the first of his Presidential rages. Truman had considered Eisenhower's promise to go to Korea as an outrageous bit of campaign demagoguery. After Election Day he had sent a telegram to the new President offering congratulations and the sentence: "By the way, if you still plan to go to Korea, I will put my plane at your disposal." Eisenhower had little interest in the advice offered by Clifford or anyone else from the Truman camp. "Ike was mad as a snake," Clifford remembers. "He was so mad he couldn't spit for two weeks." Still, Clifford made a favorable impression on Eisenhower, and Clifford's law firm continued to thrive during those lean years for Democrats.

The transition from Eisenhower to Kennedy was more gracious. Ike appointed General Wilton B. Persons from his staff to work with Clifford, and on November 14, 1960, they set up the machinery to speed security clearances for the new Kennedy people and to provide them with office space until the inaugural. Clifford was in almost daily contact with Persons, and the transition was a model of efficiency and civility.

Clifford performed his services without compensation from the Government. The sacrifice did no injury, however, to his Dun and Bradstreet rating. It is hard to conceive of a better advertising campaign for a lawyer than national publicity that he was the one who put high Federal officials behind their desks. Commented Kennedy mischievously, "Clark is a wonderful fellow. In a day when many are seeking a reward for what they contributed to the return of the Democrats to the White House, you don't hear Clark clamoring. All he asked in return was that we advertise his law firm on the backs of one-dollar bills."

The movement of Clifford from political obscurity to political power was swift but subtle. Before he graduated from Washington University Law School in 1928, he had already pushed himself into one of the most successful law firms in St. Louis: Holland, Lashley and Donnell. After hearing one of the partners, Jacob Lashley, lecture to his law school class, Clifford approached him and volunteered his services. "Sir," he said, "I would like to sit in your office library and see how the firm operates. I will work without pay, sir."

Lashley, impressed by Clifford's confidence, agreed. He also had to take notice of Clifford's ability. Clark was among 350 taking the Missouri bar examination, and he finished second. Following the pattern that landed him in the offices of Holland, Lashley and Donnell, the young attorney went out to find clients. He told judges, "If you ever have a defendant who can't afford a lawyer, I hope you'll call on me." He was soon appointed to defend a man caught in a stolen auto with a bag of burglar's tools. Clifford staged an impressive appeal to the jury, and although his client went to prison for 20 years, those who heard Clifford in the courtroom knew that great labor had gone into the defense. His luck with his cases did not show an immediate improvement. He later admitted, "I sent a steady stream of men to Jefferson City"—the state prison. Soon, however, he was winning, and the law firm began sending him to court with paying clients. In time, Washington University brought him back to the classroom to lecture on trial psychology.

Clifford had other assets that aided his career. One was his wife Margery, whom he met on a trip to Europe in the summer of 1929. She was touring with a group of Ivy-type co-eds. More taken with the girls than the sights, Clifford and a companion scrapped their own travel plans and followed the girls from Germany to Switzerland, Italy and France. Margery and Clark were married in October 1931, and she immediately set about doing the things that advance a lawyer's standing.

"Marney," as friends called her, had been a music student, and in St. Louis she quickly was elected president of the Grand Opera Guild. Clark, meanwhile, had become a director of the Symphony Society, and the Cliffords were obvious guests when Jake Vardaman began inviting music lovers to his farm on Saturday afternoons to hear the Metropolitan Opera broadcasts on his huge Capehart radio. Vardaman was a wealthy and ambitious businessman who had backed Harry Truman's successful campaign for the Senate in 1934. Clifford impressed him at the Saturday opera sessions, and Vardaman, the receiver for a bankrupt shoe firm, picked Clark to handle the legal affairs. Indeed, Clifford was so skillful at finding clients for the law firm that he was elevated to a partnership in 1938, and the firm's name became Lashley, Lashley, Miller and Clifford.

Vardaman, a Navy Reserve officer, was called to active duty shortly after America entered World War II. When he departed, he turned over all his affairs to Clifford. In 1944 Clifford decided that he, too, should join the armed forces, and Vardaman helped him get a commission as a Navy lieutenant junior grade. He was dispatched to investigate the supply jam-up in San Francisco, and the Navy found his report to be accurate and to the point. He returned to San Francisco with Atlantic Fleet chief Admiral Royal Ingersoll and transformed the supply function into an efficient program. Admiral Ingersoll gratefully boosted Clifford to lieutenant commander.

When Harry Truman became President in the closing days of the war, he remembered his old supporter Jake Vardaman, who was brought into the White House as naval aide. Admiral Vardaman, in turn, remembered his friends. When he departed for the Potsdam conference in July 1945, he summoned Clifford to Washington to hold the fort for five weeks. Clark's temporary duty lasted almost five years.

With the Presidential party away, Clifford wandered around the White House looking for work. He joined Judge Sam Rosenman, White House special counsel and a speech writer, in drafting a message to Congress. On his return, Truman discovered that Clifford could write phrases that the President could deliver. Truman's early speeches as President were audible disasters. He fumbled the well-turned phrases and classical references that FDR's ghost-writers had prepared for him. One well-written speech was reduced to such verbal rubble that its author stood in the back of the hall weeping as Truman tripped over the last transitional bridge. Clifford's prose was different; its flat, bland character was suited for Truman's flat Missouri delivery. Clifford's basically pro-business, non-New Deal outlook also made Truman feel at home.

When Vardaman was made a governor of the Federal Reserve Board, Clifford took his desk as naval aide, and was promoted to captain. Thus exalted, the handsome young naval officer finally went to sea. One of his assignments was to supervise the Presidential yacht, the *Williamsburg,* on its cruises down the Potomac. The menus aboard became a source of friction between Captain Clifford and the Commander-in-Chief. Clifford was a shrimp fancier, and Truman was not. On three consecutive cruises, shrimp appeared on the luncheon table, and Truman called his naval aide aside for a lecture.

Clifford was soon relieved of his shrimp duties. Rosenman resigned to return to private practice, and Clifford left the Navy to become special counsel for the President at $12,000 a year—less than half what he had earned in St. Louis. But the new counsel's office in the White House was only three doors from Truman's, and the traffic between the two rooms was heavy. The young, gracious Clifford was a pleasant change from the other professionals who surrounded Truman. Unlike them, he was not a product of the political machines, and he was aloof from their jokes and their pranks. Yet he could mingle with them, and when called upon, he could scald the men who were brought up on four-letter words.

Clifford's burdens were overwhelming. During his first year in the new job, he had dinner at home with his wife and three daughters only three times—on Christmas Eve, Christmas Day, and New Year's Eve. Other nights were spent working on details of the Marshall Plan and unification of the armed services, drafting more speeches, and setting up the Atomic Energy Commission and the Central Intelligence Agency. When John L. Lewis led 400,000 United Mine Workers on a strike in November 1946, Clifford astounded liberal Democrats by recommending a hard line. Urged on by Clifford, the Government got an injunction and broke the strike. Lewis was fined $10,000 and his union $3.5 million.

Clifford also joined the Bourbon and poker parties aboard the *Williamsburg*—although he had abandoned drinking as a concession to an ulcer. Coming down the Potomac with other Presidential intimates, he helped plot Truman's future. In the Congressional elections of 1946 the Republicans had seized control of both the Senate and the House, and in 1947 many Washington observers doubted that Truman would run for a full term the following year. When it became apparent that he would run, few were willing to believe he could win.

Clifford was one of those believers. On Monday nights he met for dinner at the Wardman Park Hotel with other Truman strategists. The usual group included Senator J. Howard McGrath, the Democratic chairman; Sam Rosenman, Clifford's predecessor in the White House; George Allen, the professional crony of Presidents; Oscar Ewing, the Federal Security Administrator, and Clifford. They ate well, and the bills —which often ran to $150—were paid by the Democratic National Committee. They also planned well. From these meetings emerged the strategy that put Truman back in the White House.

Clifford was the father of Truman's "give-'em hell" speeches, which he pounded out on a typewriter on the campaign train between whistle stops. With Treasury Secretary John Snyder, he made FDR's speech writer Sam Rosenman feel unnecessary and unwanted. More than any other campaigner, Clifford found favor with his chief after the dramatic victory at the polls. His proximity to the President in his work and in his thinking was quickly recognized by Washington's peoplewatchers. Clifford's influence pyramided.

On February 1, 1950, Clifford opened his own law office in Washington. He didn't have to wait for prosperity. Early clients included Allied Chemical, Grace Lines, Pennsylvania Railroad, Phillips Petroleum and Standard Oil of California. Their fees were reported to exceed $500,000.

Clifford's ability to get things done in Washington was unquestioned. No one could keep score of his victories and his defeats—Clifford's practice did not often include public appearances for his clients—but the word was passed around that here was a lawyer who understood the problems businessmen faced in the dark tunnels of bureaucracy. "I felt there was a definite need for the right kind of legal representation in Washington," he told *Fortune* magazine. "The relationship between private industry and government has grown to be very complex. It seemed to me that here was a tremendous field and that more and more attention was going to have to be given to it."

He did not give up his attention to Truman. He was still a

frequent guest at the wild-card poker parties on the *Williamsburg,* with the President dealing left-handed. When Truman feuded with his former Agriculture Secretary, Clinton Anderson, Clifford feuded, too. In the spring of 1950 he canceled plans to join Anderson for a trip to the Apple Blossom Festival in Winchester, Virginia. The relationship between Clifford and the White House did not, however, always work in Clifford's favor. In early 1950 Pan American Airways was fighting Howard Hughes' Trans World Airlines over the growing European air market. To fill gaps in its map, Pan Am moved to buy American Overseas Airlines. Hughes hired Clifford for $50,000 to protect TWA's interests. By the middle of the year, the Civil Aeronautics Board agreed with Clifford and rejected the merger. Both were right. But Truman got on the phone and begged the CAB to reconsider. In reversing itself, the CAB gave Pan Am more than it asked for, including permission to fly TWA's routes to Paris and Rome. As a sop, TWA picked up landing rights in London and Frankfurt.

Clifford may have been a liability to TWA in this case. Truman acted, insiders said, to ward off charges that the fee to Clifford had purchased Government favoritism. But this was an exception. For the most part, Clifford and his clients were on the winning side. Among his victories was an increase from a nickel to a dime for the Pennsylvania Railroad's pay toilets, over the opposition of the Office of Price Stabilization. From pay toilets he turned to gas rates. Senator Robert Kerr, in 1952, had sought to increase the price of natural gas by legislation. Kerr twisted every arm in Congress, only to see his pet bill vetoed by Truman. Clifford, representing Phillips Petroleum, went to work with Kerr and got a ruling from the Federal Power Commission that gave the oil industry almost everything it had wanted from the Kerr bill.

During the Eisenhower Administration, Clifford worked silently but effectively. Clients who needed a solid legal brief did not come to his firm. But he could offer a valuable insight into government, and he possessed powerful influence with the Democrats who controlled Congress.

As Eisenhower's term drew to a close, Clifford made one of his rare, open appearances for a client. Charles Revson, the head of Revlon cosmetics and sponsor of TV's *$64,000 Question,* hired Clifford to accompany him to the witness stand during his testimony before the House hearing into rigged quiz shows. Clifford coached his client carefully, then sat while Revson answered the questions. For this appearance, Clifford sent Revson a bill for $25,000. When Revson's Washington counsel whistled at the sum, Clifford said, "When he's down at the beach at the Fontainebleau playing pinochle with his cronies, he'll boast that Clark Clifford charged him $25,000. Then it will seem worth every penny to him."

Clifford had another encounter with the same House Commerce Committee in 1960 when it was probing the influence exerted over regulatory agencies by lobbyists. Federal Power Commissioner Frederick Stueck admitted that he had held private conversations with a number of representatives of natural gas producers, including the man in Washington for Phillips Petroleum—Clark Clifford, an old chum from law school. The meetings with Clifford, he said, consisted of "eight or ten" luncheons, but he denied that business was discussed. Clifford, who has never registered as a lobbyist, was handed a subpoena to appear before the committee. After a few discreet phone calls, Clifford was invited to visit Chairman Oren Harris in his office, and the subpoena was forgotten.

With the election of Kennedy, Clifford resumed his quiet role as Mr. Influence. Unlike some other top Washington lawyers, Clifford was not available to non-paying clients. He did, however, give generously of his time to the Government. In assessing the Bay of Pigs disaster, Kennedy set up a nine-member Foreign Intelligence Advisory Board to snoop on the snoops. As a prime mover in the founding of the CIA, Clifford was an obvious choice. Clifford became chairman of the board in 1963. He spent an average of a day a week working for it and declined the $75-a-day consultant's fee.

He also aided the President during JFK's fight with the steel industry over its price increase. Kennedy, in a moment of anger, had thundered, "My father always told me that businessmen were S.O.B.s." Clifford, whose father had told him otherwise, poured his special brand of oil on the troubled waters and helped soothe the industry's feelings as the prices were rolled back.

While Clifford was occupied with affairs of state, his law practice did not suffer. The drug investigation by the late Senator Estes Kefauver produced the occasion for another of Clifford's rare public appearances for a client. It was a duty that Clifford could not shirk—his client, the William Douglas McAdams drug advertising firm, was founded by his uncle. Kefauver demonstrated that drug advertising was frequently misleading and that doctors have often prescribed drugs that are advertised in medical publications—only to learn later that the prescriptions brought vicious side effects to their patients. The remedy demanded by Kefauver was a description of the side effects in all ads for prescription drugs. No one familiar with Clifford's potent connections was surprised when a White House-approved version of the bill omitted any reference to drug advertising.

Within 48 hours of Kennedy's assassination, Lyndon Johnson was on the phone to Clark Clifford seeking help. "Clark," the new President said, "you've become the transition expert." As Johnson became established, Clifford's phone kept ringing with 10 to 15 calls a day from the White House. Several times a week Johnson ordered an assistant, "See if Clark can come over." He always could, making the two-block trip by car, to avoid notice.

Even in his office Clifford could keep his eye on the White House. A vast picture window offered him—and his clients— an unobstructed view of Lafayette Square and beyond it the gardens and pillars of the Executive Mansion. Johnson called him "Just-a-Minute Clifford," explaining, "At the end of the discussion, when we think we're all agreed, Clark will say, 'Now, just a minute.'" He has never been afraid to say no to Presidents, and he has the ability to put things in perspective and view them without emotion. He helped Johnson plan his campaign in 1964, and, with Abe Fortas, attempted to keep reports of Presidential aide Walter Jenkins' arrest out of the papers.

The pressing demands of the White House, however, still left him with time to turn a dollar. Clifford is, of course, tight-lipped about the fee he received from E. I. du Pont de Nemours and Company for his efforts to secure a tax break for its stockholders. The industrial giant was ordered by the courts to divest itself of the 63,000,000 shares—a 24-percent interest—it owned in General Motors. After years of fighting and losing in the courts, du Pont was eager to avoid paying income taxes on its sale of the stock. Batteries of lawyers reviewed the case, and their conclusion was unanimous: Congress had to be persuaded to pass legislation giving du Pont a special tax break. Clifford was consulted on the best way of bringing Congress around. He readily admits that he evolved the plan that eventually brought du Pont its incredible windfall. Crawford Greenwalt, then du Pont's president, abandoned the workings of the corporation to underlings, and came to Washington to lay siege to Congress. The firm of Cleary, Gottlieb, Steen and Hamilton was retained to register as du Pont's lobbyist. One of its bright young lawyers, John Sharon, was assigned to guide Greenwalt to the offices of influential Congressmen.

Clifford suggested which Congressmen to contact with the proper words to say, but never came out in the open as a supplicant for du Pont. When the special legislation was passed, Sharon went to work in Clifford's firm, and rumors spread around Washington that Clifford received $1 million from his client. He scoffed at the report and said he was paid only his retainer. Men who should know insist this retainer is $100,000 annually for 10 years.

General Electric also turned to Clifford in 1962 after it was indicted for massive price-fixing. The company wound up with over 2,000 treble-damages suits for overcharges, a problem that threatened to ruin the company. Clifford advised that GE face the music and negotiate an out-of-court settlement, but also wangled a tax deduction for necessary business expenses. He also represented the J. P. Stevens Textile Company, accused by the National Labor Relations Board of systematically suppressing the Textile Workers Union in the South. The company lost the case but was eminently satisfied with Clifford's representation.

More recently Clifford worked for the $35 billion mutual-fund industry in its fight against tighter Securities and Exchange Commission regulation. Another client, International Telephone and Telegraph, sought his services when the merger between ITT and the American Broadcasting Company was challenged by the Justice Department.

From 1950 when he opened his Washington law office until his appointment in 1968 as Secretary of Defense, Clifford maintained that he was not a lobbyist. "We did no lobbying and never have," he said. "No one in the firm has ever registered. When I left the White House and resumed legal practice in 1950, I decided to have a law firm and not a lobbying firm. Sometimes, when our clients became interested in legislation, we would recommend a lobbying firm. Many corporations, especially those with broad international interests, needed counsel and advice on policies in Washington. Nowadays, to operate a large corporation, it has become important to be informed on policies and attitudes in government."

Every Secretary of Defense since the office was established in 1947 has represented the industrial-military complex that President Eisenhower warned against in his last message to the American people. Clark Clifford, who had most to do with writing the Defense Department unification act creating the job he now holds, has represented corporations that pulled down a total of $1,890,200,000 in defense contracts in the fiscal year 1967 plus $494,659,000 in research grants. When he was sworn in as Secretary of Defense, President Johnson remarked that he would now have one client—the United States. Making the transition from a tough corporation lawyer to a tough lawyer for Uncle Sam will not be easy, but some men do accomplish it. Clifford, in taking the oath of office, said he had one great debt to repay, that to the United States "which has given me 61 years of freedom and opportunity." If he repays that debt, he will be a great Secretary of Defense.

3. Sweetening the Pot

In both performance and remuneration, Clark Clifford long ranked in the top echelon of Washington's special pleaders who play all the sides and all the angles of the Federal Triangle. Indeed, he set the style for the others—some 5,000 registered and unregistered lobbyists who practice the art of gentle persuasion. Like Clifford, they have learned that it is more effective to massage egos than to twist arms. They seek to ingratiate themselves with legislators, in subtle ways that put the legislators in their debt.

The technique has been described by ex-Senator Paul Douglas: "The enticer does not generally pay money directly to the public representative. He tries instead, by a series of favors, to put the public official under such a feeling of personal obligation that the latter gradually loses his sense of mission to the public and comes to feel that his first loyalties are to his private benefactors and patrons. . . . Throughout this whole process the official will claim—and may, indeed, believe—that there is no causal connection between the favors he has received and the decisions which he makes. He will assert that the favors were given or received on the basis of pure friendship unsullied by worldly considerations."

To further these friendships, the influence-merchants eagerly provide small favors—theater tickets, imported liquors, French perfumes, free transportation: nothing so gross that the legislators could be accused of being bribed. It is the accumulation, rather than any single gift, that gradually obligates them. They can ride in style to the Kentucky Derby in the American Railroad Association's special train or take a cruise down the Potomac in the Freight Forwarders' air-conditioned yacht. "Certainly, Senators and Congressmen have been entertained on a small scale," admits the Freight Forwarders man in Washington, Stanley Sommer, "but it's nothing more than a three-hour cruise down the Potomac." When Senator Everett Dirksen and his wife wanted to spend a Labor Day weekend at the shore, Freight Forwarders was delighted to put them up at Bobby Baker's Carousel Motel in Ocean City.

Some pressure groups keep hospitality suites near Capitol Hill where Congressmen can find relaxation from the legislative grind over a short snort, a long cigar and, perhaps, a friendly game of poker. One poker session convenes regularly in gold-papered Suite 512 of the Congressional Hotel, situated conveniently across the street from the House Office Buildings. The suite is maintained by a number of cooperating lobbyists, headed by S&H Green Stamps' Robert Oliver and the Hod Carriers' Jack Curran. Across the poker chips they may score an occasional point for their clients with such regulars as Representatives Joe Pool, D-Tex., Dominick Daniels, D-N.J., and Robert Giaimo, D-Conn. Both Oliver and Curran have denied the base rumor that the Congressmen almost always win the big pots. Some members of the House Merchant Marine and Fisheries Committee have reportedly been more lucky in their card games with shipping lobbyists.

Many lobbyists keep files on the backgrounds, interests, and weaknesses of the Congressmen with whom they deal. These files are frequently more detailed—and far more fascinating—than those kept by Washington's political reporters. If a lobbyist knows that a key Congressman has a weakness for liquor, or girls, or cash in an envelope, the approach can be quick and painless. One of the most comprehensive files, kept by the National Small Business Association, contains no blackmail information, but it provides a complete breakdown on each Congressman's voting record, plus the economic, ethnic and voting patterns in his home state.

The lobbyists swarm like bees to their own hives, turning some restaurants almost into private clubs. Downtown, Duke Zeibert's and Paul Young's restaurants, less than a block apart in the heart of the fashionable Connecticut Avenue office and hotel district, are usually packed with lobbyists plying their trade at noisy lunches and quiet dinners. On Capitol Hill, the Congressional Hotel, the Rotunda and the Assembly serve as similar hangouts. And the old Bobby Baker crowd, which used to congregate in the defunct Quorum Club, has found a more discreet meeting place. They have taken over a handsome double house in Schott's Court, an alley behind the New Senate Office Building. Having learned from past mistakes, they have decided not to give their new pub a name. It is known simply by its street number—116.

The best way for lobbyists to show their appreciation for a Congressman, of course, is to contribute to his campaign. And the plunk of every donated coin, the rustle of every unfolding bill, the scratch of pen on check all add emphasis to the need for reform of the greatest evil in the American political system. For most Congressional campaigns have become financed mainly by the special-interests and pressure groups. The sad truth is that the American voter often cannot be bothered to go to the polls, let alone give money. Democracy—it's wonderful, but who wants to pay for it? Even the most honest Congressmen cannot entirely escape doing business with the special interests. Those candidates who have tried to finance campaigns from small contributions have learned quickly that the fat cats are indispensable. Indeed, it is a miracle of politics and a tribute to officeholders that the pressure groups do not wield more influence than they do.

The campaign laws require candidates to report what they collect and spend, but the laws are antiquated and riddled with loopholes. Enter the lobbyists, who have become experts in the fine art of slipping money through loopholes. Their most frequent ruse is "double billing," by which their client pays certain campaign expenses directly but shows them on the books as "business expenses." A printing bill may be picked up, or the candidate may be given a company credit card for charging his meals, say, or his air travel. Another common dodge is to channel donations through friends, relatives and employees, thus circumventing the law prohibiting contributions from corporations.

Other lobbyists have set up front groups to distribute campaign cash. The high-sounding Committee for Economic Growth, lavish with donations, turned out to be a group of restaurant owners who were fighting against tax tightening on expense accounts. Most of the committee's contributions went to members of the Senate and House committees that write tax legislation. A $1,500 contribution went to Senator Russell Long, D-La., who delivered a blistering Senate attack on the expense-account rules. Another $1,000 went to Representative John Dent, D-Pa., who introduced a bill to cancel restrictions on expense-account spending. All told, the committee gave $1,000 each to 40 Congressional candidates, another $500 each to seven candidates in 1966.

Several construction and paving contractors, working through Washington attorney Thomas Thompson, Jr., set up a campaign front called Committee for Action, taking care not to specify what action they had in mind. The contractors were known, though, to be bitterly opposed to legislation that would allow unions to picket an entire construction project when their workers are involved in only a limited phase of the work. The committee delivered its largest campaign gift in 1966, a substantial $14,000, to Senator Robert Griffin, R-Mich., who has led the fight against this legislation, known as the Situs Picketing bill, inside the Senate Labor and Public Welfare Committee.

And something called the Committee on American Leadership, it turned out, was financed by the coal lobby to reward legislators who showed the proper enlightenment toward increasing the coal depletion allowance. Among the donations distributed by the committee was $500 to Representative Elizabeth Kee, D-W.Va., and $650 to Representative John Saylor, R-Pa., who introduced bills to have the depletion allowance boosted. Since both represented coal-producing areas, perhaps they were entitled to demand the same enlarged tax loophole for coal producers that their oil and gas competitors receive.

Since a politician must have money to run for office—and he generally cannot raise it from the public—he has little alternative but to accept it from special interests. But this raises a question of propriety: which comes first, the contribution or the conviction? In the desperate struggle to fill their campaign coffers without selling their souls, candidates keep dreaming up new fund-raising gimmicks. The most productive have been the $100-a-plate dinners; some candidates start holding these dinners two years before the election. Other variations include $25-a-plate breakfasts and $50-a-plate luncheons. All these, too, have been patronized chiefly by the lobbyists. In any event, Senator Tom Dodd, who tried them all and pocketed the proceeds, has ráised a cloud over the propriety of such affairs. The House Ethics Committee, not wishing to foreclose this source of campaign revenue, has called for stricter controls. Under the Committee's proposal, future Tom Dodds could not pocket the proceeds of a testimonial function without giving clear advance notice.

Some lobbyists concentrate their attention on Congressmen who are friendly, or at least not hostile, to their own political outlook. But with most special pleaders, the only votes that count are those cast for or against the client's interests; a Congressman's voting record on other issues is a matter purely of academic interest. The voting record of Representative Eugene Keogh, for instance, coincided not at all with his roster of campaign contributors. The ruddy-faced Irishman kept his Brooklyn constituents contented with a 100-percent-liberal voting record. His rating from the National Association of Businessmen, in contrast, was a fat zero. Yet only one labor-connected organization bothered to contribute to his last campaign; his union friends were aware that Keogh's re-election in 1964 was as sure as death and taxes.

But Keogh did not lack for campaign contributors; contributions fluttered in from all over the country—Boston, Chicago, Houston, Fort Lauderdale, Philadelphia, San Francisco and Washington, to name a few. For a prominent Senator with a national following, perhaps, this pattern would not be uncommon. But for a toiler in the anonymous vineyards of the House, it took a little explaining. The explanation: Keogh had worked his way into a commanding position on the House Ways and Means Committee, and there were plenty of people anxious to buy entree to that tax-writing committee.

Two contributions—$1,000 from the Bankers Congressional Committee and $500 from the National Tax Equality

Association—emanated from the same Washington address: 1000 Connecticut Avenue. This also happened to be the address of the National Association of Businessmen, which looked with such disapproval upon Keogh's voting record. An NAB spokesman acknowledged that all three organizations were controlled by the same group of men, mostly bankers. They were able to set aside their conservative convictions and contribute to the liberal Keogh, however, in order to impress upon him the merits of "tax equality." By this they had in mind legislation to reduce the tax advantage of their chief competitors, the savings and loan associations.

Keogh's campaign coffers were replenished also by lobbyists for the National Coal Association, National Association of Electric Companies, Shoe Manufacturers Good Government Committee and the restaurant owners' Committee for Economic Growth. Deeper in Keogh's campaign finances could be found mysterious contributions, ranging from $10 to $100, from 15 high-level executives of the General Foods Corporation. Most of them gave their address as 250 North Street, White Plains, New York, the company's national headquarters, which is a long way from Keogh's liberal Brooklyn district. An even greater distance away is Cincinnati, Ohio, but Keogh collected seven contributions, ranging from $30 to $100, from the honorary chairman, president, executive vice president and four vice presidents of the Procter & Gamble Company in Cincinnati. And from Boston came five $100 contributions from the top officers of the Massachusetts Investors Trust, a $2 billion mutual fund. Out in Detroit, Henry Ford II thought so much of Keogh that he sent two contributions, one of $300 and another for $250.

All this concern for the Congressman from Brooklyn was touching, indeed, but there was no great patriotism in their motives. Three months after Keogh was re-elected, he was busy inside the Ways and Means Committee processing a tax reform bill which, among its features, sought to plug up the stock-option profits. Under the bill, they would have been obliged to pay the regular income tax rate. Among those who filed letters against this reform were Keogh's benefactors from the Massachusetts Investors Trust and Procter & Gamble. A General Foods contributor also spoke out against plugging the loophole. So did Henry Ford II. After solemn committee deliberation, the stock-option loophole remained unplugged.

4. Captive Speakers

If campaign contributions seem circuitous, there are more direct ways to pay off friendly legislators. A Congressman who is beyond bribing, for example, may be willing to accept a lecture fee. He may be able to convince his conscience that he really earned the money, though oratory can be summoned forth from the average Congressman as a reflex action. The Mortgage Bankers Association of America, to cite one pressure group, will pay perfectly good money to hear a Congressman declaim.

"We have paid honorariums to Congressmen," acknowledged a spokesman with an air of imparting a little-known fact. "Some of them will ask for it diplomatically—very diplomatically, of course—but they will ask for what the traffic will bear. The top fee my association has paid has been about a thousand." Who commands the top fee? The name most frequently mentioned in mortgage banking circles is that of Representative William Widnall, R-N.J. Like his suburban district of Hackensack, across the Hudson River from New York City, the Congressman has come up in the world since his childhood. He has developed certain views that make him a popular speaker in some moneyed circles. "Mr. Widnall," the mortgage banker's man said, "has been the nearest thing to a champion that we have, I suppose. Most of our work is through Mr. Widnall." As the senior Republican on the House Banking and Currency Committee, he is obviously a good man to work through. The savings-and-loan men know, in contrast, that the committee's chairman, Representative Wright Patman, D-Tex., views bankers with a suspicious eye.

If the bankers need friends in the House, they already have the situation well in hand in the Senate. "On the other side of the Capitol," their spokesman said, "you have an entirely different situation. There the leadership is well aware of the facts of life and the minority is not so vocal." In the 89th Congress, the Senate Banking Committee's chairman was Senator A. Willis Robertson, D-Va., who was so beloved of bankers that they set up a campaign fund to help him with his unsuccessful Democratic primary campaign against William D. Spong, Jr. The bankers think ahead, too. Robertson was never much of a star on the honorarium circuit, but his successor as committee chairman, Senator John Sparkman, D-Ala., has appeared before the United Savings and Loan League as well as the Mortgage Bankers Association.

The League's legislative director, Stephen Slipher, is forthright about his lobby's principles—if not about its pocketbook. Its customary honorarium, he said, lies "generally between a hundred and a thousand," depending on whether the speaker has to travel far to unburden himself. But crass financial considerations don't enter into these matters at all, according to Slipher. If a Congressman accepts an invitation to speak, "our outfit offers him something as an afterthought." Besides Sparkman and Robertson, his outfit has lent an ear, interest free, to the bankers' favorite, Widnall. Slipher freely admitted that his principle of selection is very simple. "We stick pretty much to the banking committees," he said.

Widnall himself claims he has never made more than $2,000 a year from honorariums, and he obviously thinks he earns whatever he gets. "Some group will ask you to fly out to Chicago for a talk on December 15—and goddammit, who wants to fly to Chicago that time of year?" Only a week earlier, Widnall complained, he had driven—with his wife—across the border into New York's Catskill resort area to address "a small investment group" at Grossinger's. "It was a long trip and we spent twenty dollars for meals and I don't know how much for gas. When I finished they never offered me even the cost of expenses, and I had to drive like fury back to New Jersey that night so that I could catch a plane for Washington the next morning. I never ask these groups for anything," the Congressman concluded virtuously, "but I think they could offer you something."

Apparently enough offers are made to keep Widnall coming back for more. Marvin Powers of the American Industrial Bankers Association regards him as one of the more prominent after-dinner speakers on Capitol Hill. But there are plenty of others. "The typical arrangement might be for the Congressman to appear in the afternoon for a cocktail reception. Then he would speak at about 7:30 or 8 P.M. during the meal," Powers explained. "It's pretty well known that the fee is important with some of them. . . . Some will do it for nothing—it all depends on how much they need the exposure. Congressman Fascell, of Miami, is an example of one that will do it just for the trip." Powers was careful not to say that Florida's Democratic Representative Dante Fascell had actually done any speaking before his group. Similarly, he didn't say the industrial bankers had paid to listen to Senator Wallace Bennett, R-Utah, who once headed the National Association of Manufacturers. What he did say was that Bennett "is developing quite a following."

Lobbyists have a way of concentrating their blandishments on legislators who are already leaning in the right direction, but the system doesn't always work that way. The United States Chamber of Commerce, according to one of its Washington representatives, has listened to a lot of Congressmen in its day—"all the principal ones"—and it does not draw the line between friends and foes. Senator Philip Hart, the Michigan Democrat who nursed the "truth-in-packaging" bill through Congress in 1966, was invited to talk to the Chamber about the bill.

Congressmen's speeches before trade associations are apt to lapse sooner or later into testimonials to the effectiveness of their lobbyists in Washington. Representative Wayne Aspinall, D-Colo., who heads the House Interior Committee, was no exception at the 1965 convention of the American Mining Congress in Las Vegas. It was always a pleasure, Aspinall began, to see old friends and make new ones at the mine operators' gatherings "and to preside at the traditional public lands session where those of us having a responsibility for public lands policy have an opportunity for public exchange of views with mining men interested in the use and development of the public lands and their resources." No one was crude enough to suggest that a mining man's interest in the use of the public domain was roughly comparable to a shoplifter's interest in a department store. Aspinall went on to add, "The cooperation of the mining industry is not a once-a-year matter; the House Committee on Interior and Insular Affairs has received, through the American Mining Congress government relations chief, Harry Moffett, prompt, complete responses whenever we have needed information, and frequently it has been furnished in anticipation of the need." In other words, don't worry, boys, your lobbyist is doing his job.

Honorariums are an old story with Congressmen, of course; the only change over the years has been the price. In the closing years of the Eisenhower Administration, the National Association of Manufacturers could spare only $700 apiece for such seasoned proponents of tough anti-labor laws as Representative Graham Barden, D-N.C., then chairman of the Education and Labor Committee; Representative Charles Halleck, R-Ind., then leader of the Republican minority, and Representative Phil Landrum, D-Ga., whose name is ritually reviled by every good union careerist for the Landrum-Griffin Act. Landrum also accepted a few fees from the American Retail Federation, which was straining to keep the minimum wage in those pre-Great Society days from rising from $1 an hour to $1.25.

The standards of selection for Congressional speakers are obscure at best, but Ray Murdock of the American Maritime Association proposes a rule of thumb. "I do believe," he said, "you can draw a graph. The more important the Congressman, the more likely he is to make speeches for honorariums." The question, of course, is what you mean by "important." Not many members of Congress can boast that their names are household words, and those who can aren't necessarily active on the honorarium circuit. Fully half of the pressure groups deny paying honorariums in any form. A good many more say their state and local affiliates sometimes do. The American Hotel and Motel Association, which has a fierce proprietary interest in keeping its employees out from under the minimum-wage umbrella, ordinarily does not pay for Congressional oratory but has made an exception for Representative Landrum, who understands them so well. More liberal organizations, from the American Civil Liberties Union to the Retail Clerks International Association, mentioned Hubert Humphrey as a prize catch before his elevation from the Senate to the Vice Presidency. The United Steel Workers' Mel Fish listed Tennessee's Senator Albert Gore, Maine's Senator Edmund Muskie and Oregon's Senator Wayne Morse—Democrats all—as past attractions and added, "Over a period of a year, we've had damn near all of them."

The Mortgage Bankers Association of America doesn't depend entirely on New Jersey's Congressman Widnall for after-dinner listening, of course. Sometimes it brings in several members of Congress at a time for a panel, mixing them up all the way from Connecticut's liberal Democratic Senator Abraham Ribicoff through Minority Leader Everett Dirksen to Senator John Tower, the conservative Texas Republican.

Dirksen has also appeared before the American Bankers Association, as has Senator John McClellan, D-Ark. House GOP Leader Gerald Ford spoke up not long ago before the American Meat Institute (he said Congress was "a weak, wet noodle"). The institute balanced the scales by asking Majority Whip Hale Boggs to speak at its next convention. The House Ethics Committee, while it would not deprive Congressmen of remuneration for the hot air they expend, has sought to keep the honorariums in line with "the usual and customary" amounts.

5. *Immediate Release*

Another form of payoff is suggested by a curious conversation between ex-Representative William Miller, R-N.Y., who departed from the House in 1964 to become Barry Goldwater's Vice Presidential running mate, and ex-Representative Frank Smith, D-Miss. The Mississippi moderate has now told how Miller offered him a public relations "retainer" of up to $500 a month not long before a crucial vote in Smith's Public Works Subcommittee on a public power project. The upstate New York Republican explained that he was the director of a company, Lockport Felt, that had just set up a new plant not far from Smith's district, and the company's president thought an ex-newspaperman who knew the area the way Smith did would be an asset to the firm's image. Would Smith like to put out a release now and then, strictly on a part-time basis? Smith asked the obvious question: "Would I be offered this work because I'm in Congress?"

"Oh, no," said Miller. "We want somebody with a newspaper background, and I thought about you simply because of that." Smith, knowing the political life expectancy of a Mississippi moderate, was tempted, and it was agreed that Lockport Felt's president would see him when business brought him to Washington in the next few weeks. Meanwhile, however, there was a subcommittee vote on the Niagara power bill. Smith voted his conviction, which happened to collide with Miller's aims, and made it clear that he would continue to vote that way. "I never heard from the president of the firm who was allegedly interested in my public relations talent," he later wrote, "and fortunately I had enough caution never to ask about it, even though it took quite some time for the idea to sink in that this had been some very direct lobbying."

The sequel to the story is interesting. Miller's connection with Lockport Felt, which paid him $7,500 a year, became a liability in his 1964 campaign when reporters learned that he had pushed legislation in the House that would have benefited the company. The connection became an asset again, however, when he was made a vice president of the company two weeks after he left Congress.

6. Merry Christmas

Just as German U-boat captains preferred to strike at dawn or dusk, the lobbyists have found that the best time to torpedo legislation is during the end-of-the-season rush. Then the legislators are so impatient to adjourn Congress and head for home that they don't often bother to scrutinize the fine print. The action is also too fast for the public to follow, and, usually, the lobbyist's hand is quicker than the public's eye.

Typical was the scramble to decorate the "Christmas Tree" bill during the closing confusion of the 89th Congress in October of 1966. The bill got its name from the goodies that the lobbyists hung on its branches as it progressed toward a final vote. It started through the legislative mill innocently enough as a tax measure to benefit the elderly. By the time it reached the Senate floor, it was loaded down with 49 riders, none of them germane, most of them intended as Christmas gifts for the lobbyists' clients. Only the elderly wound up with nothing.

Perhaps the most glittering ornament, worth an estimated $2 million to Harvey Aluminum Company, was strung on the Christmas tree by Senator Vance Hartke, D-Ind. This provided a retroactive tax reduction for the company by extending the investment tax credit to the Virgin Islands, where Harvey was building an aluminum plant. The company has no holdings in Hartke's home state, but its man in Washington, Keith Linden, has helped Hartke raise campaign funds. It was a strange present to a strange company (see page 363 for further details).

The lobbyists for three other giant metal firms—Anaconda, Reynolds Metals and Alcoa—petulantly demanded equal favors from Santa Claus. Anaconda's lobbyist, Henry Gardiner, spoke to Senator Herman Talmadge, D-Ga., about increasing the depletion allowance on the Georgia clay from which the company extracted aluminum. Reynolds and Alcoa hurried over to the office of Senator J. William Fulbright, D-Ark., and demanded similar deals on Arkansas ores which they happened to be mining. "There was agreement among the three companies, I'll be blunt about that," admitted a Talmadge aide. "We thought it would help us. Ways and Means Chairman Wilbur Mills is from Arkansas, and he was the key man on the House side." On Christmas morning, the three big metal manufacturers were not disappointed; each received a sugar plum in the form of higher depletion allowances on aluminum ores.

The clay pipe industry, feeling left out, appealed to Hartke, who did more Christmas tree trimming than anyone else. He attached an amendment tripling the industry's depletion allowance. "The suggested wording," admitted the National Clay Pipe Institute's G. A. Robinson, "came from our depletion committee." The approach to Hartke, however, was made by Edward Clements, head of Can-Tex Industries of Cannelton, Indiana, which manufactures clay sewer pipes.

While he was decorating the tree, Hartke also added an excise tax reduction for hearses. He explained to the Senate, deadpan, that the tax break was needed to revive "a dying industry." Lawyer lobbyist William Geoghegan acknowledged that he had asked Hartke to sponsor the amendment. As justification, he explained that most hearses are made in Indiana and Ohio.

A group of deprived clay, shale and slate producers from Kansas took *their* hard-luck story to Senator Frank Carlson, R-Kans., who, in the Christmas spirit, arranged a small increase in *their* depletion allowance. And Russell Long, as the Senate Santa in charge of decorating the Christmas tree, could hardly return to his native Louisiana without something for the home folks. As an appropriate bauble, Lieutenant General Walter K. Wilson, Jr., the retired chief of the Army Engineers, helpfully suggested raising the depletion allowance for clam and oyster shells. He had taken a sudden interest in the tax status of the mollusks after joining Southern Industries, which processes oyster shells for cement. To the rejoicing of Louisiana's clam and oyster shell producers, Long tripled their depletion allowance from 5 to 15 percent.

For people who had everything, Washington attorney Edward Merrigan offered a Christmas suggestion. He called upon his former next-door neighbor, Senator Eugene McCarthy, D-Minn., to plead the cause of blue-chip stockholders. For years they had been able to diversify their holdings without any annoyance from Internal Revenue by swapping individual stocks for shares in investment funds. But Internal Revenue, always slow at catching up with the tax twists on Wall Street, had finally decreed that these exchanges could no longer be tax-free. Merrigan, touching a handkerchief to his eye, explained to a sympathetic McCarthy the hardships this would cause the wealthy. So some tinsel was added to the Christmas tree for the stock swappers.

One or two Senators protested, but their voices were drowned in the adjournment clamor. "In the twenty-six years I have been here," declared Senator George Aiken, R-Vt., "the Senate never appeared more irresponsible than it does now." Senator Frank Lausche, D-Ohio, agreed. "The taxpayer," he thundered, "is being despoiled or robbed for the benefit of the few." Senator Bourke Hickenlooper, R-Iowa, held his nose. "The most odoriferous bill I have seen in years," he said. Looking down upon them from the press gallery, the Washington *Post's* George Lardner, Jr., composed a Christmas poem:

> 'Twas the night before Christmas,
> And all through the House
> Not a creature was stirring,
> Not even a mouse,
> When across in the Senate,
> There arose such a clatter;
> Russell Long was inserting
> Extraneous matter.

Some Senators squirmed a little as if the cries of protest were causing an uncomfortable draft, but most merely sat listening in studied nonchalance. Senator Long assured them, "This is a good bill," and they preferred to leave it upon his conscience. They approved the "Christmas Tree" bill by a 58-to-18 vote.

7. The Alumni Drive

Probably the most influential lobbyists are the former members of Congress who speak the raucous language of Capitol Hill and are at home in its back rooms. They have easy access to their former colleagues; they understand the intricacies of political dealing; they share the legislators' distrust of reform. Their past membership also entitles them to buttonhole legislators directly on the Senate and House floors, unless they have special interest in a specific bill being debated. They are admitted, too, to the exclusive dining areas where the members eat.

More than 100 ex-legislators have signed up as lobbyists since registration was first required in 1946; more than a few others have gently influenced votes without bothering to sign the official forms. From legislator to lobbyist would seem to be a step down. Yet for every Congressional leader who has faded into obscurity as an unsung lobbyist, there have emerged a dozen obscure Congressmen whose achievements in office pale beside their subsequent legislative feats for private clients. Representative Andrew Biemiller, D-Wis., for example, was merely a liberal Democratic voice from the back row during his two House terms. But as the AFL-CIO's chief lobbyist, he became a power on Capitol Hill. And Representative Clyde Ellis, D-Ark., cut a small but liberal swath on Capitol Hill until he became Washington panjandrum for the National Rural Electrification Association. Today he wields more power but is less liberal.

Not surprisingly, the legislators-turned-lobbyists usually specialize in influencing the committees upon which they formerly served. When Thailand sought a share of the United States sugar import quota, the Thai Government retained ex-Representative George Grant, D-Ala., to explain the need to his former colleagues on the House Agriculture Committee. They saw to it that Thailand got a piece of the action. Two other Alabama Representatives, Albert Rains and Kenneth Roberts, after their exits, lobbied for interests they had helped to regulate as members of the Banking and Commerce committees. The American Petroleum Institute's lobbyist, Texan Frank Ikard, used to deal with the oil depletion allowance as a member of the House Ways and Means Committee. And Representative Victor Knox, R-Mich., who opposed automobile excise taxes as a member of the same committee, went to work afterward for the National Automobile Dealers Association. Kenneth Keating, R-N.Y., the snowy-haired former Senator, had one of the shortest lobbying careers as special pleader for an organization promulgating birth control. He was registered precisely one month; then he quit to run successfully for New York's highest state court. Senator John Sherman Cooper, R-Ky., who kept winning special elections and losing regular ones, was on Lehigh Valley Railway's payroll for a spell between campaigns, and Senator Frank Lausche, D-Ohio, took a between-jobs retainer from the New York Central Railroad. The late Senate Majority Leader Scott Lucas, D-Ill., and former Majority Whip Earle Clements, D-Ky., served clients on the Hill after the voters retired them from Congress.

Former Congressional assistants are sometimes in demand as lobbyists, too. The late Speaker Sam Rayburn's administrative assistant, John Holton, settled down with the American Bankers Association, and onetime LBJ aide Booth Mooney found work with H. L. Hunt, the multimillionaire right-winger who is virtually a one-man interest group.

Larry King, a reformed administrative assistant who toiled for two Texas Congressmen, set up a sort of bird watcher's guide to lobbyists. In his view, the ex-Congressman who stayed to feather his nest on Capitol Hill was a Lame Duck Emeritus, with a new flock hatched every two years. King liked to tell the story of the canny ex-Senator who succeeded in pushing a client's bill through the House one year, then very quietly urged his Senate friends to drag their feet until the following year. After all, he figured, a lot of lobbyists would be looking for work if the legislative obstacle course was made too easy.

Most Lame Ducks Emeritus, being legal eagles as well, prefer to roost in the law firms around Washington. There is more dignity, it seems, in vote-influencing as lawyers than as lobbyists.

8. By Any Other Name

As each new Congress fades into history and each new Administration lays down the controls of government, they leave behind a few more prominent lawyers who don't want to go back to Pocatello. Counting those both in and out of government, Washington has more lawyers per capita than any city in the world. But the Brahmin Barristers are the celebrated holdovers, once big names on Capitol Hill and the Federal lowlands, who remain to practice law on the fringes of the Federal establishment. The line separating them from the political and policy councils is thin indeed. Washington attorneys are often called back into government as consultants; they populate the various Federal boards, committees, councils and commissions.

A few big-name attorneys, such as Dean Acheson (and Clark Clifford and Abe Fortas before their appointments to the Defense Department and Supreme Court respectively), are used as discreet troubleshooters. They might be described as fixers without portfolio who handle Presidential and Congressional assignments too delicate to be performed by anyone in an official position. They slip in the side door of the White House to advise the President on confidential matters. Their quiet counsel is whispered into the most important ears in Washington. Their phone calls are put through promptly to Cabinet officers, high officials, members of Congress.

When a White House aide was found out to be a homosexual, Clifford and Fortas were called in to handle the delicate backstage arrangements to ease him into a hospital and hush the publicity. When President Kennedy squared off against the steel tycoons, Clifford stepped in to smooth over the dispute. When the West German Ambassador talked too freely to suit Kennedy, Acheson quietly passed the word to the German Government that a new ambassador would improve German-American relations. Both Acheson and Clifford have handled repeated assignments involving high policy and deep secrecy. President Johnson, even more than his predecessors, constantly consults the Brahmins.

For this extracurricular service the attorneys generally charge the taxpayers nothing. They collect indirectly from private clients who may be impressed by their access to the high and mighty. For influence—a word Washington's Brahmin Barristers dislike mentioning—is nonetheless the *sine qua non* of their practice. They merely pretend that they use persuasion instead of pull, indulge in legalities instead of lobbying.

The top Washington law firms, like the monuments that populate the city's squares and circles, are markers of the past. Covington and Burling, the most prestigious firm in the Washington law directory, was formed by two holdovers from the Woodrow Wilson Administration. But it has kept up with the times, and its balkanized maze of more than 100 law cubicles contains a number of attorneys with excellent pipelines into the Johnson Administration and the Congress. Its most distinguished star is Dean Acheson.

Second in size, if not in influence, is Hogan and Hartson, which was put together by two Republican officials at the turn of the century. The firm gained its first notoriety when its founder, Frank Hogan, masterminded the defense in the Teapot Dome scandal. In the same tradition, Edward Bennett Williams started his courtroom spectaculars as a Hogan and Hartson defense attorney. He attracted enough headline clients to form his own law firm. But at least one member of the old firm, Edward McDermott, has an intimate acquaintance in top Democratic circles today.

The New Deal produced a whole crop of law firms whose founders built up the New Deal bureaucracy, then departed government to make fortunes helping businessmen in their dealings with the bureaucrats. Perhaps the most influential today is Arnold and Porter, a zestful firm that defended victims of the late Senator Joe McCarthy as well as blue-chip clients. It was formed by FDR's then Assistant Attorney General Thurman Arnold and then Undersecretary of Interior Abe Fortas, joined by President Truman's price administrator, Paul Porter. Fortas has been LBJ's most intimate adviser since he persuaded Supreme Court Justice Hugo Black in 1948 to overrule the Texas courts, which had barred Lyndon Johnson's name from the ballot in a dispute over his 87-vote primary victory in a contest for the Democratic Senatorial nomination.

Fortas' value to his law firm was such that he had promised his partners not to leave. Indeed, President Johnson had to draft him into the judiciary. "I've just sent fifty thousand men to Vietnam, and I'm sending you to the Supreme Court," the President told him. But even on the high bench, Fortas continued to handle occasional non-judicial chores for the President. His velvet touch was evident during the crises over the steel price hike and the transportation strike. When Ralph Lazarus, president of Federated Department Stores, announced at a meeting of the influential Business Council that Vietnam spending would soar $5 billion over the White House's public estimate, he received a phone call from Fortas at the Hot Springs, Virginia, conference. Fortas explained softly that LBJ was unhappy. Lazarus quickly modified his statement.

Fortas' move to the Supreme Court has done no damage to the standing of Arnold and Porter. The Justice's wife, Carolyn Agger Fortas, remains with the firm. It is a tribute to her tough legal mind that no one seems to notice when she lights up a cigar and blows fumes with the male partners during their deliberations.

Another New Deal law firm, which has more connections on Capitol Hill than the Chesapeake & Potomac Telephone Company, is Corcoran, Foley, Youngman and Rowe. Its stars are those two former White House brain trusters, Thomas Corcoran and James Rowe, whose records are more impressive in the back rooms than in the courtrooms. Rowe alternates between his clients and the White House, where he has helped President Johnson with political strategy. Corcoran, in particular, has a positive genius for keeping behind the scenes —a most remarkable feat in view of the delightful garrulous old Irishman's seeming open-mouth policy. He represents gas clients but never appears before the Federal Power Commission; he is retained by airline clients but studiously avoids Civil Aeronautics Board hearings; his services are sought by clients with Congressional problems, but he would not be caught in an open Congressional hearing.

"Tommy the Cork," as he is known affectionately on the Hill, is more likely to be found at the back door. When a client's papers were subpoenaed, he delivered them privately to Chairman Tom Dodd of the Juvenile Delinquency Subcommittee and exacted the astounding promise that the documents would be shown to no one else. Corcoran also pulled the right political switches to sidetrack an investigation of the drug Percodan, as he has worked to spare many another client from an embarrassing hearing. In return, he has been an energetic fund raiser for his friends in Congress. He not only steered a number of contributors to Dodd's testimonial dinners but quietly helped to mastermind Dodd's defense when he got into trouble for pocketing the proceeds. Corcoran also endeared himself to another New Englander who might be a source of help in the future: even while Dodd was under fire, "Tommy the Cork" threw a sentimental lobster bake in his suburban backyard to raise $15,000 for Senator Thomas McIntyre, D-N.H.

Another attorney who knows his way around the Capitol corridors is Lloyd Cutler, of Wilmer, Cutler and Pickering, who has represented the Pharmaceutical Manufacturers Association, General Motors and other big-money clients in the Federal city. When Robert Kennedy, as Attorney General, wanted to ransom the Cuban freedom fighters with drugs and foodstuffs, he got in touch with Cutler, who warned that tax and antitrust questions would have to be settled before the drug manufacturers would put up the ransom. He also worked behind the scenes with Clark Clifford in setting up a public-private corporation to operate communications satellites.

Many other Washington law firms specialize in political problems. A few may be able to sway a marginal decision; others merely take credit for decisions that fall their way and blame "political pressure" for the decisions they lose. A few shady law firms harbor the outright fixers and five-percenters who have given the Washington lawyer a bad name. But distasteful as it has become to be called a lobbyist, most big-name Washington lawyers engage in lobbying by whatever name they choose to call it.

The big pressure groups, of course, keep their own stables of lawyers and lobbyists. Their pressure is largely invisible, but nonetheless real. Representative Joseph Resnick, D-N.Y., discovered this during a House Agriculture Subcommittee hearing on rural America. He used the occasion to attack the powerful American Farm Bureau Federation, which, he charged, was not the simple agricultural association it claimed to be. He claimed the Farm Bureau was "masquerading before Congress, the nation and the American farmer as a farm organization deeply and exclusively devoted to promoting the best interest of the American farmer, when in reality this organization is a gigantic interlocking nationwide combine of insurance companies with total assets of more than a billion dollars." He pointed out that the Farm Bureau has opposed all Federal efforts to alleviate poverty, raise wages, promote better health, improve education, fight water and air pollution and promote community development in rural areas. A number of Farm Bureau groups, he added, have used their power to promote right-wing extremists. In Wyoming, Kentucky and Missouri, Farm Bureaus have sponsored speeches by representatives of the John Birch Society, and the South Dakota Farm Bureau engaged in ultra-right youth-training at its summer citizenship seminars.

The Farm Bureau's retaliation against Resnick was swift and harsh. On July 10, 1967, members of the Agriculture Committee received letters from Roger Fleming, second in command of the Farm Bureau. He demanded that the committee "clear the record by adopting a resolution in which it disassociates itself from the attacks on the Farm Bureau made by Subcommittee Chairman Resnick and by making known to the public at an early date its disposition." Within 24 hours, the committee began an amazing and abject surrender to the Farm Bureau. Resnick's own subcommittee met in secret without him and issued a statement criticizing Resnick. Many of the phrases used in the statement were taken verbatim from Fleming's letter. The full Agriculture Committee met behind closed doors the next day, keeping White House aide Walt W. Rostow waiting 90 minutes while it thrashed out a condemnation of Resnick that would please the Farm Bureau. By a startling 27-to-1 vote, the Committee disassociated itself from Resnick's statements.

The dynamic Resnick, a wealthy electronics manufacturer from Ellenville, N.Y., was not silenced. He stood on the House floor the next day and demanded, "Who runs Congress, the people or the lobbyists?" It was an interesting but perhaps foolish question.

9. *Win, Lose or Draw*

Another pressure group that has demonstrated its political muscle is the drug lobby. For years the drug manufacturers blocked legislation to keep drugs safe and drug advertising sane. In fact, the late Senator Estes Kefauver, D-Tenn., would have lost his long campaign for drug reforms had it not been for the tragic thalidomide scandal of 1962.

In the spring of that year, the drug lobby had every reason to believe the Kefauver reforms were safely embalmed and ready for burial. The bill had not been killed outright, of course; it had simply been amended to death on June 6 at a secret meeting in the office of Senator James Eastland, D-Miss., the slow-speaking Senate Judiciary chairman. Eastland did not attend the meeting himself; neither did the committee's ranking Republican, Everett Dirksen. But the Illinois spellbinder sent as his representatives a pair of drug industry lawyers, Marshall Hornblower and the aforementioned Lloyd Cutler, who presented a series of twelve reform-gutting amendments. Jerome Sonosky, a legislative aide who represented the Kennedy Administration at the meeting, got a long look at a copy of the drug lobby's proposals that the lawyers left behind. Later Dirksen offered precisely the same amendments, word for word, to the Kefauver bill. As originally drafted, the bill put drug plants under Federal supervision and sharply limited the claims drug manufacturers could make for their latest miracles until the drugs had been thoroughly tested. It also required the labeling of prescription drugs by generic name as well as trade name, so careful buyers could shop around for the best buy on a drug that might be sold by half a dozen manufacturers under high-priced trade names.

The bill that came out of the meeting in Eastland's office left nobody entirely satisfied. The drug people wanted no bill at all, of course; Sonosky argued in the Administration's behalf for a stronger one. Eastland warned privately that anything stronger would never get out of his committee. Kefauver himself was appalled by the amendments that had been tacked on to his effort to protect the public. He told White House aide Mike Feldman he would rather let the committee bottle up the bill and take the issue to the voters in the November election. By August, however, the temper of the nation had changed drastically in favor of drug reform. Newspaper stories and unforgettable pictures of pitifully deformed babies, whose mothers had taken thalidomide during pregnancy, broke through the massed defenses of the drug lobby and aroused a public outcry rarely paralleled in legislative history.

Dirksen, who was up for re-election, back-pedaled furiously from his two-year campaign against drug reform. When the Judiciary Committee met, Dirksen sat with folded hands, and left the industry's defense to Senators John McClellan, D-Ark., and Roman Hruska, R-Neb. They did not have to face the voters that fall.

Still the drug industry was not ready to give up. The lobbyists prepared an amendment that would have sapped the Government's power to regulate drug advertising, then lay in wait on the House side. The House Commerce Committee quietly accepted the amendment on the recommendation of the late Representative J. Arthur Younger, R-Calif. Younger had not written the amendment; it had been handed to him by a onetime Republican Representative from New Jersey, Harry Towe, who had stayed in Washington to lobby for the drug industry after leaving Capitol Hill. An industry bulletin called the "Pink Sheet" rejoiced over the committee's acceptance of the amendment on September 21 and thumped Towe on the back editorially: "The biggest job of all was done by former Representative Harry Towe, a New Jersey GOP-er, who represented *Medical Economics,* a trade journal that derives most of its income from drug advertising and was credited with the House committee language taking Rx drug advertising off the Senate hook."

When the bill reached the House floor on September 26, Towe was there to help keep his troops in line. So was another ex-Representative, Joseph O'Hara, R-Minn., even though former members are specifically barred from the floor when they have an interest in the matter under consideration. Representative John Dingell, D-Mich., chuckled tolerantly when he saw them. Nudging a colleague next to him, he said, "Look at those two. They're covering this place like a carpet."

Ordinarily Towe and O'Hara could have stayed home and congratulated themselves, for the House rarely overrules its committees' decisions. But this was no ordinary bill, and Towe's hand-tailored amendment quickly came under attack from Kefauver's allies. When Younger was named as the amendment's sponsor, he disowned it on the floor. With supporters like that, Towe might have wondered, who needs opponents? The industry's language was rejected and Kefauver got his bill.

The drug manufacturers gracefully did not hold Ev Dirksen responsible for the defeat. Although he had not been able to save them, they realized he had done the best he could, and they showed their appreciation at campaign time. Dirksen listed contributions in 1962 of $92,004.11 in his report filed with the Secretary of the Senate. Well over 5 percent of that came from nine fat cats with vital interests in the drug industry, in lumps of $250 or more. Dirksen's campaign honor roll: $1,000 each from J. M. Olin and Spencer T. Olin, whose Olin Mathieson Chemical Corporation controls E. R. Squibb & Sons, and another $1,000 from D. Mead Johnson of Mead Johnson & Company; $500 each from Alfred E. Driscoll, former Republican governor of New Jersey and president of Warner-Lambert Pharmaceutical Company, and from John G. Searle, president and general manager of G. D. Searle & Company; $400 each from three other members of G. D. Searle & Company and a comparatively stingy $250 from B. Clifford Upjohn of the Upjohn Company. Total from nine contributors: $5,450. This much at least was recorded—not bad for an off-year election.

Like the drug lobby, the tobacco interests hired a onetime member of Congress to pull strings on Capitol Hill; they picked ex-Senator Earle C. Clements, D-Ky., who had been the Senate's Majority Whip when Lyndon Johnson was Majority Leader. The industry hoped that Clements, a tobacco-state stalwart and a Presidential crony, would help preserve the *status quo*. As added insurance, however, Philip Morris, Inc.—one of the industry's six biggest cigarette makers—retained the Washington law firm of Arnold, Fortas & Porter. Abe Fortas had not yet moved up to the Supreme Court.

Benevolent neutrality was all the industry wanted from the President, but from Congress it asked something with more teeth in it: a flat prohibition on FTC regulation of cigarette advertising. The tobacco companies were even willing to put a warning label on their cigarette packs—the smaller the better, of course—if that would buy them immunity from FTC supervision. What they were *not* prepared to accept, under any circumstances, was a warning in cigarette advertising. By meddling in that area, said Bowman Gray, the board chairman of the R. J. Reynolds Tobacco Company, Congress and the FTC would be infringing on "the right to advertise—an essential commercial right." Like freedom of the press, apparently.

Unexpectedly, Senator Vance Hartke, D-Ind., led in the counterattack on the FTC. It had nothing to do with his old friend Earle Clements, according to his staff, or with the campaign money Hartke had received from the Senate's Democratic Campaign Committee when Clements was its chairman. Hartke just didn't think the committee hearings, coming on top of the Surgeon General's damning report, had proved any connection between smoking and cancer. Whatever his reasons, it was Hartke who offered the hard-line amendment that would have barred forever regulation of cigarette advertising.

On the House side, the tobacco industry's campaign was running even more smoothly: the Commerce Committee proposed to preempt cigarette advertising from the FTC's jurisdiction permanently, over the loud objections of California's Democratic Representative John E. Moss. Normally on controversial bills the House leadership gives opponents an opportunity to make their cases for the record, and as one of his party's assistant whips Moss expected to be granted that courtesy. But the bill was called up for a vote with no advance notice one afternoon when Moss was out of the country, even though he had been assured by the leadership that the bill would not be put to a vote before he got back. He was still half an hour from touchdown at Washington's Dulles International Airport when the bill was passed on a voice vote.

The tobacco lobby joined forces with the doctors' lobby, at one point, in what must have been the weirdest lobbying alliance in legislative history. Anticipating the Surgeon General's report on smoking and health, the tobacco men sought to counteract it. They offered to finance a new AMA study of the smoking hazard, thus hoping to give the impression that the Government report wasn't conclusive and that smokers need not kick the habit until the AMA results came in at some indefinite date. In return, the tobacco lobbyists promised to use their influence in Congress to block the medicare bill. The doctors were more concerned about medicare, which they fancied to be a threat to their fees, than about the threat to the nation's lungs. So it happened that those who abet and those who cure illness lay down together in millennial bliss.

After canceling an earlier tobacco study on the ground that the Surgeon General's investigation would make it unnecessary, the AMA suddenly approved a brand-new study December 4, 1963, on the eve of the great struggle over medicare. To finance the study, the AMA accepted a $10-million grant for tobacco research from six cigarette companies on February 7, 1964. Three weeks later, the AMA astounded Government doctors (and not a few of their own members) by agreeing blandly with the tobacco industry that cigarettes should not be labeled as a health hazard. The AMA's letter to the Federal Trade Commission sounded almost as if it had been written by tobacco men instead of medical men.

"More than 90 million persons in the United States use tobacco in some form," argued the AMA, "and, of these, 72 million use cigarettes. . . . The economic lives of tobacco growers, processors, and merchants are entwined in the industry; and local, state, and federal governments are the recipients of and dependent upon many millions of dollars of tax revenue." Thus by official declaration of the AMA, the doctors put the economic welfare of the tobacco industry ahead of the health of the American people. On March 19, 1964, Representative Frank Thompson, Jr., D-N.J., charged that the AMA's curious attitude toward cigarettes was part of a deal to get tobacco-state Congressmen to vote against medicare. Though the AMA issued a formal denial, the doctors' lobby and the cigarette lobby continued to work in tandem on Capitol Hill.

In the long run, however, the anti-public health lobbies were fighting a losing battle, and no one should have known it better than the American Medical Association. To get around the law against political activity by tax-exempt organizations, the AMA took a leaf from organized labor's book and organized the American Medical Political Action Committee along the lines of the AFL-CIO-backed Committee on Political Education—albeit with a different end in view. AMPAC's nonpolitical veneer cracked badly at the start when the AMA picked five Republican doctors to run it, then hastily added five conservative Democrats. In 1962 AMPAC squeezed an estimated $3 million out of the nation's affluent healers to support candidates who could be counted on to vote against medicare where it counted. In the House, that meant the Ways and Means Committee, and a dozen members who had either demonstrated their animosity toward medicare or stayed on the fence were handsomely rewarded. All together AMPAC's money went to about 80 House and 4 Senate candidates, and similar state committees gave local transfusions. Some of the AMPAC contributions went to lost causes because the doctors couldn't resist helping the opponents of Connecticut Democrat Abraham Ribicoff, who had promoted medicare as Secretary of Health, Education and Welfare, and California's Democratic Representative Cecil King, whose name was on the medicare bill that the doctors were all so hypertense about.

After the election, about all the doctors had to show for their $3 million was one defeated Ohio Democrat, Representative Walter Moeller, who hadn't actually said he was for medicare anyway. Not one incumbent who had made medicare a major plank in his campaign platform was defeated. As campaign investors, the doctors weren't nearly so canny as their patients. The National Council of Senior Citizens, which former Representative Aime J. Forand, D-R.I., helped organize in 1961 to lobby *for* medicare, had only $80,000 to spend in 1962, but it got what it paid for.

The special-interest and the pressure groups do not always win.

10. The Bay Window Brigade

Washington's most potent pressure group is probably the double-M, military-munitions lobby, engaged in the great corporate scramble for defense dollars. On Capitol Hill military appropriations are held sacred. Congressmen who challenge every detail of a $50,000 anti-poverty project will approve a $50 million Pentagon proposal with no questions asked.

Yet staggering amounts have been lavished on armaments that should have been scrapped or never should have been built in the first place. From cavalry generals to carrier admirals, the brass hats have clamored for pet weapons that have turned out to be impractical or obsolete. On occasion, the Defense Department has rushed ahead with new weapons before they have been proven. Its storerooms hold billions of dollars' worth of spare parts for canceled and antiquated weapons.

Science, moreover, has put weapons out of service faster than the advocates have been able to adjust their military thinking. Thus the generals and admirals have sometimes become obsolete along with the weapons they have commanded.

Understandably, the advocates of dubious weapons usually fight for them in all sincerity, genuinely believing them to be in the best interests of the country. And some officers argue that it is sometimes necessary to gamble in order not to get left behind in the technological race. But new weapons have been developed—missiles have been sprouting and electronic gadgets popping up like mushrooms—faster than they can be assimilated.

Each weapons system is supported by a formidable lobby, composed of the brass hats who believe in it, the contractors who manufacture the component parts, the workers who put them together, and the Congressmen whose districts enjoy the economic benefits. A canceled defense contract will bring lobbyists and constituents alike swarming like agitated hornets over Capitol Hill. They will spread dark warnings about how Federal economies in their threatened factories will undermine the nation's defense. In consequence, Congressmen who inveigh volubly against the waste of paper clips sometimes defend the most extravagant and unnecessary weapons. When North American Aviation lost a missile contract, the outcry from California Representatives was so shrill that Senator Thomas Kuchel, R-Calif., sent the Air Force an apology.

Although everyone on Capitol Hill is, of course, for God, country and economy, the average legislator favors economies in someone else's district. Thus the test has become not whether the weapon is worth the cost but whether its production will benefit the Congressman's constituency or, perhaps, whether the contract is awarded to a campaign contributor.

In the backstage wire-pulling, the wires often crisscross. Military men with vested interests in a weapon will slip up to Capitol Hill behind the backs of their superiors and whisper their case into sympathetic Congressional ears. Rival services will pour out propaganda against one another's weapons and court key Congressmen with every blandishment in the books. The Congressmen, in turn, will pound upon Pentagon doors to demand favorable action on pet defense contracts.

Behind both the military and Congressional advocates, gently nudging them on, are the pressure people from the defense industries—affable lobbyists who know the right people in Washington. For the fine art of gaining contracts depends as much on political influence as professional competence. The Navy's caustic Vice Admiral Hyman Rickover is one of the few who not only have resisted the pressure but have spoken out about it. "It is almost subversive," he once snorted, "not to want to spend Government money. The real pressure we get is to undertake more projects to spend more money." The pressure, he said, "is generally in the nature of urging me to undertake new projects which we consider not worthwhile." All too many multimillion-dollar contracts are awarded because of a bouillabaisse of political pressure, geographical appeal, corporate greed, old Army ties and cocktail parties. This fact of federal life was emphasized to the FBI—though not the taxpaying public—when it put an electronic bug in the Sheraton Carlton apartment of Fred Black, lobbyist for North American Aviation and other defense contractors. A phone call placed at 5:47 P.M. on February 13, 1963, by Bobby Baker from the Black apartment to Dean McGee, Senator Kerr's petroleum partner, told the story of how defense contractor influence works.

"Carl Albert feels he has to have something in his district to survive politically," said Baker, who went on to describe the difficulty of getting along with James Webb, director of the National Aeronautics and Space Administration, since the death of Baker's mentor, Senator Kerr of Oklahoma. "Since the old man died, this fellow Webb has gotten weaker and weaker where the state of Oklahoma is concerned. He's just not doing anything for us."

In the end, not only North American Aviation but General Dynamics opened plants in Representative Albert's Oklahoma District.

In the executive suites of almost all the top defense contractors are three or four retired admirals and generals who are on a first-name basis with the Pentagon's big brass. "In business circles," *Business Week* has reported, "the word has gone out: get yourself a General. What branch of the government spends the most money? The military. Who, even more than a five-percenter, is an expert on red tape? A General or an Admiral. So make him chairman of the board." The last time someone bothered to count them, back in 1959, there were 768 former colonels, Navy captains, generals and admirals scattered over the payrolls of 97 of the top 100 defense contractors.

Ex-Senator Paul Douglas, D-Ill., has explained how they operate: "When companies with defense contracts hire officers of high rank, some of whom negotiate with their fellow officers, or who may sit in the back room while such negotiations are going on, or who have information from their former comrades which is useful to their companies, the potential and actual abuses of the negotiated contract system are magnified." Douglas also charged that "a number of defense contractors" prepare two sets of costs—"a high cost which they submit officially and a real set of costs which they know internally." In most instances, he said, "the deception is intentional."

It has been recorded that General U. S. Grant, when he was quartermaster general in St. Louis before the Civil War, sent a message to the White House requesting a transfer "as they are getting close to my price." Today the way to a defense contract is still greased occasionally by a mixture of booze, blondes and bribes. Commenting on all the partying at military-industry conventions, *Missiles and Rockets,* the trade magazine, suggested: "Their explanations to their wives probably would make far more interesting reading than many of the technical papers presented at the meetings. . . . Industry prestige at (one meeting) was enhanced by at least one fist fight and the drunken antics of several Air Force generals, corporate presidents and vice presidents."

When George Bunker took over the management of the Martin Company, he made it a policy to provide fun in the sun for the big brass in the Bahamas. One year he picked up an $18,000 tab at the Cotton Club on Eleuthera Island. Representative F. Edward Hébert, D-La., after an investigation, suggested that Bunker's lavishness had paid off. "I can only say," said Hébert, "that when Dr. Bunker became president of the Martin Company, it was on the verge of bankruptcy. Today the Martin Company not only is high on the defense contract list, but it does not do a dime's worth of work for private business. Every nickel comes from the Government in subsidies."

Sperry Rand, for a time, leased Gardiner's Island off the Long Island coast as a private refuge—abundant in deer, wild turkey, pheasant and fish—for entertaining VIPs from the Pentagon and the Hill. One day alone, the distinguished guests bagged 4,000 pheasant, a haul reminiscent of the days when Captain Kidd was said to have buried his pirate treasures on the island.

The power of the military-munitions lobby was demonstrated in late 1967 when President Johnson ordered construction of a $5-billion anti-ballistic missile system that he really did not want. The missiles will be deployed not against the Soviet Union, the only nation that could launch an effective missile broadside, but against Red China. Not until the mid-1970s are the Chinese expected to mount a few operational intercontinental missiles. These could certainly damage, but not destroy, the United States. Indeed, they would bring a far more devastating barrage of missiles raining down upon China—terrible retaliation that should deter reasonable men from attacking. The $5 billion will be spent, however, because a few generals contend the Chinese rulers may not be reasonable.

The old Chinese revolutionaries who guide China's destiny have ranted that the United States is a "paper tiger," but they have always taken care not to look too closely down the tiger's throat. For all their mouthings, they have shown a wary respect for American firepower. The second generation of Chinese leaders is even more pragmatic than the revolutionaries, who are already fading into history. In short, the likelihood of a suicidal missile attack out of China is pretty remote.

The people who really promoted the $5-billion anti-ballistic missile system, of course, were the defense contractors whose fear of Red China appeared to be in direct proportion to the size of the subcontracts they expected to receive. With a delicate touch they applied just the right political goad to the pressure points in Congress and at the Pentagon. Providing the push were such corporations as McDonnell Douglas Corporation, which manufactures the interceptor rocket that will be used in the ABM system; Martin-Marietta Corporation, which manufactures the Sprint rocket, another component; General Electric Company, which produces the high-frequency radar that tracks incoming warheads far out in space; Sperry Rand Corporation, which developed the ABM computer system, and Raytheon Company, which manufactures the radar that guides missiles to their targets. Western Electric and Bell Telephone Laboratories, the prime contractors, issued specific orders to their lobbyists to make no approaches on Capitol Hill. This did not prevent them, however, from replying to Congressional inquiries.

The defense industries have such a stranglehold on the Capitol dome that Congressmen even began investigating their own watchdog, the General Accounting Office, when it became too critical of military spending. The GAO looked too closely into the profits of the big missile manufacturers—a step that caused the Aerospace Industries Association, representing 60 of the leading missile-space contractors, to set up a yowl. Its chief Washington lobbyist, Lloyd Kuhn, protested to Representative Chet Holifield, D-Calif., whose subcommittee is supposed to investigate Pentagon purchase practices. The audit work is done by the GAO, which submits its reports to the Holifield committee. But Holifield began investigating the GAO instead of the contractors who had been caught padding their profits.

The munitions makers bear down hardest, of course, upon the Congressmen with armaments plants in their districts. Boeing, for instance, through its home base in Seattle, is able to line up Washington State's Congressional delegation behind almost every contract it seeks. Applying this principle on a national scale, Boeing tried to head off the cancellation of its Bomarc missiles by publishing a full-page ad in Washington newspapers listing all 3,500 of its subcontractors. It wasn't necessary to spell out the message; few Congressmen missed the point that the Bomarc was bringing benefits to subcontractors in their constituencies.

Defense contractors use not only retired officers but retired Congressmen to help make the right contacts in Washington. "There is always a fertile field," acknowledged Representative Hébert, "for any ex-member of Congress who has ability to latch on to some of the defense industries." But the most resourceful lobbying of all has been achieved by the armed services, which use the Congressmen themselves. They are simply commissioned in the reserves and taken on active-duty tours of such "military complexes" as Paris, London, Rome, Madrid, Tokyo, Hong Kong and Honolulu. No other equivalent civilian group has so many reserve generals and colonels soldiering on the job.

Consider the case of Representative Robert Sikes, D-Fla., who was a soldier long before he became a Congressman. His military career was unspectacular, however, until the Democratic voters of the Florida panhandle sent him to Washington in 1940. He had spent five years in the Army reserve without rising above the rank of second lieutenant. But during the 1944 Congressional recess, as the U.S. Army was racing toward the Rhine, Sikes was given a quickie commission as a major. He dashed over to Europe for an inspection tour, then hurried back three months later for the opening of Congress. He remained in the Army on inactive duty until the war was over, finally resigning his commission in December 1945.

A month later, Sikes was reassigned to the House Armed Services Committee, where the Army likes to have friends. Suddenly he turned up in the Army reserve again, this time as a lieutenant colonel. He spent three years fighting the Army's legislative battles before he snagged an even choicer committee assignment: Appropriations. In April 1950, after he had voted dutifully for money bills the Army wanted, he was promoted to bird colonel.

The Florida Democrat waited out the Eisenhower years without promotion, but on the eve of the 1960 election he was jumped from colonel to brigadier general. Two years later, in December 1962, he was promoted to the highest rank a Congressman normally reaches: major general. His two stars put him on the same level with Senator Strom Thurmond, R-S.C., who commanded the "bay window brigade," as the Army's 90-man Capitol Hill reserve unit is irreverently known, and with then Senator Barry Goldwater, R-Ariz., who headed the now-defunct 9999th Air Force reserve squadron, which, in an emergency, would have been strained to protect Capitol Hill from the starlings. Representative Sikes, though he was as heroic a major general as ever fought for more appropriations for the Army, sadly did not get a unit to call his own.

The armed forces have handed many another Congressman an instant commission for leading their assaults upon Capitol Hill during the battle of the budget and other legislative engagements. For instance, Representative Clement Zablocki, D-Wis., an erstwhile choir director, had absolutely no military experience and had never wielded a weapon more menacing than a baton when the Air Force commissioned him as a major in 1956. Representative Harold Ryan, D-Mich., had never served a day in the armed forces before he was elected to the House in 1962. Yet the Air Force made him a colonel during his first term. This eminence turned out to be fortunate for him, since the voters declined to give him a second term.

Some Congressmen, of course, have had previous experience in uniform. Another one-termer, Representative Ed Foreman, R-Tex., declared in his official biography that he was in the Navy in 1956 and 1957. A careful look at his record disclosed that he, indeed, had been a Navy enlisted man from March 27 to October 19, 1956—when he wangled a hardship discharge after less than seven months in bell-bottoms. When the voters sent him to Congress in 1962, however, the Air Force was eager to put him in a different shade of blue. He was commissioned a captain before the voters cut his Congressional career short in 1964.

Representative G. Elliott Hagan, D-Ga., is another ex-enlisted man who made the grade—in this case, lieutenant colonel in the Air Force—the year after he arrived in Congress. Similarly, Senator Henry Jackson, D-Wash., became a major in the Army reserve the year he entered the Senate—a considerable jump from the enlisted rank he held during World War II. Now he is a lieutenant colonel.

Of all the weekend warriors in Congress, only one within memory elected to remain a mere enlisted man. Senator John Tower, R-Tex., a seaman first class, turned down a commission from the Navy because "I don't want to take a rank I'm not qualified for." The Senator was interested in bettering himself, however, after holding the same rating since the 1940s. "I'm studying the bosun's manual now," he said not long ago, "but it's slow going."

When Barry Goldwater gave up command of the 9999th Air Force squadron to seek the position of commander-in-chief of all the armed forces, the squadron was taken over by Senator Howard Cannon, D-Nev., a reserve brigadier general, and was then disbanded. Unlike the Army and Navy reserve units on the Hill, both founded in 1957, the 9999th admitted lobbyists to its ranks from its inception in 1961. This was a cozy arrangement for the lobbyists who were able to develop a special camaraderie by serving in the same VIP squadron with the men they were trying to influence.

Lining up for roll call with the Senators and Representatives were such registered lobbyists as Colonel Lyle Snader of the Association of American Railroads, Colonel Laurie Battle of the National Association of Manufacturers, Colonel Robert Poston of the National Association of Mutual Savings Banks, and Captain Jack Golodner of Actors Equity. There were other business representatives in the squadron, too, not on the official lobbyists' list: Lieutenant Colonel James Queen of Business Systems Control, Major Cyril Bendorf of Lockheed Aircraft, Captain James Konduros of IBM and Second Lieutenant George Lusk, a public-relations man for hire.

What really unites the civilians and reservists in Congress is an attack on their own privileges by the Defense Department. Even non-reservists like Louisiana's Representative Hébert denounced ex-Secretary of Defense Robert McNamara for showing "his contempt for Congress" when he ordered the military reserves merged into the National Guard. This would have abolished the VIP units on Capitol Hill and ended the semiannual junkets to such hardship posts as Paris and Hong Kong.

It was the reservists in these units, however, who exploded the loudest over McNamara's plan. Almost every reservist whose privileges were threatened joined in the outcry. Thurmond, the Army's senior retread on the Hill, deemed it "presumptuous on Mr. McNamara's part to indicate to the public that such reorganization as he describes could be accomplished without Congressional action." Senator Ralph Yarborough, D-Tex., a liberal who lost a one-fall wrestling match to the conservative Thurmond in a Capitol corridor, stood firmly alongside him on this issue—perhaps because he happened to be a colonel in Thurmond's Congressional commando unit. Yarborough, voicing his objections in typically highfalutin phrases, said the McNamara scheme "means a departure away from the long-accepted status of the citizen soldier." He did not mention the long-accepted status of the Congressional colonel.

The founding fathers certainly never foresaw a $70-billion defense budget, but they understood the dangers of trying to serve two masters. The Constitution specifies that "no person holding any office under the United States shall be a member of either House during his continuance in office." During World War II, when President Roosevelt decided he wanted his Congressmen in Washington instead of fighting the war, the Justice Department ruled that such legislators as Lyndon Johnson of Texas and Warren Magnuson of Washington could not serve in Congress and the armed forces at the same time. During the Civil War nobody had to tell Congress that. When a Kansas Senator named James Henry Lane accepted a reserve brigadier's commission in the Union Army, he was promptly ejected from Congress. Times, if not the Constitution, have changed. Instead of denying weekend warriors a Congressional seat, Americans now nominate them for President.

11. The Art of Communications

In recent years, Congress has become less and less eager to investigate the munitions lobby. This is because the individual Congressman can bring punishment on his head if he does investigate—and collect a lot of rewards if he doesn't. Defense contractors have the power to locate or close down defense plants in a Congressman's district, raise campaign funds to support or defeat him, and give him free time between elections on the radio and TV stations they own or control. The latter has become one of the most subtle and persuasive influences on Congress. The Radio Corporation of America, Westinghouse, General Electric, General Tire and Rubber, Avco and Kaiser all have bought heavily into radio and television properties—one aspect of defense-contractor influence that President Eisenhower did not mention when, in his last message, he warned the American people of the dangerous alliance between the industrial complex and a large peacetime standing army.

If our military expenditures, now 70 percent of the national budget, are ever to be curtailed, it will take an alert Congress willing to undertake salutary investigations of defense spending and the unquenchable military demand for money. But, unless interservice rivalry is involved, such as the Navy's opposition to the TFX airplane when the admirals conspired to stage an investigation, penetrating probes seldom take place. There has been no investigation of the manner in which Representative Albert Thomas, D-Texas, working through big construction contractors Brown and Root, managed to have duplicated in his home city of Houston the entire space center already built at Cape Kennedy so that when missiles or satellites are launched today, there are duplicating and sometimes confusing control systems in both Florida and Texas. And when Representative Chet Holifield of California, ranking Democratic member of the House Government Operations Committee, proposed a special commission to investigate defense spending, he met with the eloquent and effective opposition of Representative Mendel Rivers, D-S.C., who even offered members of the Rules Committee free airplane trips—courtesy of the Defense Department—if they would block Holifield's investigatory proposal. Rivers won the battle. "They were afraid of what might happen to the military bases in their districts," remarked one member of the Rules Committee.

In 1938, before defense contractors had acquired so much power, Representative Will D. McFarlane of Texas charged the Radio Corporation of America with bribing a Federal judge on behalf of RCA and was promptly defeated for re-election when RCA's general counsel, Frank Wozencraft, the former mayor of Dallas, substantially backed an opponent, Edward Gossett, later counsel for Texas Southwest Bell Telephone. But in 1940 Senator Charles Tobey of New Hampshire, a Republican, took up the defeated McFarlane's charge against RCA and uncovered the lobbying influence of two fellow Republican Senators. The case of RCA and its use of Congressmen, retired military officers and its radio-television network, the National Broadcasting Company, is an apt illustration of the power of the military-industrial complex that President Eisenhower warned against in his last message to the American people. RCA has long followed a consistent pattern, beginning with payments to two Republican Senators, George Moses of New Hampshire and Dan Hastings of Delaware, in the Hoover Administration; the use of a Democratic Senator, Pat McCarran, in the Truman Administration; and another Democrat, Senator Dodd, in the Kennedy-Johnson Administrations. RCA also used Clark Clifford, now Secretary of Defense; Margaret Truman, though she didn't realize she was being used; and Major General Harry Ingles after he retired from the Signal Corps. The man directing this blatant use of influence—RCA Chairman David Sarnoff—who is himself a retired brigadier general, has a record of manipulating Congressional influence dating back to the closing days of the Hoover Administration when the Justice Department, in one of the biggest antitrust cases in American history, tried to break up control of the radio patents Sarnoff had corralled for RCA, through licensing agreements with General Electric, Westinghouse, American Telephone, and United Fruit.

RCA had obtained postponement after postponement until after three years of foot-dragging, Special Justice Department

Counsel Warren Olney II would accept no further delays, The trial date was set for October 1932. Sarnoff confided to his counsel that he was sure the Hoover Administration would be defeated in November and his friend Franklin D. Roosevelt would be elected. So, in an ultimate effort to delay the antitrust case, he journeyed to New Hampshire on October 1 to buy the influence of one of the leading Senate Republicans, George Moses, and paid him $8,000. Cross-examining Sarnoff afterward, Senator Tobey got from him the unique explanation that he had paid Moses to do "a study for us of the Balkan situation, economical and political." Moses, incidentally, had never been in the Balkans.

He advised Sarnoff not on the Balkans, but to retain Senator Dan Hastings, Republican of Delaware, the state in which the antitrust case was to be tried. Hastings admitted on the witness stand that he was paid $7,500 by RCA and that he thereupon summoned Henry C. Mahaffy, clerk of the U.S. District Court in Delaware, to the Waldorf-Astoria in New York, where it took only ten minutes to convince Mahaffy of the need of postponing the antitrust case. Mahaffy went back to Wilmington and subsequently telegraphed the Justice Department: "JUDGE [John J.] NIELDS IS INDISPOSED. TRIAL OF UNITED STATES AGAINST RADIO POSTPONED. NEW DATE WILL BE FIXED AT EARLIEST OPPORTUNITY." Testimony disclosed that thereafter Mahaffy was definitely paid $2,500 by RCA attorneys (though the Senate committee heard conflicting evidence and there were some indications that he was paid as high as $25,000). When Senator Kefauver of Tennessee introduced a resolution calling for the impeachment of Judge Nields, the judge retired, as did clerk Mahaffy. The trial of RCA never took place. Hoover was defeated by Roosevelt, just as Sarnoff predicted, and three weeks later the Justice Department threw in the sponge with a weak consent decree.

In November 1954, the Justice Department again brought a civil suit and later a criminal action against RCA on a charge of patent monopoly. A total of more than 10,000 patents was involved. Four years later, in October 1958, after much maneuvering, procrastination and wire-pulling, General Sarnoff agreed to another consent decree. The evidence against RCA was so overwhelming that it pleaded *nolo contendere* and paid a total fine in the criminal case of $100,000.

Meanwhile, Sarnoff had become involved in a charge of

usurping one of the most important military patents for radar developed between the First and Second World Wars. The manner in which RCA expropriated the radar patent is a valuable illustration of how defense contractors write their own ticket. The Sarnoff story was disclosed in testimony before Senator Paul Douglas, D-Ill., and the Senate Committee on Labor and Public Welfare during the 82nd Congress.

In the early 1930s, England, Germany and the United States were experimenting with the first glimmerings of radar. In the United States, radar was developed at Fort Monmouth, New Jersey, under the direction of Lt. Colonel William Blair, working with a young physicist named William D. Hershberger, who early in the 1930s conceived the idea that by using a heavy filament tube, radio waves could be bounced against an object and its distance away from the sending point calculated in the process. Experimenting on a Signal Corps launch, Hershberger found that passing boats could be detected by such micro-rays, and his tube became known as the VT-67, basic to the advancement of radar.

In 1936 Hershberger decided to return to college to finish work on a degree and, before leaving, summarized his findings in a memo for the Signal Corps. After six months at the University of Pennsylvania, Hershberger submitted his resignation to the Signal Corps in the fall of 1936 and the following year joined the staff of the Radio Corporation of America. In December 1937, RCA had voluntarily proposed to the War Department that it submit three proposed patents to see if there was any objection to their registration. The War Department examined the applications and informed RCA that any public disclosure of the principles of radar would be against the public interest. The Secretary of War further wrote RCA in April 1938 requesting an assignment in trust to the Army for two applications for radar patents.

No reply to the Secretary's letter was received. Instead, the War Department discovered that earlier, on January 11, 1938, RCA had already filed with the U.S. Patent Office for patents on the basic radar tube, listing as joint inventors William D. Hershberger and I. Wolff, an RCA laboratory man who had done some previous work with Hershberger.

The Signal Corps was flabbergasted. In 1938 it was increasingly apparent that war in Europe was imminent. Yet RCA not only filed publicly for an all-important military patent in the United States but proceeded to apply for patents in Japan, a potential enemy, and Germany, where Hitler had started wholesale persecution of the Jews—a persecution similar to one that drove David Sarnoff's parents out of Russia.

The Signal Corps considered suing RCA in 1938 but finally decided such a step would only focus attention on the importance of the radar patent. Instead, it asked the Patent Office not to make the application public. But it was impossible to prevent blueprints from being published in Japan, Germany, Australia, New Zealand, and other foreign countries where RCA had filed.

Only after making the patent public did RCA bother to ask the Army whether the invention of radar was still secret. It was a preposterous inquiry. RCA's scientists, wearing special armbands, had been admitted with special clearance to hush-hush radar demonstrations inside a fenced-in enclosure; RCA must have known the highly classified nature of the new discovery. Replying to RCA's belated inquiry regarding publication of the patent, the Signal Corps wrote, on March 3, 1938:

"While employed at SCL [Signal Corps Laboratories], Mr. Hershberger prepared a memorandum on November 22, 1933, disclosing the principles of a method for locating a metal object by means of reflected radio waves. . . . It indicates that Mr. Hershberger was cognizant of such operation as early as 1933.

"Mr. Hershberger's notebook, page 31, dated June 27, 1936, shows a circuit for producing voltage pulses which was applied [a detailed description followed] . . . In any event this invention should be classified as secret.

"As indicated in the detailed descriptions above, it appears that patent applications RCV-D-5293, RCV-5591, and 5709 consist largely of work done by Mr. Hershberger while at these laboratories or work done by other personnel either at these laboratories or at the Naval Research Laboratory at Bellevue, to the results of which he had access. These three patents should be kept in a secret category until such time as the entire project 12-F [radar] is removed from this classification."

The letter was signed by Captain David E. Washburn, director of the Signal Corps Laboratories.

Nevertheless, RCA filed for patents in Germany, Japan and the major industrial countries of the world.

No disciplinary action was taken against Sarnoff, and he continued to be treated with deference on his frequent visits to the War Department.

In April 1946, after the war, General Harry Ingles, then chief of the Signal Corps, wrote a letter to the Justice Department to request an investigation of the RCA radar patent case with a view to prosecution. But mysterious things started happening. General Ingles resigned as chief of the Signal Corps on March 31, 1947, and took a job with RCA, the company he wanted to prosecute. After that, the Signal Corps seemed to lose all interest in prosecution. (By now Sarnoff had been promoted to the rank of brigadier general. And when he retired from his reserve status on April 24, 1956, he was given a full-dress retreat parade at Ft. Meyer with Secretary of the Army Wilbur Brucker in attendance.)

Though the Army wanted to forget the radar patent case after General Ingles was hired by RCA, its original complaint had reached the hands of an indignant commissioner of patents, Casper W. Ooms, who sent it to Assistant Attorney General J. Graham Morison, who had called a grand jury to investigate various RCA activities. Morison had stepped into the position once occupied by John F. Sonnett, who had leaped rather precipitously from the Justice Department to become a partner in the law firm defending RCA from various antitrust prosecutions.

Morison was subjected to all sorts of pressures, but persevered in the face of Sarnoff's continued maneuvers. Sarnoff had already hired Sonnett. He also retained Clark Clifford, former counsel to President Truman. Finally he gave a contract to Margaret Truman to sing for the National Broadcasting Company. There had been nationwide debate over Miss Truman's singing ability, and most of the critics were not charitable. Sarnoff knew that nothing could send his prestige higher where it counted most—the White House—than his network's recognition of Margaret's singing. The NBC contract so endeared him to the President of the United States that Truman invited Sarnoff to a family luncheon at the White House on December 4, 1950, despite the fact that British Prime Minister Clement Attlee had hastily flown the Atlantic the day before to persuade the President not to use the atom bomb in the Korean War. The Prime Minister was kept cooling his heels while Truman entertained the man who had given his daughter a singing contract.

But Assistant Attorney General Morison still refused to drop the action against RCA. Sarnoff applied new pressure. His next move illustrates what sometimes happens when a conscientious bureaucrat tries to do his duty—a Senator goes over his head. In the Hoover Administration, Sarnoff had paid two Republican Senators to go over the head of the Justice Department counsel pursuing RCA. Now, with a Democratic President in office, a Democratic Senator, Pat McCarran of Nevada, approached Attorney General Howard McGrath with the demand that the case against RCA be dropped. As chairman of the Senate Judiciary Committee, McCarran held a whip hand over the Justice Department. McGrath referred him to Morison, who says the conversation went this way:

"I'll be glad to study the matter, Senator." ·

"I'm not telling you to study the matter. I'm telling you what to do."

"No one is going to tell me what to do."

"I'll get your hide," was McCarran's parting threat.

He did. Shortly thereafter, Attorney General McGrath resigned, and James P. McGranery, a former Democratic Representative from Pennsylvania, was appointed in his place. Before his appointment could be confirmed, he had to pass the hurdle of the Judiciary Committee, over which McCarran reigned supreme. In return for confirmation McCarran demanded that McGranery drop the case against RCA.

When the new Attorney General McGranery questioned Morison about the RCA case, Morison stood his ground. McGranery said little. But a few days later Morison was fired.

RCA has never been prosecuted criminally or civilly for grabbing the Signal Corps' radar patent. Today it ranks as one of the nation's bigger defense contractors and twenty-second in receiving free research grants from Uncle Sam—a total of $52,964,000 in 1966. Its National Broadcasting Company division escaped scrutiny by Senator Dodd's Juvenile Delinquency Committee investigating violence in television programming. And who should turn up as the chief attorney defending Senator Dodd from Senate censure but John Sonnett, the one-time member of the Antitrust Division who jumped from the Justice Department to defend RCA from antitrust prosecution.

12. *Metal Muscle*

It would be unfair to suggest that members of Congress are chiefly to blame for military lobbying, which annually swells the national budget by unnecessary billions that inevitably influence the foreign policy of the nation toward war. Lobbying is a two-way street. If it were not for the tremendous economic stakes involved and for the provisions for enormous tax deductions in the alleged interest of the national defense, Congressmen would not be ensnared or tempted by the ruthlessness of defense contractors.

The events leading up to the $2-million tax refund finagled by Senator Vance Hartke, D-Indiana, for Harvey Aluminum (see page 333) is a case in point. Hartke is a Senator with a record of battling courageously for the public good—most of the time. He has bucked the oil and gas lobby on pipeline safety and the military lobby on the issue of appointing military men to civilian Government posts. Yet he did a $2-million favor for a company that was nurtured on the weapons of war and has parlayed gall and Government money to become the fourth largest aluminum manufacturer in America.

It began in World War II when Harvey Aluminum, then operating a small plant in the Los Angeles suburbs under the name of Harvey Machine Company, Inc., was caught making an offsize testing gauge for 20 mm. shells in order to slip "oversize projectiles past inspection," according to United States Navy inspectors. Following an FBI and a Navy investigation, the case was turned over to James E. Harrington, chief of the Justice Department's War Frauds Division, with a recommendation for criminal prosecution.

The Harvey family, however, was not prosecuted. It had contributed to too many politicians in southern California. Not only were the Harveys not prosecuted, but in September 1951 they had come within a hair of receiving a $46-million Government loan to build an aluminum plant at the Laughing Horse Dam in Montana when Secretary of the Interior Oscar Chapman learned of the Navy's earlier charges and canceled the contract.

Harvey's political angels at the time were the late Millard Tydings, former Senator from Maryland, who was paid for his aid; former Assistant Secretary of the Interior Gerald Davidson, who was also paid; and California's Representative Cecil King, who as a member of Congress could not be paid for his lobbying aid. All three were Democrats. In 1952, the Harveys retained the most powerful Republican on the political horizon—Thomas E. Dewey—and made it their business to contribute handsomely to the Eisenhower campaign. They also hired away Representative King's administrative assistant, an adroit and personable young man named Keith Linden, whom they put in charge of their Washington office and later promoted to the rank of a Harvey vice president. They also formed a liaison with Bobby Baker, powerful secretary of the Senate, and with Baker's ally and associate, Wayne Bromly, partly to influence legislators, partly to reelect friendly legislators. And finally, the Harvey family maneuvered to have Leo Harvey's daughter, Carmine Warshaw, appointed chairman of the Democratic National Committee for Southern California.

Thus buttressed politically, the Harveys wangled a deal whereby Army engineers spent $2 million to dredge a channel up the Columbia River from Bonneville to The Dalles, where the Harveys were constructing an aluminum plant. Oregon Representatives Edith Green of Portland and Al Ullman of Baker, both Democrats, helped promote this Harvey bonanza as an asset to Oregon.

With the Korean War over and the aluminum market glutted, the Eisenhower Administration signed a contract with Harvey in late 1955 to produce more than 200,000 tons of aluminum for the national defense stockpile. Credit was given to Tom Dewey for this feat, considered all the more remarkable since the Government was already stuck with a stockpile of 765,000 tons of aluminum. Despite that, the United States Government paid Harvey $90,092,625 over a period of eight years for purchases of aluminum.

In the early 1960s, Harvey began looking for new worlds to conquer and began negotiating with Governor Ralph Paiewonsky of the Virgin Islands to locate a bauxite reduction plant in St. Croix for the processing of bauxite imported from Guinea in West Africa. The move caused great consternation.

"We are against the establishment of big industry because this is not a heavy industrial area and should not become one," decreed the St. Croix Chamber of Commerce on December 15, 1961. "Our tourists come here to get away from industry and enjoy a tropical island. They come here to see the hills and beaches, not large industrial plants. We need every bit of land on these islands to be put to its best possible means in planning the future of government-owned land, not disposing of it in segments to powerful groups. We are for progress, not calamity."

Though sentiment in St. Croix and the rest of the islands was overwhelmingly against Harvey Aluminum, Governor Paiewonsky was not. His family controls many liquor stores and gift shops on the islands. With the help of John J. Kirwan, in charge of Virgin Islands affairs in the Interior Department, and his father, Representative Mike Kirwan of Ohio, he got the Harveys the permit to process bauxite in the Virgin Islands.

It was after the plant began operation that Senator Hartke produced his big tax bonanza for the Harveys. Keith Linden, the ex-aide to Representative King and then a Harvey vice president, had served as secretary to the Senate Campaign Committee, of which Hartke was chairman. Linden was a singularly successful money-raiser, and the Harveys were one of his chief sources of supply. They took a $15,000 full-page advertisement in the Democratic National Committee's 1965 yearbook, and three of the Harveys—Lawrence M., Herbert and Leo A.—had subscribed a thousand dollars each to the President's Club, a group of business executives friendly to the President. And so on October 23, 1966, as Congress fretted toward adjournment, Hartke tacked an amendment onto the "Christmas Tree" bill that had the effect of forgiving $2 million of taxes for one company and one company alone— Harvey Aluminum—for its operations in the Virgin Islands.

The public did not know, because the fine print of criminal indictments is seldom studied, that the January 5, 1966, Federal indictment of Bobby Baker (Nos. 39–66 and 40–66) charged in part that he had failed to declare and pay taxes on $10,000 received from his aide, Wayne Bromly. The checks had been made out to Bromly by Harvey Aluminum. Bromly performed no services for Harvey; he merely endorsed the checks and passed them on to Baker. There has been no explanation of what the funds were for. Baker was later convicted, partly on the above charge. But Harvey got away with its $2-million gift.

13. The Religious Lobby

Only one religious body complies with the lobbying act by registering with the Clerk of the House of Representatives—the Society of Friends. Maintaining a Washington office at 245 Second Street N.E., under the name of the Friends Committee for National Legislation, the Quaker delegation of Frances Neely, David Hartsough and Raymond Wilson patiently makes the rounds of Congressional leaders and pleads one general case—peace. They urge Congressmen to vote for smaller military expenditures and greater expenditures to fight poverty, to improve race relations and to feed hungry people. The Congressmen who listen—and most of them do—are polite and patient but usually continue voting heavy military expenditures. The Quakers are persistent, respected, but not very successful lobbyists.

Far more successful in the past has been the Methodist Board of Temperance located just across Capitol Plaza in the Methodist Building at 100 Maryland Avenue, from where the late Bishop James Cannon used to keep a watchful and critical eye on the lack of sobriety of Congressmen and their poorly disguised yearning to repeal the Volstead Act and the Eighteenth Amendment. It was Bishop Cannon and the Protestant clergy of his day who were largely responsible for persuading Congress to vote for prohibition in the first place. The waning strength of the Methodist lobby, together with certain changes in the Methodist Church and the growing power of the beer and whisky lobby, contributed to the end of prohibition.

All of that, however, was before there was a lobbying act, before petitioners to Congress were required to register. Today no church lobby aside from the Quakers registers, chiefly because they would thereby jeopardize their tax-exempt status. Such a consideration, though, does not dissuade them from petitioning Congress. The most successful among the religious lobbyists are the Catholic Church and various Jewish organizations. The latter, however, rarely lobby as a group. For instance, when Representative Martha Griffiths, D-Mich., was pushing a bill to regulate stockyards and secure more humane slaughter of animals, the orthodox rabbis came to Washington to lobby for their right to continue rabbinical slaughter of chickens, lambs and cattle. They approached Speaker John McCormack of Massachusetts and succeeded in getting an amendment inserted in the legislation permitting certain types of bloodletting when required by the rituals of the Jewish faith. And when Ogden Reid, former publisher of the New York *Herald Tribune,* was nominated by President Eisenhower to be Ambassador to Israel and faced opposition from Senator Fulbright, chairman of the Senate Foreign Relations Committee, the Israeli embassy exercised its discreet lobbying influence. It would have been unwise and illegal for the Israel Government to approach any Senator, but certain powerful Americans of the Jewish faith were free to approach members of the Fulbright Committee to pressure for Reid's eventual confirmation. Fulbright remarked that he had never realized the Israeli lobby was so powerful.

Far and away the most powerful religious lobby on Capitol Hill, however, is the one conducted by the Catholic Church. Its members have no hesitancy in approaching Congressional leaders on such vital issues as continued support for dictator Franco of Spain or the allocation of Federal funds for Catholic schools and colleges. Members of the clergy have called on Supreme Court Justice William Brennan, a Catholic, to tell him how he should cast his vote. He has politely shown them to the door. A priest once stood in the doorway of the House Democratic cloakroom urging entering Congressmen to vote for a bill to aid Spain. Representative Wright Patman of Texas had to ask "Fishbait" Miller, the doorkeeper, to remove the priest. And when 60 members of Congress sent a telegram of congratulations to the Loyalist Cortes in Madrid for its opposition to Generalissimo Franco in 1960, they were so vigorously condemned by Catholic leaders that all but 17 retracted. Msgr. Michael J. Ready of the National Catholic Welfare Conference described the telegram as "incredible," and veiled threats were made that those who stood by the telegram might suffer in the coming elections. Even Representative Usher Burdick of North Dakota, an independent Republican and father of a newly elected Senator from North Dakota, meekly announced that he had made "a serious mistake" by signing the anti-Franco telegram.

The boldness of the Catholic lobby stems, in part at least, from the fact that during a long succession of Protestant Presidents and predominantly Protestant Congresses, Catholics were in both a political and numerical minority and to combat this position had to organize militantly. Their resentment deepened after Al Smith's defeat in 1928 by Herbert Hoover, and they came out in full force to join Franklin D. Roosevelt in defeating Hoover in 1932. Roosevelt won in large part because he appealed to the big-city vote, largely Catholic in composition. The Irish, the Italians, the Poles, all second-generation voters, lined up solidly behind FDR.

With Roosevelt in power, it was only natural that Catholics should seek to make up for long years of political impotence on the Federal level, and some of them began to propose policy as if they, not Roosevelt, were running the United States. Evidence of the power of the Catholic bloc: domestically, Roosevelt permitted the Church to censor American magazines; and, in foreign affairs, he applied an embargo against arms to Spain deliberately calculated to help a Fascist Government, even at a time when he knew that the democracies faced an eventual showdown with the dictators of Europe.

Church censorship was applied through Postmaster General Frank Walker, a Catholic, who all but abrogated to Bishop John F. Noll of Fort Wayne, Indiana, the power to deny second-class mailing privileges to magazines that offended the National Organization for Decent Literature. How tight Catholic control was over magazines read by all religious faiths was illustrated by the following letter written by William Smith, head of the Washington office of NODL, to Bishop Noll in April of 1935:

YOUR EXCELLENCY:

During the past week, Mr. Selinka, Counsel for the Dell Publishing Company, brought to me a revised dummy of Modern Romances magazine. Since they made the changes which I suggested I have already written to Your Excellency that this magazine does not violate the code.

Mr. William H. Fawcett, accompanied by the new editorial director of their Confession magazines, Mr. William H. Lingel, called on me with the dummy of Romantic Story. I carefully read this dummy, made a few minor changes in it, but had to object to one of the stories. Mr. Lingel assured me that this story and the others I objected to would be changed. . . .

I talked to Mr. Hassel, Counsel in the Solicitor's office of the Post Office Department. He told that the following magazines had been cited for hearings to show cause why their second class mailing privileges should not be revoked. They are: Special Detective Cases, Romantic Story, Crime Confession. I shall of course attend these hearings.

The Post Office Department is apparently trying to avoid as much publicity as possible with regard to these hearings because no news releases were sent out naming the magazines or giving the dates and times of the hearings.

Most respectfully yours,
WILLIAM SMITH

Acolyte, the official organ of the National Organization for Decent Literature, hailed with rejoicing a long list of magazines barred from the mails by the Catholic Postmaster General: "The U.S. Post Office Department has recently revoked or denied the second-class mailing privilege to certain magazines. The Department is to be commended for its vigilance and efficiency in citing these magazines and in refusing to grant second-class mailing privileges to offensive publications." Then followed the list of magazines, all but two of which were cited by the NODL before Postmaster General Walker had announced the roster of proscribed publications, including: *College Humor, Real Screen Fun, Squads Riot, Flynn's Detective, Front Page Detective, Amazing Detective, Film Fun, Spotlight Detective, Argosy, Gripping Detective,* and *Exclusive Detective.*

14. Catholics Left and Right

Before any chronicle of the Church's role in U.S. relations with Spain over the past 30 years, it should be noted that there have been two Catholic lobby groups—one vigorously active in Washington, the other not. The lobbying group was headed by the late Francis Cardinal Spellman of New York, and his spokesmen in Congress included Senator Thomas J. Dodd of Connecticut, Senator John O. Pastore of Rhode Island, House Speaker John W. McCormack, Representative John J. Rooney of Brooklyn, and Representative James J. Delaney of Long Island City, New York. Opposed to using political influence with Congress is the liberal wing of the Church, of which Richard Cardinal Cushing of Boston is the leader and which follows the ecumenical movement of the late Pope John XXIII. Cardinal Spellman followed the doctrines of the late Pope Pius XII, and many of Spellman's representatives in Congress, including Speaker McCormack and Senator Dodd, have been frankly worried by the liberal policies of John and his successor, Pope Paul VI, who, they feel, have been too ecumenically minded and too tolerant of Communism.

Long before Pope John and Pope Paul made it clear they were not in sympathy with the Catholic hierarchy of Spain, the reactionary wing of the Catholic Church in the United States had been conducting one of the most efficient lobbies ever to operate on Capitol Hill. It was able to reverse completely American policy on Spain. During the Spanish Civil War, Thomas G. Corcoran, a member of the Roosevelt brain trust, worked effectively at the White House to keep an embargo on all U.S. arms to both sides—a move that had the effect of denying American arms to the Spanish Loyalist Government while in no way hindering the flow of arms to Franco from Mussolini and Hitler, both anxious to establish a Fascist dictatorship on their Iberian Peninsula.

After the Spanish war was over, President Roosevelt attempted in 1939 to lift the general embargo against arms to Europe. By that time Hitler was already in Poland, and Roosevelt was concerned not about Spain but about the protection of France and England. The Catholic lobby came close to defeating him. Copies of the *Sunday Visitor,* the Catholic weekly, containing a full-page editorial and an article by Gertrude Coogan, formerly associated with Father Coughlin, were sent to Congressmen. In Brooklyn all priests took a firm stand against lifting the arms embargo. Mail began to pour into Congress. Delegations from New York and Boston came to Washington. The Christian Front, supporters of Father Coughlin, and the Paul Revere Society in Massachusetts packed the halls of Congress. As they entered the House Office Building, one husky young delegate was heard to call out, "Smash the furniture, boys—we're going to take over this place." The Paul Revere Society was so unruly in its visit to Representative Thomas A. Flaherty, D-Mass., who earlier had voted to lift the embargo, that employees in adjoining offices summoned the police. A bus driver delegate, shaking his finger under Congressman Flaherty's nose, demanded, "We want a yes or a no answer. No pussyfooting. How are you going to vote on the embargo? We know how you stood last session, and the people of your district don't like it. Now how are you going to vote?"

"Listen here," remonstrated Flaherty, "I'm not going to be browbeaten by you or anyone else. I'm representing the people—"

"You can't get away with that," yelled the bus driver from Boston. "Tell us what you are going to do."

After the war, conditions changed somewhat. Harry Truman, a thirty-second-degree Mason, was in the White House. Generalissimo Franco was still in power in Spain, but aid from his fallen Fascist allies had been cut off, and his economic situation was perilous. The Western allies were indignant over the bases he had provided for Nazi submarines along the Spanish coast to prey on Allied shipping. Thirteen top Spanish generals, in a showdown with Franco, had told him pointedly they would no longer support him. Finally, two great Catholic prime ministers, Georges Bidault of France and Alcide de Gasperi of Italy, had taken strong positions against him. Politically, Francisco Franco was hanging by the skin of his teeth. He urgently needed a loan from the United States.

At this point he retained as his Washington lobbyist Charles Patrick Clark, once attached in a minor capacity to the staff of the Truman investigating committee in the Senate, who was able to convince many people, including the Spanish embassy, that he had influence with the Truman Administration. He did have influence—but on Capitol Hill, not with Harry Truman. Truman continued to oppose aid to Franco to the bitter end. So did his Secretary of State, Dean Acheson. Clark nevertheless managed to reverse the entire foreign policy of the United States by one of the most extraordinary lobbying efforts in American history.

He accomplished this first by working through Senator Pat McCarran, R-Nev., whose sister was a nun, and later through Representative Eugene Keogh of New York, a power in the House and a friend of Cardinal Spellman; Speaker McCormack; Senator Owen Brewster, R-Maine; and Senator Styles

Bridges, R-N.H., who was highly interested in collecting campaign contributions for the Republican Party.

It was Senator McCarran, powerful member of the Senate Appropriations Committee, who in the summer of 1949 slipped a special $50-million gift to Spain into the appropriation for Marshall Plan aid to Europe—a step that caused Paul Hoffman, administrator of the Marshall Plan, to write to Senator Arthur Vandenberg of Michigan:

> *Because no work has yet started on a recovery program for Spain, it would be most unwise to attempt to gear such a program immediately into the present European Recovery Program. It would also violate the program of European initiative. Furthermore, it would create the most difficult political problem to us if we were to attempt to force the OEEC [the Marshall Plan] to admit Spain. The admission of new members should, it seems to me, be initiated in the OEEC itself.*
>
> *Before granting or loaning Spain money we should first request that Spain herself develop a recovery program; just as we have insisted that the participating countries develop their recovery program. This program should then be studied, screened and laid before the Congress as a separate project exactly as was done in the case of Korea. Congress should then make its decision on a rational, informed basis. Any other course would constitute reversion to a practice which in past years has proved wasteful.*

The Catholic lobby, however, was powerful—so powerful that the Appropriations Committee handed dictator Franco a $50 million share in the Marshall Plan without even requiring him to tell how he was going to use the money, as was required of all the other participating nations. What the Catholic lobby failed to achieve, however, was a time limit as to when the $50 million should be used. President Truman simply would not, and did not, spend the money.

But in 1950 lobbyist Clark induced Senator McCarran to put another $50 million back in the appropriations bill, this time as a loan, not a gift. Truman was so indignant that he summoned Congressional leaders to the White House and tried to persuade them to eliminate the loan. He argued that the loan would be a slap at countries like France and Italy—

both Catholic—which had argued strongly to the State Department against any aid for dictator Franco. "A loan," President Truman said, "might seriously hurt the cause of democracy in these two Allied nations where Communist elements already are too strong for comfort. It would also plant fear among anti-Communist people in France and Italy that the United States was deserting them with a plan to make the Spanish Pyrenees the last line of defense against Communism in Europe."

Truman was very grim, very earnest. But his plea fell on deaf ears. The lobby was too strong. Senator McCarran made sure that aid to Spain remained in the appropriations bill. Lobbyist Clark, meanwhile, was working with Spanish Ambassador Count José Félix de Lequerica y Erquiza, who had served as wartime ambassador to the Vichy Government of France, and Counselor Pablo Merry del Val, nephew of the late Cardinal Rafael Merry del Val. To prove his strength with the Church, Clark helped obtain an honorary degree for Count Lequerica from Catholic University in Washington and boasted to his staff that he had secured it merely by giving a $100 contribution to St. Anne's Orphanage in Washington. Patrick Cardinal O'Boyle, chairman of the board of trustees of the university, was so flabbergasted when he learned of the degree that he did not believe it.

Franco now faced a devastating drought as well as the stirrings of democracy inside Spain. It was even reported that Catalan Communists had successfully infiltrated the Spanish Falange. With Franco desperate for American aid, Clark staged his strongest drive to make sure that aid to Spain was not only included in the Senate Appropriations Committee recommendation but remained in the bill during the House and Senate debates. In March and April of 1950 Clark began paying Congressman Keogh of Brooklyn checks averaging about $1,000 a month, allegedly for advice on a Federal tax case (though it is against the law for a Congressman to accept fees in a Federal tax case). When the matter was brought to the attention of the Justice Department, Keogh hurriedly returned the money to Clark.

Congressman Keogh had been elected to the House of Representatives in 1938 and for 11 years thereafter had taken no appreciable interest in Spain. But he visited Spain in 1949, received an exclusive audience with Franco and, according to the Associated Press, had $5,000 in cash stolen from his pocket when he placed his pants too near the window of a Spanish sleeping car. Then suddenly, simultaneously with his visit to Spain, Keogh began making pro-Franco statements on the House floor or inserting favorable editorials about Spain in the *Congressional Record*. He interrupted Congressional debates to defend Spain and offered an amendment to include Spain in the Marshall Plan.

During 1950, the year Spain finally managed to crash the Marshall Plan, Clark received a total of $108,250 from the Spanish embassy. On April 25, 1950, Clark received embassy check No. 4417 for $500 to cover "expenses." On the same day he made out check No. 3393 for $1,000 in cash and asked his secretary to cash it at the Mayflower Hotel in $100-bills. Clark told his secretary that he had a date to play gin rummy with Senator Owen Brewster that evening. He also remarked, "Hurry up and get the cash or Brewster will be hopping mad."

Two days later, April 27, Senator Brewster introduced an amendment to the Marshall Plan appropriation to include Spain. He delivered a speech on the Senate floor supporting the amendment and entered into the debate that followed. At its conclusion, Brewster was given an additional two minutes to speak in support of the Spanish amendment. The Senate, however, voted him down, 42 to 35. Four months later, after continued efforts by Brewster, Keogh, McCarran and an assist by another paid lobbyist, Max Truett, son-in-law of Vice President Barkley, the Senate tacked a rider on to an appropriations bill authorizing $62,500,000 for Spain through the Export-Import Bank.

Asked whether he had made any financial or political contributions to Senator Brewster immediately prior to the Brewster amendment for aid to Spain, Franco's lobbyist Clark replied, "Oh, there's nothing to that. I have known Brewster a long time. I don't work that way."

"Why did you get a thousand dollars in cash on April 25?" he was asked.

"I cash checks that way all the time and for even bigger amounts. I have had furniture to pay for and a lot of other things."

But, he was reminded, he saw Brewster later that same day.

"I saw Brewster a lot of times," Clark replied.

Clark was paid an extra $5,000 for breaking the ice on the first loan to Spain. He earned the bonus. For this was the first money for the Spanish dictatorship to be authorized by Congress, and it passed despite the opposition of the President, the Secretary of State, and our NATO allies. In 1951 Clark received $103,499.55 from the Spanish embassy. In return, he managed to wangle another $120 million out of Congress, again with the help of McCarran, Keogh and Brewster. The money was voted even though Franco was still balking about granting the United States air or naval bases on his territory. Finally, in early 1954, a lopsided base agreement was signed by which Spain was not committed to fight on the American side in case of war or even let the United States Air Force use the bases in case of war. Spain, furthermore, could throw the United States out after ten years and take over the bases herself at a figure equivalent to their value in scrap. In return, the United States was committed to rebuild Spain's broken-down railroads and highways, revamp and re-equip her military forces, pump in economic aid, lay a 570-mile pipeline across three-quarters of the country, and pour over $200 million into building air bases, port facilities, and communications systems. All this, thanks in large measure to the power of a paid foreign agent and the Catholic lobby in Washington.

A wing of the Catholic lobby also heavily influenced American foreign policy on Vietnam. It would, of course, be unfair to charge Catholics generally with responsibility for our involvement in Vietnam, because many Catholics have fiercely opposed American intervention there. Most of them did not know, however, that Cardinal Spellman planted the seeds of our position in Vietnam.

Spellman's powerful influence was first felt shortly after the signing in the summer of 1954 of the Geneva Agreements, dividing French Indochina into four separate countries with the proviso that the North Vietnamese could move into South Vietnam and South Vietnamese could move north. Cardinal Spellman flew to Saigon shortly after Christmas in 1954 to present a check for $100,000 from Catholic Relief to help care for these refugees. Returning to Washington, he enlisted the support of Vice President Nixon for a substantial amount of U.S. aid for South Vietnam as well as military advisers. There were a million Catholics in the north, Spellman argued, who would need help and protection while migrating south.

Nixon had been active earlier that year in urging the Eisenhower Administration to intervene militarily to help the French but had been overruled by Eisenhower. Now, however, Eisenhower went along with Nixon's and Spellman's subsequent appeal for aid to South Vietnam. He dispatched approximately 1,000 American military advisers.

Meanwhile Ngo Dinh Diem, who came to be described as a sort of "Catholic mandarin" while he was President of South Vietnam, arrived in the United States to study at Maryknoll, the Catholic seminary outside New York City, before he had taken power back home. Diem had come to know Cardinal Spellman, who in turn introduced him to Joseph P. Kennedy, the father of the man who was to become President of the United States. He went to Washington, where he induced young John F. Kennedy, then a Senator, to make a Senate speech in 1954 warning against any negotiated peace in Vietnam. Thus, John Kennedy first served as the Senate spokesman of the Catholic mandarin whom he was later to support with 30,000 American troops. The Kennedy family—the son in the Senate and the father in New York—had worked with Cardinal Spellman in 1954–1955 to set up a press and political campaign to support Diem's Catholic rule in Vietnam, a country 80-percent Buddhist. Harold Oram, crack public-relations counsel, was retained at $3,000 a month to build up the Vietnam lobby under the guidance of Cardinal Spellman, who helped Oram organize the "American Friends of Vietnam." Spellman served as a director, as did Msgr. Robert C. Hartnett, an editor of the Jesuit magazine *America*.

Ramparts magazine, edited largely by lay Catholics, described the operation of the Spellman lobby in its July 1965 issue:

> Diem's American advisers took care that his speeches were liberally salted with democratic clichés despite the fact that during the three years of office he had managed to crush rival religious sects and independent politicians and surround himself with a group of American advisers— Michigan State University professors, military advisers, AID officials, Catholic welfare aides.
>
> Everything that Diem did or attempted was described as a miracle. Articles appeared in magazines building the miracles of political stability and reform, refugee settlement and

economic development allegedly achieved by the Diem regime. But the miracle was actually only a miracle of public opinion.

Ramparts also told how the Vietnam lobby manufactured the refugee myth:

> The dramatic story of one million refugees fleeing to the South from the Communist North supported the theory of the North Vietnam leaders as "devils" and Diem's regime as the sanctuary of freedom. Naïve, well-meaning publicists like Dr. Tom Dooley projected this view with extraordinary success in the United States. What Americans were not told was that the refugees were almost all Catholic, many of whom had fought with the French against Communist Vietnam and who realized that they could get better treatment under the Catholic Diem. These refugees were settled and well cared for through extensive American aid, becoming a privileged minority in South Vietnam. But Diem had to use repressive police measures to keep in line the remainder of the population—13 million—which did not share the Catholics' hatred of communism, and in fact were sympathetic toward the Vietminh.

To the credit of the Church, it should be noted that Pope Paul has been a consistent critic of the war in Vietnam, as have many Catholic clergymen in the United States and around the world. Unfortunately, their criticism came only after the Spellman lobby had thoroughly and secretly accomplished its work. In September of 1961 President Kennedy, stung by failure at the Bay of Pigs and by his Vienna meeting with Khrushchev, increased the American commitment in South Vietnam from the small core of military advisers authorized by Eisenhower to an American army of some 30,000 men. The die was cast. The United States had embarked on a policy that was to produce incalculable agony in coming years.

15. *The Bishop from Boston*

Prior to the Kennedy Administration, the chief Congressional proponent of aid to education was Representative Graham

Barden, D-N.C., chairman of the House Education and Labor Committee and a former schoolteacher. Supporting him was the then chairman of the Senate Labor and Public Welfare Committee, Elbert Thomas, R-Utah. But when Thomas, in April of 1949, tried to get Catholic cooperation for an aid-to-education bill, he found the red flag raised by Senators Howard McGrath of Rhode Island and James Murray of Montana, both Catholics and both Democrats with long records of enlightened battling for social reform. They warned that if the Catholic hierarchy took a stand against the education bill, they would have to reverse themselves. Senator Brien McMahon of Connecticut, one of the most liberal Democrats of his day, and a Catholic, promptly joined in the roadblock tactics against Federal aid to public schools. As a result, aid to education got nowhere in 1949. And after 1954, when the Supreme Court decision desegregated schools in the South, it lost its chief backer in the House of Representatives—Graham Barden of North Carolina.

It was not until the election of the first Catholic President that serious consideration of Federal aid to public schools was revived. The Catholic hierarchy, foreseeing that a Catholic President would be under pressure to stand firmly against his own Church, had begun six months before Kennedy was nominated in 1960 to level criticism at him. Senator Kennedy had written an article for *Look* magazine in which he quite bluntly stated that if elected President, he would observe the Constitutional provision for the separation of church and state. The reaction was virulent. "We were somewhat taken aback by the unvarnished statement that 'whatever one's religion in his private life . . . nothing takes precedence over his oath,' " wrote *America*. "Mr. Kennedy really doesn't believe that. No religious man, be he Catholic, Protestant, or Jew, holds such an opinion. A man's conscience has a bearing on his public life as well as his private life." The Reverend John Sheering, a Paulist priest, wrote in the *Catholic World:* "In my opinion the most significant and most regrettable statement by Kennedy was his opposition to aid to parochial schools. . . . Kennedy's statement is unacceptable. . . . The whole text is bound to irritate Catholics. He seems to imply that the first amendment is 'infinitely wise' in barring the use of Federal funds for parochial schools." With the exception of *Commonweal*, the lay Catholic magazine, almost every Catholic publication in the United States jumped all over the young Senator who sought to be the first Catholic President of the United States.

President Kennedy was the target of another barrage of criticism from the Catholic press when, in March of 1961, he carried out his pre-election pledge and proposed Federal aid to education excluding aid to parochial schools. Father Charles M. Whelan, writing in *America*, charged that Kennedy's statement regarding the unconstitutionality of aid to Catholic schools was "erroneous, inopportune and unnecessary. We could and did expect a silence respectful of the problem," wrote Father Whelan. "As President of the United States . . . he should avoid unnecessary pronouncements on delicate Constitutional issues." The *Transcript* of Hartford, Connecticut, was also caustic: "It is no part of the President's business to rule them [parochial schools] out pre-emptorily. The President gave ample evidence here of unbecoming haste and judgment and a dismaying lack of fairness." The *Transcript* then asked all readers to write letters to their Congressmen. Again, only *Commonweal* went to the defense of the new Catholic President of the United States.

Running into the stone wall thrown up by the Catholic lobby, Kennedy began to waver by June of 1961. His most effective opponent was Cardinal Spellman, his father's old friend, who had been the recipient of at least a million dollars in gifts from the Kennedy Foundation. His most effective opponent in Congress was Speaker John McCormack, D-Mass., whom Kennedy privately labeled "the Bishop of Boston," and who was determined that Congress give financial aid to parochial schools if any was to be given to public schools. Bowing to the Catholic lobby, the Senate had worked out a compromise by which the school bill was divided into two parts, one for construction and teachers' salaries for public schools only, the other, a national defense education bill providing money to construct Catholic school buildings for the teaching of mathematics, science and foreign languages. The Senate had passed the first part of the bill, but at this point it encountered the opposition of the most powerful Catholic in Congress, Speaker McCormack. McCormack had a long record of voting for the common man. Under Roosevelt and Truman he had pushed legislation for public housing, slum clearance, old-age pensions, medical aid for the elderly and civil rights for

Negroes just as hard as he had battled to preserve the uneconomic Boston Navy Yard. He had gaveled down such bigots as Representative John Rankin of Mississippi for referring to Israel as a "sinkhole." And early in his career he had seen the danger of Nazi propaganda in the United States and exposed the manner in which the German Railways' tourism office in New York had served as a screen for Hitler's propaganda; as a result, Congress adopted the Foreign Agents Registration Act requiring all foreign propagandists to register with the Justice Department.

Yet John McCormack was first, last and foremost an Irishman. He once persuaded President Roosevelt to lend him the U.S. Army band for a St. Patrick's Day parade in Boston on the ground that it would celebrate FDR's wedding anniversary. And he once adjourned the House of Representatives to celebrate the fact that the Irish Minister in Washington was promoted to the rank of Ambassador. So when the first Catholic President proposed an education bill to aid public schools, John McCormack made certain that the second part of the bill giving some types of aid to Catholic schools would not be dropped. Using his friend Representative Thomas P. O'Neill, Jr., of Boston and Spellman's friend Jim Delaney of Long Island City, McCormack managed to slow up aid to education. His chief ally, however, proved to be a Protestant Virginian, Representative Howard W. Smith, chairman of the House Rules Committee. Smith, a nominal Democrat who voted Republican almost as frequently as he supported a Democratic President, was delighted to cooperate with the Speaker in sidetracking any type of aid to schools, whether public or parochial. Smith was no champion of the Catholic Church; he was just a devout believer in keeping the Federal Government out of education.

It was Cardinal Spellman who had sold Kennedy advisers on the idea of including aid to Catholic schools that taught mathematics, science and foreign languages on the ground that these subjects were an aid to national defense and the principle of the separation of church and state in the Constitution would not therefore be violated. At first Kennedy balked. But finally, faced with the unrelenting opposition of his own Church and the rapidly deteriorating standards of public schools, he bought it.

When word of the Spellman compromise leaked out, Protestant churchmen began to smolder. They accused the new President of going back on his pledge and argued that to build a Catholic school with Federal funds to teach science, mathematics and foreign languages was not only a violation of the Constitution but would create a police state where the Federal Government would have to inspect schools to make sure no other subjects besides these three were taught in Federally financed buildings. Senator Morse, chairman of the Senate Education Subcommittee, was called to the White House, where he warned that a long list of Protestant witnesses had demanded an opportunity to testify before his committee against the Spellman compromise. He then proposed the strategy of dividing the bill into two parts—one providing aid to public schools, the other a national education defense bill to include loans, not grants, to parochial schools for teaching the three key subjects. The White House bought the compromise, and the Senate, in the spirit of that compromise, passed the first section of the aid-to-education bill.

At this point Speaker McCormack, working in close touch with the archdiocese of New York, took over. The first section of the education bill, aiding public schools, got as far as the House Rules Committee—and stayed there. The Rules Committee was delicately balanced between Republicans and Southern Dixiecrats on one side and Northern liberals on the other. Ordinarily the Northern liberals had the balance of power. But McCormack's two Catholic allies on the Committee—Congressman Delaney and O'Neill—switched over to the Dixiecrat-Republican coalition. They had fought valiantly against the Dixiecrat-Republican coalition on such matters as housing, slum clearance, medical aid and minimum wages, and Delaney had introduced some excellent health bills and voted consistently for progressive measures aiding children, the aged, Negroes, and the poor. But when it came to aiding the education of children in public schools, he remained the faithful representative of Cardinal Spellman. "We are legislating discrimination," Delaney told one closed-door session of the Rules Committee during the hectic debates in June and July of 1961. "All children should be treated alike."

One Catholic on the committee vigorously opposed him. Representative Ray Madden, an Indiana Democrat, representing a heavily Catholic, industrial constituency, told Delaney at a closed-door session, "How silly can you get? About two weeks ago we adopted a motion deferring considering of all school legislation until the national defense education bill [containing parochial school loans] was reported by the Education and Labor Committee. I opposed the motion, because it was like holding a gun at the head of the Education and Labor Committee, blackmailing the committee, if you will. Nonetheless, it was clearly understood by everyone that we members of the Rules Committee would immediately begin hearings on the general aid-to-education bill, once the other bill, the defense education measure, also was cleared by the Education and Labor Committee.

"That was the agreement," continued Madden. "But now you have gone back on the agreement by this motion today. You are making a liar out of the Rules Committee. . . . We may as well admit it. We are breaking our word."

"Cardinal Spellman killed the bill as surely as if he had come here and voted against it," remarked Representative Carl Elliott, D-Ala.

Thus ended all attempts to pass a Federal aid-to-education bill until after the death of President Kennedy. He had made a valiant attempt, but then compromised beyond the point that Protestant churchmen and millions of Protestants had believed he would when they voted for him in 1960. Even so, he was unable to push an aid-to-education bill past Cardinal Spellman and the key bloc of Catholic Congressmen who wielded such substantial power in the House Rules Committee.

13

LOBBYISTS: FOREIGN

1. Minus Cloak and Dagger

At last count by the Attorney General's office, there were 473 registered and active—some exceedingly active—foreign agents in the United States. And their ranks continue to grow.

Registered foreign agents differ from unregistered foreign agents in at least two notable ways. First, they are not here, ostensibly anyway, to steal state secrets. Second, they are not foreign—or most of them are not. Instead, they are American citizens retained by foreign Governments and industrial interests for the purpose of prevailing upon the U.S. Government to act with kindness toward their clients. And sometimes that kindness is translated into economic advantage for the client nation or company, which, in all likelihood and for a substantial fee, will then continue to engage the services of its favorite registered foreign agent in Washington.

The typical foreign agent, then, is a variation on the legendary domestic lobbyist. Instead of promoting a special sector or interest or facet of the American political kaleidoscope, he pitches for a foreign power or enterprise whose call on the American Government is likely to be even less legitimate and open to even more suspicion than the hardly ennobling entreaties of the home-grown variety of pitchman. Which is another way of saying that what the foreign lobbyist seeks for his client may not coincide with the interests of the American people.

A major part of the lobbying effort by foreign agents is aimed, naturally enough, at Congress, with its tight hold on the Federal purse. On Congress, therefore, falls a large part of the obligation to screen out the legitimate pleas of foreign agents from the mass of blatantly self-serving requests. But an unsettling number of Congressmen have, over the years, been responsive to overtures—and campaign contributions—from foreign agents whose missions have better served their clients' interests than those of the people who elected the Congress.

No foreign agent has represented his clients in Washington over the past two decades with more single-minded zeal than a stubby, Chicago-born public-relations man named Julius Klein—Major General (Ret.) Julius Klein—now in his late sixties. If, in the ceaseless pursuit of his clients' interests, he has also fattened his own bank account, no one can accuse him of sinning—only of the most brazenly self-serving and insensitive effort of modern times to curry Congressional favor.

2. "Say Something Nice About Me"

In the Chicago office of Julius Klein Public Relations, Inc., hanging upon a paneled wall, is a framed quotation from the Bible. It is the second verse of the twenty-seventh chapter of Proverbs:

> *Let another man praise thee, and not thine own mouth; a stranger and not thine own lips.*

Julius Klein, manicured, pressed and pomaded, likely had this Biblical injunction in mind as he fidgeted behind the rostrum in the spring of 1963, snorting expensive cigar fumes. He had brought his old friend, Senator Tom Dodd, to Chicago to address an Italian-American dinner. When the Senator was halfway through his speech, Klein could hold back no longer. He tugged at the Senator's coattails and, in a hoarse, clearly audible whisper, pleaded, "Say something nice about me, Tom."

Klein has been trying to get people to say nice things about him all his life. For those who hesitate over what to say, he will eagerly provide the right words. Julius Klein Public Relations, Inc., has produced reams of laudatory speeches, letters and releases about Julius Klein. From this great outflow, now and then, a favorable notice has appeared in print. No matter where it may turn up, be it the *Congressional Record* or the Keokuk *Clarion,* he will pounce upon, reproduce it and circulate it to a wide mailing list.

If this immodest process should seem to violate his own Biblical rule against self-praise, it must be blamed upon his irrepressible nature. He is caught up in the vision of his own grandeur. He is quite incapable of carrying on a long conversation in his animated German-accented speech without bringing up the subject of Julius Klein. He views himself as an international mover and shaker. He ended postwar German-Israeli hostility, according to his version of history, by playing peacemaker between the two nations. Konrad Adenauer, then West German Chancellor, negotiated a restitution treaty with David Ben-Gurion, then Israeli Prime Minister. "I got Adenauer and Ben-Gurion together in New York," Klein has revealed. The close relationship between Adenauer and John Foster Dulles, the late Secretary of State, was an important factor in shaping United States postwar foreign policy. What history has failed to record is that Klein brought it all about. Correcting this oversight, he has confided, "It was I who brought these two great statesmen together."

Klein doesn't merely drop names—he dribbles them like a basketball. His private Who's Who is enough to stagger any potential client. The walls of his offices in Chicago, Washington, New York and Frankfurt are covered with pictures of the high and mighty. There are Presidents from Herbert Hoover to Lyndon Johnson, Vice Presidents from Richard Nixon to Hubert Humphrey, generals from Douglas MacArthur to Omar Bradley, admirals from Chester Nimitz to William Halsey—and, of course, a host of Senators and Representatives. The pictures of President Johnson and Cardinal Spellman are signed "Best wishes." Tom Dodd's reads "With good wishes and high admiration." Senator Wayne Morse signed his "Best wishes always." Dwight Eisenhower's picture is autographed not by Ike to Klein but, incredibly, by Klein to Ike. Just about the only mug shot of any importance missing from Klein's celebrities' gallery is that of Adlai Stevenson. "He was an appeaser," Klein has explained.

The impetuous Julius, who has more the look of a roly-poly teddy bear than an international intriguer, readily produces biographical data about himself that would have put Baron Munchausen to shame. The Julius Klein legend, as immortalized in his own press handouts, portrays him as a "distinguished war correspondent" at age thirteen, a "doughboy" in the American Expeditionary Force in World I at age seventeen, a "member" of the U.S. Military Commission in Berlin at eighteen. Klein later married a countess, so his story goes, and became a Hearst "editor" during the *Front Page* days of Chicago journalism. By the time he was thirty-three, he was a "$75,000-a-year" movie executive in Hollywood. During World War II, there was service with General MacArthur, medals for "heroism," and eventually the two stars of a major general.

Klein seems to have persuaded himself that this remarkable record is true. On his official "Officer's Qualification Card Copy," which he filed and signed on August 15, 1945, he claims to have been a "reporter, foreign and war correspondent, editor and radio commentator" with Hearst newspapers at a salary of $2,000 a month. His secondary civilian occupation, he stated, was "motion picture producer, scenario writer, investigator, editorial writer on foreign affairs," and World War I author "specializing in military intelligence." He also mentioned his childhood stint as a war correspondent, 1914–18, and his service on the U.S. Military Commission in Berlin, 1918–19. The legend takes on additional luster after V-J Day. He became a cold war "consultant" and an adviser to Congress, to foreign officials, and to the Republican party. He also acquired, according to Vice President Humphrey, whose name Klein likes to drop, "more friends in the Senate and House than any man I know." Julius Klein Public Relations, Inc., saw that Humphrey's statement was distributed throughout the United States and Europe.

Klein's heroic past, subjected to independent research, loses some of its luster. The son of a fur importer-exporter with offices in Chicago and Berlin, Julius was born in Chicago but reared in Berlin, with the result that his tongue has never been fully Americanized. He was not exactly a war correspondent during World War I; he wrote for his school newspaper. One of his articles has been preserved from the school paper; it was about Kaiser Wilhelm's declaration of war. Young Klein, in a style that was later to become his stock in trade, wrote that the Kaiser "spoke glorious words to his people in this dreadful hour of need." Klein has yet to furnish the public with samples of any of his dispatches.

By lying about his age, an act that was to plague him later, Klein got a job with the U.S. Army in Berlin about one month after the war ended in 1918. He was later employed by the U.S. Military Commission for eight months in some undefined clerical capacity. But the Defense Department has no record of his ever having been a "member" of the Commission or, for that matter, a World War I "doughboy." Hearst also has no record of Klein's employment with the defunct Chicago *Herald-Examiner,* but Walter Trohan, who now heads the Chicago *Tribune's* Washington bureau, remembers Klein well. "He was a promoter," Trohan has said.

One of his promotion stunts got him a punch in the face. The *Herald-Examiner* in the late 1920s sponsored a relief train for the victims of a Florida hurricane. It was a circulation-building promotion stunt, but Klein managed to sneak a picture of the train into the composing room and plant it in one edition of the paper's unamused rival, the *Tribune*. The train was draped with a banner that read: HER-ALD-EXAMINER MERCY TRAIN. The stunt almost cost the job of a *Tribune* picture editor, and the next time Trohan saw Klein, he knocked him down. Klein likes to tell this story on himself as evidence of his swashbuckling role in the rollicking journalism of Chicago in the twenties.

Claiming he was the model for "Dutch" in the Ben Hecht–Charles MacArthur play *Front Page*, Klein tells a couple of other colorful stories of the era. One has him volunteering in 1926 to pose for pictures strapped in the first electric chair to be installed in the Chicago Criminal Courts Building. The warden, unaware that the electric chair was not plugged in, fainted dead away when someone threw the switch. The other story, also probably apocryphal, has Klein heading for New York and a personal confrontation with William Randolph Hearst after having been fired from the *Herald-Examiner*. In the big town, Klein is supposed to have rented a dress suit and crashed a party that Hearst was attending. The publisher was said to be so impressed with the young man's nerve that he re-hired him on the spot and brought him back to Chicago in a private railroad car.

Trohan also recalled that during this period Klein had a sideline. He published a German-language newspaper that appeared only at election time and circulated around Republican campaign headquarters. The paper introduced him to the world of politics, which, in 1932, he decided to crash. He ran for Congress as a Republican and got buried in the Democratic landslide. (His last lunge at public office was in 1954, when he ran ninth in a field of 11 candidates for the Republican Illinois Senatorial nomination.)

His career as a $75,000-a-year "motion picture producer, scenario writer" and "story editor of Universal Studios and RKO" apparently left no impression on Hollywood. The *Motion Picture Encyclopedia*, produced by the copyright office at the Library of Congress, contains no picture credits for Klein. Indeed, his name is not even listed. Old-timers at the Motion Picture Association dimly recall that he once served as a publicity man for the late Louis B. Mayer, head of M-G-M.

Klein, though, definitely is a major general (retired)—there is no disputing that. He returned from World War II adorned with the Soldier's Medal, usually given, according to Pentagon sources, to enlisted men for acts of bravery in peacetime. Klein won it because he was supposed to have salvaged one or more trucks on the South Pacific island of New Caledonia when an ammunition dump accidentally caught fire (though one witness has sworn to us that Klein showed up at the scene, puffing heavily, after the fire had already been put out). Thus bemedaled, Klein advanced to general's rank in a manner worth recording. On February 15, 1949, Major General Joseph A. Teece, commanding general of the Illinois National Guard, prepared an efficiency report on Klein, who aspired to become a brigadier general. General Teece's report stated:

B. DESCRIPTION OF OFFICER RATED AND COMMENTS:

Comments of rating officer: An officer of high intelligence with marked ability in promotional and public information field. However, self-centered, egotistical, and disloyal—would go to any length to further his own interest. Not professionally qualified to his present assignment.

When a commanding officer refuses to endorse the promotion of one of his staff, his recommendation is customarily followed. Julius Klein, however, has never been easily held down. In a letter to Teece's chief of staff, General Kenneth Buchanan, Klein fumed: "All I can say—my friend—is that I will not take this lying down. It is his privilege to challenge the professional abilities of MacArthur, Richardson, Eichelberger, Plank, Lincoln, Patterson and Haffner, who were my superior officers, and under most of whom I commanded AAA." Klein's claim that he commanded antiaircraft artillery cannot be verified from his official Pentagon record. Most of his active duty, it appears, was spent with truck units. He had no combat arms assignment during World War II.

Klein, it turned out, had an ally in General Buchanan, who urged General Teece in a letter: "I would like to see this matter settled amiably by conference between you and General Klein. I do not expect you to take disrespect and certainly you are not expected to be apologetic to any officer. I believe, however, that these factors will not enter and that if you can see your way clear to settle the issue in some form of conference, the Illinois National Guard and all concerned will be much better off." Buchanan, who was later to become the high-salaried general manager of Julius Klein Public Relations, Inc., added to Teece: "This letter has been written as a duty of my position and it must not be interpreted as a plea for General Klein. He would resent it if it were."

The conference between General Teece and Colonel Klein was held the night of March 14, 1949, in the Illinois National Guard's headquarters at 205 West Monroe Street in Chicago. Klein came to the headquarters at 9:30 P.M. and asked to see General Teece, who later made special notes on the conversation which were forwarded not only to Governor Adlai Stevenson but also to Army headquarters in Washington to be included in Klein's permanent file. Colonel Klein came right to the point. "General," he said, according to Teece's report, "I'm greatly disturbed over my personal situation and would like a frank expression from you as to what you think of me as a general officer."

Teece replied, "I want to be perfectly frank with you. . . . While I have nothing against you personally and you have always been cordial and friendly to me, I don't believe that you are professionally qualified to be a general officer [the military term for all generals from one to four stars] in the National Guard of the United States."

Klein started dribbling names. "I might state that my good friend of long standing, Jake Arvey [then a power in Illinois Democratic politics] phoned me and asked me to come to his office today and upon doing so he gave me information to the effect that a special report has been made to Washington on my qualifications."

"It's true," Teece replied, "that I turned a special efficiency report in on you but I said nothing more in this report than I have passed on to you both verbally and in letter form in the past."

Klein bounced a few more names into the conversation. "General Teece," he said, "do you mean to say that recommendations by Generals Richardson, MacArthur, Marshall, and others on my ability are not proof enough to you that I am qualified for this job? . . . I am not only going to be a brigadier general of the Illinois National Guard, but also a major general and will eventually command all of the Guard of Illinois."

Such a brassy performance seemed to confirm General Teece's original appraisal. He said again, "I repeat that I do not think you are professionally qualified, that you have been most disloyal to me and as far as I know the only officer of the Illinois National Guard that has ever used political influence to further his own interest."

The charge had no visible effect on Klein, who blithely went on with his bragging: "Pete Green [former Illinois Governor Dwight H. Green] and I are the closest of personal friends. I was one of his sponsors and have been one of his advisers in all matters relating to the Illinois National Guard. I was the one instrumental in having General Haffner appointed as first commanding general and it was through my influence that you were made major general to command the new division. . . . Governor Green was most anxious to make me a major general in command of the Guard when it was reactivated and I begged him to allow me to go along as a colonel and to give the assignments to General Haffner and yourself."

General Teece, cordially agreeing that Klein had pulled wires with Governor Green, added a few particulars Klein hadn't mentioned. Teece charged that Klein had used his influence with the Governor to have General Buchanan assigned to Fort Sheridan; that Klein had persuaded Green to give him an extra administrative assistant; that Klein had wangled a Buick rather than a Ford staff car out of Green, and that, on more than one occasion, he had persuaded the Governor to rescind certain orders issued by Teece. "You failed to adhere to the chain of command in working out matters that would be of direct benefit to you," Teece complained. "I repeat that you are the only officer in the entire Illinois National Guard to my knowledge that has ever willfully violated this strict military procedure."

Unabashed, Klein stuck to his theme: "You fail to understand that Governor Green is my close friend. I was his adviser on matters relating to the Guard, and he looked to me for direction in his duties as commander in chief."

Teece refused to be impressed. "Regardless of what you say," he replied coldly, "I still feel that you are not qualified to become commanding general of our antiaircraft artillery brigade. This, of course, is up to the examining board in Washington, and I am merely outlining my own opinion. The report given you is correct, and I am ready to stand back of every statement I said."

Klein had the last word. "All right, General, that's your privilege, but I'll still qualify, and I'll eventually become the commanding general of the Illinois National Guard. Nothing will stop me."

Klein continued his political tactics until the exasperated Teece, on May 5, 1949, sent him this notice: "For the best interest of the service and all concerned, I recommend that you tender your resignation in the Illinois National Guard. Sending this communication through regular channels." General Teece was backed by a majority of the ranking officers in the Illinois National Guard. Yet on February 20, 1950, he received a telegram from Colonel Frank X. Meyers, executive officer of Klein's 109th AAA Brigade. The telegram read:
BRIGADIER GENERAL JULIUS KLEIN WILL BE SWORN IN TONIGHT AT 8:45 AS BRIGADIER GENERAL OF THE LINE NGUS. U.S. APPELLATE COURT [now Governor] OTTO KERNER WILL ADMINISTER THE OATH OF OFFICE IN THE CLUB ROOM OF THE ARMORY AT 5917 BROADWAY. YOU ARE CORDIALLY INVITED TO BE PRESENT.

How did Klein do it? Politics. He prevailed upon the late Senator Robert A. Taft, by adroitly pulling the right strings, to demand his promotion. It was this sort of political intervention that has brought the National Guard to the point of facing abolishment.

Militiaman Klein was a great admirer of General Douglas MacArthur's style. A few years before his own not entirely spontaneous elevation to the rank of general, Klein bade farewell to the officers and enlisted men under his command in the Quartermaster Corps with a flourish befitting a tin-medal MacArthur. Transferring his military skills to the antiaircraft artillery units of the Illinois Guard, the Colonel with the owlish face and the cherubic shape wrote a letter to his former charges so full of bombast and blarney that another colonel dourly recommended it be "transmitted to the Library of Congress to be preserved for posterity in the Hall of Archives, with the Declaration of Independence, Constitution and other important papers." Colonel Klein's Farewell to his Troops proclaimed, in part:

As your Commanding Officer, I thank you from the bottom of my heart for your loyal support. I shall at all times consider you my buddies. . . . Never forget that the Quartermaster Corps has played a most important and vital part in winning the recent war. You kept 'em rolling in spite of all odds.

Good luck and God Bless You All—and Keep 'Em Rolling.

It is not surprising, then, that when Harry Truman fired Douglas MacArthur a few years later, an agitated brigadier general named Julius Klein caught the first plane to San Francisco, squeezed his way up to his hero and, on his own authority, invited him to come to Chicago. Klein promised that the Illinois National Guard and the city itself would welcome him lavishly, with the ceremonies to include a 17-gun salute from the guard. But the big guns never boomed. Instead, there was a political backfire; Klein's Guard unit was abolished. Klein, striking a MacArthur-like pose, charged that the abolishment of his unit by Adlai Stevenson had robbed Chicago of its air defenses and would open it to enemy attack. He also charged that Stevenson had deactivated the unit—and Klein along with it—because of Klein's personal loyalty to MacArthur. Pressed for issues in 1951, the Republicans seized on the Klein charge. The GOP solemnly demanded that Klein be restored to his job as general and that the AAA battery be reinstated.

Major General Harry L. Bolen, who commanded the Guard's 44th Division, impatiently called Klein's charge "a damned lie." He said that Klein's AAA unit "couldn't shoot down a kid's box kite. . . . We need [that unit] like I need a damned buggy whip on my jeep. . . . That kind of man is dangerous, and we can't have him in the Illinois National Guard and I threw him out. Stevenson didn't, and I am a Republican."

In the same manner that he was bounced out, Klein bounced back in 1952 after William Stratton, a Republican, was elected governor. Julius not only got back his old job; Stratton also promoted the promoter to major general. He never quite fulfilled his boast, however, that he would one day command the Illinois National Guard.

After he returned from World War II, adorned with his

Soldier's Medal, Julius Klein went to work briefly for Secretary of War Robert Patterson as a publicity man. Then came the turning point in Klein's life. In 1947 he founded Julius Klein Public Relations, Inc., and was elected national commander of the Jewish War Veterans. Klein promptly took advantage of his new eminence to go calling in Washington. Among those he visited was General Dwight D. Eisenhower, who subsequently sent Klein a laudatory telegram concerning the Jewish War Veterans. Julius Klein Public Relations, Inc., reproduced the telegram and distributed it throughout the nation.

Thus was launched Julius Klein's *modus operandi.* Anyone who smiled twice at him was likely to get a follow-up letter. If the return letter was civil, Klein kept up the correspondence. He went on to develop more Congressional pen pals in this manner than probably any promoter who ever assaulted Capitol Hill. Presenting himself as a national Jewish leader and offering his eminent military rank as a further credential, he could get inside almost any door. His letters and calls would rarely be snubbed. He learned to derive more mileage out of a word of praise, a small honor or a friendly newspaper notice than anyone working the back corridors of the Capitol. Indeed his firm's chief product appears to have been letters to and from important men. Klein would avidly circulate the most routine replies, the autographed photographs, the inserts in the *Congressional Record,* all of which served as documentary evidence of his intimate ties with the world's great men. As the years went on, a number of big clients were clearly impressed.

Klein's position with the Jewish War Veterans increased his political as well as his financial fortune. In 1948 he was named "defense consultant" to the Republican National Committee and was also selected as an Illinois delegate to the GOP National Committee. As a delegate, he went down the line for Senator Robert A. Taft's nomination, an act that endeared him to conservatives. Kein, in fact, calls himself a "Taft Republican." When he tried to arrange the abortive Chicago salute for MacArthur in 1951, he further cemented his relationships with the GOP's conservative wing. In 1954 Styles Bridges, then chairman of the Senate Appropriations Committee, named Klein as an unpaid "consultant" and dispatched him on a 10-week tour of Europe. Bridges was a big money-raiser for, and Klein a big contributor to, GOP causes. Upon his return, Klein wrote a fulsome report on global affairs and strongly recommended that the United States should take another look at its policy on the wartime seizure of German property. The report had scarcely come off the Senate presses when Klein landed a $40,000-a-year contract with the Cologne Society for the Protection of Post World War II Investments.

Klein's involvement with the German war reparations effort did not sit well with the Jewish War Veterans—especially after they learned that one of the leaders of the Cologne society was Herman J. Abs. Though Klein claimed Abs was a poor victim of Hitler, the fact is that Abs was one of the top bankers in the Nazi era, a director of I. G. Farben, a director of the Deutsche Bank, and active in wresting property away from Jews under Hitler. A confidential cable sent to Washington by U.S. political adviser Robert Murphy in 1948 reported:

ABS COOPERATED HAND-IN-GLOVE DURING THE THIRD REICH WITH LEADING POLITICAL PERSONALITIES OF THE GOVERNMENT, INDUSTRY AND [Nazi] PARTY CIRCLES. HE BECAME PROMINENT IN 1937 AS CHIEF OF THE FOREIGN DEPARTMENT OF THE DEUTSCHE BANK AND WAS IN MANY CIRCLES CONSIDERED TO BE THE MOST BRILLIANT AND ENERGETIC OF THE DEUTSCHE BANK'S BOARD OF DIRECTORS. SUBJECT TOOK IMPORTANT ROLE IN IMPERIALISTIC EXPANSION OF DEUTSCHE BANK FOLLOWING NAZI POLITICAL AND MILITARY ABSORPTION.

These disclosures caused numerous uncomfortable situations that led Klein to resign from the Jewish War Veterans. But he helped to take the anti-Semitic curse off the Abs group. Klein was able to get a plug for the return of German property into the journal of the International Investment Law Conference and later got the same blurb inserted into the *Congressional Record*. Soon Klein began to pick up more German accounts—Bayer aspirin, Daimler-Benz, Mannesmann, and Flick. But the most important account he landed was the Society for German-American Cooperation, formed in Wiesbaden. The society paid Klein a fat fee of $150,000 a year; to this day the society's exact function remains cloudy, its membership unknown, and its financing secret.

Just what Julius Klein did for the society to earn his $150,000 is equally vague. In a nonstop sentence he later told the Senate Select Committee on Standards and Conduct—then investigating his curious hold on Senator Tom Dodd—that "the society was founded to promote the new image of the new Federal Republic in Germany that the Hitler terror naturally justifiably damaged all over the world and some bankers and others got together to form this society independently of the Government to promote the better trade and economic and cultural relations with the United States and other countries."

After World War II, it was decreed that never again should the great steel industry of the Ruhr and Rhineland be permitted to build another war machine. This was the one point on which there was no disagreement among the American, British, Russian and French allies. Scarcely had this been written into the peace settlement, however, when the powerful German industrialists—together with their friends the American bankers who had lent them money, and their friends the American industrialists who had exchanged patents with them—began to maneuver to undercut the peace terms. Klein was an ideal agent for this purpose. He was a Jew who could not be accused of pro-Nazism, and—to underline his anti-Nazism—he was also a former commander of the Jewish War Veterans, a fact he never let anyone forget.

As his business prospered, the dumpy, unmilitary figure of Julius Klein, puffing on his Corona Coronas, would bustle down the halls of Congress and grab the hand of any Congressman within reach. Congressmen will shake hands with almost anybody; there might be a vote at the other end of the arm. The air Congressmen inhale in their musty House and Senate chambers, moreover, seems to go through some mysterious chemical process that causes it often to come out hot and gaseous. Indeed nothing is in such abundance on Capitol Hill, and so readily dispensed, as hot air. Congressmen will praise almost anything or anybody at the slightest instigation, blowing out the superlatives in rosy cumulus clouds. Anyone who doesn't admit to beating his mother or belonging to the Communist party can get a little harmless flattery inserted in the *Congressional Record*—a fact not universally known in this country and certainly less well known overseas. Building a name on the strength of such bloated rhetoric, Klein added a number of important clients—including, for a time, Pan American Airways and Euratom—to his German accounts.

For all his apparent success, it would strain the imagination to picture Julius Klein as a sinister international intriguer, with tentacles reaching from his Chicago office on East Wacker Street into the Capitol in Washington and the Bundeshaus in Bonn. Rather, he simply relished the good life his success was bringing him.

He liked his chauffeur-driven limousine in Chicago with the privileged JK 109 license plate (the number of his old antiaircraft artillery brigade). He liked his $700-a-month suite at the Essex House overlooking Central Park in New York and the $625-a-month apartment overlooking Lake Michigan in Chicago. He liked to entertain guests in Washington at the Mayflower, the Sheraton Carlton and the Army-Navy Club. Most of all, Julius Klein liked to be liked, to be respected, admired—especially if the admiration came from the great. (Once Klein went to the Pentagon, moving from one office to another, chatting a bit. At each office he announced that if anyone phoned, he could be reached in the Office of the Secretary of Defense.) He used what one Republican politician who has known him for 30 years calls "unlimited guts and gall" to maintain that good life. Peering up at you through his bifocals, Julius Klein seems a most unconvincing troublemaker. But there are those in high office whom he has caused a good deal of trouble.

3. "Friendship Is a Two-Way Street"

Senator Thomas J. Dodd claims he doesn't remember when he first met Julius Klein. But Klein remembers. "It was in the office of Secretary of War Robert Patterson," he quickly told the Senate Select Committee on Standards and Conduct, convened in 1966 to look into Senator Dodd's affairs. "I would say I have known Senator Dodd for twenty years. He wasn't a U.S. Senator then and he wasn't a Congressman either."

But the curious correspondence between the two indicates that Klein saw more advantage in the friendship *after* Dodd entered Congress. On September 4, 1959, for example, Klein sent the Senator a "Dear Tom" letter, virtually demanding that he deliver a eulogy to West German Chancellor Konrad

Adenauer. A fulsome speech, written by Harry Blake of the Klein staff, was helpfully enclosed. "As soon as you have edited the copy," Klein instructed the Senator, "please deliver it and have Jack Fleischer [Dodd's press man] release it, not only to the American press, but also the German correspondents accredited to the National Press Corps, and send a copy over to the press attaché of the German Embassy, including Minister Krapf, so that this will get the widest circulation in Europe."

Down at the bottom of the letter is a scrawled comment in Dodd's handwriting: "Not too keen about this." But he later wrote Klein that he had used the material "in a congratulatory message I sent on Adenauer's tenth anniversary [in office as Chancellor]."

Meanwhile, Klein's lie to the Army in Berlin about his age had caught up with him. He had informed the Army that he was born on September 5, 1895. He later decided the true date was September 5, 1901. Going by its records, the Army retired him on his fifty-fourth birthday. He tried to correct the record but wound up instead with an official reprimand for lying about his age. Dismayed, Klein complained, "The reprimand by the Secretary of the Army was unwarranted and gives an erroneous picture of my service to my country." Julius also called on his friend, Tom Dodd, who helped remove the tarnish from Klein's two stars by interceding with the Pentagon.

Dodd did other chores for Klein, who, when dissatisfied, did not hesitate to rap the Senator's knuckles. In 1961, for instance, Dodd wrote President Kennedy that Klein was just the man to fill an opening on the American Battle Monuments Commission. "I believe you could not make a finer appointment," Dodd wrote, "because General Klein has indeed distinguished himself as an outstanding military man." Klein was pleased over "such a warm endorsement." But the post, alas, went to another. Julius was back at Dodd's door for the next honor that came around—a spot on the U.S. Advisory Commission on Information. "I am sure you will want to add your endorsement," Klein wrote Dodd on July 14, 1962. "But what is more important, couldn't you take this up personally with President Kennedy and with Lyndon Johnson so that we not lose this opportunity by default, as happened last time?"

Dodd dutifully fired off a letter to President Kennedy and

received a bare acknowledgment from Lawrence F. O'Brien, then a White House aide. Again, the post was given to another. Disappointed, Klein wrote bitterly to Dodd, "You know, Tom, friendship is a two-way street. I don't blame you for what happened, but what I am more disappointed in is that I didn't hear from you at all, either way. I am confident that had I been in your place and the roles had been reversed, I would have been in constant touch with you." This got Dodd's hackles up, and he fired back a testy reply: "I did what I said I would do, but I am sure you will understand that I cannot guarantee any performance." Although still sulking, Klein decided to give Dodd another chance. He wrote, "Tom, I never expected you to guarantee any performance. . . . Anyhow, this is water over the dam."

In any event, Klein had other performers on Capitol Hill willing to give voice to the puffery that came off his assembly line. Essentially his operation is not unlike that of the fabled emperor's tailors who snipped the air to their royal client's measure and persuaded him the ethereal garment was the finest fashion. Klein produced speeches dear to the ears of his clients and processed them through the Congressional mill. His foreign clients, unaware that the *Congressional Record* is crammed with trivia, happily supposed that the speeches were commanding the attention of Washington. Usually the glorious superlatives remained unspoken and were merely inserted into the *Record*.

Typical were the drafts of two speeches prepared by Klein's office in January 1961. The speeches were duly spread upon the *Record,* almost word for word, by Representative Emanuel Celler, D-N.Y., and Representative Roland Libonati, D-Ill. Celler topped off his speech by inserting into the *Record* an article by Chancellor Adenauer entitled "I Owe My Life to the Jews." Libonati hailed Adenauer's "powerful leadership" in stamping out "neo-Nazi propagandists." These were followed on January 26, 1961, by an interoffice memo from the Chicago to the Washington office of Julius Klein Public Relations, Inc. The memo read:

Subject: *Congressional Record* inserts and reprints.
Celler and Libonati.
We are sending you under separate cover a copy of a letter which we received today from Congressman Libonati.

Were the Celler-Libonati reprints ordered? Did you discuss this with General Klein? If so, please keep us posted. Here is what General Klein has in mind:

We will need about 2,000 reprints ordered. Two hundred copies will be sent to Chancellor Adenauer; 200 copies also will be sent to Globke. As soon as we know what is what, we will tell Adenauer and Globke to send reprints to their own American mailing list.

Brentano should get 100 copies of the reprint, and as soon as we know that this is being handled, we will write to tell him so.

Have the German Embassy in Washington ship these three packages via the diplomatic pouch. They will recall that Brentano authorized such direct shipments of important material.

"Globke" referred to Hans Globke, who held the title of State Secretary in the Adenauer Government until forced to resign because of his Nazi past. Heinrich von Brentano, later to serve as Foreign Minister, was then majority leader of the West German parliament. No doubt they were properly impressed with the speeches, which Klein thought sufficiently important to go in the German Embassy's diplomatic pouch to Bonn. But in Washington the speeches had about the same impact on U.S. foreign policy as might the comments of a taxi driver to a junior Foreign Service officer.

By 1963 Julius Klein had about perfected his techniques. By then he was a master at persuading Congressmen to say nice things about him. He would simply mail them the nice comments of others; they were encouraged to match these comments or risk being thought an ingrate by Klein, who was always willing to say nice things about them and, perhaps, even contribute to their campaigns. Senator Bourke Hickenlooper, R-Iowa, wrote a typical letter to Klein on December 31, 1963. "I have noted the enclosures," he said, "which include commendatory statements by Senators Morse, Symington, Dodd and Javits. These indeed are excellent statements attesting their personal regard for you." Under the circumstances, the Senator from Iowa was not likely to contradict his colleagues in the upper chamber of Congress.

But by 1963 Julius Klein had also gone as far as he could go without being called down for his methods. That year, the

Senate Foreign Relations Committee, under Senator Fulbright's chairmanship, reviewing the activities of non-diplomatic representatives of foreign powers in the United States, singled Klein out for special attention. He was cited as an example of a public relations practitioner who "by exaggeration or misuse of his relationships with members of Congress can for his own purposes create for foreign governments, officials or business interests a mistaken and sometimes unflattering picture of how our governmental institutions function."

The skill with which he had accumulated at least the lip-service support of the high and the mighty in the Capitol was demonstrated at this moment of travail. Intending to disprove the charges against him, Klein submitted evidence of his manipulation of friendships on Capitol Hill in the form of endorsements he had managed to extract during his tribulations with the Fulbright committee:

Said Senator Stuart Symington, D-Mo., "As you know, I have always had confidence in you and am sorry that anything this committee did hurt your business."

Said Senator Abraham Ribicoff, D-Conn., "During the many years I have known you, you have never made any request of me. I have always found you to be a man of honor and integrity. You are an extremely able citizen who has been a credit to his country, both in public and private life."

Said Senator Hugh Scott, R-Pa., "I can say for my own part at no time since I have been a member of Congress have you attempted to impose on or abuse our relationship. I hope you are successful in making your position clear."

Said Senator Albert Gore, D-Tenn., "I am sorry indeed for the embarrassment you suffered from unjustified publicity. As you say, the correction seems never to overtake the erroneous first impression or charge."

Said Senator John Sparkman, D-Ala., "Just let me remind you that I was not one who ever leveled any criticism at you."

Senator Kenneth Keating, R-N.Y., went so far as to link Fulbright with Communists for embarrassing Klein. Wrote Keating: "This is a wholly disgraceful effort on the part of the Communists to discredit you. Actually, it looks to me like good evidence of your effectiveness that they belabor the point so much."

Nevertheless, Klein emerged from the Fulbright hearings with bubble gum on his face. German newspapers played up the story, and some of the hot air went out of the heroic image Klein had created of himself. Suddenly he began to lose accounts. First to shy away was the Bayer account. Then the Mannesmann firm canceled, followed by the Flick and Daimler-Benz. Klein was hurt in both pocketbook and pride. In desperation, he turned to Tom Dodd.

But the Senator's political instincts had cautioned him to back off. A letter enclosing a resolution that Klein had wanted Dodd to introduce had been produced at the Senate hearings. When advance proofs were submitted to Dodd for his comment, he wrote Chairman Fulbright: "I have found the original of the letter dated May 14, 1962, in my files, but the letter bears a notation that the resolution alluded to was never received. General Klein's letter was never answered, and the resolution referred to was not introduced by me." Dodd concluded with this cold request: "I think it appropriate that my reply to you be made a part of the official record and I hereby request that this be done." When Klein got the printed report and read Dodd's letter, he was horrified. He sputtered that Dodd's reply was not based on fact, and he complained in a hurt tone that "you did not even add a few remarks about our personal friendship so that there should be no reflection on me." Once again Tom had failed to say something nice about Julius.

Klein remonstrated further. "I asked you to be present at the executive session. You promised me the night before that you would attend—but you were not there. I wired you to be present at the public hearings—you were not there either. What are you afraid of?" Klein demanded. "Do you consider friendship a one-way street? All I can say is I am ashamed of you. With this, Tom, I close the chapter for good."

Chastened, Dodd dictated a "Dear Julius" letter that blamed the response to Fulbright on an unnamed staff member. "The lamentable fact is," Dodd claimed (erroneously, according to people in his office), "that the letter was prepared for my signature, and on the day it was put on my desk for signature, I was harried and deeply concerned about another matter. As a consequence, I did not take time to read it carefully, and it went out without a full awareness on my part." Dodd enclosed a copy of a second letter that he had sent to Fulbright. This one had some nice things to say about Julius. "I have known General Klein for many years, and I consider him to be a man of sterling character and of great competence," ran Dodd's testimonial. "In addition, he is one of the most patriotic Americans I have ever met, and he is dedicated and devoted to the best interests of our country." He is also, the Senator added, "a man of unblemished honor and integrity."

But Tom Dodd once again was too late—purposely, some cynics in his office suspected. Senator Fulbright replied: "Unfortunately, your letter was received after the hearings had gone to press, and it was impossible to include your letter as a part of the permanent record." The mollified Klein, having reopened the chapter he had closed for good, searched the permanent record eagerly for Dodd's letter. Though he was distressed not to find it, he had a solution. "I suggest," he wrote to Dodd, "that you insert your letter in the *Congressional Record*, with appropriate remarks. This should give you an opportunity to say a few extra words." Once again Tom had the opportunity to say something nice about Julius.

On December 17, 1963, the public relations expert complained about his own public relations in a confidential letter to Dodd: "The aftermath of all these distortions in the press was the cancellation of the Mannesmann contract which called for $50,000 a year. There are, in addition, two options with my German clients that are up in December, neither of which has been renewed as yet." Then Klein put the poser to Dodd. "Now the next question is," he wrote, "what should be done?"

On December 23 Klein fired off another letter to Dodd with a postscript that implored him to "answer the committee smear against me." By January 20 Julius Klein was in Europe seeking to salvage his remaining accounts. Meanwhile his brother Max, a minor functionary in the Klein setup, kept the pressure on Tom Dodd with telephone calls and letters. A plan had been formulated whereby Dodd would go to Germany to join in the rescue operation. After one call, Max Klein wrote the Senator: "Since we have received cancellations of two more German accounts, [Julius] is especially anxious to discuss these matters with you before you talk with any of our German friends so that he can brief you and bring you up-to-date. . . . I would be deeply grateful if you would phone me co lect when your plans are firmed so that I can cable Julius. He is anxiously waiting word about your trip."

The telephone and telegraph pressure continued. On January 29 Julius wired Dodd from Düsseldorf: "UNDERSTAND YOU CANNOT BE IN GERMANY UNTIL AFTER FEBRUARY 12. . . . I WILL REARRANGE MY SCHEDULE TO MEET YOU UPON ARRIVAL AND HAVE THEREFORE DELAYED MY RETURN PASSAGE TO THE UNITED STATES UNTIL THE LATTER PART OF FEBRUARY. . . . I WOULD LIKE TO SEE YOU AND BRIEF YOU BEFORE YOU SEE OUR MUTUAL FRIEND. . . ." Another telegram from Klein informed Dodd that the vice president of the "international division" of Julius Klein Public Relations, Inc., would serve as Dodd's interpreter and assistant. "HOPE YOU HAVE CABLED YOUR FRIENDS IN BONN REGARDING APPOINTMENTS," Klein wired. "ALSO LET ME KNOW WHEN AND WHETHER YOU WILL LEAVE SO I CAN ALERT MY FRIENDS."

But the Senator from Connecticut was beginning to hedge. On February 14, 1964, he wrote to Klein:

> As you know, I have been trying and trying to get away to join you. . . . It now looks as if I will be unable to get away until some time in March. I wanted to let you know this right away, because I certainly do not want you to wait around for me, especially since my schedule is so uncertain. Anyway, I have been thinking about this, and I believe that I might be more successful with the people in Germany if I talk to them alone. I don't think it is at all necessary for you to accompany me and there is a chance it might be misunderstood. You know how anxious I am to help you, and it is for this reason that I want to present your case in the best possible light.

By return mail, Klein expressed his disappointment and reminded Dodd that "you were gracious enough to tell me in New York that you could come any time, even if it were to fly here for a weekend." Klein went on to recount the loss of contracts. Then he came to the crux of Dodd's proposed trip: "The most important contract of course is the Committee for German-American Cooperation of Wiesbaden. This is my No. 1 client and their contract is still in doubt. They fell into the trap opened up by the distortions in the German press as a result of the Fulbright hearings."

Next on the things-to-be-done list for Tom Dodd was whom to see. In a memorandum, Klein instructed the Senator to "ask for the following appointments when you are in Germany: (1) Chancellor Ludwig Erhard, (2) Dr. Konrad Adenauer, (3) Dr. Heinrich von Brentano—former Foreign Minister, (4) State Secretary Karl Carstens—a Yale graduate. You met him in Washington, (5) Minister Gerhard Schroeder.

"Your good friend Dr. von Brentano is now at home in Darmstadt—Stenberweg 25—recuperating from his operation. He looks forward to seeing you. You should see Dr. Globke first. He will brief you so that you will understand the 'new' German picture." Klein's final admonishment to Dodd was: "I suggest, Tom, that you see each person alone, without anybody from the Embassy or the foreign office."

But Julius Klein, a registered foreign agent, was not content to tell a United States Senator whom to see. He also sketched, without sparing the adjectives, what the Senator should say. Klein enclosed a set of briefing memoranda on nine of West Germany's most influential statesmen and industrialists and directed the Senator to keep the memos in front of him to "refresh your memory." These extraordinary memos told Dodd exactly what nice things to say about Klein. There was the memo, for instance, on Secretary of State Professor Dr. Karl Carstens. Klein had this to say about him:

> Carstens was the man who gave support to the German group—the Society to Promote German-American Cooperation, Wiesbaden—that engaged me to handle political public relations. He is the key to this problem as without the support from his office, the Wiesbaden group could not function. In talking to Carstens use the same arguments as set forth in the Erhard memorandum. You have to be very emphatic with him.

The argument Tom Dodd was supposed to use with Carstens was this modest summation of Klein's talents, as supplied by Klein:

> We in the Congress who are working day and night have to rely on the assistance and help of General Klein in giving us proper briefings, research material and other vital information of interest to the United States in regard to the German Federal Republic.

The interest of the United States is of course uppermost in the mind of General Klein when he talks to us. Fortunately, the Federal Republic and the United States are allied in their fight against Soviet aggression, and their respective positions on Berlin and free Germany are one. In the most trying days after World War II, while still an active U.S. general, it was General Klein who was the prime mover for a quick reconciliation of the new Germany in our fight against Communism.

What else should Tom Dodd say of Julius Klein to such German leaders as then Chancellor Ludwig Erhard, Foreign Minister Gerhard Schroeder, and Dr. Gerhard Hempel, the former lord mayor of Weimar and the Secretary General of the all-important Wiesbaden society? Klein suggested:

He has handled skillfully political public relations. He deserves not only our gratitude but yours—and your continued support. This is the reason I am here to explain. We hope that this pleasant relationship will continue. We were very disturbed to hear that certain of our friends in Germany have used the distortions in the press to hurt General Klein's standing and reputation, his influence and the constructive work that he has performed in the interest of both countries. Your predecessor, Chancellor Adenauer, with whom we all worked and former Foreign Minister von Brentano were pleased with the support and cooperation General Klein gave us at that time. We Democrats hope that this will continue under your regime.

The same extraordinary set of briefing memos instructed Dodd to see Dr. Hans Globke first. Klein's memo said:

When in Bonn, see him first to brief you. Dr. Globke is your devoted friend. He will ever be grateful to you for the courageous stand taken in your Senate speech of 1960. . . . To refresh your memory, attached is a marked copy of your speech.

Globke was the liaison man with whom I worked closely while working with Chancellor Adenauer and Dr. von Brentano. He knows the problem from A to Z. He is already working on my problem. He will brief you exactly and give you all the assistance that you need. Dr. Globke will support and guide you 100 percent in my behalf. You can show him everything and discuss everything with him. He might add some points to the prepared memos for your discussion.

Julius Klein likes to describe himself as a "practicing Jew" and a deeply religious man. There is a certain irony in the fact, therefore, that Dr. Hans Globke was the expert in Hitler's Interior Ministry who wrote the decree singling out Jews for discriminiation. Adolf Eichmann, on trial for his life in Israel for his role in the extermination of German Jewry, testified on June 21, 1961, that Globke was responsible for the Nazi measures depriving German Jews of citizenship. According to *The New York Times* of June 22, 1961, "Eichmann implied that Dr. Globke, while he was in the legal department of the Nazi wartime department of interior, had been responsible with an official named Hering for supplemental decrees of the Nuremberg racial laws. A final decree in 1943 deprived Jews of access to the courts and left them wholly at the mercy of the police." *Cross Currents,* a book by Arnold Forster and Benjamin Epstein, charges that "Hans Globke, credited with drafting the Nazi legal justifications for the Nuremberg racial laws, was later placed in charge of Adenauer's federal press and chancellery offices. In 1936, Globke made this official contribution to German racial legislation: 'The Jew is completely alien to us in character and blood. . . . The Nuremberg laws will form a permanent blockade against further penetration of Jewish blood into the German nation.' " Less than thirty years later, Julius Klein, a former national commander of the Jewish War Veterans, was counting on Globke to help him save his $150,000-a-year political account.

While Senator Dodd kept delaying his trip, Klein grew nervous. The more nervous he grew, the more pressure he applied. And when Dodd delayed his trip again until April, Klein wrote petulantly:

Had I known that your schedule would have kept you in Washington, I would have asked either Senator Humphrey or Senator Symington to make a quick trip here on a weekend to speak on behalf of their Democratic colleagues just as Javits did for Dirksen and other of his Republican colleagues.

The Senator finally left for Bonn on April 6, 1964. He spent the night before his departure, according to registration card No. 08328, at the Essex House, in Klein's New York apartment. He took off abruptly, it should be added, in the middle of a Senate filibuster on civil rights. He was needed in the Senate to answer quorum calls. Any time a full quorum couldn't be mustered, the Southerners could recess for the day and win a delay. He was, furthermore, a squad captain in charge of the debate on one section of the civil rights bill. He took off anyway on Lufthansa flight 401, which left Kennedy International Airport at 8 P.M., one hour late.

What urgent business did Dodd have in Germany that required him to abandon his Senate duties? He later explained that he had hurried across the Atlantic to interview B. N. Stashynsky, a confessed member of the Russian murder apparatus, whose grim business was to eliminate political victims. But Stashynsky, serving an eight-year prison sentence in West Germany, was not going anywhere. He could have kept the date just as conveniently later. The case also was not so hot that Dodd needed to drop everything to rush to Germany. It had been hanging fire for more than two years. He later explained to the committee that investigated him, "One of the most difficult tasks . . . has been to make people aware that there is such a murder apparatus and terror apparatus in the world." Yet two years earlier, *Life* magazine had given the Stashynsky case a big spread. The article was more widely read than the dull official report that Dodd eventually produced in 1965, a full year after his emergency trip to Germany. In an America nurtured on James Bond thrillers, in any case, few could have been surprised at news that the Soviets were operating a murder apparatus.

Senate Ethics Committee Chairman John Stennis, D-Miss., frankly skeptical about Dodd's excuse for the trip, wondered aloud at the 1966 hearing, "What did you get out of the trip that you did not already have before you went?"

Dodd gamely insisted the trip *had* been necessary. "I came away with a far better understanding," he said. "You learn it by looking a man in the eye and asking him questions."

Unconvinced, Stennis pointed out that Dodd had summed up all he learned in Germany about "Murder International, Inc." in less than three pages of a report that was not issued until a year later. "Anyway," Stennis concluded, "you did not get anything new over there from any of the agencies of our Government."

Stennis had reason to be politely skeptical of Dodd's purpose in hurrying off to Germany. Not only did the Stashynsky excuse appear a bit contrived in view of the extensive Dodd-Klein correspondence, but it was also contradicted by the testimony of witnesses. Mrs. Marjorie Carpenter, Dodd's secretary at the time of the trip, testified that she had handed the Klein instructions to the Senator on the eve of his departure and had watched him slip them into his bag. They reappeared in the "out" box behind his desk, she said, immediately after his return from Germany. Dodd, of course, denied with much Senatorial sputtering that he was even aware of the instructions. "I never saw any such papers or knew that they existed," he protested at the 1966 Senate Ethics Committee hearing. If his testimony is to be believed, he must also not have read his incoming wires. The record shows that on March 22, 1964, he huddled with Klein at the Essex House. The meeting was followed next day by a happy telegram from Klein including a reference to Professor Carstens, one of the six people Klein had urged Dodd to see in Germany. "You have his dossier in your folder," advised the telegram.

David Martin, the anti-Communist expert and baggage-handler who accompanied Dodd on the trip, was produced by Dodd at the Senate hearing to attest that the Klein papers had been left behind. But Martin, possibly having missed what the Senator said about not knowing the papers even existed, testified that the two had discussed the Klein memos at the airport before the takeoff. And James Boyd, Senator Dodd's former administrative assistant, testified that Martin, after returning from the trip, pointed to the Klein folder and groaned, "I had more trouble over that." Boyd also quoted Martin as saying, "I was very upset and concerned that the Senator brought those things with him and consulted them. I was always afraid, as he has a habit of leaving things behind, he would leave these documents behind either on a plane or in a hotel room and that perhaps a CIA agent or some embassy person would make a note of them, and it would be later used to discredit him."

While Julius Klein had been waiting for his dilatory U.S. Senator to show up, he encamped at the Königshof Hotel in

Bonn. The town, which curves along the west bank of the Rhine, has been described as being half as big as the Chicago cemetery and twice as dead. Across the river is the Siebenge-birge, or seven hills, where Snow White is said to have lived with the Seven Dwarfs; Klein, looking not unlike an oversized Grumpy, bustled between the huge L-shaped building housing the West German Presseamt and the American Embassy hulking on the banks of the Rhine in Bad Godesberg. He bad-gered officials of both nations and frequently invoked the names of his powerful Washington friends. A high German official, remarking on that performance, said Klein "is a hairy question here."

It has been established that Dodd, while in Germany alleg-edly for the sole purpose of interviewing Stashynsky, saw most of the people whom Klein had asked him to see. After-ward the Senator, eyes heavenward, vowed he had not dis-cussed Klein with any of them—except for a two-minute conversation with the aging Adenauer, who, Dodd allowed, brought up the subject. Martin, during his turn on the witness stand, eagerly concurred; Dodd had discussed only matters of state with all Klein's friends except Adenauer. The Senator merely told Adenauer, recalled Martin, that Klein had been accused of no crime, that the Senate investigation had been misrepresented by German newspapers, that it was an inquiry into the general subject of foreign agents and that Klein was well thought of by people on both sides of the Senate. Though Martin may not have intended to, he was saying that the Sen-ator had told Adenauer exactly what Klein had instructed him to say.

Whether or not the same spiel was repeated to the others on Klein's list, Julius was eminently satisfied. He got a person-al report from Dodd on the German trip a few days after the Senator's return. "It was good seeing you last week," Klein wrote to "Dear Tom" on April 21, 1964. "I had a very nice letter from former Chancellor Adenauer and am very pleased." But Julius, hoping for some frosting on the cake, added, "I presume, Tom, you will write the various people you saw over there and if you do, I would appreciate it if you would add a PS: 'I was indeed glad to discuss with you also the fine work of our mutual good friend General Klein.' . . . Once again, my thanks for your true friendship, and I am always ready to be of service to you in the interest of our country and good government."

The following August, Tom had another opportunity to say something nice about Julius. Klein's public-relations account with the Wiesbaden group was still in danger. Klein needed support from Ludger Westrick, a new Cabinet member in the Erhard administration and a power in the Wiesbaden Society to Promote German-American Cooperation. In July of 1964, Dodd had promised to write to Westrick in Klein's behalf, then had fibbed that a letter had been sent. On August 10, Klein called the bluff:

> I think somebody in your office must be kidding you. It's now six weeks that you wrote the letter to Westrick. . . . Last week you said you had your office mail me a copy of your letter. I never received it.

This time Dodd didn't bother to blame it on his luckless staff, but merely offered this weary alibi:

> I think I have been mixed up about the Westrick letter. Apparently, you and I have been talking about two different matters.

Two days later, Dodd received a draft of what he should write to Westrick. Klein explained:

> It appears that the Westrick letter was never sent. I regret this very much because the Chancellor went on vacation for the month of August. When I returned from Europe in July, you were good enough to say that you would write such a letter. . . . To save you time, I am enclosing herewith a rough draft. . . . Please get the letter out on Monday. You can say that you were so burdened with various foreign relations problems and are only now trying to catch up with your correspondence. . . .

As a postscript, Klein scrawled across the bottom in the best cloak-and-dagger fashion:

> Please destroy this letter—I made NO copy.

The proposed letter to Westrick was another testament of Klein's unshakable admiration for himself. In part, Klein wanted Dodd to tell Westrick:

> From Speaker McCormack who admires you, and from our mutual friend, General Julius Klein, I know of your splendid record, your close association with Chancellor Erhard in the reconstruction of Germany, and your fight against Soviet aggression. Incidentally, I saw General Klein recently who, as you know, works hand in hand with all of us. He has the confidence of my Republican and Democratic colleagues and is especially close to our leaders—like Senators Dirksen and Humphrey. It is for this reason that we all regretted the distortions in the German press and the slander which originated in the press behind the Iron Curtain as General Klein has been rendering a great service not only to our nation but also to your country. His advice has always been most valuable to us Democrats—as it was and is to his Republican friends. . . .

With only an inconsequential change, Senator Dodd signed the letter and mailed it to Minister Westrick. Unaware that the letter had been ghosted by Klein, Westrick responded warmly:

> I was extremely interested in hearing your opinion of General Julius Klein and to learn from your letters that the Speaker of the House Mr. McCormack joins you fully in your opinion. Mr. Klein visited me recently, but we have not yet reached a result that is to his satisfaction.

Westrick's reply might have been more reserved had he known that Klein supplied not only Dodd's opinion about Klein but McCormack's opinion as well.

Julius was momentarily delighted with Westrick's reply, but he never seemed to be satisfied. On November 21, 1964, he wrote to Dodd:

> I am grateful to you because apparently your discussion and letter got the ball rolling again even though the matter has not been settled yet. . . . Therefore, I am taking the liberty of preparing for your consideration a draft of a letter which

I wish you would send in reply. It will be very helpful in getting this matter straightened out once and for all.

The draft was quick in arriving along with an added word from Klein:

This letter from Minister Westrick to you gives you a great opportunity to reply to him as per the enclosed draft. . . . Please do this on Monday, because I am leaving for Europe on Wednesday.

The Senator, though willing to do Klein's bidding, liked to do it in his own good time. When Klein put out to sea on Wednesday, the letter still had not been mailed.

That Wednesday morning, December 2, 1964, Dodd's office received an urgent phone call. A secretary later placed this note on the Senator's desk:

General Klein (aboard the S.S. *United States*) called. (1) Has the letter gone out yet? (2) His apartment is at your disposal for the next three weeks.

Dodd remained unhurried. Not until December 11 did he get around to Klein's letter. Once again Klein was unstinting in praise of himself, and once again the Senator from Connecticut allowed himself to be used by a registered foreign agent. Klein wrote and Dodd signed the following:

I note that you had a visit with General Klein and all of us, of course, shall appreciate it if his problem, in the interest of both countries, is solved to mutual satisfaction. I also have spoken to General Klein since receiving your letter, and he told me that he had been in touch with you. I don't have to repeat the high regard we have for the General and the great help he has been to us in the past, but most important we value his advice and counseling.

I assure you that my and my colleagues' friendship and my desire to underline General Klein's values as advisor and counsel is a purely unselfish one, and it is based on our feelings that he is an understanding bridge between our countries. These statements are not only shared with my Democratic and Republican colleagues, but also with our newly elected Vice President Hubert Humphrey who recently stated how he will need the advice and counsel of his friend Julius Klein.

Months before that letter was written, Hubert Humphrey had drawn the line on Julius Klein. Like others who had accepted his fund-raising help, Humphrey was badgered repeatedly for statements of his undying friendship to Klein. "Julius Klein is the most persistent man I know," Humphrey once said wearily. "I get more letters from him than from my own mother." But Humphrey's patience finally wore out, and on January 10, 1964, he wrote to Klein: "I can't believe that it is necessary to give a personal testimony again and again as to our friendship and as to my respect for you. You have that in writing many times and you have the demonstration of such respect by many personal acts on my part."

What sort of acts? Humphrey had written the usual eulogies that Klein never tired of receiving; he had met the clients Klein brought around to impress and had co-hosted an occasional luncheon for German officials. Yet there was a limit to Humphrey's acquiescence. In the same 1964 letter he added:

Now in reference to the date with Senator Dodd and Ambassador Knappstein. I was called to the White House on that noon without any advance notice and simply couldn't return to the office of Senator Dodd in time for that conference. Yes, I should have called, but I simply didn't have the time. . . . I did receive a letter from Ambassador Knappstein, and I thought it was in very poor taste. I hesitated to answer the letter lest I be too abrupt and candid with him. He wrote to tell me that he disliked my remarks concerning the Federal Republic of Germany and its policy of selling to the Eastern bloc communist countries. All of the Ambassador's explanations will not erase the fact that Chancellor Adenauer criticized the United States for its intention to sell wheat to the Eastern bloc communist countries at the very time that business interests in Germany were selling large quantities of wheat and flour to those same countries. I don't need any lecture from the German Ambassador.

Nevertheless, Humphrey went on, almost dutifully, to repeat to Klein: "You perform your duties well. You have many friends in the Congress. You have given the outstanding service to your clients. You have nothing to apologize for and much to be proud of." A politician without personal wealth does not dismiss a campaign contributor too cavalierly.

That, though, was the last kind word Julius Klein has had in writing from the Vice President of the United States. Helen Batherson, a former secretary to Klein, told the Senate Ethics Committee how "the General" had tried repeatedly to reach Humphrey after the 1964 election, but Humphrey, she said, never answered the calls or agreed to see Klein. "We had worn out our welcome," she said, "and it got to be embarrassing to keep calling, but the General insisted on it."

4. The Office Joke

Senator Tom Dodd either did not know or did not care that he was wrongly advising a high official of a foreign Government when, in his dilatory but still dutiful letter of December 11, 1964, he wrote that Julius Klein was in high favor with the newly elected Vice President. More important, though, than the Senator's misrepresenting the position of Hubert Humphrey was the basic question put to Dodd during the 1966 Senate hearings on his conduct. Senator James Pearson, R-Kan., asked it. His voice rising on a note of incredulity, Pearson asked Dodd, "What was the relationship between a Senator in the U.S. Senate and General Klein that would permit him to put pressure upon you, both in the letters here and in regard to the trip to Germany, that would permit him to write the things he wrote to you in the correspondence?"

Tom Dodd, looking in repose like a bust of Caesar come to life, sucked on his pipe. "Well, there are some people like this in the world, and he is one of them. . . ." The committee chairman, Senator John Stennis, still could not understand. He shook his head sadly, then told Dodd, "I don't know of any reason why he should write to you as he did there in that letter, or why you should let him do it. Do you want to explain that?"

Dodd slowly fingered his sculptured profile. "I cannot explain how another man writes a letter," he said, "but there are many people who do. . . . He is this kind of human being; he writes that kind of a letter. I overlooked it because, as I have said, I have had a liking for him. I found that he was a decent human being."

Julius, at the moment, was bouncing around Germany still trying to save his $150,000-a-year contract. It took protracted overseas negotiations to bring him home to testify. After a month's delay, including sailing time (since Klein does not like to fly), he brought his comedy routine back to Capitol Hill. In his previous appearance he had sworn to tell the whole truth and nothing but the truth and then had told the Fulbright committee, "I have never asked a Senator for a favor because I have no favors to ask."

This time the General was at his best as a master dissembler. He began his testimony outside the hearing room, the flow of words like audible exhaling. He spoke English as if he thought in German, then translated it verbatim. But if his meaning was largely unintelligible, there was no mistaking his tone of righteous indignation. Still talking between puffs on his Corona Corona, he entered the hearing room and took his place at the witness table. For the remainder of the day, the committee was bathed in verbal smoke and cigar fumes. Klein was asked what he did for the Wiesbaden group to earn his $150,000 a year. "I point out to them," he said learnedly, "the good and bad public relations to the present image, make suggestions how they can improve it, and book to speak to various groups." Master of the non sequitur, Klein added, "My job over there is chiefly in Germany, more so than here in the United States." What did he do for the society in the United States? Klein tried to explain: "First of all, visitors come over here from Germany, industrialists and others. I try to meet them or my staff meets them. We advise them who's who. We point out to some of our friends in the United States the problem that Germany is facing. I deliver a lot of talks in this country myself."

Helen Batherson, who had been with Klein for 12 years, reduced it to simpler terms. "We didn't do anything for them that I can recall," she told the Washington *Post,* "except to arrange lunches with Senators and people when they would visit here."

Throughout the hearing, Klein stoutly denied any wrongdoing. His attitude alternated between indignation and pain that his virtue should be questioned, but more often he came across like a dialect comedian at a burlesque house. Once, reaching for *Othello* but not quite making it, he intoned, "As a great Englishman said, 'You steal nothing when you steal my money, but when you steal my reputation you steal everything.'" Chief counsel Benjamin Fern, citing Klein's repeated lamentations about contract cancellations, asked whether he also might have had money on his mind. "I am a businessman," Klein admitted. As for Dodd's trip to Germany, Klein blandly denied that he had brought any pressure upon the Senator. This was more than Fern could swallow. "In view of the testimony and the documentary evidence received by this committee of some twenty letters and cables and many phone calls from you, and in view of the additional representations of two of your senior employees, Kenneth Buchanan and Max Klein, in view of the bulging packet of briefing materials which were specifically tailored for Senator Dodd, all of which had been undertaken over a period of a few months before the German trip, and all of which appears to have been calculated to salvage your disappearing clients, how," he demanded, "can you describe this as anything other than pressure?" By the time he had finished his question, Fern was glaring at Klein.

Klein's jowls puffed up. "I don't call this pressure," he barked back in his best major-general voice. "I don't know a single U.S. Senator who can be pressured. I exercised my right as an American to petition a Senator or Congressman to correct a grave injustice. If there are thirty letters, a hundred letters, if I have to write a thousand I would do it, but I wouldn't call it pressure, no, sir. It is my right and I will continue doing so."

Among others Julius Klein said he had solicited to correct the grave injustice done him was Senator Jacob K. Javits, R-N.Y., one of his favorites in Congress. Javits not only had responded to Klein's SOS to bail him out of trouble with his German clients but had flown to Germany on a rescue mission. Javits also required no laborious briefing, Klein added approvingly, so it was unnecessary to prepare any dossiers for him. "Senator Javits is completely indoctrinated on this issue, and he wouldn't need a memo. He knows exactly what happened and defended me and rightfully so," said Julius Klein, somewhat to Javits' discomfort. Only Tom Dodd, the bumbler, had to be spoon-fed what to say to German officialdom.

Javits tried awkwardly to deny Klein's compliment without

offending Klein. Only a few weeks earlier, Klein had produced a Dodd-like letter from Javits to get him out of his latest swirl of hot water with the Jewish War Veterans. The organization had become embarrassed by its erstwhile commander not only because of the revelations coming out of the Dodd investigation but because of one of Klein's more odious clients. It had leaked out that Klein represented Rheinmetall, Hitler's second biggest arms supplier, which had used Jewish slave labor during the war but had refused to pay restitution to the survivors. Klein had helped Rheinmetall land a big piece of a $75-million contract from the Defense Department to manufacture a 20-mm. cannon for the U.S. armed forces. The Pentagon received a protest from Adolph Held, president of the Jewish Labor Committee, who charged that Rheinmetall "sought out and employed concentration camp inmates for exploitation in its arms factories. A special camp for Jewish women and girls recruited from Buchenwald by Rheinmetall was built by Rheinmetall at Sommerda in Thuringia. Over 1,200 Jewish women were employed in that camp alone. The evidence is overwhelming that they were forced to work under the most inhumane circumstances." Yet Klein's client had refused to pay restitution to the survivors as other Nazi companies, including Krupp and I. G. Farben, had paid. Klein not only pleaded Rheinmetall's case passionately before the Defense and State departments, but Government officials said they understood he even advised Rheinmetall to stand pat and not pay restitution to the slave labor camp victims.

Javits, an able and intelligent Senator, was fully aware of the seriousness of the claims against Rheinmetall. In answer to his own query about the case, he received a letter, dated March 7, 1966, from Assistant Secretary of State Douglas MacArthur II outlining Rheinmetall's record. The letter read, in part:

It appears that of the five present principal officers of the Rheinmetall AG, three were members of the Nazi party during World War II. Of these five officers, two, including one of the Nazi party members, were plant directors of Rheinmetall Borsig AG during the war. The degree of active involvement in Nazi party activities by the three wartime members is not known. . . . As regards the financial claims by slave laborers against Rheinmetall, the Department of

State was advised of these claims some time ago. We brought them to the attention of our own Defense Department as well as to that of the German ministry of defense, which has in turn discussed them with Rheinmetall. There may be as many as 1,000 claims by former slave labor employees involved.

Javits prepared a speech criticizing the award of a $75 million U.S. arms contract to a company that had refused to compensate its former slave laborers. But he never delivered it; he explained lamely that others had already made the same points. Later, when Klein suddenly found his popularity slipping with the Jewish War Veterans at the height of the Dodd revelations and the Rheinmetall case, Javits wrote a letter almost as astonishing as those revealed at the Dodd hearings. Javits wrote to Klein on April 21, 1966:

> The present controversy surrounding you within the Jewish War Veterans is, as these things always are, unfortunate. However, it is my present understanding that the controversy is on its way to a just solution; I fervently hope so. Within the context of your repatriation of West German business concerns and individuals—which is itself a matter of your business judgment and your personal disposition and not for me to pass on—I feel you have done your utmost to secure justice for the victims of Nazism and a measure of reparation through aid to Israel.

The jubilant Julius triumphantly circulated the Javits letter throughout his world.

At the same time, Javits' brother Ben brought pressure upon the New York *Post* not to run the Pearson-Anderson columns on Klein's conduct. Ben Javits not only telephoned the *Post* himself but persuaded others to do the same. When Klein hired Ben to represent him at the Senate hearing, however, Senator Javits discreetly phoned his brother and asked him to withdraw.

Thus, to feed his hunger for praise and prestige, to impress and help keep his foreign clients, to bail him out of troubled waters, Julius Klein has been able to call upon a steady supply of U.S. Congressmen whenever he needed them. The question, then, remains: how did this stubby figure, so ludicrous in his protestations under the white glare of the Senate's klieg lights, wield his strange power over Capitol Hill?

It is possible, of course, to ascribe the success of Julius Klein to his magnetic personality. But there seems to be no corroborating evidence for such a view. A more plausible answer is that Julius Klein didn't exactly wield power on Capitol Hill—he wheedled it out of Congressmen who, to one extent or another, were grateful to him for campaign contributions or other fund-raising efforts in their behalf. And some Congressmen, just like the people who elect them, are more pliable than others. Hubert Horatio Humphrey, for example, was long known to have the sort of good nature that is easily imposed upon; in his personal relationships he found it painful to offend, easy to forgive. He was grateful to Klein for his fund-raising activities in his behalf and was reluctant, moreover, to offend a man he supposed to be a prominent Jewish leader. And so, for much of his career in the Senate, he let himself be imposed upon by the indefatigable promoter.

Senator Jacob Javits has a harder crust than Hubert Humphrey and is less likely to have let himself be imposed upon for sheer love of humanity. Asked by the authors to explain his services in Klein's behalf, Javits tried to shrug off the relationship with a big grin and a quick quip. He described Klein as "an office joke" and claimed that no one in the office took the downpour of Klein's letters seriously. "You know Julius," Javits said with a grin. "He's always bothering me and Hubert Humphrey and his other Senate friends." Asked why he would write letters and do favors for a man he considered "an office joke," Javits said he felt Klein had done some good work, particularly in using his contacts with the Adenauer Government to help secure reparations payments for Israel. Others felt that Germany had agreed to pay reparations without any prodding from Klein. Also, Humphrey had closed his door on Klein after becoming Vice President, and other Congressional "friends" had abruptly dropped him after the Dodd-Klein exposé; only Javits was still writing letters defending him as late as April 21, 1966. Wasn't that an excessive political risk to take, Javits was asked, for an "office joke"? Javits stopped grinning, said he hadn't thought of the April 21 letter in that light and agreed he might have been unwise to write it.

But the fact is, whether one ascribes it to a perverse sort of

loyalty or some less attractive motive, the letter was written—
as many before it had been—at the behest of a registered
foreign agent with a peculiar power over members of the
United States Congress. That agent, presumably, will go on
asking the Tom Dodds and the Hubert Humphreys and the
Jacob Javitses of the world to say something nice about him.
But it's not praise he really craves—at least not in his own
mind. As he told the Senate committee's counsel on July 19,
1966, "You always use the words 'praise me.' I never make
such a request. The request was to state the facts about me."

5. Hook, Line and Sinker

Although Julius Klein later gave the impression that the 1963
Fulbright hearings had been called solely to get him into trouble with his bankrollers in Bonn, the retired Major General
was only one of the propaganda purveyors who paraded before the Foreign Relations Committee. Klein's operations, if
the most blatant, were on a smaller scale than those of some
of the others who came to light as Fulbright bored into his
witnesses.

One witness was Kenneth T. Downs, a vice president of the
New York public relations firm of Selvage & Lee, Inc., which
had been authorized to draw up to $500,000 to polish the
American image of Portugal and its dictator, Premier Antonio Salazar. Like Klein, Downs insisted that his firm was never
directly in the employ of a foreign government. Yet when G.
Mennen Williams, then Assistant Secretary of State for African Affairs, was about to visit Angola, Downs went into a two-
hour huddle with Portuguese Government officials to figure
out what to do with him. The decision, as revealed in a memo
from Downs in Lisbon to his boss on August 6, 1961:
"Agreed he [Williams] gets red carpet and is kept constantly
on the hop, busy from morning to night."

Important as the Williams visit was to the Portuguese,
Downs apparently set even greater store on good relations
with the Congressmen who breezed through Portugal. In another memo from Lisbon he wrote:

Forgive me if I keep harping on this business of visiting
Congressmen, but this I think is of absolute top priority

importance, if we can do it. They make news while they are here, after they come back, and they are established "experts" that we can continue to use.

The kind of usage Selvage & Lee had in mind was evident in a memo dated October 10, 1962, from Downs, now in Washington, to the man who had replaced him in the Lisbon office:

> I am sending Dr. Pinto Basto copies of the *Congressional Record*. You might explain to him that we wrote some twenty speeches. Much of the material in some of the speeches was ours. Joe Martin, Speaker of the House under Eisenhower, for example, used Sam's stuff without change apart from abbreviation. You might point this out to Dr. Pinto Basto and tell him that it required a great amount of work on the Hill to get the time allocated for these speeches. Patrick Clark [General Francisco Franco's man in Washington for 15 years] recently did the same thing for Spain, but he paid for his. We didn't put out a penny. In all fairness Comacho should be given a great deal of credit on this one. It was his tireless pressure on some of the Massachusetts Congressmen that made it possible, and he is the one who at the last minute got Speaker McCormack into the act.

Downs was so busy dropping names in this memo that he got one of them wrong. "Comacho" was Martin T. Camacho, a Madeira-born Boston attorney who was put on the Selvage & Lee payroll at $400 a week because of his Portuguese-American connections. At the public relations firm's suggestion, Camacho formed the Portuguese-American Committee on Foreign Affairs, a front group with himself as chairman and sole spokesman. At the Fulbright hearings, Camacho admitted that he didn't tell the other members of the Portuguese-American Committee he was in the pay of Selvage & Lee. Nor did he consult them about a letter he sent on committee stationery in the spring of 1962 to every Tennessee newspaper he considered worth the postage. This letter condemned Senator Albert Gore, D-Tenn., for suggesting that the United States should make sure its aid to Salazar's Portugal wasn't being used to "kill, punish or intimidate Africans" in the shaky Portuguese colonial empire. "We feel your Senator has been misled," the letter read, adding that the uprising in Angola a few weeks earlier had been "misrepresented by forces which wish to break the Western alliance asunder and, eventually, destroy both Portugal and the United States." Not only had the other member of his makeshift committee never seen the letter, Camacho told Fulbright later, but the attack on Gore had been drafted by Selvage & Lee.

Fulbright's sharp questioning of Selvage & Lee executives developed persuasive evidence that he was himself a victim of an attempt by Portugal's paid agents to paint him as an integrationist in the eyes of the red-neck voters back in Arkansas. After establishing that a certain free-lance writer was getting $5,000-a-year retainer from Selvage & Lee, the chairman produced copies of three articles the writer had done the previous October, castigating Fulbright and the Kennedy Administration under the title "Africa and the South." Had these racist attacks been written as part of the writer's duties for Selvage & Lee?

Sam Bledsoe, the vice president in charge of Selvage & Lee's Washington office, said definitely not. Then why, Fulbright demanded, had the writer's expenses for the three months before the articles appeared been charged up to Selvage & Lee's Portuguese account? Bledsoe said he didn't know. He was equally fuzzy about the duties of a former newspaperman who had drawn $600 a month from Selvage & Lee in the latter half of 1962. Bledsoe could say only that the ex-newsman was "attached to" the Senate Republican Policy Committee and "a close friend" of Senator Bourke Hickenlooper, the bedrock conservative Iowa Republican. "It made him happy to be given $600 a month for doing nothing?" Fulbright prodded.

"Well," said Bledsoe, "I don't think it made him angry, Senator."

The Gore and Fulbright incidents demonstrated that foreign agents could show their teeth to Congressmen who opposed them. Selvage & Lee's custom-tailored Portuguese-American Committee could growl menacingly at unfriendly newsmen, too. After the National Broadcasting Company aired a television documentary on the Angola uprising of 1961, Camacho fired off identical letters to three Senators, accusing NBC of "unwittingly serving the Communist cause" with a "biased and malicious document." Letters went to the two Senators in a position to investigate the networks, Senate Commerce Committee Chairman Warren Magnuson, D-Wash., and Communications Subcommittee Chairman John Pastore, D-R.I. The third letter went to Connecticut's Tom Dodd, who was quick to investigate anyone accused of serving the Communists.

The Fulbright hearings never did make it entirely clear what Camacho had done to get House Speaker John McCormack "into the act," as Downs had put it in his memo to his successor in Lisbon. But another Massachusetts Congressman who had been subjected to Camacho's "tireless pressure" did take the trouble to write to Fulbright. Former Speaker Joseph Martin said nobody had told him that Camacho was a paid agent for foreign principals. "I have always been interested in the welfare of the Portuguese-American community," Martin wrote. "Many of these people live in my district. But I know nothing about these public relations people serving Portuguese interests." When Fulbright was finally done questioning Downs about that memo to Lisbon, the Selvage & Lee man was obliged to concede that it had been "very carelessly written."

Another man about Capitol Hill who sold his services to a foreign Government was John O'Donnell. He could have been a character out of a John O'Hara novel—a tough Irish Catholic boy from Scranton, Pennsylvania, who broke away from the coal country to earn a law degree at Georgetown University and land a job afterward with the Interstate Commerce Commission. An enlisted man in World War II, he went to the Judge Advocate General School and came out of the war a major.

But O'Donnell's career really took off after Harry Truman named him in 1947 to the three-man Philippine War Damage Commission. Before the commission went out of existence early in 1951, it doled out $400 million in private claims to compensate for the ravages of war. After that, O'Donnell continued his career of giving away Uncle Sam's millions in a private capacity—charging fees as high as 10 percent from the big Filipino claimants whom Congress could be persuaded to reward. Legislation was passed that brought him close to $300,000 in fees from the Catholic Church and other clients in the Philippines. Still, O'Donnell testified on behalf of a new Philippine claims bill every year from 1959 to 1962 before the House Foreign Affairs Committee. He spoke as a former member of the War Damage Commission and kept quiet about his if-and-when fee arrangements with the claimants. Finally, in 1962, Congress passed a bill that had been introduced in the House by Representative Clement Zablocki, D-Wis., granting the Philippines an additional $73 million. O'Donnell's clients would have got more than $3 million of that, according to a later estimate, and the erstwhile poor boy from Scranton stood to collect $150,000 as his share—enough to have bought a great many of the white carnations he often sported on his lapel.

But on March 1, 1963—before the $73 million was actually appropriated—the Fulbright committee caught up with the gregarious O'Donnell. He appeared behind closed doors, then was invited back for a public hearing a few weeks later. But his doctor said he was too sick. When the committee released his earlier testimony, O'Donnell must have felt even sicker. The transcript revealed that O'Donnell's Philippine clients had sent him $18,000 to be spread around where it would do the most good in the 1960 Congressional campaign. O'Donnell said he hadn't expected his employers to be so generous; something in the neighborhood of $5,000 would have been ample. "I was completely flabbergasted," he told the committee. But he had made a quick recovery, and soon he was laying out campaign contributions with a lavish hand. With each contribution went a letter that said: "Knowing your reputation . . . for unqualified fairness in dealing with causes in the public interest, I need not emphasize that neither I nor my friends in the Philippines, for whom I occasionally speak, are expecting any favored position by reason of my small help."

Zablocki got the biggest slice of the pie: $2,000. He had been doing "a lot of work on this Philippine War Damage bill," O'Donnell explained, "And he was very friendly to the Philippines and it was in the best interest of the Philippines that he be returned to the Congress." But the second biggest handout, $1,000, went to a candidate who was running for Attorney General of Massachusetts, not for Congress. Why O'Donnell's Philippine employers should care about the election of Edward McCormack to state office in Massachusetts was a mystery, of course—unless it had something to do with the fact that McCormack's uncle was House Majority Leader John McCormack, now the Speaker and a loyal son of the

Catholic Church. He had been most sympathetic toward war-damaged Catholic institutions in the Philippines.

Other O'Donnell contributions were on a smaller scale. Representative George P. Miller, D-Calif., a co-sponsor of the bill that passed in 1962, got $500 because he was "the oldest living member of the old Insular Affairs Committee that handled all Philippine matters when it was a Commonwealth." Another $500 went via Senator Eugene McCarthy, D-Minn., to Senator Humphrey, who became Majority Whip after the 1960 election and introduced O'Donnell's bill in the Senate. In Humphrey's Minnesota, however, O'Donnell was careful to play both sides of the fence. He also gave $500 to Representative Walter Judd and $200 to Representative Albert Quie, both conservative Republicans.

The only other Republican on O'Donnell's gift list was Maine's Representative Clifford McIntire, who got $400. Except for $500 each to two Democratic Senators, West Virginia's Jennings Randolph and Delaware's J. Allen Frear, Jr., the rest of the contributions were for $300 or less. Representatives John Dingell of Michigan and Robert Levering of Ohio each got $300. Representatives Pat Jennings of Virginia, Earl Hogan of Indiana, Eugene Keogh of New York and Daniel Flood of Pennsylvania were given $200 apiece. And $100 checks were sent to Senators Patrick McNamara of Michigan, E. L. Bartlett of Alaska and Paul Douglas of Illinois, also to Representatives Stanley Prokop of Pennsylvania, James Delaney of New York and Thomas P. O'Neill, Jr., of Massachusetts. O'Donnell tried to give $300 to Texas Representative W. R. Poage, but apparently the check was never cashed. And the prodigal Philippine agent partly made up for neglecting individual Republican candidates by passing $500 to New York's Representative William Miller, then the Republican Congressional Campaign Committee chairman. Finally, there was a $200 check to a member of Florida Senator George Smathers' staff—reimbursement, according to O'Donnell, for tickets to some $100-a-plate dinner he couldn't recall.

The General Accounting Office, trying to make sense of O'Donnell's murky bookkeeping, tabulated that he spent—or had tried to spend—$9,100 on political contributions to 24 Congressional candidates, employees, or their relatives. That was just the way these things were done, O'Donnell told Fulbright's committee. "I do not believe," Fulbright said, "that if the Administration and the Congress had been informed of the true facts as we now know them, the legislation which was actually passed would have been enacted." Before the 88th Congress was over, Fulbright proved his point: the war claims bill was amended to prohibit successful claimants from paying fees to anyone who had been a member of the Philippine War Damage Commission. It still cost the American taxpayer $73 million, but at least John A. O'Donnell didn't get any of it.

6. Whose Benefactor?

Some foreign agents have the audacity even to contribute directly to the campaign of U.S. Presidential candidates. A $10,000 kick-in for John Kennedy's Presidential drive was traced to the Somoza family, which operated Nicaragua for years like a private estate. President Luis Somoza's registered agent in Washington—Frank Barry—was the donor for the record. While he was at it, he shelled out something like $1,500 for Representative Daniel Flood, D-Pa., who also got $200 that year from John O'Donnell's Philippine fund. Flood was a persistent booster of a canal through Nicaragua as an alternative to the Panama Canal, but he assured reporters this had nothing to do with the Somozas' campaign subsidy. It just happened that he and Barry both came from Wilkes-Barre, Pennsylvania. The hometown tie is evidently strong in the anthracite coal region of Pennsylvania.

Probably the champion foreign influence-seeker of all time, though, was Rafael Leonidas Trujillo Molina, the vainglorious Dominican Republic dictator who spent a fortune trying to convince Americans he deserved the title he gave himself— the Benefactor. Even the Trujillo millions could not make a lovable lamb out of this wolf. But before he was assassinated, Trujillo gave employment to a lot of needy Americans. Among them was ex-Representative Albert L. Reeves, Jr., who stayed on in Washington when he left public office. His law firm got $2,000 a month to represent the Dominican Republic's embassy, and Reeves was the chief liaison man. Franklin D. Roosevelt, Jr., another ex-Representative, got a $60,000 fee for a year's service as special counsel to the Dominican Republic in partnership with the flamboyant Charles Patrick Clark, who apparently had some spare time left after duty as chief lobbyist for Franco of Spain. Roosevelt's contract called for a second year on the Trujillo payroll, but he abruptly pulled out early in 1957—too late for his political ambitions, which to this day have been clouded by the Benefactor's shadow.

The one piece of legislation guaranteed to make every Caribbean agent's mouth water is the sugar bill that, periodically, sets sugar import quotas. Domestic cane and beet growers, who produce only 60 percent of the sugar Americans consume, demand that their prices be pegged by the Agriculture Department above the world rate. To accommodate the domestic sugar lobby, the Government restricts imports so that the supply won't outstrip the demand and prices won't go down. But to keep the restricted foreign growers happy, too, kindly Uncle Sam pays them a premium, over and above the world price, for the sugar that is admitted into the United States. The result, of course, is a furious struggle for the biggest quotas, and nobody ever struggled harder than the Benefactor's men in Washington.

The Fulbright committee's 1963 investigation threw some light on the infighting over the sugar bill of 1956, a typical year, when Trujillo retained the astute Washington law firm of Surrey, Karasik, Gould and Green to obtain an even larger share of the great American sugar bowl than the 30,000-ton quota then allotted him. For every ton the quota was increased, up to 100,000 tons, Trujillo's men in Washington were supposed to get $1. For every ton above 100,000 the bonus would drop to 50 cents. In addition the law firm was guaranteed a $95,000 retainer for less than a year's work.

To earn its fee, the Surrey firm "made contact," as one of the partners delicately put it in a memo, with a "powerful law firm" in the home state of Senator Harry Byrd, the tight-fisted Virginia Democrat who headed the Senate Finance Committee. The Virginia firm was well positioned to influence the Senator, the memo went on, since its senior member was "the executive officer of the Senator's political machine," a second partner was the "son of the Senator's first campaign manager," and the third was the Senator's "private confidential attorney." And all three had agreed to visit the Senator and "engage his sympathy for the position of the Dominican Republic with respect to sugar legislation." For this day's work, said the memo, the Virginia firm wanted a $2,500 bonus if the

Dominican Republic's sugar quota was satisfactorily increased. Trujillo's share of the American market ultimately was upped from 30,000 tons a year to 60,000.

Perhaps the dictator's men never got to Harry Byrd, but Trujillo certainly made a favorable impression on some other Dixie Senators. Senator Allen Ellender, the globe-trotting segregationist from Louisiana, paid a visit to the Dominican Republic in 1960. When he got back to Washington, his Mississippi neighbor and fellow Democrat, Senator James Eastland, engaged him in the following sprightly dialogue on the Senate floor:

EASTLAND: Is it not true that Trujillo has been a friend of the United States?

ELLENDER: I do not believe there is any doubt about that. . . . There is not one country in South or Central America which, since 1952, has shown greater economic progress than the Dominican Republic.

EASTLAND: Did the Senator from Louisiana find that the people there were happy and contented?

ELLENDER: I saw no evidence of unrest. . . .

EASTLAND: Is it not true . . . that Trujillo has given the country stability—something it never had before?

ELLENDER: There is no question about that.

EASTLAND: Is it not true that it takes a strong arm to rule in countries of that sort . . . ?

ELLENDER: That is certainly true in many instances.

EASTLAND: If it were destroyed and if a vacuum were left, who would march in?

ELLENDER: Another Castro, without a doubt.

EASTLAND: Is not Trujillo the foremost enemy of Communism in Latin America?

ELLENDER: I never met anyone there who so often and vocally professed his opposition to Communism.

Still another Senator with a soft spot for the icy-eyed Dominican Republic dictator was fashion-plate George Smathers, D-Fla., who visited Ciudad Trujillo in 1960, at a time when criticism of the regime was building to a roar. Shrugging off the fact that Trujillo had ruled with an iron fist for three decades, he came back with a report that free elections were promised within two years. "We are always a little naïve," Smathers said tolerantly, "in thinking that because we have democracy in our own country, and because of our love for humanity, people in other lands should have exactly the same type of government we have." What the public did not know was that Smathers' Miami law firm represented the dictator's Dominican steamship line.

Testimonials are nice, of course, but they cannot be deposited in numbered Swiss bank accounts. And no matter how many Senators were on Trujillo's team in Congress, in the pinch there was just one man who really counted at sugar time on Capitol Hill. He was Representative Harold Cooley, the touchy North Carolina Democrat, who headed the House Agriculture Committee until his defeat in 1966 after 31 years in Congress. He regarded sugar legislation as his divine right. "There aren't five men in Congress that understand it," a sugar lobbyist once confided. "I never talked to an individual member of Congress save one: Harold Cooley." Fully agreeing, the committee chairman, who learned his law at Yankee Yale as well as the University of North Carolina, suggested that Congress ought to accept his drafts of sugar bills "on faith."

Trujillo realized long before the sugar legislation came up for review in 1956 that he could not afford to neglect Cooley. But rather than single out the chairman for special attention, the Benefactor grandly invited the entire committee—and its staff—to visit his tight little island. Cooley was too busy to get away, but among those who did make the trip were his sister, Mrs. Mabel Downey (who happened to be a clerk on the committee staff), and his son and daughter-in-law. When they got back, Mrs. Downey wrote a nice thank-you note in appreciation of Trujillo's "thoughtfulness and generosity."

None of this had any influence on Cooley's handling of sugar legislation, according to the chairman himself. Yet in 1960, after a Trujillo-inspired attempt to assassinate the President of Venezuela, Cooley blocked President Eisenhower's request for authority to reduce the Dominican Republic's sugar quota. The sugar bill of 1962 was a bigger free-for-all than ever, because Fidel Castro's takeover in Havana meant the Cuban quota was up for grabs. Two dozen sugar-growing nations spent an estimated $500,000 in fees and retainers alone. The list of foreign agents in Washington included Ralph Gardner, an able young attorney whose father used to be governor of Cooley's home state. Representative W. R. Poage, D-Tex., the man who said he never cashed John O'Donnell's $300 campaign contribution, broke into one of the committee hearings to announce that he didn't even know where Gardner's client, the island of Mauritius, was located. Thumbing through an atlas, he finally found it in the Indian Ocean.

A curious thing about the 1962 sugar legislation was that it opened up the American market to nations that had never grown any sugar and never would. The ban on Cuban sugar imports didn't apply if the sugar was refined in some other country. Thus, under the 1962 bill Ireland could import raw sugar from Cuba, refine it and ship it back across the Atlantic to sell at the premium rate in the United States.

In 1965, the last time the law was revised, Cooley maneuvered to put another nation in the sugar business in spite of the continuing world sugar surplus. The bill he pushed through Congress called for a 10,000-ton quota from the Bahamas. The entire Bahaman quota, it turned out, would be produced by the American-owned Owens-Illinois Glass Company, whose business had always been glass, paper and plastics, not sugar. But Owens-Illinois had to do something with its property on Great Abaco Island, where the pulpwood it had been cutting was just about gone. The experts who sampled the soil and climate advised the company to grow sugar.

Fair enough—if Owens-Illinois had been willing to sell its sugar in the free market, where the going price was about 1.75 cents a pound. But the company wanted a bite of the American quota, which was then paying a 5-cent premium above the world price for sugar. The difference amounted to $100 a ton—or $1 million a year—for Owens-Illinois. The company's president, Raymond Mulford, told us, "We are the largest employer in the Bahamas. We feel quite a responsibility for the five hundred people we employ on Abaco." Neither he nor Cooley mentioned any responsibility to the American taxpayers who were expected to line Owens-Illinois's pockets to the tune of $1 million a year.

At about the same time the 1965 bill was being worked out, the Venezuela Sugar Association sent three young emissaries to Washington to see about raising their country's import quota. After checking in at the Venezuelan embassy, they headed straight for Cooley. "What you need is a lawyer," the chairman told them affably. The Venezuelans asked him to recommend one, and Cooley mentioned Charles Patrick Clark. Taking the hint, the three men from Caracas called on Clark and were surprised to find that he expected them. Certainly he would represent Venezuela's sugar interests in Washington—for a fee of $125,000 spread over two years, plus certain expenses. His visitors agreed on the spot.

When they got back to the embassy to report, Ambassador Enrique Tejera-Paris was dumbfounded. Not only had Clark been the chief lobbyist for Franco's Spain for 15 years; he had also worked for the Dominican Republic's dictator Trujillo, who had masterminded the 1960 assassination attempt against the freely elected Venezuelan President Rómulo Betancourt. Worst of all, Clark had been retained by Venezuela's own hated ex-dictator, Marcos Pérez Jiménez, then in jail awaiting trial. The ambassador hastily informed Caracas he had had nothing to do with hiring Clark, and the Minister of Commerce went on television at home to explain what had happened. After all the uproar, however, Clark earned his generous fee. His clients had asked him to get the Venezuelan sugar quota jacked up from 2,500 tons to 20,000. Clark did much better. The bill Cooley wrote raised the quota to 30,000 tons—more, incidentally, than Venezuela could produce. Later the Senate, overruling Clark and Cooley, scaled down the quota to 21,564 tons.

When Cooley was drafting the 1965 sugar legislation, he invited lobbyists Irvin Hoff of the Cane Sugar Refiners and Phil Jones of the Beet Sugar Association to sit in at the committee sessions, despite the fact that they were closed to the public and the press. In the House Rules Committee, the next step toward passage, Cooley spoke up sharply for his scheme to report the sugar bill to the House floor under a rule barring amendments. This would have forced the opposition to settle for his bill or no bill at all. Representative Richard Bolling, D-Mo., asked Cooley at the closed Rules Committee hearing why he had ignored the Agriculture Department's recommendations on the bill and had written his own instead.

"We didn't write this bill for the Agriculture Department," Cooley retorted. Bolling kept probing, and finally Cooley lost patience and snapped, "We didn't write this bill for you."

Nobody ever found out whom the bill had been written for, but it certainly wasn't the taxpayers. Cooley's bill not only allowed more sugar into the country than the Agriculture

Department wished but also allocated the quotas to countries with the best political connections rather than the most need. Nevertheless, Rules Committee Chairman Howard Smith, D-Va., sided with Cooley on the no-amendment rule and called for a show of hands. Six went up for the ayes; six for the nays—because Representative John Young, D-Tex., didn't vote. The bill went to the floor under the rule Cooley demanded, and it passed on October 13, 1965, by a 348-to-147 vote. And that's what happens to the taxpayers' interests when they collide with the lobbies in the back rooms of Congress.

V

═══════

STRAIGHT
AND
NARROW

═══════

14

THE GOOD GUYS

1. Telling Right from Wrong

Most of the members of the Senate and House who have
made their way into this book are, to one degree or another,
villains in the drama of government. They are self-seekers
who put personal aggrandizement above public service, whose
independence has been bartered away for the rewards of private interests, who wait eagerly for the next temptation. These
men are a minority in Congress, but, unfortunately, they often
attract more attention than the honest, hardworking members.
Nor is it always easy to separate the Congressional wheat from
the chaff. The sellout one day may be the holdout the next. For
even the worst rascals on Capitol Hill have their moments of
righteousness.

One of the Senate's most conscientious members—J. William Fulbright, D-Ark.—votes down the line for the oil and

gas interests. Talking privately to friends, he once explained apologetically that he could not be re-elected in Arkansas if he bumped his head against the powerful oil bloc. His likely successor would be the racial demagogue, Orval Faubus. "I am vain enough," said Fulbright, "to believe I make a better Senator than Faubus." Few reasonable men would disagree.

The first duty of every member, Representative Adam Clayton Powell once quipped, is to get himself re-elected. It would be difficult indeed for a Congressman to win re-election if he ignored the wishes of his constituents. But do the voters always know what is best for them? Edmund Burke, the great eighteenth-century English liberal, insisted that they do not, and he told them so in a classic letter to the electors of Bristol. "Your representative owes you, not his industry only," Burke declared, "but his judgment; and he betrays instead of serving you if he sacrifices it to your opinion."

A more typical legislator's view, perhaps, was expounded more recently by another liberal, Representative Emanuel Celler, D-N.Y., who observed that "the elected representative who *wholly* subordinates the selfish requirements of interest groups to the furtherance of abstract principle, who ignores the felt needs of people in *exclusive* pursuit of high ideals, falls as far short of fulfilling the legislative function as the legislator who sells his vote. And I must add that he enjoys a substantially poorer expectancy of survival in office."

Three years after Burke wrote his letter, Bristol denied him re-election to Parliament. Manny Celler's Brooklyn district has sent him to the House in every election since 1922.

The plain fact is that Congressmen are expected to serve some special interests. As the New York City Bar Association observed in its landmark 1960 study, "It is common to talk of the Farm Bloc or the Silver Senators. We would think odd a fishing-state Congressman who was not mindful of the interests of the fishing industry—though his campaign funds come in part from this source. This kind of representation is considered inevitable and, indeed, is generally applauded."

Thus it is possible for legislators, without loss of integrity, to represent the legitimate special interests of their constituencies. There remains a subtle, difficult-to-define line, of course, beyond which a conscientious Congressman doesn't press a local cause. Meanwhile, the good are sometimes damned along with the bad by the press and the public. Honest men in public life, who have made great personal sacrifice to serve the nation, can suffer from guilt by association. The good legislators deserve to be noticed; their rewards are too few. Two men of granite integrity who are entitled to public approbation have come to be known as the Damon and Pythias of the Senate.

2. *Mike Mansfield:*
The Painful Excercise of Power

Washington was coming to life. The cars and buses, converging on the bridges from Virginia and moving down the arteries out of the Maryland suburbs, were massing for an assault on the city streets. It was eight o'clock on a summer morning, and the sun was already poised to sear the tempers and the flesh of those whose offices were not air-conditioned.

At the Capitol, young law students and older, less ambitious men, in the uniforms of the Capitol's own patronage-staffed police force, took up their stations around the Senate and House office buildings to protect the parking spaces of the privileged from the plundering tourists. The side streets on Capitol Hill were still quiet, and the policemen could lounge against the marble buildings.

Down in the basement of the New Senate Office Building, the food handlers in the cafeteria roused themselves to wait on a tall, lean man who pushed his tray past the steam tables. He chose the items for his breakfast with care, then walked across the big room to a table where a smaller man was already seated. The newcomer carefully removed the food from his tray and aligned it on the table; he murmured a greeting to the other man, who answered without looking up from his morning paper.

This rather cold ritual is one of the bonds between two of the Senate's warmest friends. The man pulling out his chair to sit at the table was Mike Mansfield of Montana, the Democratic Leader. Across the table, behind the paper, was George Aiken of Vermont, a Republican. Their prestige bridges both parties.

The Democrat from the West, spare and solemn, towered over the Republican from the East, who is short and gnarled and has an elfish twinkle. The two have been breakfast partners for years. Both feel the necessity to be at work in their offices by seven in the morning, handling the problems of their states before the rest of Congress arrives to work on the problems of the nation.

As the Majority Leader, Mike Mansfield is as different from his predecessor, Lyndon Johnson, as ginger ale is from a martini. When LBJ ran the Senate, he *was* the Senate, wheeling and dealing, delighting in his triumphs and grousing over the smallest obstacles in his grand plans. Mansfield believes in putting on the pressure only when it is needed, in treating the 99 other Senators as individuals. He has been criticized on occasion for not pushing the Senate hard enough, for not squeezing out legislation fast enough. He is one of those rarest of politicians who care nothing for power or publicity. He is guided only by conscience and duty, and in politics the demands of the one do not always coincide with the demands of the other.

The power and prestige of his job are trappings that Mansfield never sought and never dreamed of possessing in his bleak, difficult youth. He was born in 1903 of Irish immigrant parents in the Hell's Kitchen section of Manhattan and was sent off at age three to live with relatives in Great Falls, Montana, after his mother died.

In the Senate, Mansfield is known for his unwavering honesty, but he admits to at least one deceit of major proportions in his youth. At fourteen, he lied about his age to go to sea with the Navy during World War I. This made him the youngest man from Montana to serve in that war. He later enlisted in the Army and Marines, never rose above private, and at nineteen was rich in military adventures but poor in the experiences that help men earn their way in the world. He went back to Montana and wrestled a living from the earth as a mucker in a copper mine. Somehow it was discovered that the tough, lean young man had the talent and intelligence for leadership, and he was promoted to work with the mine engineers. Soon the dropout was hungry to expand his knowledge.

Mansfield was accepted at the Montana School of Mines and later transferred to Montana State University. He was thirty when he graduated; he also received a high-school-equivalence certificate at the same time. In his senior year at Montana State, he married Maureen Hayes, a schoolteacher who had been helping him make up his high-school English courses.

With his B.A. degree, Mansfield became a history instructor at Montana State and, after classes, worked on his master's degree. He specialized in Latin American and Far Eastern history, and his students found inspiration in their soft-spoken professor, whose gentle manner was but the moss on a character of granite. A corps of students rang doorbells and passed out literature for Mansfield when he ran against Republican Representative Jeannette Rankin, the only member of Congress to vote against America's entry in both World War I and World War II.

Installed in the House, Mansfield acquired none of the airs, mostly hot, that inflate many newcomers to Congress with self-importance. Once, when his daughter Ann was a student at the swank Marymount School, Mansfield dropped by to pick her up after a high-school party. Other fathers were there, and their clothes reflected their economic success. Mansfield was wearing a wool shirt and a crumpled hat. "Who is that?" one pompous parent whispered. "That," he was told, "is Congressman Mansfield. He never tries to impress anybody."

In 1952 Mansfield ran for the seat of Senator Zales Ecton, R-Mont., a dull, droning ultraconservative. Ecton brought in Senator Joseph McCarthy, R-Wis., then at the height of his influence, to help deflect Mansfield's challenge. McCarthy trotted out his anti-Communist clichés. Mansfield, he said, was "either stupid or a dupe," and McCarthy accused him of "Communist-coddling practices." Never ashamed of dirty politics, which he considered part of the game, McCarthy greeted Mansfield with a slap on the back in the Senate after Ecton was beaten. "How are things in Montana these days, Mike?" he asked jovially. Mansfield eased himself out of McCarthy's grasp and answered coldly, "Much better since you left."

The likable Mansfield rose quickly in the Senate's inner circle. Johnson, looking for a balance wheel, picked him to be Majority Whip in 1957. When Johnson moved on to the Vice Presidency four years later, Mansfield moved up to the leadership.

Mansfield seldom finds party policy a block to expounding his own views on foreign policy. On several occasions his words on Vietnam—one of his fields of expertise since he made three trips to Indochina during the wars against the French—have been interpreted by Senate watchers as shifts in Administration policy. There was no such reflection; Mansfield was merely speaking his mind.

Speaking his mind is one of the few luxuries in which Mansfield frequently indulges. He makes his decisions, however, with great gravity. He never speaks on a subject without long and deep thought. He never rushes into any action. All important decisions are committed to paper. When he is called to the White House with other Congressional leaders, he pulls out a written statement and reads from it.

Some men seek power, enjoy and employ it. Some have power thrust upon them and accept it only from a sense of duty. Frequently they find its exercise painful in the extreme. Such a man is Mike Mansfield.

3. George Aiken: Deeds to Match His Words

George Aiken has been an elected official—first as a state legislator, then governor for two terms, then Senator—since 1931, but the road that runs past the house he has owned in Putney, Vermont, since the 1920s is still unpaved. That is a measure of the importance Aiken attaches to the trust Vermont's voters have placed in him. In the years since he came to the Senate in 1941, Aiken has been independent from every pressure except his people back home.

His independence and his integrity are such that his voice is heard in both parties, and he does not hesitate to endorse Democratic programs that he believes are worth while. "As Republicans, let us not be afraid of the 'me too' charge which is sometimes leveled against us," Aiken lectured. "If a Democrat says we need better health, I am not going to come out for poorer health just to disagree with him."

In Washington, Aiken has lived frugally on his Senate salary, staying in a $150-a-month, one-bedroom apartment across the street from the Senate Office Building. Until she died in 1966, Beatrice Aiken, his wife for 52 years, stayed home in Putney to help keep the expenses down, waiting for Aiken's frequent visits to Vermont. Without her, Aiken's loneliness magnified, and he remarried in mid-1967. His bride was Lola Pierotti, who had been his assistant for many years.

Aiken was born in 1892 and grew up on a farm where, he admits, he spent much of his free time admiring the beauty of wildflowers. He was one of the first to engage in the commercial cultivation of them and published a book on the subject, *Pioneering with Wildflowers,* in 1933. It was dedicated to "Peter Rabbit in the hope that flattery will accomplish what traps and guns have failed to do and that the little rascal will let our plants alone."

Peter Rabbit paid no heed to Aiken, but a lot of people did. Aiken has maintained the New England virtue of terseness, yet his few public words are almost all worth while. In 1953 he issued a statement on prospective Presidential candidates that was both concise and explosive. Said Aiken, "How often do we hear people say, 'I'm supporting So-and-so for President because he'll do the things I want done.' What so many overlook is the fact that the President is not elected to do the things which we as individuals want done—nor even to do the things which he himself would like to do.

"In our kind of government, it is the duty of the President as Commander-in-Chief of the armed forces to protect the security of the United States; to conduct our affairs with foreign countries through the making of treaties and appointments of ambassadors; to appoint judges and other Federal officials; and to administer laws and carry out programs as determined by the Congress. As I see it, it is far more important to elect a person of integrity and ability to the Presidency—one who will conscientiously perform the duties of the office as prescribed by the Constitution—than it is to elect one on the premise that he may agree with our particular viewpoint."

Aiken's deeds are as good as his words. He is consulted by President Johnson more often than any other Republican except the Senate GOP Leader, Everett Dirksen, and his advice is as terse as Dirksen's is overdrawn. Aiken sometimes feels dismayed, however, when Johnson does not follow his counsel. "If Mr. Johnson did what I've told him," Aiken once said, eyes twinkling, but only in half jest, "he'd be the best President in history."

Aiken does not feel, of course, that his word is infallible. He has not been afraid to support programs that go against his original positions, and once defended Franklin Roosevelt's

New Deal before the Republican National Committee. He urged his party "to accept in general the social aims which the opposing party has had the wisdom to adopt, but has lacked the ability to put into efficient operation."

In 1954 Aiken gave up the 13 years' seniority he held on the Senate Labor and Public Welfare Committee to take a post on the Foreign Relations Committee. His purpose: if he had not taken the seat, it would have gone by default to Joe McCarthy, a man for whom Aiken had contempt.

Aiken is one of the Senate's old men, but he is still vigorous physically and mentally. His views on Vietnam are frequently a rallying cry for today's college students. "I was against bombing up there in the first place, and I was against the resumption," he said. "There are about three times as many men infiltrating into South Vietnam now as there were before the bombing started, and the supplies have increased also."

Aiken and Mansfield do not always agree on the measures before Congress, but they are seldom at odds about each other. Said Mansfield, "George Aiken is probably the most solid man in Congress. He has honesty, humaneness and, above all, independence." Aiken showed all of these traits when he returned from his 1967 honeymoon and his bride asked for his advice on groceries. "I think I'd like some peanut butter," the Senator told her.

"Well, how do you like your peanut butter—with jelly?" questioned Mrs. Aiken.

The Senator thought a moment before answering. "I don't know," he said. "I've never been able to afford the luxury of peanut butter and jelly both."

4. Profiles in Integrity

Political courage is not always easy to measure. Sometimes it takes more courage to compromise than to cling stubbornly to a principle. For without compromise, our democratic processes would become brittle and shatter. It would also be naïve to suppose a politician could stay in office without making some concessions to campaign contributors, local interests, pressure groups and party leaders. No member of Congress, however independent, can wholly escape the political pressures. Perhaps the true test of a Congressman's worth is not only the courage to stand up for his convictions but the common sense to compromise when it will serve the general good.

Admittedly, the line between courage and compromise is difficult to draw. To what extent, for example, should a Senator from du Pont-dominated Delaware champion the interests of du Pont? For Senator John Williams, R-Del., this has not been just a rhetorical question. He has supported the du Pont interests when it benefited his state. But he has refused to accept the notion that what is good for du Pont is necessarily good for Delaware.

Consider the 12-year antitrust battle that culminated in a court order to du Pont to divest itself of $3.5 billion worth of company-owned General Motors stock. Hardest hit was the du Pont family, who faced taxation at the going rate on the income from the forced sale. For anyone in the du Ponts' tax bracket, this meant many millions. But the company easily persuaded Delaware's Senator J. Allen Frear, Jr., to introduce a bill fixing the tax on the sale of those General Motors shares at a gentle 7 percent. Both Frear, a Democrat, and Williams, a Republican, conveniently sat on the Senate Finance Committee. Frear naturally voted for his bill. When the tally clerk got to Williams' name, the committee was split, 7 to 7. Williams took a deep breath and voted against the bill. "It would have put the stockholders in the position of making money by losing a court case," he explained later.

Texans still do not vote to cut the oil depletion allowance, just as West Virginians do not vote against bituminous coal. A few courageous Southerners, however, have risked antagonizing their constituents to support civil rights bills. The evening before the showdown on the voting-rights bill, Representative Hale Boggs, D-La., told a few friends he had decided to vote for the bill. His daughter "Cokie" walked over to her father, kissed him and said she was proud of him. "I'm not only going to vote for it," said Boggs, "I'm going to make a speech for it."

Next day, his colleague from Louisiana, Representative Joe D. Waggonner, Jr., leaped into the debate on the side of the segregationists and declared that Louisiana was being maligned by this legislation and that there was little discrimination in his state. Boggs, born in Mississippi, reared in Louisiana, rose to reply. "I wish," he declared, "I could stand here as a man who loves his state, who has spent every year of his life in Louisiana since he was five years old, and say there has not been any discrimination. But unfortunately, it is not so. . . . I shall support this bill because I believe the fundamental right to vote must be a part of this great experiment in human progress under freedom, which is America."

There are other cases on record of Congressmen who opposed powerful interests in their own states. Senator Frank Church, D-Idaho, took on the local lumber and mining barons who were bitterly against a bill to create wilderness areas. Representative Edith Green, D-Ore., once voted to build a hospital in Alaska instead of Oregon because the need was greater there. Senator Thomas Kuchel, R-Calif., whose home state probably has more extremists per capita than any other in the nation, led the Senate crusade against the right wing. When the right-wing claque circulated an unspeakable smear against him, accusing him of sexual perversion, he was told he would only advertise the charge by answering it. Yet he dared to fight back, and he forced the culprits to eat their filthy words in court. They were convicted.

Unaccountably, Oregon legislators seem more concerned than most about higher standards on Capitol Hill. Senator Maurine Neuberger, elected to her husband's seat after his death in 1960, carried on his campaign for disclosure of Congressmen's income, assets, liabilities and stock-market trading. Senator Wayne Morse, that free-lance dissenter on practically every question, has been pushing for disclosure since 1947 and regularly makes his own financial dealings public. And Mrs. Green has fought for conflict-of-interest reform in the House, where it has even fewer friends, if that is possible, than in the Senate. But Mrs. Green, wary of simple answers, raised some hard questions on the House floor:

What are the proper limits on the power of a Member of Congress to appoint his staff from among his family? What kinds of outside employment and income are compatible with what kinds of committee assignments? How far should a Member of Congress go in voting on matters in which he has a personal stake?

Now I suppose that no one believes a Member of Congress should disqualify himself from taking part in a housing bill because he owns a house. But what if he is president or a member of the board of directors of a local urban renewal agency or a large residential construction company?

No Member of Congress should disqualify himself from taking part in legislation involving oil or gas because his house is heated by gas or oil. But what if he is a major stockholder or officer in a gas transmission line, or the owner of a dozen oil wells?

No Member of Congress should disqualify himself from taking part in legislation involving our major carriers because he travels to and from his state to Washington by train. But what if he might sit on a committee that deals with this legislation and at the same time maintains connections with a law firm that has a major railroad as a client?

No Member should disqualify himself from shaping commodity legislation because he owns a farm or a ranch. But what if this Member serves as a consultant to an economic interest that seeks to knead and shape the legislation to its own ends?

Members of Congress should not disqualify themselves from accepting campaign contributions or speaking out on legislation before professional and trade organizations. But what if the speaking fee received is so inordinately large that it points to the conclusion the fee is, in effect, a campaign contribution not reported?

What of the Member of Congress who is defeated for election and then suddenly evidences during his lame-duck period a great interest in visiting the countries of the world? Is there legitimate work to justify such an expenditure?

And what of the Member who, ostensibly traveling abroad on Congressional business, spends more time seeing night sights than sighting on the business at hand, and using taxpayers' dollars or counterpart funds while doing so, and later has printed at taxpayers' expense a voluminous, vacuous account of his travels?

What of the Member who may represent business interests on a retainer fee, and also is required by committee assignment to vote on tax bills ostensibly with complete objectivity?

Where should the lines be drawn?

The Congressmen who have disqualified themselves from voting under House Rule VIII because of "a direct pecuniary or personal interest" could caucus in the back of the Minority Leader's limousine without having to pull down the jump seats. The standard alibi for voting on matters involving an obvious conflict of interest is that it's not fair to deprive constituents of a voice on a vital issue simply because their elected Representative has a stake in it himself. New York's Senator Jacob Javits, a liberal Republican with a thriving law practice, objects to disqualification on purely practical grounds. "We in Congress vote on everything under the sun," he told the Senate. "If we tried to disqualify ourselves because of any relationship we have to any of these matters we vote on, we probably would sit here mute and voteless most of the time."

Still, some Congressmen do disqualify themselves on some issues. One is Representative James Scheuer, D-N.Y., who has built urban renewal projects in Washington and half a dozen other cities and is one of the country's ranking experts on housing. When he entered Congress, however, Scheuer put his real-estate holdings in an irrevocable trust for his wife and children. He turned down a seat on the Banking and Currency Committee, which handles housing legislation. And when bills dealing with Federal housing programs came up for a vote, Scheuer cited Rule VIII and voted present. Senator William Fulbright, to cite another example, abstains from voting on postal-rate bills because his family owns a small newspaper in Fayetteville, Arkansas.

Integrity in Congress, of course, knows no party, no political creed, no regional boundary. Probably the most far-out extremist in the Senate, Strom Thurmond, R-S.C., is a model of personal integrity. After he was elected to the Senate in a 1954 write-in campaign, he dissolved a $200,000-a-year law partnership, severed his connection with the Aiken Federal Savings and Loan Corporation, and sold his few stock holdings. He lives on his Senate salary, though this has meant a reduced standard of living. Even his speaking fees wind up in a loan fund for needy students at Winthrop College in Rock Hill, South Carolina.

Few are as scrupulous, however, as Representative Carl Perkins, D-Ky., who once learned that a piece of personal mail had been franked out of his office by mistake and was receiving free postal handling reserved for official mail. He ran down the letter in the House post office and attached a five-cent stamp to it. Perkins also flatly refuses to accept campaign contributions from anyone he has helped in Washington—a degree of self-denial almost unheard of on Capitol Hill. The decision has cost him contributions as high as $500. It has also given him some delicate problems in etiquette. After he helped a disabled World War I veteran get a disability allowance, the pensioner gratefully knitted a handsome white shawl and brought it to Perkins' office in his wheelchair. Perkins was out of the office when the gift was delivered. When he saw it, he was touched by the sentiment, but he stuck to his rule. "We'll have to send it back with a note of thanks," he told an aide. "I did a favor for that nice old gentleman."

Ex-Senator Paul Douglas made it a practice to send back all gifts worth more than $2.50. Formerly a university economics professor, he enlisted as a private in the Marine Corps during World War II and was wounded twice during some of the Pacific's most ferocious fighting. Yet he refused to accept the disability pension he earned on Okinawa and Peleliu because "it was obvious that the wounds did not interfere with my ability to serve." To help maintain the expense of two homes, he gave lectures and wrote articles for pay. But if he spoke before a partisan political audience—a labor union, for instance—he did not keep the fee. Only university and nonpartisan checks went into the Douglas household account. "For the most part," he said, "this is clean money."

It is a sad commentary on the American political system that men like Douglas, towers of integrity, who refuse to bend their principles, have a low survival rate in Congress. One of the factors that defeated Douglas in 1966, ironically, was a last-minute charge by his opponent, Charles Percy, that Douglas was engaging in a smear campaign. The basis for the accusation was the circulation by the Douglas camp of a civil rights position paper that Percy had passed out in Chicago's ghettos. Douglas' campaigners, realizing that the white backlash was hurting their candidate in a number of white areas, sent copies of Percy's pamphlet to the white suburbs. "These tactics represent a deplorable attempt to appeal to both racial hatred and bigotry," Percy complained loudly.

The hulking, white-maned Douglas was shocked and shaken. "Never before in my eighteen years in the United States Senate has anyone questioned my integrity," he replied sadly. His answer never caught up with the charge, and Percy took over Douglas' Senate seat. The change was a disappointment to those who for so many years had depended upon Douglas for moral leadership.

Another stalwart left Congress in 1966, but his departure was of his own choosing over a question of conscience. He was Charles Weltner, D-Ga., who cut off his promising career in the House rather than endorse the candidacy of extremist Lester Maddox for governor. Maddox had become a national symbol of defiance to the civil rights laws by brandishing an ax handle against Negro citizens who attempted to eat in his Atlanta restaurant.

If Weltner's decision not to support his party's candidate came as a surprise to some, it was typical of the man. He would not compromise a philosophy that had been growing since he first became interested in politics in 1954—the same year the Supreme Court outlawed segregation in public schools. He explained his view: "If the South is to stop losing and start winning, our first goal must be to close the 'Southern gap'—to eliminate all disparities in education, income, public services, health standards and economic opportunity. The Federal Government offers the major opportunity for closing the Southern gap. Realistic Southerners will acknowledge this. And their own realizations must be reflected in the representation they send to Congress. If the South is to win, it must see that all levels of government perform at maximum efficiency."

The Congress has been the making or breaking of many men. Some Representatives have already formed their political philosophies before they arrive. Others become equivocators and vote against their consciences for political advantage or personal gain. A Congressman's first duty is to his constituents, but his interests cannot remain purely regional in the face of larger national problems.

Congress was not entirely the making of Charles Weltner.

His philosophy had evolved over the years from the time of the Supreme Court school decision, when he could say blandly, "There was no race problem—at least so far as I was concerned, Negroes were merely poor." Ten years later, when he arrived in Congress, the young Southerner was saying, "The South can never attain equality as long as one-fifth of her people live in poverty. The entire economy of the South will continue to suffer because of Negro unemployment, Negro poverty, and Negro dependency. To close the Southern gap will require the elimination of those practices which have produced and preserved wide disparities between whites and Negroes." This was a new breed of Southerner speaking.

Throughout his career, Weltner had backed all civil rights legislation "as precepts of law." On July 2, 1964, when the civil rights bill was returned to the House for final amendment, it was time, at last, for his conscience to speak. Earlier that year he had voted against it. "I still was reluctant to accept the means adopted by the bill to secure equal rights. Yet the goal of equal rights was something I had long ago accepted, and found in accord with my understanding of the Constitution."

The House was crowded the day of his excruciating decision, with the galleries jammed to capacity. Carl Vinson, the senior Representative from Georgia, approached him. "I understand you are planning to vote for this bill?" he asked. When Weltner admitted he was, Vinson, who had served in the House for 50 years, scowled: "Well, profiles in courage and all that. But I hate to see you throw away a promising career."

"He spoke out of genuine concern for me," Weltner recalled, "for which I shall ever be grateful. Vinson returned a few minutes later. 'I understand you are planning to *speak* for this bill?' 'Yes, sir,' I said. He fixed me with a keen eye, looking down his fierce nose. Somewhat sadly, and wonderingly, he shook his head and moved off."

Weltner's two-minute speech in favor of the bill urged Americans and Southerners to cast their lot with the law of the land and the "new reality." "I would urge that we at home now move on to the unfinished task of building a new South. We must not remain forever bound to another lost cause." Reaction at home was swift and violent. It was an election year, and Weltner was campaigning hard. Everywhere he went, he was asked the same question: "Why did you support the civil rights bill?" He recalled that at one political rally an acquaintance came over to him and said, "Charlie, when you voted for that bill, were you prepared to be thrown out of office over it?" Weltner said he was prepared for such an event. "Well, you are a nice fellow personally, and you have a lot of friends. But we are going to do everything we possibly can to see that you never go back to Congress."

Weltner saw that election campaign as more than the routine biennial ritual. In his eyes, this election would answer the question of whether a Southern district would try to accept the new way. "In 1964 the people at home came face to face with the race issue," said Weltner, and he was returned to Congress.

Then in 1966 he made his deepest commitment to conscience, and dropped out rather than declare party loyalty to Maddox.

These are only a few of the men in Congress who have put their consciences ahead of their bank balances and even their political careers. There are many others who deserve mention. One who has fought for higher Congressional standards is Representative Charles Bennett, D-Fla. To quiet the public wrath over the Adam Clayton Powell case, the House finally accepted his proposal in 1967 to establish a House Ethics Committee. But Speaker John McCormack quietly euchred Bennett out of the chairmanship and put a safer man, Representative C. Melvin Price, D-Illinois, in charge. The Speaker made it clear he wanted no embarrassing investigations.

The House was always willing, of course, to pay lip service to Bennett's ideals. In 1958 it adopted a "Code of Ethics for Government Service," which he introduced. This code—a kind of bureaucrat's Ten Commandments—put Congress firmly on record against sin. Anyone in government service, it declared firmly, should "engage in no business with the Government, either directly or indirectly, which is inconsistent with the conscientious performance of his governmental duties." Furthermore, a Government employee should "expose corruption wherever discovered." When four employees exposed corruption in the office of Senator Thomas Dodd eight years later, Speaker McCormack, who had voted for the code, ordered one of them fired from his new House job. Meanwhile the Speaker has arranged for copies of the code, printed up in gold, red, white and blue, to go out by the car-load from the House mailing room.

The code's author, Congressman Bennett, is a World War II Silver Star winner who was crippled by polio while a guerrilla fighter in the Philippines. Like Paul Douglas, he refuses to accept his disability pension. He gave up his law practice when he entered Congress in 1949 and has not missed a House roll call since June 4, 1951. Although his Jacksonville constituents are among the least progressive in any big Southern city on racial matters, Bennett voted in 1965 for the voting-rights bill because "this is a question of basic American rights, not of mixing."

In short, Charles Bennett is an honest, courageous Congressman who is willing to go beyond the late Senator Claude Swanson's first two maxims for polifical success and follow the third. Swanson, a Virginia Democrat who served in Franklin Roosevelt's Cabinet for a time, said this was his formula: "First, be bold as a lion on a rising tide. Second, when the water reaches the upper deck, follow the rats. And third, and most important, when in doubt, do right."

For many members of Congress, the third maxim gets lost under the pressure of a tremendous work load and unrelenting demands on time and purse. It is not easy to recognize that you're doing wrong when everybody else seems to be doing it too. The men cited in this chapter have set an example under pressure. The question is: can the rest of Congress be persuaded to abide by the same high standards?

15

THE AGONY OF REFORM

1. *Our Lethargic Press*

The great majority of Senators and Representatives serving in the United States Congress, we believe, are honorable men. But too often they let themselves be victimized by a system that puts almost irresistible pressures on men in high places who will do almost anything they can get away with to stay there. The costs of getting elected in the first place, of maintaining residences in Washington as well as in their home districts, of traveling constantly, of going back to the people regularly for votes of confidence in the form of re-election—all these produce heavy burdens on talented men who might well be earning substantially more money if they were not serving in government. Yet many Congressmen do manage to live meticulously within their means. It is a pity that these upright men are blemished by the dishonesty or the clearly compromising practices of the rest of Congress. However unjust such guilt by association may be, though, there is no condoning the remarkable lethargy that afflicts Congress when it is suggested that Congress must set its house in order itself or face the continuing scorn of the public.

Traditionally the press has been charged with the job of monitoring the ethical conduct of public officials in this country. But the performance of the press as a watchdog has left a good deal to be desired. Its lack of diligence in this regard is perhaps best illustrated by newspaper coverage of personal expense funds raised to help two prominent Senators in recent years—Richard Nixon and Thomas Dodd. More money was contributed to Dodd's personal fund between 1958 and 1967 than to Nixon's while he was running for Vice President in 1952, but the principle involved was similar. The punishment, however, was not. Dodd was censured by the Senate despite an emotional appeal to his peers. Nixon made a similar emotional appeal to the American people on television, and was elected Vice President of the United States. Probably the basic reason for the differing outcomes to the cases was the way the press reported the stories.

An account of Nixon's $18,000 personal expense fund, contributed by 76 of his friends, was first published September 18, 1952, by the New York *Post* and the Los Angeles *Daily News,* both with Democratic editorial policies (the latter is now defunct). A revelation of this kind would normally have rocked the nation. No such slush fund had ever figured in a Presidential race. Yet Midwest newspapers, almost all of them Republican in their editorial affiliation, smothered the story so completely that the general public scarcely understood the seriousness of the charge against the Republican candidate for Vice President. The Omaha *World-Herald*, for instance, played the story on page 56 and used a headline that made it appear that Nixon was the beneficiary of an insurance trust fund.

With the exception of the St. Louis *Post-Dispatch*, a Democratic paper, no newspaper subsequently dug into the ramifications of the Nixon fund and demonstrated the benefits that had been received by those who secretly contributed to it. Under the rules of Congress, a member is at liberty to help his constituents but at no time is he entitled to receive remuneration for that help. On the contrary, there is a clear-cut statute making it a criminal offense for him to receive any remuneration for any representation he makes before the United States Government. A member of the Congress is a servant of the Government, paid by it and not by private individuals. He is required, furthermore, to serve all his constituents without favor, not merely those who secretly contribute funds to help defer his expenses. But the Nixon case was marked by gratitude expressed in the form of campaign contributions for favors done and votes cast while he served in Congress.

Dana Smith, who collected the $18,000 fund, earlier had a personal tax case before the Justice Department involving a $500,000 tax refund that he was demanding from the Government. Nixon sent a member of his office staff to the Justice Department's tax division to apply pressure on Smith's behalf. In the summer of 1952 the same Dana Smith lost $4,000 on a gambling spree in a Havana nightclub, gave his check for that amount to the nightclub owner, and then stopped payment on the check. The owner sued to collect, whereupon Nixon wrote the American Ambassador in Cuba and asked that he intervene on behalf of his friend Dana Smith. The Ambassador replied that protecting gamblers was not among his official duties.

Among the 76 millionaires who kicked in to the Nixon fund were 15 oilmen, 11 real-estate executives and a cross section of bankers, milk-products men and munitions and armaments contractors. All had had heavy stakes in legislation on which Nixon had voted. On issues of concern to the oilmen who contributed to his fund, Nixon voted their way down the line: against cutting the 27½ percent oil depletion allowance, for the oil companies' basing point bill (facilitating price-fixing in monopoly-dominated industries and promoting concentration of industry), and for the tidelands oil bill. Nixon even sent out literature in favor of the tidelands bill under his Senate frank on behalf of the oil companies. Similarly, Nixon voted on housing bills in a way that obviously pleased his fund contributors from the building and real-estate industry—in favor of reducing the number of public housing units provided (from 50,000 to 5,000 units in one bill), in favor of speeding up the expiration of wartime rent controls by four months, in favor of giving local communities the option to impose or lift rent controls around military installations and defense plants, and in favor of an amendment he himself introduced to a defense bill in 1951 aimed at sidetracking public housing. Some of his votes, it is safe to say, contributed to the decay of big cities only now being recognized as a national crisis.

The facts regarding the conflicts of interest were all available to the press during the 1952 election; but American newspapers, of which 80 percent are Republican and which later tracked down Adam Clayton Powell, a Negro and a Democrat, like a pack of bloodhounds in full cry, were not interested in serving as watchdog for the operations of a white Republican Senator running for Vice President.

The fact that Nixon got away with his $18,000 personal expense fund, due in large part to the failure of the press to put the fund in proper perspective, may have contributed to complacency in Connecticut regarding the Dodd funds and to the naïveté of Senator Charles Percy, R-Ill., in proposing a $100,000 private fund to pay his alleged office expenses. The disclosure of that fund during his first year in the Senate, in contrast to the efficiency with which former Senator Paul Douglas represented the state of Illinois on his own modest income, may have seriously dampened Percy's chance of national leadership. The Percy fund was officially dismantled in January 1968.

Lethargy on the part of the press undoubtedly contributed to another bizarre money-raising scheme in 1960 when the Nixon family was again involved in a flagrant conflict of interest. On October 25, as the Kennedy-Nixon campaign was moving down the homestretch, our "Washington Merry-Go-Round" column disclosed that Nixon's brother Don had received a $205,000 loan on December 10, 1956, from Howard

Hughes, the airplane manufacturer who was then chief stock-holder of Trans World Airlines. The loan, secured by a mortgage on Lot 10 on Whittier Boulevard in Whittier, California —a piece of real estate that no bank would have accepted as security for a loan of that size—was apparently never repaid. The Hughes Tool Company was an important defense contractor. TWA had applied for an extension of its route from the Philippines to Japan. Hughes himself faced an antitrust suit. And he had other problems, none of which were likely to become aggravated by the fact that the family of Richard Nixon, a man who might become President of the United States, was beholden to him financially.

Again, a large number of newspapers failed to exercise their role as watchdog for the public. Subsequently, New England newspapers selected three veteran newsmen—Norman Isaacs, editor of the Louisville *Courier-Journal,* Carl Lindstrom, former editor of the Hartford *Times* and author of the book *The Fading American Newspaper,* and Edward Rowse of the Washington *Post*—to survey why they were losing influence with the public. The panel picked the Nixon-Hughes loan story as a case in point and reported that of the 43 New England papers that normally run "Washington Merry-Go-Round," only three ran the column breaking the Hughes loan story—the Waterbury (Connecticut) *American,* the Springfield (Massachusetts) *Daily News,* and the Portsmouth (New Hampshire) *Herald.*

"There was no wire-service treatment of the loan story until late in the day of October 26," the editorial panel reported. The Associated Press lead was a strong denial of the column by Robert Finch, Nixon's Washington campaign manager, who called the story "an obvious political smear" and denied the loan was from Hughes. The United Press also carried Finch's denial but farther down in the story. Despite the availability of these two wire-service accounts, the three editors noted, 19 of the 43 papers being examined passed up the news story.

When the wire services carried a story on October 28 saying that the Justice Department denied that the loan to Donald Nixon was in any way linked to its having dropped an antitrust suit against the Hughes Tool Company, the Providence *Journal* headlined it: JUSTICE DEPARTMENT NAILS PEARSON

CHARGE. The Boston *American* headline read: WRITER HIT IN NIXON SMEAR TRY.

In a follow-up that was sent out for distribution October 27, "Washington Merry-Go-Round" charged that the Nixons had gone to great lengths to keep the Hughes loan a secret and to avoid paying capital gains taxes on the difference between the purchase price of the property in 1923, $4,000, and the $205,000 sale price taxable at 25 percent—or $50,250 in taxes. The Portsmouth *Herald* was the only New England newspaper to run the follow-up column.

In the panel's judgment, the matter of news censorship "passed beyond any debate stage on October 30 when the AP sent a dispatch from Los Angeles at 5:38 P.M. reporting that Donald Nixon had admitted that the $205,000 loan had originated from the Hughes Tool Company. But nothing of this could be located in nine of the [New England] morning papers." A later, fuller AP story, moved on October 30, reported that Finch admitted he was misinformed when he had at first denied that the loan came from Hughes. "The Finch story raises a problem," the panel of editors went on. "Twenty-two papers did not carry the first wire stories in which Finch denounced Pearson's charges. But what of the 21 newspapers which had carried the earlier Finch denials? Giving thoughtful weight to the principle of equity of news treatment, the committee can find no excuse to justify the omission of the October 30 Finch [admission] statement by these 21 newspapers."

Thus, here was a man running for President of the United States whose brother had received a loan of almost a quarter of a million dollars from a top Government contractor under circumstances no responsible bank would countenance, yet the majority of the Republican-owned newspapers in one thoroughly analyzed sector of the nation either suppressed the news or carried denials of the truth. Though Nixon is now back in the news, the newspapers again have not bothered to report that the Nixon family lot is now registered in the name of the Hughes Tool Company.

The story of Senator Dodd's personal expense fund in all its ramifications was aired rather fully by the press, but only after the Senate Ethics Committee swung into action. The wide press coverage presumably contributed to public pressure on the Senate to censure Dodd. The one place in the country where news of the case was suppressed was the Senator's home state of Connecticut, where the press is inclined to be Democratic in its leaning or to favor a local boy. Robert H. Yoakum, a Connecticut resident and frequent contributor to the *Columbia Journalism Review,* surveyed the press coverage of the Dodd case in Connecticut and concluded, "If ever a man had reason to be grateful to the press, that man is Thomas J. Dodd."

Yoakum, noting the indifference of the 1,400-man Washington press and broadcasting corps, reported that "in the three months from the first Pearson-Anderson column on January 24, 1966, until the Ethics Committee announced hearings on April 29, 1966, the Dodd employees [who offered evidence against the Senator] were interviewed by only two people: Sarah McClendon, representing some Texas newspapers, and James Canan of the Gannett Newspapers, which take in the Hartford *Times.*" The wire services were hardly more conscientious than the newspapers, Yoakum added, remarking that the UPI's dispatches "often sounded as though they had been processed in Dodd's office. 'For eight years, he has been one of the most respected members of the Senate,' a UPI background story reported inaccurately in April 1966, compounding the error later in the piece by referring to Dodd as '. . . a man respected for his views on foreign affairs.' " His indignation rising, Yoakum wrote: "A Senator was up to his clavicle in ill-gained dollars, but the wire services were unable to spring even one of their 141 Washington reporters to interview the ex-employees who had the story."

The Connecticut press was even more dilatory, considering that the story had as pertinent a local angle as a news story can have. Two exceptions to the pattern were the Waterbury *American* and Charles B. Lenahan, publisher of the Hamden *Chronicle,* who wrote a column in mid-April of 1967 titled "Connecticut's Silent Press." Just back from a visit to Saigon, Lenahan wrote:

> . . . Senator Dodd was spread all over the front pages of such disparate papers as the Bangkok *World,* the Saigon *Post,* Hong Kong's *South China News,* and Tokyo's *Ashai Evening News.* This was a bigger story in the English language press of the Far East than it evidently was in the Connecticut press.

This is a condition that has existed from the beginning of the Dodd revelations. . . . There is no doubt that the [Connecticut] state press has held back on the Dodd story. The question is why. . . .

Whatever the reason, the newspaper-reading public of the state has been subjected to a remarkable example of nonreporting, of quite self-conscious evasion of an important public matter.

Calling Connecticut editors to find out why they had failed to delve into the story, to interview the principals, to write indignant editorials demanding a speedier and broader Senate investigation or to investigate whether state laws had been violated, Yoakum got no satisfaction. "Connecticut's oldest newspaper, the Hartford *Courant,* was as spry as its age [203 years] in reporting the Dodd case," Yoakum observed. "The *Courant* maintains a full-time Washington correspondent, Robert D. Byrnes, who has been with the paper for over 40 years and in Washington about 25. Byrnes broke no new ground, however, not even bothering to interview the employees who defected. The home office did no better. Local angles were multitudinous—Dodd's home office is there, so is his law firm, and so are several industries with whom Dodd traded favors, not the smallest of which is insurance—but the *Courant* missed it all."

By all odds the most astonishing conflict-of-interest case to be ignored by the press in recent years involved President Eisenhower. The conflict involved gifts to his farm in Gettysburg and the way the upkeep of the farm was handled.

Fletcher Knebel in the Des Moines *Register* carefully listed the numerous gifts presented to the Eisenhower farm, including a John Deere tractor with a radio in it, a completely equipped electric kitchen, landscaping improvements and ponies and Black Angus steers—worth, all together, more than half a million dollars. Compare this outpouring to the $1,200 deepfreeze—and the resulting uproar over it—given to President Truman by a Milwaukee friend of General Harry Vaughn. But no newspaper dug into the highly compromising fact that the upkeep of the Eisenhower farm was paid for by three oilmen—W. Alton Jones, chairman of the executive committee of Cities Service; B. B. (Billy) Byars of Tyler, Texas, and George E. Allen, director of some 20 corporations and a heavy investor in oil with Major Louey Kung, nephew of Chiang Kai-shek. They signed a strictly private lease agreement, under which they were supposed to pay the farm costs and collect the profits. Internal Revenue, after checking into the deal, could find no evidence that the oilmen had attempted to operate the farm as a profitable venture. Internal Revenue concluded that the money the oilmen poured into the farm could not be deducted as a business expense but had to be reported as an outright gift. Thus, by official ruling of the Internal Revenue Service, three oilmen gave Ike more than $500,000 at the same time he was making decisions favorable to the oil industry. The money went for such capital improvements as: construction of a show barn, $30,000; three smaller barns, about $22,000; remodeling of a schoolhouse as a home for John Eisenhower, $10,000; remodeling of the main house, $110,000; landscaping of 10 acres around the Eisenhower home, $6,000; plus substantial outlays for the staff including a $10,000-a-year farm manager.

How the money was paid is revealed in a letter dated January 28, 1958, and written from Gettysburg by General Arthur S. Nevins, Ike's farm manager. Addressed to George E. Allen in Washington and B. B. Byars in Tyler, Texas, it began, "Dear George and Billy" and discussed the operation of the farm in some detail. It said, in part:

> *New subject*—The funds for the farm operation are getting low. So would each of you also let me have your check in the usual amount of $2,500. A similar amount will be transferred to the partnership account from W. Alton Jones's funds.

In the left-hand corner of the letter is the notation that a carbon copy was being sent to W. Alton Jones.

During his eight years in the White House, Dwight Eisenhower did more for the nation's private oil and gas interests than any other President. He encouraged and signed legislation overruling a Supreme Court decision giving offshore oil to the Federal Government. He gave office space inside the White House to a committee of oil and gas men who wrote a report recommending legislation that would have removed natural-gas pipelines from control by the Federal Power Commission. In his appointments to the FPC, every commissioner Ike named except one, William Connole, was a pro-industry man. When Connole objected to gas price increases, Eisenhower eased him out of the commission at the expiration of his term.

On January 19, 1961, one day before he left the White House, Eisenhower signed a procedural instruction on the importation of residual oil that required all importers to move over and sacrifice 15 percent of their quotas to newcomers who wanted a share of the action. One of the major beneficiaries of this last-minute executive order happened to be Cities Service, which had had no residual quota till that time but which under Ike's new order was allotted about 3,000 barrels a day. The chief executive of Cities Service was W. Alton Jones, one of the three faithful contributors to the upkeep of the Eisenhower farm.

Three months later, Jones was flying to Palm Springs to visit the retired President of the United States when his plane crashed and Jones was killed. In his briefcase was found $61,000 in cash and travelers' checks. No explanation was ever offered—in fact none was ever asked for by the complacent American press—as to why the head of one of the leading oil companies of America was flying to see the ex-President of the United States with $61,000 in his briefcase. Yet the press resumed its vigilance in such matters and editorialized at great length when it was belatedly disclosed that Lyndon B. Johnson, a Democrat, received a hi-fi set for Christmas in 1959, when he was in the Senate, from the then Senate Secretary, Bobby Baker.

2. *"Left to Its Own Devices . . ."*

If the press cannot ultimately be relied upon to chronicle the misdeeds of Congressmen and political figures in general, the public must then depend on the Government itself to do the policing. The Justice Department would be the logical agency to carry out such a task, but the Justice Department is often ultra-political in its composition and might too easily be manipulated by political pressures radiating from the White House. There is a very real question, moreover, of jurisdiction. After Representative Thomas Johnson. D-Md., together with Representative Frank ("Everything Is Made for Love")

Boykin, D-Ala., was convicted in 1963 of conspiring to defraud the United States, the U.S. Court of Appeals for the Fourth Circuit (affirmed in 1966 by the United States Supreme Court) reversed the conviction on the ground that the evidence used against him violated the provision of the Constitution that "for any Speech or Debate in either House [Congressmen] shall not be questioned in any other place." Boykin, who did not appeal, was granted a pardon by his old friend President Johnson.

The court, however, and the American public, too, apparently, have little idea of how difficult it has been to persuade members of Congress to act against their colleagues. Examples of Congressional reluctance in this regard are legion.

The Senate was fully aware, for example, that its Republican colleague from Ohio, John W. Bricker, drew money from his Columbus law firm paid to it by the Pennsylvania Railroad largely if not solely because Bricker was the chairman of the Senate Commerce Committee and therefore in a position to influence railroad legislation. Yet no one in the Senate spoke up about it, even when Bricker was nominated for Vice President on the 1944 Republican ticket. Only when the acid-tongued Stephen Young, fellow Ohioan and a Democratic candidate for the Senate, publicized the facts about Bricker's law practice did the Senator receive a vote of nonconfidence from the electorate and go down to defeat.

Similarly, and as suggested earlier here (see Chapter Five), it was widely known that Senator Robert Kerr, D-Okla., was one of the wealthiest oil and gas men in the United States, yet he never hesitated to push legislation to exempt natural gas from Federal regulation and otherwise advance legislation in the interests of the oil and gas lobby. Yet only Senator Wayne Morse, D-Ore., spoke out against Kerr. Almost every member of the Senate knew that Tom Dodd was engaged in clearly questionable practices, yet only Senator J. William Fulbright, D-Ark., among all Dodd's 99 colleagues, raised his voice in protest before a full-dress hearing was forced on the Senate by a growing public clamor. And Fulbright's remarks were stricken from the *Congressional Record* because they were critical of a fellow Senator. What happened to Representative Don Edwards of California when he tried to call the House's attention to the blatant conflict of interest involving Representative William Miller, R-N.Y., and his efforts to promote the interests of the Lockport Felt Company was recounted in Chapter Eight. What is particularly interesting about the pressures brought to bear upon Edwards to keep quiet is that some of it was exerted by two of Edwards' fellow Democrats —John Rooney of New York and Chet Holifield of Edwards' own California delegation—who warned him that he would be blackballed on choice committee assignments and would never get his private bills passed if he persisted in his efforts to have Congressman Miller disciplined.

Just how anxious Congress is to avoid censuring its members—except for nonconforming non-members of the club— can be gathered from the responses made to letters of inquiry from the public following disclosures that Representative Mendel Rivers, chairman of the House Armed Services Committee, was a flagrant alcoholic who was hospitalized on several occasions because of excessive drinking. Without exception and regardless of party, members of the House rallied around Rivers. The authors surveyed Congressional opinion at the time of the disclosures and obtained samples of the letters that Congressmen wrote their constituents on the Rivers matter.

Representative Charles E. Bennett, D-Fla., who was campaigning for a code of ethics for the House of Representatives, wrote to John H. Wolters of Jacksonville, Florida: "As far as I know, Rivers has not had a drinking problem since I have been on his committee. I have never seen him take a drink or under its influence."

Representative James B. Utt, R-Calif., wrote to Douglas F. Davis of La Jolla, California: "I am very proud of Congressman Rivers as a man and as a distinguished chairman of the Armed Services Committee."

Representative William L. Scott, R-Va., wrote to Dr. Paul McFarlane of Broad Run, Virginia: "I have no personal knowledge of the allegations regarding the conduct of Mendel Rivers, and I do not think it would be prudent to form an opinion on the basis of hearsay."

Representative Charles M. Teague, R-Calif., wrote Merlin Kersey of Santa Paula, California: "I have no first-hand knowledge concerning these allegations."

Representative Walter S. Baring, D-Nev., was expansive in defending Rivers: "In all these years I have never seen Congressman Rivers out of order, quite the contrary. He is always a gentleman of the old school. You see the trouble with Congressman Rivers is that he has the nerve to speak his mind."

Said Representative Alton Lennon, D-N.C.: "I have never seen Mr. Rivers take a drink of any alcoholic type of beverage. . . . To my personal knowledge, there is no more able, hardworking or dedicated member of Congress than Mendel Rivers."

These, in the face of the facts about Rivers' drinking problem, almost universally known in Washington. Representative Alvin O'Konski, R-Wis., was a bit more candid in writing constituent Donald O. Peterson of Eau Claire: "Regarding the person you wrote about who is chairman of the Armed Services Committee, I am happy to state that for the past year and one-half he has completely stopped drinking, and I hope and pray that he will continue on this path." Alcoholics are automatically tabbed as security risks and not permitted to serve in the State or Defense departments or other sensitive agencies. But Mendel Rivers, in a similarly sensitive position as head of the House Armed Services Committee, enjoys the protection of the club.

"Left to its own devices," says Senator Clifford Case, R-N.J., "Congress will not take action to do the job of self-reform which urgently needs doing. Too many members have vested interests in maintaining the status quo."

Case is right. Yet a small band of Senators and Representatives, Case among them, is dedicated to the reform of campaign contribution laws and the overall improvement of ethics in Congress. Besides Case, the most avid reformers in the Congress are Senators Clark of Pennsylvania, Gore of Tennessee and Williams of Delaware. In the wake of the Bobby Baker, Tom Dodd and Adam Clayton Powell cases, many more Congressmen have begun to show belated concern. In 1962, when a bill providing a long-overdue overhaul of the Corrupt Practices Act was thrown into the Senate hopper, it did not even get a hearing. In August of 1966, after being pigeonholed for five years, the bill designated S. 2451 ("A Bill to Revise the Federal Election Laws, to Prevent Corrupt Practices in Federal Elections, and for Other Purposes") was dusted off by the Senate Rules and Administration Committee under the sponsorship of Senator Howard Cannon, the Nevada Democrat whose law firm represents a great many small airlines in his vast and underpopulated state. It was bumped along to the Senate floor without full hearings. A weak bill, it was, at least, a start. It reached the Senate shortly after President Johnson sent Congress his own election reform bill, plugging some of the loopholes in the Cannon bill. The Administration bill covered primary elections—a provision Southern Senators have opposed because in the South it is the primaries into which the heaviest campaign outlays are funneled. It also called for reports on contributions to political committees operating within a single state and demanded that members of Congress report all gifts of more than $100 and all sources of campaign income to the Secretary of the Senate or the Clerk of the House.

"Outrageous," fumed Senator Joseph Clark when Cannon pushed his own bill out of the Rules Committee ahead of the Administration's tougher bill.

"There is still plenty of time to hold hearings on the Administration's bill," replied Cannon.

"This year?" demanded Clark.

"I can't promise you that," replied the Senator from Nevada.

Clark's outrage was particularly directed to the vacillations of Rhode Island's Senator Claiborne Pell, a Newport aristocrat whose personal fortune would probably be found to compare favorably with Clark's if he ever consented to disclose it as Clark has his. After a remarkable demonstration of parliamentary befuddlement over whether hearings should be held on either the Cannon bill or the Administration bill or both—or neither—the Rules Committee voted 5 to 4, with Pell for and Clark against, to report out the Cannon bill. The Senate ignored it, and it died with the 89th Congress.

The House Administration Committee, meanwhile, held hearings on election reform, and the subcommittee on elections approved a reform bill exactly five weeks before Election Day that was so strong it startled the Senate. The subcommittee chairman, Representative Robert T. Ashmore, D-S.C., and its ranking minority member, Representative Charles E. Goodell, R-N.Y., introduced identical bills that would (1) amend the Corrupt Practices Act of 1925 to require that primary campaign spending be reported, (2) extend such a requirement not only to Congressional and Presidential primaries but to nominating conventions for Congressional and Presidential candidates, (3) require reports from any political committee that receives or spends more than $1,000 to help elect a candidate even if the committee operates within one state, (4) let the voters know—15 days and again five days *before* they cast their ballots—how much money has been spent during the campaign and how it was spent and what debts have been incurred, (5) set up a five-member Federal Elections Committee to receive such reports instead of the Secretary of the Senate and the Clerk of the House, with no more than three of the members belonging to the same party, (6) place such reports on file in Federal district courts all over the country instead of keeping them locked up in Washington, (7) force candidates to report all gifts and honorariums of $100 or more and require all Congressmen to do the same even in years when they are not running, (8) remove all ceilings from campaign spending on the theory it doesn't matter how much a campaign costs as long as everyone can see who is spending how much and for what, and (9) retain the $5,000 limit on individual campaign contributions.

"Although final action in this Congress is doubtful," Democrat Ashmore and Republican Goodell acknowledged, "we strongly believe the favorable reporting by the subcommittee lays a solid foundation for early and effective action in the next Congress." As predicted, the bill expired when Congress went home.

3. Progress

With the specter of the Dodd case hanging over them, members of the 90th Congress finally got down to producing reform legislation. The Senate Subcommittee on Privileges and Elections under Chairman Howard W. Cannon, D-Nev., brought out a new and strengthened Administration bill, the tightest bill to clear the Rules Committee in a decade.

The new bill contained most of the tougher provisions of the Administration's bill from the previous session and the Ashmore-Goodell House election reform plan, including (1) reporting on all intrastate political committees spending more than $1,000 in a given year, (2) filing of financial statements by candidates with the clerks of the U.S. district courts where the candidates reside, (3) a limit of $5,000 on the amount a contributor can give any candidate *or any of his committees*, thus doing away with multiple contributions to different committees raising funds for the same candidate, (4) a ban on political contributions from potential Government contractors, and (5) the reporting of campaign contributions and expenditures in party primaries and conventions. In September 1967 the bill passed the Senate by an 87-to-0 vote. Public indignation over the conduct of Senator Dodd thus brought the first strengthening of the Corrupt Practices Act in 42 years. (As this book is written, the bill is awaiting hearings in the House.)

But the single most important provision in the Administration's proposed law—mandatory disclosure of any gift received by any member of Congress valued at more than $100—was knocked out. "This [provision] is an impertinence and an outrage," stormed Senate Republican Leader Everett Dirksen, R-Ill. "It should be roundly defeated."

It was. The vote was 46 to 42. Its defeat demonstrates the consistent determination of the Congress to refuse to do what it demands of members of the executive branch—full disclosure of its assets, gifts, rewards and emoluments. The issue reached a critical stage during the Truman Administration when, as a result of the deepfreeze and mink-coat scandals, Newbold Morris had been entrusted by the President to wage a cleanup campaign and recommended that every member of Truman's cabinet file a report of his assets. Attorney General J. Howard McGrath flatly refused to comply—and Truman demanded (and, as Presidents usually do, got) his resignation. The issue did not arise again until President Kennedy, and later President Johnson, required all Cabinet members and Presidential appointees to file lists of their assets with the Civil Service Commission. If President Eisenhower had followed this practice, he might have avoided the embarrassing conflict-of-interest cases that marred his Administration (though his own case might have proved the most embarrassing of all).

The issue of public disclosure by Congressmen came to a boil on November 19, 1963, when Senator Case was pressing his colleagues on the Committee on Rules and Administration to stop sitting on his proposed bill requiring financial disclosure by virtually every Federal employee who made more than $15,000 a year, members of Congress included. Except for Federal Judges, who are supposed to disqualify themselves from hearing cases in which they have a personal interest, the Case bill would have required all upper-echelon Government workers to reveal their incomes, capital gains, assets, stock or commodity dealings, and real-estate transactions. The penalty for failure to comply would have been $2,000 in fines and five years in prison.

"Mr. President," Senator Case began that November day in 1963, "Congress is now midway in the eleventh month of the longest session in years. Unfortunately, the unusual length of the session is the only distinction—and a dubious distinction indeed—that this Congress has so far achieved." Case then drew a bead on the Bobby Baker investigation, at that time in the dawdling hands of the same Senate committee that was sitting on the Case full-disclosure bill. "It appears, however, that we may be on the verge of still another dubious distinction—a new low in public confidence in the integrity of Congress as a whole. The resignation of the Majority Secretary [Baker] and subsequent developments reported in the press have cast a reflection on the Congress as an institution, members as well as staff."

Unlike some high-minded bills, which are left at the Clerk's desk for any and all Senators to attach their names to, Case's bill had only two co-sponsors, Senator Clark and Oregon's Senator Maurine Neuberger, elected to the seat held by her husband, liberal Democrat Richard Neuberger, after he died of lung cancer in 1960. He had been one of the earliest advocates of financial disclosure by Congressmen. "I fear that it has a corroding effect on government generally," Dick Neuberger once wrote, "when a member of the President's Cabinet can be ordered to jettison his corporate portfolio by Senators who may themselves be dabbling in oil, cotton futures, television, hotel chains or uranium."

On the Senate floor the day Senator Case was calling for action on the disclosure bill, Senator Clark echoed the late Dick Neuberger's words. "We cannot, like so many ostriches, put our heads in the sand," Clark said, "while we insist on the most rigorous conflict-of-interest requirements with respect to all appointees of the executive arm of government whose nominations must be confirmed by the Senate." Maurine Neuberger added, "We accept that procedure for appointees but we are unwilling to do the same for ourselves. So long as we believe it is necessary for a member of the President's Cabinet, it seems to me we should be willing to undergo the same scrutiny."

This was too much for Everett Dirksen. "The gentlewoman from Oregon forgets," he rumbled, "that members of the Senate are screened by the electorate before they ever get to the Senate. They are confronted by people at election time. . . . If the voters are on their mettle and want to know something about a Senator's personal affairs, they are perfectly free to ask." The Minority Leader did not add, of course, that Senators are perfectly free to ignore the question.

Anyone who confronted him with such a question, Dirksen added, would be given an answer. "But I am not going to see it done by compulsion. That is the spirit of prohibition."

Clifford Case likes to relax at the piano when he has time, but he prefers Bach and Mozart to Dirksen's Wagnerian kettledrums. "I see no relevancy whatever in the prohibition amendment," Case said tartly. "The opposite is true. The purpose is not to make anything illegal, but merely make it possible for the facts to come out, so the public may make a judgment." The Senate then passed on to other matters, and three days later an assassin's bullet in Dallas turned the nation's attention away from Congressional reform. Yet Everett Dirksen has never explained why a Secretary of Defense should be willing to sell $2 million worth of General Motors stock, as Charles E. Wilson did on joining the Eisenhower Cabinet, when the Minority Leader of the Senate thinks public office isn't worth it if he is required merely to reveal what stocks he owns (see page 113).

Other Senators disagree with Dirksen. Wayne Morse, who has been dropping disclosure bills in the hopper since 1947, says briskly, "If we do not wish to live in a glass bowl, we should not enter politics."

Ohio's outspoken Democrat, Senator Stephen Young, who gave up his law practice when he entered Congress, became the first member of the Senate who voluntarily listed his stock holdings and other assets. Among the stocks in Young's portfolio were 11 oil companies. As a stockholder, Young regularly got form letters with his dividends that urged him to write his Congressman opposing any reduction in the 27½-percent oil depletion allowance. Young had been for cutting the allowance to 15 percent, a position he staked out during his years in the House.

But no Congressman has gone quite so far in setting an example of full disclosure as Pennsylvania's Joseph Clark, who, starting in 1962, has stood at his desk in the back row of the Senate and recited the list of all his assets as well as every source of income down to the $21.38 annual dividend he gets from the Franklin Life Insurance Company and the honorariums he receives for lectures (from a low of $100 at the University of Pennsylvania to a high of $750 at Wheaton College in Massachusetts, where his audience presumably included fewer potential Clark voters and no Philadelphia newspaper reporters).

Senator Hugh Scott, Joe Clark's Republican colleague from Pennsylvania, reluctantly followed Clark's lead in listing his holdings to avoid being outmaneuvered by Clark. Other Senators, with the Baker, Dodd and Powell cases in the open, have been eager to prove their own innocence by disclosing their assets and income in the *Congressional Record.* Some 30 Congressmen have done so, and the prospects of Congress facing up to its ethical obligations are brighter now than they have been within recent memory.

Indeed, the membership of both the Senate and House, having been scorched by scandal, sought to absolve their sins before going home to face the voters in 1968. With a great outpouring of piety, each house adopted its own code of conduct in early spring. The lofty language, however, was merely the incense that disguised the smell. For the new standards, in the name of ethics, legitimized practices that previously had been considered unethical.

The Senate, for example, gave its blessing to "slush funds" of the sort that Richard Nixon had made famous. Professing self-abnegation, the majority solemnly voted that it will be entirely ethical hereafter for Senators to solicit money from the special interests to pay their Senate expenses. This provision was offered by Senator Ralph Yarborough, D-Texas, who thereby sanitized his own slush fund. For years, he had been collecting expense money from the labor unions at the same time that he headed the Senate Labor Subcommittee.

The loudest objection to having his ethics regulated came, predictably, from Senator Everett Dirksen, who thumped his desk and thundered in self-righteous wrath. "The fact that I

went out and got elected does not make me a class-B citizen,"
he cried, repeating a refrain he had sounded in past battles
against Senate reforms. He took vociferous umbrage, in particular, to an amendment that would have required Senators
to make full public disclosure of their outside income and assets. Presumably, he did not want the voters to learn too
much about his Peoria, Ill., law business, whose clientele includes a number of corporations that have benefited from
Dirksen's influence in Washington (see Chapter Four).
Moved by his basso profundo, the Senate rejected the disclosure requirement for the third time in twelve months.

The Senate Republican leader, in the name of women's
rights, also persuaded the Senate to exclude wives from the
code of ethics. "For a hundred years," he boomed, "we have
been laboring at the business of emancipating women in this
country. . . . Now it is proposed to say here, 'Well, you are
going to have to account for what your wife owns.' " Dirksen
kept to himself a personal reason for championing the privacy
rights of Senate wives. Most of his own holdings are in his
wife's name; she handles the family finances and keeps the
ledgers.

Senator Allen Ellender, D-La., who once was able to buy
four choice acres outside Houma, La., from the South Downs
Sugar Company for half the price of surrounding real estate
(see Chapter Nine), was troubled by another point. "Am I to
understand," he demanded of Senate Ethics Chairman John
Stennis, D-Miss., "that when a report is made by a Senator,
no matter what the property cost him, he must more or less
state the market value at the time he makes his report? Is that
not what it amounts to?" Stennis assured him that the code,
while requiring a confidential listing of real estate worth more
than $10,000, would not demand any embarrassing figures.
"Senators do not have to state what it is worth," said Stennis.

Senators are inclined to look upon themselves as distinct
from lesser human beings. This was expressed by the Ethics
Committee in its official report advocating formal standards:
"A Senator is extended an extraordinary measure of trust and
confidence not given to ordinary members of society." As an
act of public penitence in the aftermath of the Bobby Baker
and Tom Dodd scandals, however, the Senate at last adopted
a code of ethics, albeit one riddled with loopholes.

The new standards require Senators to report their outside

income and assets, but the information is submitted in sealed envelopes that can be opened only by the Senate Ethics Committee. Senators are also free to accept law fees under $1,000 and honorariums under $300 without making any disclosure at all. And their wives, of course, can accept mink coats and deepfreezes untroubled by the code.

House members, their political antennae always slightly more sensitive to the public mood, imposed slightly tighter restrictions on their conduct. The House code at least requires partial financial disclosure. "Putting it in some sealed envelopes doesn't mean a thing," said Representative Charles Halleck, R-Ind., who led the fight for ethics. It was a curious assignment for Halleck. "I've always been a live-and-let-live sort of guy," he explained to his bemused colleagues. But the demands for disclosure, he said, were overwhelming. He did not, however, wish to carry reform too far. When Representative Richard Ottinger, D-N.Y., introduced an amendment demanding full disclosures, Halleck snorted: "We have all had copies of this amendment. It's not going anywhere." The House, as he had predicted, rejected the amendment.

Representative John Kyl, R-Iowa, suggested that the house-cleaning should include "the numbers racket, sports pools and similar gambling" that flourished "in every building" on Capitol Hill. The House finally approved a code that calls for a public accounting of law fees over $1,000, outside income over $5,000, and investments above $5,000 in companies doing "substantial" business with the government. Congressmen may still keep strictly secret their investments in companies with an interest in legislation—although this would seem to be the area of greater conflict. Both the Senate and House placed modest restrictions on honorariums and testimonial dinners.

Representative Peter Frelinghuysen, R-N.J., cast the lone vote against the House code of ethics. He felt its provisions were too vague, and he could see "nothing to be gained" from adopting them. The lone dissenter in the Senate, Vermont's gnarled George Aiken, was more outspoken. "I will not be a party to the perpetrating of a fraud upon the American people by making them think that we are trying to purify ourselves, when we are really making ourselves look worse," he declared.

But on both sides of the Capitol, the majority were more

interested in embracing the form rather than the substance of ethical conduct. They assured one another that, as the people's chosen representatives, their characters had already been vouched for by their constituents. Halleck gave voice to the sentiment in the cloakrooms: "There is nothing wrong with Congress that a good election won't cure."

Still, the record of Congressional malfeasance, misfeasance and nonfeasance, as this book perhaps has convinced some of its readers, has been so appalling that both houses of Congress must move with dispatch to impose truly stringent ethical standards on their membership. For Congress to do less is to face a continuing crisis of confidence in its relationship to the American people. When the representatives of the people weaken or fail, then the whole fabric of democratic-republican government weakens and fails. Can there be doubt that when our elected leaders thus betray the confidence bestowed upon them by the people they are contributing to a decline of ethical standards throughout the nation? We submit that this failure of Congress to act nobly—to stand as a beacon casting its bright light across the American land—is not unrelated to such signs of national demoralization as our terrifying crime rate, the frustration of our young people, the revolt of the far-out left and the rancor of the far-out right.

4. Ten Modest Proposals

To restore that confidence, we propose, finally, that Congress give immediate consideration to the following ten reform measures—and, after considering them, act positively on them:

1. Every second year, Congressmen shall disclose all assets and all sources of income and file such disclosures with the General Accounting Office. Such a step not only would help the public detect any undue enrichment but would protect members of Congress. (It would also show that many of them lost money while serving in Congress.)
2. No Congressman shall practice law before any Federal Court or any Federal agency. Congress should adopt the practice of former Representative Andrew Jacobs, Jr., the Indiana Democrat who said, "When I was elected to

Congress, one of the first things I did was take a razor blade and scratch my name off the door of my Indianapolis office. I have only one client now—the Eleventh Congressional District of Indiana."

3. All letters and all phone calls to regulatory agencies shall be made public as a matter of law.

4. No Congressman may serve as a director or an official of any corporation, partnership or organization doing business with the Federal Government.

5. No Congressman who serves as a member of the Armed Forces Reserve shall accept promotion while in Congress. As proposed by Representative Charles A. Vanik, D-Ohio: "A member of Congress should be subject to no other command but his own conscience."

6. A record of all trips from Washington to the home district, if taken on other than regular commercial carriers, shall be filed with the Clerks of the House and Senate. Or if the trip is paid for by any organization or individual, the name of the donor shall be filed.

7. The names of all relatives on a member's payroll shall be filed and published in the annual reports of the House and Senate.

8. No member shall use on his staff any person not paid by him except for students provided by academic institutions as temporary summer employees.

9. Members shall disclose any pecuniary interest in a bill on which they vote. Such a measure would not preclude their voting but would give the public an opportunity to judge whether votes were influenced by pecuniary interests.

10. A commission of five members shall be created—two from the House and two from the Senate, serving under a chairman appointed by the President—for the purpose of enforcing these reforms.

In addition, we recommend increasing Congressional salaries according to a cost-of-living escalation clause, giving members a $9,000 tax deduction instead of $3,000 for living expenses while in Washington, and tightening both the Lobbying Registration Act and the Corrupt Practices Act.

Aaron Burr, who in 1801 came within one vote of being elected President of the United States by the House of Representatives, later gave this farewell message to the Senate over which he had presided as Vice President:

> "This House is a sanctuary; a citadel of law, of order, and of liberty; and it is here, it is here in this exalted refuge, here, if anywhere, that resistance will be forever made to the storms of political frenzy and the silent arts of corruption; and if the Constitution be destined ever to perish by the sacrilegious hand of the demagogue or the usurper, which God avert, its expiring agonies will be witnessed on this floor."

At the end of his address the entire Senate was in tears, and it was necessary to recess for fifteen minutes so the legislators could regain their composure. Because speeches were not transcribed during executive sessions in those days, a number of Senators sat down together and agreed from memory on the language quoted above. We commend this language and its goals to the current Congress.

INDEX

465

v